THE HOLY CATHOLIC CHURCH

THE HOLY CATHOLIC CHURCH

HISTORY AND MISSION OF GOD'S PEOPLE

Ave Maria Press   AVE   Notre Dame, Indiana

The Subcommittee on the Catechism, United States Conference of Catholic Bishops, has found that this catechetical high school text, copyright 2025, is in conformity with the *Catechism of the Catholic Church* and that it fulfills the requirements of Core Course IV of the *Doctrinal Elements of a Curriculum Framework for the Development of Catechetical Materials for Young People of High School Age*.

Nihil Obstat: Reverend Monsignor Michael Heintz, PhD
    Censor Librorum

Imprimatur: Most Reverend Kevin C. Rhoades
    Bishop of Fort Wayne–South Bend
    Given at Fort Wayne, Indiana, on 16 January 2024

The *Nihil Obstat* and *Imprimatur* are official declarations that a book or pamphlet is free of doctrinal or moral error. No implication is contained therein that those who have granted the *Nihil Obstat* or *Imprimatur* agree with its contents, opinions, or statements expressed.

Scripture texts in this work are taken from the *New American Bible, revised edition* © 2010, 1991, 1986, 1970 Confraternity of Christian Doctrine, Washington, DC, and are used by permission of the copyright owner. All Rights Reserved. No part of the *New American Bible* may be reproduced in any form without permission in writing from the copyright owner.

English translation of the *Catechism of the Catholic Church* for the United States of America copyright © 1994, United States Catholic Conference, Inc.—Libreria Editrice Vaticana. English translation of the *Catechism of the Catholic Church: Modifications from the Editio Typica* copyright © 1997, United States Catholic Conference, Inc.—Libreria Editrice Vaticana.

Textbook Writer
Kevin Schmiesing

Educational Consultant
Sara Burmeister, PhD
Assistant Clinical Professor
College of Education
Marquette University

Cover image "Handing Over the Keys to St. Peter" by Pietro Perugino. Photo by Realy Easy Star / Alamy Stock Photo.

Cover design by Christopher D. Tobin.

Text design by Andy Wagoner.

Printed and bound in the United States of America.

Sacred art is true and beautiful when its form corresponds to its particular vocation: evoking and glorifying, in faith and adoration, the transcendent mystery of God—the surpassing invisible beauty of truth and love visible in Christ, who "reflects the glory of God and bears the very stamp of his nature" (Heb 1:3), in whom "the whole fullness of deity dwells bodily" (Col 2:9). This spiritual beauty of God is reflected in the most holy Virgin Mother of God, the angels, and saints. Genuine sacred art draws man to adoration, to prayer, and to the love of God, Creator and Savior, the Holy One and Sanctifier.

—Catechism of the Catholic Church, 2502

We will begin each chapter with a short study and reflection on a piece of sacred art in order to visually portray an important aspect of our faith and to pass on this wonderful tradition of our Catholic faith.

CONTENTS

The Church
Gives Life

Handing Over of the Keys

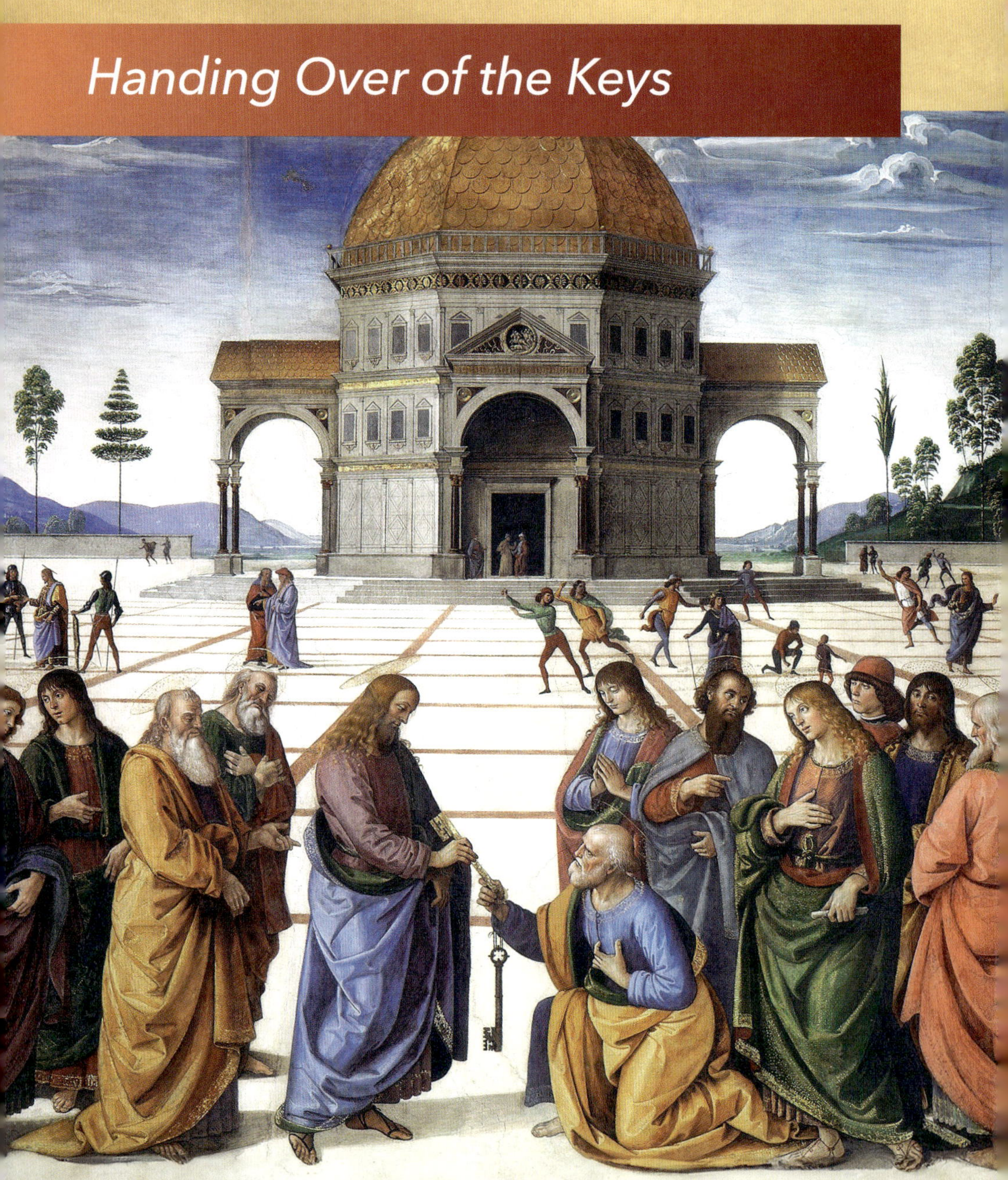

Pietro Perugino

Returning to the region of Caesarea Philippi, Jesus asked his **disciples**, "Who do people say that the Son of Man is?" At first no one got it right, misidentifying him as John the Baptist, Elijah, Jeremiah, or another prophet. When Simon Peter spoke up and identified Jesus as "the Messiah, the Son of the living God," Jesus commended Peter and promised he would build his Church upon him. Peter would be the rock of the Church and given the keys of the kingdom (see Matthew 16:13–28). The painting, *Handing Over of the Keys*, by Pietro Perugino (1446–1523), an Italian Renaissance painter, is part of a series of frescoes known as the Stories of Christ painted on the north wall of the Sistine Chapel at the Vatican.

Pietro Perugino learned his craft among illustrious Renaissance painters. First studying in his hometown of Perugia in local workshops sponsored by artists such as Bartolomeo Caporali and Fiorenzo di Lorenzo, he later transferred to the larger city of Florence, where he served as an apprentice alongside rising artists, including Leonardo da Vinci. Later, he was himself a teacher of the artist Raphael.

Pietro was among the earliest artists to perfect oil painting, and he used that style to create several frescoes for a convent—eventually destroyed by fire—in Florence. *Handing Over of the Keys* was produced between 1481 and 1482. Pietro Perugino died in 1523.

Note the details in the foreground of the painting. Christ is handing the silver and gold keys to Peter, who is kneeling. The other Apostles are present, all depicted with halos. It is said that Pietro used his contemporaries as models. The fifth figure from the right is thought to be his self-portrait. In the background, there is a depiction of the Jerusalem Temple, serving to center the scene. In the middle background are two scenes from the life of Christ: an illustration of his teaching to "repay to Caesar what belongs to Caesar and to God what belongs to God" (Mt 22:21) on the left and his being stoned on the right.

In total, the painting represents Jesus setting the foundation of his Church with Peter, the Apostles, and their successors.

If you would like to learn more about the Stories of Christ *series of frescoes at the Sistine Chapel, see Chapter 1 Review, Chapter Project 1.*

---

disciples From the Latin for "learners," those who learn from and follow Jesus Christ and who accept a share of his ministry in the world.

What is the purpose of the Church?

A CHURCH OF INTIMACY AND SELF-GIVING

We are not *compelled* to believe in and follow God; God made us free so that we can make the choice for union with him on our own. Nevertheless, God provides us with his grace so that we can desire him, and there is a biological aspect to this desire. Within our bodies he has made us so that we long to participate in the eternal love of God, the type of love shared between the Three Divine Persons: Father, Son, and Holy Spirit. We experience something similar to our yearning for God in our sexual drive to be intimately connected to another person, expressed in the Sacrament of Matrimony.

While not a perfect image of the intimate love God has for us, marriage *is* a wonderful demonstration on earth of how God wants to love us. Think about what you have witnessed in a holy marriage between a man and woman. First, their love is unconditional. They promise to love each other in sickness and in health, in poverty and in wealth, and in good times and in bad times. The man and woman love each other unselfishly, placing the needs of the other first. One way this is expressed is in conjugal love that does not separate the unitive dimension of sexual intercourse from the procreative dimension. "Expressed in a manner which is truly human, these actions promote that mutual self-giving by which spouses enrich each other with a joyful and a ready will" (*Gaudium et Spes*, 49).

Whether you will ever be married or not, you are called to a spousal relationship with Christ. In his Letter to the Ephesians, St. Paul compared the love husbands and wives share with how Christ loves the Church. Paul went on to describe the Church as Christ's beloved Bride for whom he gave himself up so that she would be holy (see Ephesians 5:21–32). "The Church," wrote Pope John Paul II, "cannot . . . be understood . . . unless we keep in mind the 'great mystery' . . . expressed in the 'one flesh' of marriage and the family."[1]

As you begin to study the meaning of the Church in more depth, keep the intimacy and life-giving sharing that exist between a man and woman in marriage in the forefront of your thoughts. This is the type of deep physical, emotional, intellectual, and spiritual union God desires to have with you. In the same way that God has gifted you with your life in this world and sacrificed himself so that you have the possibility of eternal happiness with him in the next world, he wants to share his life with you right now through his presence in the Catholic Church. He also wants you to share your life with him through your own self-giving.

Examples of Self-Giving

A husband and wife give of themselves unselfishly to each other in many everyday ways. For example, a wife getting ready for work a few minutes before her husband uses the light of her phone to find her clothes in the closet so as not to disturb him by turning on the bedside lamp. Then, upon rising himself, the husband gets the coffee brewing for his wife and goes out to the garage to warm up her car. Unselfishness and self-giving are also prominent in larger decisions in a marriage. Imagine the wife who orchestrates several family moves from place to place to support her husband's career, or the husband who passes up a new job because it would leave less time for him to spend with his wife and children.

We have been created by an unselfish God who gave of himself in becoming not only human, but a *poor* human who ultimately gave up his life for the benefit of sinners. Christians ever since have attempted to imitate this trait of self-giving. Consider these two examples.

"To Die in His Place"

Maximilian shuffled into line along with the other prisoners. He was miserable, and so was everyone else. The sweltering sun burned overhead while insects buzzed in their faces. Awful odors of filth and dirt and death reached their nostrils. The cruel soldiers marched up and down the ranks, explaining the ugly truth of their situation. A prisoner had escaped overnight. In retribution, ten prisoners would die, and they would die slowly and in agony.

It was 1941, and the men were prisoners at the infamous Nazi concentration camp of Auschwitz. The commander chose the ten helpless men randomly, calling out their prison numbers. They were all terrified and stepped forward with looks of despair on their faces. But one of them broke down completely. He fell to the ground wailing, "I have a wife and two boys. What will become of them?"

Then Maximilian stirred to life. He walked directly up to the commander and stood in front of him. "What do *you* want?" the officer snarled. "I want to die in his place," Maximilian replied. The German was stunned. When he learned that Maximilian was a Catholic priest, he agreed. The father's life was spared that day.

Maximilian was taken with the nine others to a bunker, where they slowly starved to death over the next two weeks. He encouraged and cared for the others until he was the last one alive. Then he was injected with poison to hasten his death.

Maximilian was a Franciscan friar who was later canonized by the Catholic Church and is today known as St. Maximilian Kolbe. The man he saved, Franciszek Gajowniczek,

St. Maximilian Kolbe

Franciszek Gajowniczek

Franciszek Gajowniczek, prisoner number 5659, the Polish sergeant whom Maximilian Kolbe saved, spent five years, five months, and nine days at Auschwitz after being transferred from another Nazi prison in Tarnów in southeastern Poland. He had been captured while crossing into Slovakia following a defeat of his military unit during the 1939 invasion of Poland by the Nazis.

Gajowniczek's wife, Janina, said of her husband, "Ever since the war he had a deep sense of Kolbe's presence and a feeling Kolbe will know when to take him." Gajowniczek died at the age of ninety-four in 1995. Gajowniczek was a special guest at both the beatification of Maximilian Kolbe in 1971 and his canonization by Pope John Paul II in 1982.

was reunited with his wife and lived another fifty-three years, telling everyone how grateful he was for the heroic sacrifice of Maximilian Kolbe.[2]

"Saint Mommy"

Gianna faced an impossible choice. As a physician herself, she knew her doctor was right: if her pregnancy continued, her own life was in peril. But she could not bring herself to end her little baby's life.

St. Gianna Molla with her daughter.

Gianna and her husband, Pietro, lived in northern Italy. They had been married for more than six years, and she was already the mother of three children. They were excited about the addition to their family, looking forward to filling their home with even more joy. Then came the bad news. There was a tumor growing in Gianna's womb that posed a threat to her life and the baby's life. Removing the uterus would likely save the mother, but it meant certain death for the baby. Gianna had been a doctor for more than ten years and understood well the consequences of the choice she faced. She decided to have the cancerous tumor removed but insisted that the baby be protected at all costs.

Because of the risk level of the pregnancy and Gianna's choice to protect her unborn child, it became necessary to deliver the baby via caesarean section. The day before Easter, Gianna went into surgery and a healthy baby girl was born. A week later, on April 28, 1962, the mother of four died of complications from the operation.

Like Maximilian, Gianna has been recognized by the Church as a saint: St. Gianna Molla. Her fourth child, Gianna Emanuela, the girl born on Holy Saturday, grew up to be a doctor like her mother.∞ She also shares her story with the world, expressing her gratitude for the generosity and example of the woman she calls "Saint Mommy."[3]

No Greater Love

Jesus said that there is no greater love than to give your life for another person (see John 15:13). At some level, everyone—Christian or not—understands this. We all hold in esteem the firefighter who rushes into a burning building to save a person who cannot get out, or the person who gives up an organ for a relative who needs a replacement. Likewise, the radical love shown by St. Maximilian Kolbe, St. Gianna Molla, and many other saints throughout history who not only sacrificed their lives for others but did so in the name of Jesus Christ is universally admired. In these latter cases, they not only allowed others to have life in this world but inspired many others to do what it takes to gain eternal life in the next world.

At the head of all those who have given their lives for others stands Jesus himself. Because he refused to deny the truth about who he was, Jesus suffered and was killed. But Jesus's Death on the Cross was both different from and more than the other examples previously covered.

St. Maximilian Kolbe and St. Gianna Molla had the opportunity to give another person life in this world, which is an amazing gift. But Jesus did something greater. He gave us life *for eternity*. Because Jesus is the Son of God, when he gave his life for us, he made a sacrifice that had the power to save everyone, everywhere, for all time. His Death gave us the chance to live forever.

∞ Note

Gianna Emmanuel Molla chose Springfield, Illinois, as the location of a spiritual pilgrimage center to honor both her mother and her father. The center will include a replica of the spousal home of Gianna and Pietro as it was in Ponte Nuovo of Magenta in Milan, Italy; a pilgrim center; a replica of the original Chapel of Our Lady of Good Counsel with attached rectory as it was at her parents' parish in Ponte Nuovo; a shrine church of St. Gianna; and a rectory for visiting clergy.

Some people who witnessed what Jesus did and understood what his Death meant were willing to follow his example. In the first three centuries of the Church, many Christians were martyred for their faith when Christianity was illegal in the Roman Empire. They were the followers, or disciples, of Christ, the beginning of what we now call "the Church." Catholics today belong to this same Church, whose members, when first initiated at Baptism, are "baptized into his death" (Rom 6:3). This is quite a challenge to accept.

In this course, you will explore what it means to belong to the Church of Jesus Christ by taking a close look at the Church's teachings and how her members through every age have attempted to live them out. You will encounter many diverse examples of Catholics who came before us and found ways to follow Christ in their own circumstances. The intimate marriage-like relationship God wants with you begins with your participation in the Catholic Church because Jesus, who is at the center of the Church, is the source of that relationship and of your call to eternal life. Catholics who take up Jesus's Cross and follow him (see Matthew 16:24) do so with the intention of living in close intimacy with God now and in the future.

SECTION Assessment

Comprehension

1. Why did the Nazi guard accept Maximilian Kolbe's offer to substitute himself for Franciszek Gajowniczek's death sentence?

2. How did Maximilian Kolbe die?

3. What was the difficult choice that Gianna Molla had to make?

4. How did Jesus's Death on the Cross differ from the sacrifices of St. Maximilian Kolbe and St. Gianna Molla?

Reflection

5. How do you imagine a relationship with God even more intimate than that between a husband and wife in marriage?

HEARING THE CALL OF THE CHURCH

In the late days of the Roman Empire, in the mid fourth century, a brilliant young man was living a lost life. Augustine had always been a searcher, looking for something he couldn't seem to find. He had tried to find happiness in partying, in sexual relationships, and in dominating others with his intelligence and sharp tongue. When all that failed, he looked for comfort in strange religious ideas, including *Manicheism*, the beliefs of a heretical group that did not acknowledge the legitimacy of the Old Testament for Christians, but none of it worked. "I searched about for something to love," he lamented, "but my soul was far from well."

Then he heard someone calling. It was the singsong voice of a neighborhood child chanting the lyrics of a song that went "Take up and read." There was a book near Augustine, a collection of the Letters of St. Paul. Augustine followed the message of the lyrics and began to read from the Scripture.∞ Then he experienced a different sort of calling, an internal sense of what his purpose in life was. As he finished reading the passage, he recalled, "All the darkness of doubt vanished away." In the teachings of Jesus as recounted by St. Paul, Augustine finally began to find what he'd been looking for.

> **∞ Note**
>
> Augustine described picking up the Letters of St. Paul: "I seized it and opened it, and in silence I read the first passage on which my eyes fell: 'Not in carousing and drunkenness, not in sexual excess and lust, not in quarreling and jealousy. Rather, put on the Lord Jesus Christ and make no provision for the desires of the flesh' (Rom 13:13–14)" (*Confessions*, VIII, 12).

Augustine began a process of conversion.∞ He prayed more and followed the laws of Christian morality. He was baptized and, despite his previous life of sin and aimlessness, went on to become a bishop and one of the most important theologians in the history of the Church. St. Augustine of Hippo shared his story of conversion with others by writing a book known as his *Confessions*, which is still in print and popular more than 1,500 years later. In the *Confessions*, St. Augustine described his experience in what has become perhaps the most famous line in all of Christian literature. Addressing God, he wrote, "Our hearts are restless until they rest in you." St. Augustine had been restless because he wasn't listening for God's voice. He started following Christ because he heard the call to do so.[4]

Origins of the Church

Hearing a call as St. Augustine did is at the heart of the experience of being a member of the Church. The English word *church* comes from a Greek word, *ekklesia*, which means "people called together." *Ekklesia* was used in the Greek translation of the Old Testament to refer to the Jewish people when they were gathered together at Mount Sinai to receive the Ten Commandments. The people of Israel were called by God to come together to receive his teaching, leading them to be known as the "Chosen People." They had been called, or chosen, by God to be witnesses to the rest of the world of God's identity and teachings.

The Ten Commandments were a sign of God's continuing **covenant** with the Chosen People. The covenant God established was an irrevocable bond. God promised his love and care and in return expected the Chosen People to respond in gratitude by way of ethical living, summarized later by Jesus in the Great Commandment to love God and to love one's neighbor (see, for

---

∞ Note

The *Catechism of the Catholic Church* defines *conversion* as "a radical reorientation of the whole life away from sin and evil, and toward God" (Glossary).

---

covenant A binding and solemn agreement between humans or between God and people, holding each to a particular course of action.

apostates Baptized Christians who deny Christ and repudiate the Christian faith.

example, Matthew 22:37–40). The accounts of key figures in the Old Testament—Adam and Eve, Noah, Abraham, Isaac, Jacob, David—tell of God's People repeatedly turning away from him. Yet God remained faithful, calling them back and renewing his covenant with them multiple times. As St. Augustine found out centuries later, there is always a chance to make amends with God and start over.

These Old Testament accounts also reveal the way God gradually prepared the world for the founding of his Church. In the time of Noah, the ark served as a vessel for saving those who followed God's commands—an image of the role of the Church in the world today. St. Cyprian, a third-century North African bishop, recognized that the Church, like Noah's Ark, was the one and only place God could save us. He wrote that "the one ark of Noah is a type of the one Church."[5] He said this in reference to the *lapsi*, that is, **apostates** who had denied Christ during the time of the Roman persecutions. He advocated for their forgiveness and return to the Church after Christianity was legalized in 313.

After the waters of the Great Flood had receded, God established a covenant with Noah and his descendants, promising never again to destroy the earth's inhabitants in that manner. This covenant was renewed and strengthened when God promised to make a great nation from the descendants of Abraham. The gathering of the Israelites in the time of Moses and God's gift of the Law on Mount Sinai definitively established them as the People of God, the Chosen People. It is easy to recognize how the Church today is rooted in the experience of the people of Israel. Like the Chosen People, the Church consists of those called by God to gather and receive his Word. Here are some ways the Church resembles the Chosen People:

▶ The commandments given to the people gathered at Mount Sinai—worship the one true God; honor your parents; do not kill; do not lie—still serve as the foundation for living a Christian life.

▶ Rejecting the false teaching of the Manicheans, Christians still recognize the Old Testament as part of their Sacred Scriptures.

▶ The first followers of Christ were Jews—descendants of Abraham who had been formed as a people in the time of Moses.

Today, there is a great focus on individualism. There is nothing wrong with promoting and celebrating your individuality: God created you uniquely in his own divine image. Individualism is only a problem when it drives people apart from one another. When this happens, the individual creates his or her own definition of self and the world. This leads to people rejecting a crucial function of the Church: to call people who believe in God to come together to worship, pray, socialize, and serve. People with an individualistic philosophy often reject this call to come together when there is disagreement between the individual's definition of self and the Church's understanding of what it means to be human. The bottom line is that many people today do not feel that belonging to the Church is vital to maintaining a relationship with God.

"Here Comes Everybody"

Contrary to the negative aspects of individualism, God intends for all people to come together and participate in the human family and in his own life via the Church. In the famous passage from the First Letter to the Corinthians, St. Paul wrote: "As a body is one though it has many parts, and all the parts of the body, though many, are one body, so also Christ" (1 Cor 12:12). The Catholic Church not only calls all people to belong; she needs all people to do their part to make the Church function ideally.

Those who are not Catholic sometimes view the Church as an exclusive club with rigid rules that, if broken, cast a person out. This isn't so. Twentieth-century priest and sociologist Fr. Andrew Greeley pointed out that the Church has always had a "rich, complex, diversified, pluralistic heritage." The purpose of the Church is to cast "her boundaries out as far as possible, to include everyone she can." Greeley cited Irish poet James Joyce, who is known for defining the Catholic Church as "Here comes everybody."[6]

Because Christ's Death on the Cross was intended to win salvation for all—Jews and Gentiles who accepted him and those who didn't—and because his Church is the instrument he chose to perpetuate his presence in the world, all

people have a connection with the Church and are called to participate in the Church. This means that anyone who is seeking to live according to God's design is thereby connected in one way or another to the Catholic Church. This is why the truths discussed in this course are relevant to all students, Catholic or not.

To clarify further, those who are baptized as Catholic and practice their faith are clearly members of the "visible" Church. They are located within the boundaries of the Catholic Church and form an identifiable group of Christ's disciples, but the Church is not reducible to her visible boundaries. The Church is also a spiritual reality that extends her reach into all hearts who long for God. Those who are baptized into a Christian tradition other than Catholicism, such as Protestant and Orthodox Christians, are still closely connected to the Church. They have received the Sacrament of Baptism, which brings them into the family of God and identifies them as followers of Christ. Those who adhere to one of the other "Abrahamic" religions, Judaism and Islam, also have ties to the Church. They recognize the one God and see the beginning of God's covenant with humanity in the call of Abraham.

Even those who follow other religions or do not identify with organized religion at all have access to the saving power of Jesus and his Church. Pope John Paul II declared that "the universality of salvation means that it is granted not only to those who explicitly believe in Christ and have entered the Church. Since salvation is offered to all, it must be made concretely available to all." He observed that "today, as in the past, many people do not have an opportunity to come to know or accept the gospel revelation or to enter the Church. The social and cultural conditions in which they live do not permit this, and frequently they have been brought up in other religious traditions." For non-Catholics such as these, "salvation in Christ is accessible by virtue of a grace which, while having a mysterious relationship to the Church, does not make them formally part of the Church but enlightens them in a way which is accommodated to their spiritual and material situation" (*Redemptoris Missio*, 10).

The reality of the Church is therefore relevant to all. Catholics, non-Catholic Christians, and others are all called to embrace the truth about God and his relationship with us. We are all called to knowledge of the Church, which can lead us to understand how the Church facilitates our growth in wisdom, grace, and unity with God and others and brings about the salvation of our souls and a path to eternal life.

SECTION Assessment

Comprehension

1. What did St. Augustine read when he picked up the Bible after hearing the child sing?

2. What is the meaning of the Greek word *ekklesia*?

3. Name three ways that the Church resembles the Chosen People.

4. How are non-Catholic Christians, Jews, Muslims, and those who do not identify with any religion nevertheless connected to the Church?

Vocabulary

5. What is the two-sided nature of a *covenant*?

6. Define *apostate*.

Reflection

7. Explain the meaning of St. Augustine's most famous quotation, "Our hearts are restless until they rest in you."

8. What are one positive and one negative aspect about individualism when it comes to participating in the Church?

9. How does the James Joyce quotation "Here comes everybody" describe the Catholic Church?

JESUS CHRIST FOUNDED THE CHURCH

As chronicled in the Old Testament, God acts over and over to form a people who are chosen not because of merit, but simply because of his compassion and love for them. Although the Israelites (later called "Jews") as a people frequently abandoned the demands of a loving relationship with God, he refused to abandon them. They were a people bound by a promise, a covenant, that was not of their making.

In fact, in spite of their ongoing sinfulness, God announced through the prophets a new and eternal covenant. He was committed to the Jewish people as a faith community from which his own Son, Jesus, would be born. When the proper time came, God himself became a member of that community. The only Son of God was entrusted not only to this Chosen People, but to humanity itself. In the Incarnation, the Second Person of the Blessed Trinity came down from heaven and assumed human nature. It was through this event that God instituted the **New Covenant** through Christ and specifically through his **Paschal Mystery**: "He called a people together made up of Jews and Gentiles, which would be one, not according to the flesh, but in the Spirit, and it would be the new people of God" (*Lumen Gentium*, 9).

Whether you have considered the following statement many times before or only now, it's important to acknowledge that no matter your level of belief, the following is objectively true: *Jesus, besides being truly God, was a historical*

New Covenant The climax of salvation history; the coming of Jesus Christ, who is the fullness of God's revelation.

Paschal Mystery Christ's work of redemption, accomplished principally by his Passion, Death, Resurrection, and glorious Ascension. The mystery is commemorated and made present through the sacraments, especially the Eucharist.

person who lived in a particular time and place (first-century Palestine). It isn't possible to prove every detail of Jesus's life, Death, or Resurrection, and people will continue to debate those matters until the end of time, but the findings of historians show that it is reasonable to believe the accounts of the Gospels. The Gospels do not contradict what we know from history, and they provide strong evidence for the truth of the Church's claims about Jesus: that he was the Son of God who died and rose from the dead. By doing so, Jesus showed that God has power over death.

The Church, therefore, is not founded on an idea or a myth or a legend but on a real, historical person. Jesus founded the Church, and by his words and actions shaped her form and structure. For example, even as the twelve tribes of Israel were the backbone of the Jewish faith and nation, so the Twelve Apostles chosen by Jesus were the "foundation stones of the new Jerusalem," the Church (*Catechism of the Catholic Church*, 765). In instituting his Church, Jesus ushered in the Kingdom of God on earth.

The Kingdom of God Is Present in the Church

What is meant by "Kingdom of God"? You might think of it as "the world as God would have it be." Or think of it this way: The Kingdom of God is a state of "already, not yet." What this means is that in Jesus of Nazareth the Kingdom of God is already present in a new, unprecedented way. At the same time,

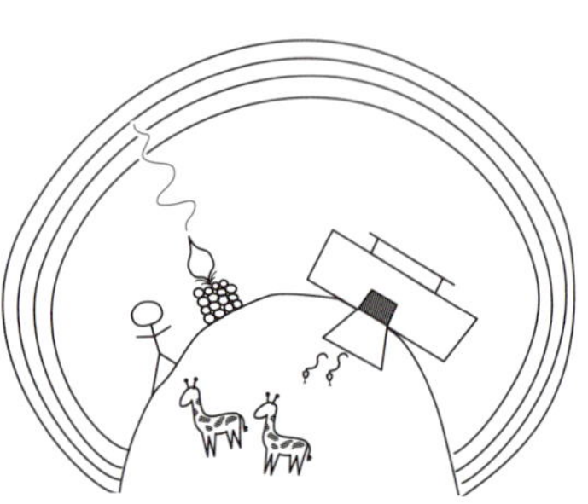

Noahic Covenant

Abrahamic Covenant

Mosaic Covenant

Davidic Covenant

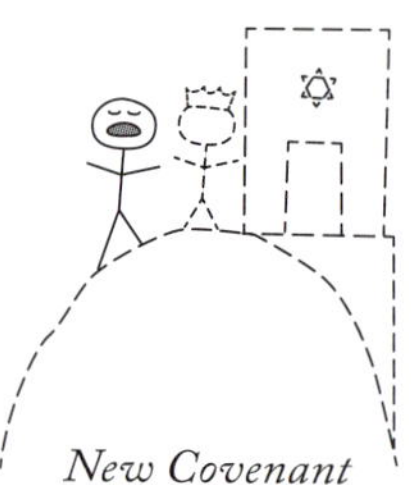

New Covenant

God's Kingdom has not yet transformed all creation; that will not take place until the end of history. In the meantime, the Church is the way to salvation. This "already, but not yet" quality of the Church is evident in many of the parables that Jesus told about the Kingdom. For example, in one parable Jesus said that the Kingdom of God "is like a mustard seed that, when it is sown in the ground, is the smallest of all the seeds on the earth. But once it is sown, it springs up and becomes the largest of plants and puts forth large branches, so that the birds of the sky can dwell in its shade" (Mk 4:31–32).[7]

It is also important to understand how the Chosen People and the Law of Mount Sinai from the Old Testament are related to Jesus, the Church, and the Kingdom. Christ did not come to abolish the Law of Mount Sinai, also known as the Mosaic Law or the Old Law (see Matthew 5:17). But he did preach a radically new understanding of it. Jesus explicitly taught that the love of God and neighbor must guide all of the laws. The "Good News" that Jesus preached to the world was therefore not merely a new written code to replace the faithful application of the 613 laws of the Torah.[∞] The Good News is more *who Jesus is* and *what he did*. By his own life—his suffering, dying, and rising—he repaired the damage done by sinfulness and defeated the wages of sin—that is, death—that had been present since Adam and Eve.

The Church Was Born on the Cross

You may have noticed that Catholics wear around their necks or display in their homes a crucifix instead of a plain cross. What's the difference? A crucifix has the *corpus* (body) of Christ on it, and a plain cross does not. The intention is to be mindful that there is no resurrection of the bodies of the saved without the Death of Jesus on the Cross. St. Augustine wrote: "The death of the Lord our God should not be a cause of shame for us; rather, it should be our greatest hope, our greatest glory." Similarly, the use of a crucifix

---

∞ Note

The number of 613 laws is mostly symbolic. Third-century AD Jewish Rabbi Simlai came up with the number of 613 precepts of the Mosaic Law: 365 negative precepts, corresponding to the number of solar days in a year, and 248 positive precepts, corresponding to the number of "limbs" (joints, or bones, covered with flesh and sinews) in a man's body.

Why Is the Church a "She"?

Focus Question: What is the purpose of the Church?

You may already have noticed that the pronouns used for the Church in this text are feminine ones: *she* and *her*. Why give personal pronouns to the Church at all, you may wonder, and why make them feminine?

The use of feminine pronouns for the Church comes directly from the Scriptures. In the Letter to the Ephesians, St. Paul assigns a female pronoun to his description of the Church. In a famous passage comparing the relationship between husbands and wives to the relationship between Christ and the Church, he writes: "Husbands, love your wives, even as Christ loved the church and handed himself over for her to sanctify her, cleansing her by the bath of water with the word, that he might present to himself the church in splendor, without spot or wrinkle or any such thing, that she might be holy and without blemish" (Eph 5:25–27).

There are other New Testament passages that emphasize the feminine description of the Church. In the Second Letter to the Corinthians, Paul compares the community to a bride that will be presented "as a chaste virgin to Christ" (2 Cor 11:2). In the Book of Revelation, the Church is once again described as the bride who is in a covenant relationship with God: "For the wedding day of the Lamb has come, / his bride has made herself ready" (Rv 19:7).

The image of the Church as the bride and Christ as the Bridegroom has been taught by the Church in all the centuries since her founding. "The Church is the spotless bride of the spotless Lamb" (*CCC*, 796). For these reasons, the Church continues to be referred to with the feminine pronouns *she* and *her* over the impersonal *it*.

Further Study and Reflection

- In your own words, explain how Christ's relationship with the Church is like a husband's relationship with his wife.
- Read John 3:28–30. How does this passage support the feminine identification of the Church?

Pope Benedict XVI was known for arranging the altar with a crucifix and six candles. He said this arrangement greatly helps the celebrant and the faithful alike to perceive and thus to reverence the greatness of the altar of sacrifice, and, in that connection, to turn their interior gaze to Jesus Christ, who stands at the very center of the liturgical action.

is obligatory during the celebration of Mass and is to be clearly visible to the congregation.∞

Pope John Paul II said that the Church, in a certain sense, was "born on the Cross," reiterating the teachings of the Second Vatican Council: "For it was from the side of Christ as He slept the sleep of death upon the cross that there came forth the 'wondrous sacrament of the whole Church'" (*Sacrosanctum Concilium*, 5). The *Catechism of the Catholic Church* adds: "As Eve was formed from the sleeping Adam's side, so the Church was born from the pierced heart of Christ hanging dead on the cross" (*CCC*, 766).

However, the full meaning of Christ's saving work does not end with the Cross. Jesus was crucified to atone for human sinfulness. A mystery of the Cross is that it finds its fulfillment in the Resurrection of Jesus. It is in the Resurrection that the power of God's love, incarnate in Christ, triumphs over the power of death. Today, Jesus remains truly present in the Church, though not in flesh and bone. The Church is the Body of Christ; Christ himself is the head: "Not only is she gathered *around him*; she is united *in him*, in his body" (*CCC*, 789). Jesus's presence in the Church is a great blessing. He is present in the Church in several ways but "most especially in the Eucharistic species" (*Sacrosanctum Concilium*, 7). This is called the **Real Presence**.

∞ Note

Note, however, that the altar itself has precedence over the crucifix at Mass. The altar represents both the sacrifice of Christ and the table of the Lord. Wrote St. Ambrose: "The altar represents the body [of Christ] and the Body of Christ is on the altar" (quoted in *CCC*, 1383).

Real Presence "The unique, true presence of Christ in the Eucharist under the species or appearances of bread and wine" (*CCC*, Glossary).

It is through Baptism that Catholics are "incorporated into Christ and integrated into the People of God" (*Lumen Gentium*, 31). It is through the Church, where Jesus is present, that he continues to invite all people into a relationship with God and to know and experience what he revealed about God:

- Jesus came from the Father.

- Jesus and the Father are one.

- Jesus has returned to the Father.

- All are invited to share in God's love through participation in the Church.

The benefit of this participation in the love of God—fueled and guided by the Third Person of the Trinity, the Holy Spirit—is salvation. This raises the question: What does it mean to be saved?

SECTION Assessment

Comprehension

1. What did Jesus teach about the Law of Mount Sinai?
2. What is the connection between the Church and a crucifix?
3. Name four things that Jesus revealed about God.

Vocabulary

4. On what occasion was the *New Covenant* instituted?
5. What is meant by the *Real Presence*?

Reflection

6. How important is knowing that Jesus was a historical person to your faith in him?
7. Explain the "already, not yet" dimension of the Kingdom of God in your own words.

WHAT *DOES* IT MEAN TO BE SAVED?

Put simply, salvation means "the forgiveness of sins and restoration of friendship with God, which can be done by God alone" (*CCC*, Glossary). Today, before many can accept the definition of salvation, they first have to accept a belief in sin. Due in part to **relativism** and a lack of belief in objective truth, there are many people today who live by the premise that "whatever is right for an individual person" is the source of that person's own truth and that people should not be judged by any other person, let alone by God. Likewise, to accept the need for salvation one must first believe in God. In addition to subscribing to relativism, some people today have created a system in which science alone dictates their beliefs, making it difficult for them to accept either God or the need for salvation. Japanese doctor **Takashi Nagai** was just such a person before his conversion.

The Church Is Necessary for Salvation

Traditionally, the Church has stated that the Catholic Church is necessary for salvation and that "outside the Church there is no salvation" (*CCC*, 846, quoting St. Cyprian). This is so because Jesus is necessary for salvation. Without Jesus, who has made the Church his Body, there is no salvation.

All who recognize that the Church is the Body of Christ are called to be part of that Church. If, knowing that the Church is the Body of Christ, they reject the Church, they are rejecting salvation. This does not mean that those who, through no fault of their own, do not know Christ or his Church have rejected salvation. There are certainly people in the world who have not heard

relativism A belief that knowledge, truth, and morality exist only in relation to culture, society, or individuals and are not objective or absolute.

TAKASHI NAGAI

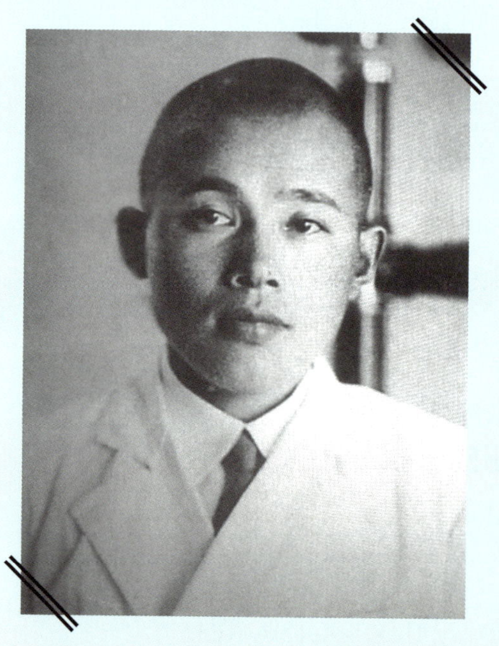

Takashi Nagai believed in science. His father had been a medical doctor, and Takashi followed in his footsteps, dedicating himself to understanding the human body and how to fix it. What he could see and touch—the physical matter of this world—is all there is, Takashi thought. He didn't believe in God.

Although Takashi was sure he was right about there being no spiritual world, he wasn't happy. When he wasn't studying, he was lonely and discontented. He started drinking heavily to try to ease the bad feelings.

Things began to change for Takashi when he watched his elderly mother die. As he pondered her fate, he started to think maybe he had been wrong. He could not believe that such a kind, beautiful person could just *cease to exist*. Maybe there was something after this life. Maybe there was more to the world than physical matter.

While he studied in medical school in Nagasaki, Japan, Takashi stayed in a spare room in a family's house. He got to know the family well, especially the pretty and thoughtful young daughter, Midori. He saw in Midori and her family a peacefulness and joy that he lacked. Midori didn't need alcohol to be happy. Takashi wondered what her secret was.

Gradually, he figured it out. Midori's family was Catholic. There were very few Catholics in Japan, but there was a small community of Catholics in Nagasaki. The faith had been passed down for three hundred years, from the time when St. Francis Xavier had brought Christianity to the island kingdom in the sixteenth century (see subsection "Jesuit Missionaries of the Sixteenth and Seventeenth Centuries" in Chapter 5, Section 4).

Takashi began to understand. There was more to this world than could be seen or touched. Humans also possessed a spiritual dimension called a soul. Takashi came to understand that our souls needed nourishment just like our bodies needed food. He converted to Catholicism and married Midori in 1934. "Here was a scientist who converted to Christianity, not despite being a scientist, but because he was a scientist," said Dominic Higgins, director of the 2016 movie *All That Remains*, which is based on Takashi's life.

Takashi's conversion and marriage didn't mean that Takashi and Midori lived happily ever after. There is a dimension of suffering to living out the Catholic faith that the couple would experience as World War II approached. This dimension of their faith and the conclusion to their story will be shared in Chapter 8.

of Jesus and even more who have not had Jesus and his Church explained to them. You might recall the story, told in the Acts of the Apostles (8:26–40), of the Ethiopian eunuch who was reading from the Book of Isaiah. The Apostle Philip asked him if he understood what he was reading. "How can I, unless someone instructs me?" the man replied. Jesus and the Church are necessary to God's plan for salvation; however, through ways known only to God, the Holy Spirit can lead those who know neither Jesus nor the Church to unity with the Father.

In order to be faithful to Christ and to truly be his Body on earth, the Church must reach out with compassion to everyone; the Church must also challenge Catholics to live as Christ lived and to attend to how the Holy Spirit reveals that Christ's teachings are to be applied. Mahatma Gandhi, a Hindu known for leading a peaceful resistance to the British in India, is said to have said, "I like your Christ. But your Christians are so unlike your Christ." Of

St. Philip and the Ethiopian.

course, such a statement is not true the majority of the time. Without good Christian examples, few would be attracted to Christ and the Church, which is not the case. But Gandhi's reminder is an important one. The Church is a sign and the instrument of God's love for humanity—a sacrament. As a sign, the Church must strive for perfection; as the instrument, the Church must offer God's all-encompassing love to all.

Salvation Is a Lifelong Process

We need signs along the course of our life in order to recognize and understand God's presence. You may already have experienced many such markers in your own life. Perhaps you had an inspiring teacher who, in the course of one uplifting conversation, inspired you to fulfill a talent that you possess. Or maybe, in helping a sibling or class-mate who faced a special challenge, you felt the presence of God working through you. It's up to us to take a step back and recognize how God is with us.

The Church herself is the sacrament of our union with God and oth-ers, meaning that the Church—the people, the prayers, the saints, the

---

Seven Sacraments "Efficacious [effective] sign[s] of grace instituted by Christ and entrusted to the Church, by which divine life is dispensed to us through the work of the Holy Spirit" (*CCC*, Glossary). The Seven Sacraments are Baptism, Confirmation, Eucharist, Penance or Reconciliation, the Anointing of the Sick, Holy Orders, and Matrimony.

buildings—is a concrete demonstration of what is going on in the spiritual realm. "The Church is essentially both human and divine, visible but endowed with invisible realities" (*CCC*, 771, quoting St. Bernard of Clairvaux). The **Seven Sacraments** are unique in that they are clear and concrete signs, instituted by Christ, which we can perceive with our senses, but which point to a spiritual reality that is happening at the same time. For example, the signs of ordinary bread and wine that we perceive with our senses (sight, taste, touch, smell, and so on) point to the spiritual reality of Christ's Real Presence when they are consecrated in the Sacrament of the Eucharist.

We are not left to wonder whether we are making spiritual progress, growing in grace, and traveling the road toward eternal life: we can *see* these things happening through our participation in the sacraments and the life of the Church. "Christ, the one Mediator, established and continually sustains here on earth His holy Church, the community of faith, hope and charity, as an entity with visible delineation through which He communicated truth and grace to all" (*Lumen Gentium*, 8).

When St. Paul and his missionary companion were asked, "What must I do to be saved?" they replied, "Believe in the Lord Jesus" (Acts 16:30–31). Believing in Jesus is the first step toward salvation, but Jesus also asks us to cooperate in our salvation. He asks us to listen to him, to believe his words, and to apply his teaching. This is the way to salvation. Jesus said, "I am the way and the truth and the life" (Jn 14:6). The purpose of the Church is to continue Christ's way on earth by bringing the message of salvation to all. Like Takashi, we are called into the Church by people like Midori. We are then called to be like Midori in leading others to Jesus and the Church. Salvation, then, is a lifelong process.

SECTION Assessment

Comprehension

1. What were two events in Takashi Nagai's life that caused him to reconsider the spiritual dimension of life?

2. Why has the Catholic Church stated that "outside the Church there is no salvation"?

Vocabulary

3. Why might people who ascribe to *relativism* be more unlikely to be concerned about salvation?

4. How are the *Seven Sacraments* different from other everyday signs of God's presence?

Reflection

5. Comment on both the truth and the untruth of Gandhi's statement that Christians are so unlike Christ.

6. How would you answer the question posed to St. Paul, "What must I do to be saved?"

7. Give an example of how God has recently been at work in your life.

THE STUDY OF THE CHURCH

This course may appear in your school's curriculum as "Ecclesiology" or, simply, "Church." Recall that *ekklesia* is the Greek word for *church*. The suffix *-ology*, as you likely know, means "study of." From this root word and suffix we get the term *Ecclesiology*. This textbook supports a course on "the study of the Church." Here are two important points to be aware of for now.

First, *Church* refers to the "Church of Christ," that is, the "one, holy, catholic, and apostolic Church" that was founded by the Divine Person Jesus Christ, who became incarnate in history. Today, the proper term for the Church is the *Catholic Church. Catholic* means "universal." The Catholic Church is the universal Church in union with the bishop of Rome, the pope, who is the successor of St. Peter, the "rock" upon whom Jesus promised to build the Church (see Matthew 16:18). The name "Catholic" was associated with the Church as early as the second century. In 107 when St. Ignatius, the bishop of Antioch, was arrested and brought to Rome, he wrote a letter before he was martyred that said, "Where the bishop is present, there is the Catholic Church."[8]

Second, studying the Church is different from studying any other human institution, like a nation or an empire, or a historical period like the ancient era or the Middle Ages. The Church is a different kind of institution because she has both a divine dimension and a human dimension.

The divine dimension is explained like this: From the time of creation, when God the Father created the whole universe and then created humans to share in his divine life, he had the Church in mind. The Church is truly "a plan born in the Father's heart" (*CCC*, 759), foreshadowed or "already present in figure at the beginning of the world" (*Lumen Gentium*, 2). An early Christian writing stated, "The world was created for the sake of the Church."[9]

The Church is also the place where Jesus Christ, the Son of God, remains present and the place where God continues to share his revelation to the world. Because of God's presence in the Church from her beginning to her end, the Church transcends history even though she is part of historical time. In other words, the Church both takes part in human history *and* surpasses human comprehension of her meaning just as God himself both takes part in human history *and* surpasses human comprehension. The divine dimension of the Church is what makes studying the history of the Church different from other history courses you take in school and what makes the Church different from any other institution. Think of it this way: Some people who don't participate actively in the Church come to the Church for the sacraments like Baptism, First Holy Communion, and Matrimony. Even if they only do so in order to create an event where they have a party with cake and presents to follow, or to have a wedding in a beautiful place without understanding the transcendent nature of the sacraments, God is still present with them and acts with those receiving the sacraments. It is impossible for the human experience of the sacraments to take place without the divine presence. God gives his *grace*—a share in his life—to all who receive the sacraments worthily in faith.

The human dimension of the Church is what most people are familiar with. The Church is certainly an institution made up of a community of people and a hierarchy of structure. The pre-Christian era focused on preparation for the coming of Jesus Christ and the establishment of the Church. The Old Testament recounts this preparation through the experiences of the Jewish people. The New Covenant established by Christ gave rise to a new People of God, a community of believers not restricted to any particular ethnic, cultural, or political group. This community of believers, the Church, instead is formed from those who have faith in Christ and are baptized in his name. Christ is the head of this Church and remains present with her. After his Resurrection, Jesus commissioned his disciples to continue his work and promised them, "I am with you always, until the end of the age" (Mt 28:20).

The Light of the Church Overcomes the Darkness

Christ's promise to be present in the Church for all time ensures the Church will always have a divine dimension. God will never abandon his Church. Even when there is confusion, darkness, and difficulty in the world, truth, light, and grace can be found in the Church.

"I speak of the Church as if it were a field hospital. It's true: there are many, many wounded! So many people need their wounds healed! This is the mission of the Church: to heal the wounds of the heart, to open doors, to free people, to say that God is good, God forgives all, God is the Father, God is affectionate, God always waits for us." —Pope Francis

What about when this darkness invades the Church herself, when people in the Church do terrible things? We know this will happen because it has happened in the past and happens today. The Church is made up of human beings, who are sinful and who fail. Telling the history of the Church honestly means not only celebrating the triumphs of some of the Catholics who went before us but also admitting the failings of others. "Let us think of the history of Christians, even the history of the Church with the many sins, the many scandals, with many bad things, throughout these two millennia," Pope Francis said. With all of these problems, the pope wondered, why did the Church not fall? His answer: "Because God is there."[10]

If you have rejected the Church recently or in the past because of the sins by some of her members that you have witnessed, rethink this response. The Church is filled with sinners who come to the Church for healing, not to strut their righteous works. In one of his first homilies as pope, Pope Francis described the Church as a "field hospital that cleans and heals wounds." We all have wounds, and we all need them healed. The Church has a wide-open door for "everybody" (in the words of James Joyce), especially sinners. Twentieth-century convert Dorothy Day,∞ a founder of the Catholic Worker movement to serve the poor, said that she was first attracted to Catholicism after visiting Catholic churches in New York City and seeing rich and powerful people praying alongside the poor and ordinary.

Another Catholic convert of the early twentieth century, English writer G. K. Chesterton,≈ told a story of when he was considering whether to be Protestant or Catholic. He would leave his umbrella in the back of each church when he went inside for a worship service. In the Protestant churches, his umbrella was always there when the service ended, but in the Catholic churches he often found his umbrella missing after the service. Surprisingly, Chesterton wasn't angry. He said that if the Catholic Church had such an open door for thieves, the impoverished, and sinners, this was the place for him. He found that the Catholic Church really was "for everybody."

G. K. Chesterton

To "walk in darkness" is to be lost, as St. Augustine was lost. In contrast, the story of the Church is the story of God working through his people to

∞ Note

Dorothy Day (1897–1980) was a peace and social activist. The Catholic Worker movement is still active today; Catholic Worker houses serve the poor in many cities, and the *Catholic Worker* newspaper, aimed at an audience of the poor and suffering, remains in publication, still at the cost of one cent.

≈ Note

G. K. Chesterton (1874–1936) was a literary author, Christian apologist, philosopher, and art critic. He wrote of the Catholic Church: "It is impossible to be just to the Catholic Church. The moment men cease to pull against it, they feel a tug toward it. The moment they cease to shout it down, they begin to listen to it with pleasure. The moment they try to be fair to it, they begin to be fond of it."

bring light to the world. Jesus said, "Whoever follows me will not walk in darkness, but will have the light of life" (Jn 8:12). In spite of human sinfulness and frailties, the Church brings light to the world because it reflects the light of Christ. This is why the Church Fathers used the image of the moon to describe the Church. It has no light or power of its own, but it shines brightly in the darkness nonetheless, because it reflects the light of the sun. To "have the light of life" is to live in the hope that eternal life awaits us at the end of our journey on earth. Through the Church, we have access to that hope, which is grounded in belief in the saving power of Jesus Christ.

Why Be Catholic?

Most people today, Catholics and non-Catholics alike, understand that there is a connection between Jesus and the Catholic Church, but many people seem to believe that living the Christian faith and participating in the Catholic Church can be separated. You may hear comments like these:

- "I believe in God, but I have no use for the Church."

- "As long as I accept Jesus, the question of belonging to the Catholic Church or any church is irrelevant."

- "Commitment to any church gets in the way of real faith."

On the other hand, many young people who choose the Catholic Church say they have done so because of her continuity with the past. One recent convert stated: "If you won't build on the knowledge and understanding of the generations that went before you, you end up spending all of your time reinventing the wheel. For the most part, churches that want to reconsider the basics of faith and apply it to every generation never have the time and energy for service to the rest of the world." Another Catholic in her twenties said that she finds comfort and security in the presence of the **papacy**. For her, the papacy provides assurance that the Catholic Church will not be reduced to a conglomeration of independent congregations who work in opposition to one another almost as much as they work in cooperation.

---

papacy The supreme rule and ministry of the pope as the shepherd of the whole Church. The pope is the successor of St. Peter, the bishop of Rome, and the Vicar of Christ.

Pope Francis greeted thousands of Catholics at the opening of the 2023 World Youth Day in Lisbon, Portugal.

New Catholics and Catholics who are at Mass every Sunday make a profession of faith by reciting either the Nicene Creed or the Apostles' Creed. When you do so, you are saying by your words and actions that you believe in one God—the Father, Son, and Holy Spirit—and that you are committed to joining with others in the Church to make God known in the world.

SECTION Assessment

Comprehension

1. What is meant by the "Church of Christ"?

2. What is meant by *catholic* in the name "Catholic Church"?

3. What are two dimensions of the Church?

4. How is studying the history of the Church different from studying the history of other institutions or eras?

5. What did G. K. Chesterton learn about the Catholic Church by having his umbrella taken from the backs of churches?

Reflection

6. What is a plan you have for your future life that is born in your heart now?

7. Give an example of Pope Francis's image of the Church as a "field hospital."

8. How would you counter an argument that one of your peers has for not wanting to be a member of the Catholic Church?

CHAPTER 1 REVIEW

Section Reviews

Focus Question

What is the purpose of the Church?
Complete one of the following:

- Meet with a partner and take turns brainstorming words associated with the Church. Write down all the suggestions and circle the three that seem most prominent to you. Choose one of the words and write about what that word says about the meaning of *Church.*

- Write a short profile of a person you know who, through some twists and turns in life, has come to know and believe in God. What is a lesson you have learned from this person that you can use to further your own search for God?

- Read the Nicene Creed (see the Appendix). Write down one statement from it that you think you understand well and one statement that you would like to know more about.

Introduction
A Church of Intimacy and Self-Giving

Review

God wants to have an intimate, loving relationship with each person that magnifies the love between a husband and wife in marriage. God wants to share his life with people through his presence in the Church, and he wants people to share their lives with him through their own self-giving. Christians in every age have exemplified this offering in their own actions.

Assignment

Write about a saint not mentioned in the introduction section who gave up his or her life for another.

Section 1
Hearing the Call of the Church

Review

The meaning of *church* (*ekklesia*) is "people called together." The origins of this community are found in the Chosen People, formed from the family of Abraham. The Law of Mount Sinai remains foundational to the Church today, as Christians continue to recognize and use the Old Testament as part of Sacred Scripture. All people—practicing Catholics, non-Catholic Christians, Jews, Muslims, and others seeking to live according to God's design—are called to know Christ in the Catholic Church.

Assignment

How are you able to maintain your individuality while still seeking out communal identity in your family, peer group, and school? What individual gifts do you have that can benefit the Church?

Section 2
Jesus Christ Founded the Church

Review

Jesus, the Son of God and a historical person, founded the Church by his words and actions and shaped her form and structure. The Kingdom of God is present in the Church, although the complete transformation of creation that begins in the Church will not take place until the end of time. The Church was born of Christ's self-giving on the Cross. It is through the Cross that Christ brings salvation to the world.

Assignment

Read *Lumen Gentium*, 9 (see www.vatican.va). Transcribe two sentences that best summarize the content of Section 2.

Section 3

What Does It Mean to Be Saved?

Review

Salvation is the end goal of creation. It refers to the forgiveness of sins and the restoration of our permanent unity with God and one another. Salvation is made possible through the life, Death, and Resurrection of Christ. The Church is necessary for salvation because Jesus is necessary for salvation and Jesus is the head of the Church. This statement applies to people in different ways based on their knowledge of Jesus and their instruction in the Church. Achieving our salvation is not a one-time event; it is a lifelong process that we can measure by our participation in the life of the Church.

Assignment

Write a short profile of a person you know whom you consider to be a good representative of Christ and the Church.

Section 4

The Study of the Church

Review

Ecclesiology means "the study of the Church." The Church of Christ is known today as the Catholic Church. Studying the Church is different from other historical studies because the Church has both a divine and a human dimension. The divine dimension guarantees that God will always be present in the Church. Through our participation in the Church, we have access to Jesus Christ.

Assignment

Based on your study in this chapter, answer this question: What is the purpose of the Church?

Chapter Projects

Choose and complete at least one of the following projects to assess your understanding of the material in this chapter.

⚙ 1. *Write a Report on the North Wall of the Sistine Chapel*

The north wall of the Sistine Chapel displays a series of six paintings known as the Stories of Christ. However, there are other scenes and elements on the north wall. Read and report on what is contained on the north wall. Include mention of the following information in your report:

- What does Michelangelo's *Last Judgment* have to do with the Stories of Christ series?

- What are lunettes?

- What is the purpose of the false drapes?

- What legend is associated with Perugino's *Handing Over of the Keys* and the election of popes?

- How many events make up the Stories of Christ series?

- How is the Series of Pontiffs connected to the Stories of Christ series?

- Which artists created the Stories of Christ paintings?

⚙ 2. *Document a Conversion Story*

Create a minidocumentary on video (approximately five minutes in length) in which you interview two converts to Catholicism. Use questions like the following in your interview, as well as some questions of your own. Edit the video, adding music and other effects as you choose. Turn in the video on a platform that can be accessed by your teacher.

- What attracted you most to the Catholic Church?

- Can you name a specific occasion when you knew you wanted to become Catholic?

- How is the Catholic Church different from other churches?

- What was the most difficult issue you wrestled with before becoming Catholic?
- What do you love most about being Catholic?
- How do you share your faith with others?

⚙ 3. Compose Key Questions on Issues Facing the Church

Listed below are ten issues facing the Church today. Do the following: (1) Write a one-sentence summary of each issue as it applies to the Church. (2) Write three questions that are facing the Church on each issue (see example). (3) Answer the questions you formulated for one of the issues.

- Gospel witness

  How can American Catholics remain true to the vision of Jesus in a pluralistic and increasingly secular society that accepts as "normal" behaviors and lifestyles contrary to the Gospel? How can the Church best remind people of the reality of sin and the need for conversion? How can the Church challenge national leaders to work for peace in just ways in the midst of a world besieged by terrorism?

- Ecumenism
- Immigration
- Leadership
- Parish life
- Religious education
- Catholic schools
- Vocation crisis
- Women
- Loyalty to the pope

⚙ 4. Draw Early Symbols of Christianity

Two early symbols of Christianity were the *ichthys* and the Chi-Rho. *Ichthys* is the Greek word for "fish." This symbol was used to identify Christian homes when Christianity was illegal in the Roman Empire. The Chi-Rho refers to the first two letters of *Christ* in Greek. It became a symbol after Christianity was legalized. Roman soldiers often used this symbol on their shields in battle.

Draw these early symbols for Christianity on separate pieces of paper. Include a detailed caption below each symbol explaining more about its origins, history, and meaning. Finally, research a third symbol of Christianity from the first three centuries of the Church. Follow the same format with the third symbol as you did for the other two.

⚙ *5. Create Icons for Six Models of the Church*

Cardinal Avery Dulles (1918–2008) was a Jesuit priest and theologian. He is associated with describing and explaining the Church by using six models: (1) mystical communion, (2) sacrament, (3) servant, (4) herald, (5) institution, and (6) community of disciples. Write an introduction with a description of Cardinal Dulles and the origins of his six models of the Church. Next, create a three-column table in which you name each model, write a definition of each model, and create an icon to represent each model.

CHAPTER 1 REVIEW

Faithful Disciple
Mary, Mother of the Church

Mary's special role in the Church is based in Scripture. Elizabeth's address to Mary as "the mother of my Lord" (Lk 1:43) is the basis of Mary's most preeminent title, "Mother of God" (*Theotokos* in Greek). The angel's greeting to Mary in Luke 1:28—"Hail, favored one!"—is further evidence from the Scriptures of the importance of Mary's role in the Church. "Hail, favored one!" is translated in the Latin edition of the Bible as "Hail, full of grace!" If Mary is full of grace, then she is also able to dispense grace to others. Mary can share what she herself has been given.

In the early Church, Mary was also understood as a link between the Old Covenant and the New Covenant. The Old Testament contains several examples of foreshadowing of Mary. For instance, Mary is called the "New Eve," the mother prophesied in Genesis 3:15 who will strike at the serpent as her Son atones for the sin of Adam and Eve. She also embodies the qualities of the female heroines in the Old Testament. Mary also parallels the Ark of the Covenant: as the Mother of Jesus, the Son of God, she is the receptacle of the New Covenant.

By the third century, devotion to Mary was quite strong. Christian graves that were decorated with the images of saints and martyrs interceding on behalf of the deceased usually featured Mary in a place of honor. A prayer fragment from the third or fourth century underscores Mary's role as a powerful intercessor. It reads: "Mother of God [hear] my supplications: suffer us not [to be] in adversity from danger."

Pope Paul VI stressed in his 1974 apostolic exhortation *Marialis Cultus* (*Marian Devotion*) that Mary is not a timid and submissive woman, but a strong and brave woman who is willing to risk everything because she trusts and loves God. He emphasized her title as "Mother of the Church," writing that whether we turn our gaze to either the primitive Church or the Church today, we always find Mary. "The Church desires to live the mystery of Christ with her," Pope Paul wrote. "Devotion to the Blessed Virgin should become a concrete and deeply-felt love for the Church" (*Marialis Cultus*, 11).

Comprehension

1. How is Mary the "New Eve"?
2. How does Mary parallel the Ark of the Covenant from the Old Testament?
3. What does the prayer fragment from the third or fourth century teach about the Church's devotion to Mary at that time?

Reflection

"If Mary is full of grace, then she is also able to dispense grace to others." Explain the meaning of this statement and what impact it might have on your life and the lives of others today.

Prayer

The Benedictus is one of three canticles (hymns) in the opening chapters of Luke's Gospel (the other two being the Magnificat of Mary and the Song of Simeon). The Benedictus takes its name from its first word in Latin, which means "blessed." Also known as the Canticle of Zechariah (the father of John the Baptist), it is recorded in Luke 1:68–79. The Benedictus is addressed to the Israelites about their hopes for a Messiah, but it is also applicable to Christians who have welcomed Jesus, the Christ, and who anticipate his Second Coming.

The Benedictus

> Blessed be the Lord, the God of Israel;
> he has come to his people and set them free.
> He has raised up for us a mighty savior,
> born of the house of his servant David.
> Through his holy prophets he promised of old
> that he would save us from our enemies,
> from the hands of all who hate us.
> He promised to show mercy to our fathers
> and to remember his holy covenant.
> This was the oath he swore to our father Abraham:
> to set us free from the hands of our enemies,
> free to worship him without fear,
> holy and righteous in his sight all the days of our life.
> You, my child, shall be called the prophet of the Most High;
> for you will go before the Lord to prepare his way,
> to give his people knowledge of salvation
> by the forgiveness of their sins.
> In the tender compassion of our God
> the dawn from on high shall break upon us,
> to shine on those who dwell in darkness and the shadow of death,
> and to guide our feet into the way of peace.
> Glory to the Father and to the Son and to the Holy Spirit,
> as it was in the beginning, is now, and will be forever. Amen.

2

The Church Sets Her Foundation

► *Sieger Köder*

German artist Sieger Köder (1925–2015) was a Catholic priest and artist. During World War II, Köder was imprisoned for joining a Catholic youth movement that was in opposition to the Nazis. When he was forty-one, he began his studies for the priesthood. Fr. Köder was ordained in 1971. He combined his life as a parish priest and his work as an artist for the rest of his life.

His Pentecost image shown here is on a stained glass window of St. Bartholomew Church in the Berchtesgadener district of Bavaria in Germany. It shows Peter leaning out an open door to share the Gospel. The church is situated on the western shore of the Königssee Lake and can only be reached by ship or by a long hike through nearby Watzman mountains. The first church on this site dates from the twelfth century. In 1697 a church was rebuilt in the Baroque style featuring two domes and a red-domed roof, fittingly corresponding with the Pentecost image.

Köder completed a fuller and updated painting called *Pentecost (I Will Pour Out My Spirit)* in 2007, when he was eighty-two. Both the window and the painting focus on the meaning of Pentecost.

Pentecost (I Will Pour Out My Spirit) contrasts the Pentecost story in which the Jews gathered outside the window of the upper room were able to hear and understand St. Peter's words to them in spite of language differences (see Acts 2:1–13) with the Old Testament story of the Tower of Babel (see Genesis 11:1–9) in which God scrambled the one language of the people when they tried to build a tower to reach him in heaven. In the middle of the painting, St. Peter comes through an open door, holding a book with the Greek word *evangelion*, meaning "Gospel" or "Good News." Directly behind Peter, the Apostles can be seen with tongues of fire above their heads. The open windows allow Peter, filled with the fiery, red glow of the Holy Spirit, to share the Good News in his Pentecost sermon (see Acts 2:14–41) with the sad, gray figures beside him who are sitting in the scaffolding of the abandoned Tower of Babel. Köder also included an image of Pope St. John XXIII, who conceived of the Second Vatican Council as opening up a new spirit of **ecumenism** in the Catholic Church.

---

ecumenism The movement, inspired and led by the Holy Spirit, that seeks the full and visible unity of all Christians.

How did the Church grow and prosper in spite of persecutions?

Introduction

Love Is the Source of the Church

Section 1

The Holy Spirit Is Present in the Church

Section 2

St. Paul: From Persecutor to Apostle

Section 3

A Church of Martyrs

Section 4

Foundations of Belief and Practice

LOVE IS THE SOURCE OF THE CHURCH

Asked to love one another in the way that God expects of us as members of his Church, we can use the deep love between a husband and wife as a facsimile to help us understand the intimacy, care, devotion, and commitment that are necessary, but married love is not the source of love itself. We are only able to love one another because "love is of God; everyone who loves is begotten by God and knows God" (1 Jn 4:7).

In other words, God is the source of love. Think about that statement. How is God a *source* of love? How could God "create" love without experiencing love? Who is the object of God's love? If God is the source of love, the object of his love cannot originally have been people or the created world since neither was present from all eternity. Nor is God consumed in a selfish, solitary love for himself. Contemplating how God is the source of love leads us to the mystery of the Holy Trinity, Three Divine Persons in one God. Think of the Holy Trinity the way that Pope Francis explained it: "God is a 'family' of Three Persons who love each other so much as to form into one." For all of time, God loved in relationship.

In his words and actions, Jesus revealed this surprising identity of one God in Three Divine Persons. He referred to God as *Abba*, Father. In Jerusalem for the Feast of the Dedication of the Temple, Jesus explained to his listeners that his power is a gift from the Father. He said clearly, "The Father and I are one" (Jn 10:30). At the Last Supper, Jesus told his Apostles that the Father would send in his name "the Advocate, the holy Spirit" who is "the Spirit of truth that proceeds from the Father" and who would testify on Jesus's behalf (Jn 14:26, 15:26).

This revelation of God as Father/Creator, Son/Savior, and Holy Spirit/Advocate was one of the first mysteries that Christians pondered in order

This is a diagram of the Blessed Trinity, Three Divine Persons in one God. The Latin translates to "the Father is not the Son and the Son is not the Spirit" and vice versa.

to understand God's nature in Three Persons. Early Church Fathers and teachers of the faith understood that *Creator*, *Savior*, and *Advocate* were human terms for understanding God's actions within the created universe, especially his interactions with humanity. They also realized that God must understand himself in a way beyond human terms. In trying to understand the mind of God and think about how God understands himself, the Church described God's knowledge of himself in the Greek terms *Archē* (Source), *Logos* (Word), and *Pneuma* (Spirit). It is the divine source, the First Divine Person of the Trinity, the Father, who knows himself with infinite knowledge. He speaks this perfect knowledge in a Divine Word that completely reveals itself in another person, the Second Divine Person of the Trinity, the Son. These two Divine Persons look at each other and love one another. Their love for one another is breathed out in the Third Divine Person of the Trinity, the Holy Spirit.

After Jesus ascended into heaven, the Father sent the Third Divine Person, the Holy Spirit, to guide the members of the Church. Through the Father's sending of the Holy Spirit to the Church his Son had founded, we glimpse the loving relationship between the Three Divine Persons of the Trinity that had been in place for all time, before the creation of the world. The Church was founded in this love.

Led by the Spirit

The Holy Spirit revealed the Church to the world at Pentecost, when "the Church was publicly displayed to the multitude [and] the Gospel began to spread among the nations by means of preaching" (*Ad Gentes Divinitus*, 4). The coming of the Spirit to the Apostles at Pentecost can be seen as the "birth" of the Church, because from that point forward the followers of Jesus sought to continue his mission on earth.

It was on the first Pentecost that the Holy Spirit came in a special way to "the Twelve,"∞ the Apostles who had been chosen by Jesus to be close to him, to hear his teaching, and to lead the rest of his disciples in the way he intended. The Apostles played a crucial role in the early Church, preaching and witnessing to the reality of Jesus's Passion, Death, and Resurrection. Their example stamped the Church with the *apostolic* character that it has possessed ever since.

The Apostles had many collaborators in their mission to spread the Gospel, none more important than St. Paul, a Jewish convert and Roman citizen who visited local churches, wrote letters of instruction and exhortation to these new Christian communities after he left, and ultimately was arrested and martyred for his faith. St. Paul is known as the "Apostle to the Gentiles" and as one of the Church's greatest theologians. His writings and example had a formative and lasting impact on the character of the Church.

St. Paul wasn't the only early Christian to suffer persecution and death. Christians were under constant threat by the hostile Roman government in the Church's first three centuries of existence. Why didn't the Christians simply hide their faith? Because Jesus had told them not to. He taught that faith in him was a much-needed light to the world, explaining that a person does not "light a lamp and

The Conversion of St. Paul

After the betrayal of Judas on the eve of Jesus's Crucifixion, there were in fact only eleven Apostles, but Scripture consistently uses "the Twelve" to refer to the remaining group, and their number was replenished when, shortly after Pentecost, the Apostles selected Matthias to take Judas's place.

Fr. Walter Ciszek, SJ

World War II started when the German army invaded and conquered the nation of Poland. In eastern Poland, meanwhile, the Soviet army moved in to counter the German move. A Jesuit priest from Pennsylvania, Walter Ciszek, was there, serving the Eastern Church Catholics of the area. The Soviet invasion presented an opportunity for Fr. Ciszek: He could disguise himself as a laborer, get hired to work in a factory, and travel deep into the nation of Russia itself.

Ciszek was ecstatic. Yet he knew he had to temper his enthusiasm and examine his emotions. He needed to pray, to make sure that he was listening to God. "Wasn't I merely following my own desires and simply calling them God's will for me?" He had second thoughts, doubts, and worries, but he continued to pray "to be totally open to God's will, to hear his voice, and

The annual Fr. Walter Ciszek Day Mass at St. Casimir Roman Catholic Church in Shenandoah, Pennsylvania.

to leave self out of it." Then his answer came. "There came flooding back that sense of peace, that feeling of joy, that confidence in the simple and direct faith expressed in trusting him alone. I knew then what I must do." In his deliberation and confusion about what to do, Ciszek experienced the work of the Holy Spirit. He found that "God's will can be discerned by the fruits of the spirit it brings," and that "peace of soul and joy of heart are two such signs." Ciszek discovered that "there are movements of the soul, deeper than words can describe and yet more powerful than any reason, that give a man to know beyond question or arguing or doubt that *digitus Dei est hic* (the finger of God is here)." "Only in the decision to go to Russia," he concluded, "did I find the joy and the interior peace that are marks of God's true intervention in the soul."[1]

then put it under a bushel basket; it is set on a lampstand, where it gives light to all in the house. Just so, your light must shine before others, that they may see your good deeds and glorify your heavenly Father" (Mt 5:15–16). The Christian way of life is meant to be an example to all and to draw all toward Jesus.

Instead of hiding their faith, Christians boldly continued to share the Gospel, pray together, and live according to the moral teaching of Jesus. They believed that being marked as followers of Jesus—as members of the Church that Christ founded—was essential for salvation, and they held fast to the truth of the faith in the face of every difficulty. The first Christians set the pattern for the Christian way of life from that time forward. They exemplified the Church as "the People of God gathered together." They lived in community, sharing and tending to each other's needs. They gathered in prayer, especially for the "breaking of the bread" (Acts 2:42), the Eucharist, where they re-presented the sacrifice of Jesus and received him in Communion. Despite persecutions, the Church continued to spread and grow.

The two millennia since the first Pentecost in the Church are filled with examples of the Spirit at work in Christian saints and other ordinary people of faith. For example, **Fr. Walter Ciszek**, an American priest, was convinced that his fifteen years spent in a Siberian prison camp after World War II were directed by the Holy Spirit. He said: "I had no doubts, no fears, no hesitation. It was as if my whole life, in God's plan, had pointed to this moment." The same Holy Spirit present as the Third Person of the Holy Trinity from all eternity and sent to the Apostles as an Advocate at Pentecost has remained with the Church from her very beginning and is present today, providing us with the peace and joy of Christ along with courage to persevere in inevitably difficult times.

SECTION Assessment

Comprehension

1. What human terms are used to describe the Father, Son, and Holy Spirit?

2. Why is the first Pentecost understood as the birth of the Church?

3. What was the pattern for Christian life established by the first Christians?

4. How was Fr. Ciszek able to get into Russia during World War II?

Reflection

5. Explain the love between the Divine Persons of the Holy Trinity in your own words.

6. What is a difficulty of assigning human terms to how God understands himself as Father, Son, and Holy Spirit?

7. What is similar about St. Paul's and Fr. Walter Ciszek's motivation for ministry?

THE HOLY SPIRIT IS PRESENT IN THE CHURCH

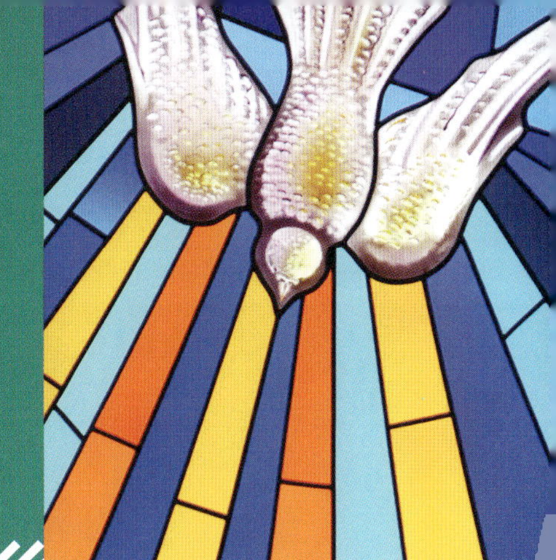

The Acts of the Apostles is the first Christian history book. The likely author of Acts is St. Luke, who also is credited with writing the third Gospel. The style, language, and organization of the Gospel of Luke and Acts are very similar. Both the Gospel and Acts are addressed to Theophilus, a name that means "friend of God" (see Luke 1:1–4 and Acts 1:1–2).

The Acts of the Apostles focuses on the early years of the Church. In its first two chapters, it describes the very beginning of the Church. After Jesus's Resurrection, **St. Peter** and the other Apostles prayed together for fifty days. This period of preparation gives us the term *Pentecost*, meaning "fiftieth." Pentecost was also the Greek name for a traditional Jewish harvest feast at the end of spring, on the fiftieth day after Passover. We can imagine the Apostles being afraid before Pentecost. After Jesus's Ascension (forty days before Pentecost), they were left without their Master and Teacher. The Jewish and Roman leaders who concocted accusations against Jesus that resulted in his arrest, trial, and Crucifixion were likely to seek out his followers to hand out the same type of punishments.

They weren't left hopeless, however. Before ascending into heaven, Jesus told them what would happen: "You will receive power when the holy Spirit comes upon you, and you will be my witnesses in Jerusalem, throughout Judea and Samaria, and to the ends of the earth" (Acts 1:8). On Pentecost, while the Apostles were gathered with Mary, the Mother of Jesus, in the same upper room in Jerusalem where the Last Supper was held, the Holy Spirit came suddenly "like a strong driving wind, and it filled the entire house. . . . Then there appeared to them tongues as of fire, which parted and came to rest on each one of them. And they were all filled with the holy Spirit" (Acts 2:2–4). The Apostles quickly discovered what it meant to be "filled with the Holy Spirit."

Pentecost, *by Emil Nolde.*

Because it was a Jewish feast day, Jews from all over the Mediterranean region were gathered in Jerusalem, celebrating together. They spoke many different native languages. When Peter, whom Jesus had chosen to be the "rock," or foundation, of the Church, began preaching the Gospel to this diverse group, the listeners were "astounded and bewildered" (Acts 2:12) because they were all able to understand him.

The reaction that Peter generated on the first Pentecost has been common throughout the ages wherever the Gospel is preached. Some who heard him recognized that they were witnessing a miracle and understood that God was trying to get their attention. Others who couldn't believe that an uneducated fisherman accompanied by other commoners could have anything valuable to say dismissed the spectacle, arguing that Peter's exhilarating speech could only be explained by his being intoxicated, even though it was only nine in the morning. In other words, some heard the Gospel message and embraced it; others rejected it and went on with their lives.

The Jews who *were* receptive to the words of Peter "were cut to the heart" and asked the Apostles what to do. Peter was ready with his response: "Repent and be baptized, every one of you, in the name of Jesus Christ for the forgiveness of your sins; and you will receive the gift of the holy Spirit" (Acts 2:37–38). The Holy Spirit was not reserved for a select few. Here, at the very beginning of the Church, the Apostles made it clear that the Good News was intended for *all* people *everywhere*. All were called to gather together to follow the Lord and to be his Church.

Without the Holy Spirit, the Church would be not much more than a fraternal club that meets socially and for community service. With the Holy Spirit, God is actively present in the Church, both in the **Magisterium** and in the lives of all her members. The Holy Spirit manifests to different people in different ways, inspiring each person to contribute to the work of the Church in his or her own, unique way. St. Paul called these manifestations "fruit of the Spirit" and listed them as "love, joy, peace, patience, kindness, generosity, faithfulness, gentleness, self-control" (Gal 5:22–23). According to the *Catechism of the Catholic Church*, "by this power of the Spirit, God's children can bear much fruit" (*CCC*, 736).

"Make Disciples of All Nations"

Just before Jesus ascended into heaven, he gave to his followers what is known as the *Great Commission*. Jesus commanded them to "Go, therefore, and make disciples of all nations, baptizing them in the name of the Father, and of the Son, and of the holy Spirit, teaching them to observe all that I have commanded you" (Mt 28:19–20). Make disciples of *all nations*! The followers of Jesus were to spread his message to the entire world. This was a daunting task for a handful of fishermen and other misfits who lacked wealth, power, and influence.

The Apostles knew that the task was impossible to achieve by their own efforts alone, but they believed that "for God all things are possible" (Mt 19:26). Through the prompting of the Holy Spirit, they set about making the

---

Magisterium The living, teaching office of the Church whose task it is to interpret the Word of God; the bishops in communion with the successor of Peter, the bishop of Rome (the pope). Jesus bestowed the right and power to teach in his name on Peter and the Apostles and their successors.

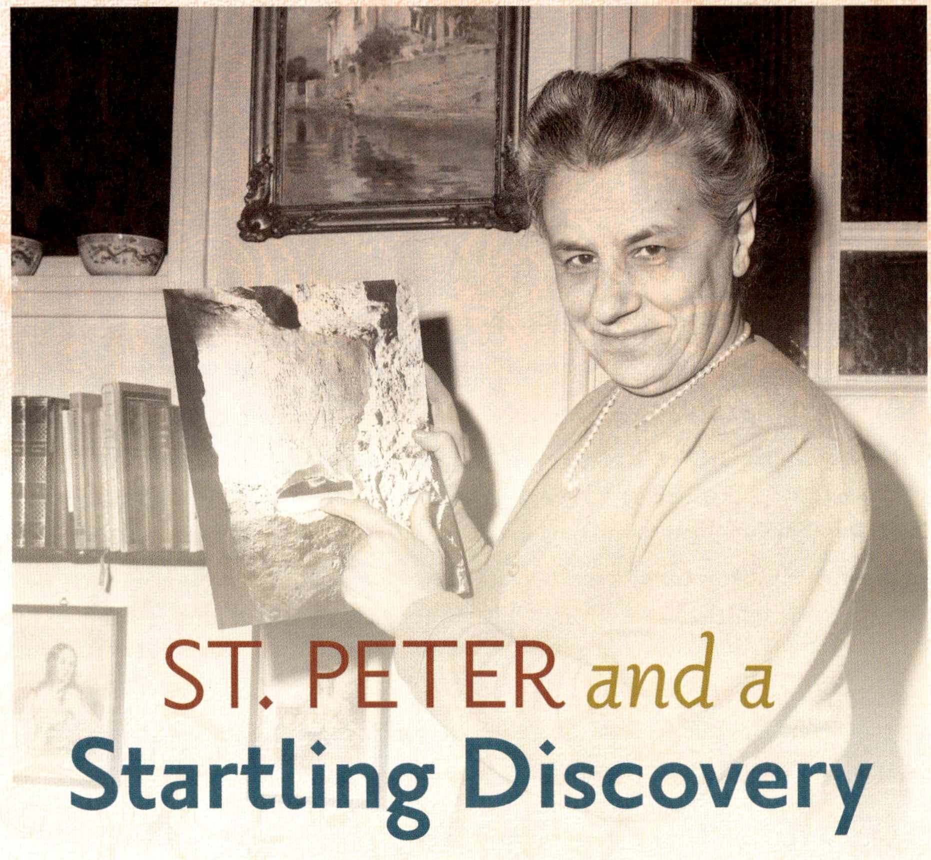

ST. PETER *and a*
Startling Discovery

Dark and dank earthen walls enveloped Dr. Margherita Guarducci as she descended into the ancient underground burial site. An expert in ancient languages and symbols, she had been working at the site for months, trying to decipher graffiti that appeared near one of the tombs. Desperate for clues to the meaning of some of the unusual inscriptions, she asked a nearby workman about a cavity in the graffiti wall, whether anything had been found there.

The worker had by chance been present when the contents of the gap had been removed. He led her to a wooden box in a nearby storage room. In the box were a number of bone fragments. Guarducci insisted that the box be placed in more secure storage and examined. She suspected that the importance of the box's contents had not been adequately appreciated. She was right.

The archaeological dig on which Guarducci was working was the search for the bones of St. Peter. Underneath the magnificent Basilica of St. Peter in Rome, there is a burial chamber known as the Sacred Grottoes. After the death of Pope Pius XI in 1939, plans were made to enlarge the chamber by excavating its floor. To the surprise of everyone involved, the construction workers who began digging out the floor unearthed a lost chapter of history. When they uncovered a series of burial sites *underneath* the "modern" burial chamber, the construction project suddenly became an archaeological dig.

St. Peter's Basilica is an old church—about five hundred years old—but in the vast scope of Church history, it's relatively young. Before the church that sightseers gawk at today was built, there was on the same site a different church—the "old" St. Peter's Basilica, built by the emperor Constantine in the fourth century. Everyone knew that the builders of the sixteenth century had torn down and covered up the old basilica, so it wasn't surprising that the foundations of the old basilica were found beneath the new basilica. But no one remembered what was beneath the old basilica when it was built long ago in the waning days of the Roman Empire.

As the Vatican workers continued to dig, the picture got more interesting. The old basilica had been built on the slope of a hill, over the top of an existing cemetery. To build on such terrain had required an immense amount of labor and materials, and to build over a cemetery violated Roman law and custom. It would have been difficult and controversial. Why had the emperor Constantine gone to such trouble to place the church at precisely that spot?

Church tradition held that St. Peter had been killed and buried on this very hill, but there was little hard evidence justifying this belief. The findings under the new St. Peter's, however, began to back up the claim. The altar of the old St. Peter's was directly under the altar of the new St. Peter's, and that old altar was directly above a cemetery where Christians were buried. The placement of the old basilica supported the idea that the spot had been honored as the tomb of St. Peter from at least the third century.

A cache of bones was discovered within the tomb thought to be Peter's, but scientific tests showed that they did not match what was

Pope Francis holds the bone fragments said to belong to the first pope, St. Peter, during a ceremony on the Solemnity of Our Lord Jesus Christ the King at St Peter's Square on November 24, 2013, at the Vatican.

known about the fisherman. Shortly after Margherita Guarducci's discovery of the neglected wooden box, however, the pieces started to come together. Making a breakthrough in her decoding work, Guarducci discovered that one of the inscriptions on the graffiti wall read, "Peter is within." At some point, the bones of the Apostle had been moved from the tomb into a niche in the wall near it, probably to protect the remains from flooding.

Following exhaustive scientific examination of the bones in the wooden box and the gravesite surrounding it, Vatican authorities had enough evidence and certitude to make a public declaration. In June of 1968, nearly thirty years after the excavation began, Pope Paul VI announced the stunning discovery to the world. After lying hidden for almost two thousand years, the remains of St. Peter had been found![2]

The discovery beneath St. Peter's in the twentieth century affirmed that the Apostles—St. Peter chief among them—held an honored place in the early Church. That these men called by Jesus were central to the life of the newborn Church was clear from her very beginning at Pentecost.

Great Commission a reality. The newborn Church began growing immediately. Peter's preaching was successful on Pentecost: some three thousand people decided to be baptized and join the new movement (see Acts 2:41)—three thousand out of a world population of about three hundred million.[3] Making disciples of all nations still seemed far-fetched, but it was a start.

It was a world in some ways receptive to the Good News. The Roman Empire was open to ideas that came from other cultures. It copied the arts and literature of the Greek civilization that it had conquered and borrowed architecture from Egypt. Roman religion permitted additions to be made to its *pantheon*, or collection, of gods. Many Romans were attracted to the strong theology and moral code of Judaism but were discouraged by the rigidity of Jewish law. Christianity offered a path to know the one true God without the burdens of the Old Law.

In other ways, it was a world that presented challenges to the new faith. While Roman authorities were lenient about worshipping a variety of gods, they were nervous about a religion that denied divinity to the rulers of Rome. Centuries of persecution had created powerful cohesion in the Jewish community, and thus many Jews were dismayed by the prospect of a religion that embraced Gentiles. A devout Jew would have seen Christian belief in the divinity of Jesus as blasphemy, a serious sin against the First Commandment.

The task of navigating through both the promise and the peril of the first-century world fell above all to the recognized leaders of the early Church, the Apostles.

The Apostolic Nature of the Church

The importance of the Apostles is so great that it is etched into the very identity of the Catholic Church. Theirs along with the teachings of St. Paul, St. Ignatius of Antioch, and St. Irenaeus, in particular, were formalized in the Nicene Creed (see the Appendix) in the early fourth century. In 381 at the First Council of Constantinople, the words "I believe in one, holy, catholic, and apostolic Church" were officially added to the creed. These characteristics are known as the **four marks of the Church**. The four marks of the Church, and how they are manifested throughout the history of the Church, help to

---

four marks of the Church The attributes (also called notes) of the Church mentioned in the Nicene Creed: "We believe in one, holy, catholic, and apostolic Church."

explain how the nature of the Church is an expression of the nature of Jesus Christ. Through the Holy Spirit, Christ makes the Church one, holy, catholic, and apostolic. The apostolic nature of the Church originates, naturally, with the Apostles, especially in three ways (see *CCC*, 857):

1. **The Church is built on the foundation of the Apostles**, the twelve men Jesus chose to spread the Good News.

2. **The Church hands on the teaching of the Apostles**, as expressed in the Deposit of Faith, considering it to be the faithful account of the teaching of Christ himself.

3. **The Church is to be "taught, sanctified, and guided by the Apostles until Christ's return."** This is accomplished in a concrete way, through the appointment of the pope and bishops, successors to the Apostles, who continue to serve the Church as the Twelve Apostles did.

The word *apostle* comes from the Greek word for "emissary"—the representative of a king who acts in his name. Jesus appointed the Twelve, "[whom he also named apostles] that they might be with and he might send them forth to preach" (Mk 3:14). The first task for the Apostles was to go forth and preach—a mission that was confirmed in the Great Commission.

This foundational role of the Apostles can be seen throughout the early history of the Church, especially in the Acts of the Apostles. This first Christian history book shows how the Apostles built up the community of believers through three main actions: *preaching*, *teaching*, and *witness*. These actions are explained in the following sections.

Preaching

After his preaching from the window of the upper room on Pentecost, Peter and the other Apostles continued to share the Gospel widely for the rest of their lives. In the face of opposition from Jewish religious leaders, Peter and John defended the position that Jesus was the Messiah and the Son of God. When the Jewish elders insisted that they stop preaching, they answered, "It is impossible for us not to speak about what we have seen and heard" (Acts 4:20).

Acts also reports that "many signs and wonders were done among the people at the hands of the apostles" (Acts 5:12). Large numbers of sick people were cured when they were brought into the presence of Peter and the other Apostles. *Miracles*, amazing healings or other beneficial events that science cannot explain, had been a key feature of Jesus's ministry. The Apostles demonstrated both Jesus's concern for those in need and his power to help them. Although many people in the modern era doubt the validity of miracles, there is solid evidence that they have occurred in every era. Miracles continue to occur in the contemporary life of the Church today, and they have been analyzed and documented using modern scientific techniques (see Chapter 6).

While we don't know exactly where and how the Apostles preached after they left Jerusalem, there is some evidence in the Scriptures and other early Church writings that they were ultimately martyred in places that were early centers of the Church. John, the Beloved Disciple, was the only Apostle who did not suffer a martyr's death.[4] Matthew may have traveled and preached in Ethiopia. The Apostle Andrew is associated with bringing Christianity to present-day Ukraine. Simon and Jude evangelized in Persia and Mesopotamia—present-day Iran and Iraq. There is a strong tradition that Thomas spread the faith in India. Some groups of Indian believers still call themselves "Thomas Christians" and honor the tomb of St. Thomas in the city of Chennai

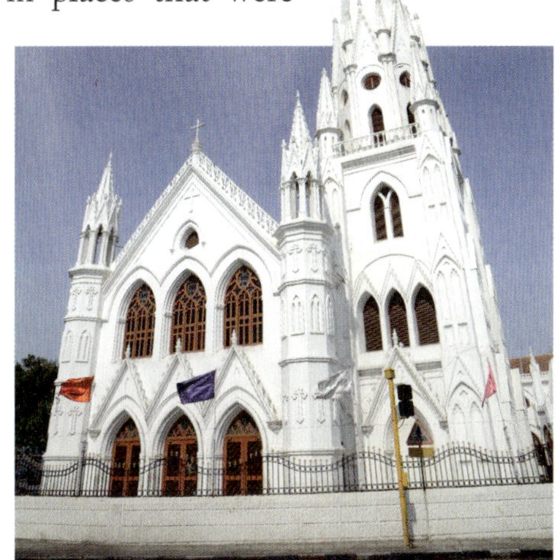

San Thome Basilica was built in the sixteenth century over the tomb of St. Thomas in Chennai, India.

in southeastern India. The example the Apostles left is that the Gospel is meant to be shared. This is what is meant by **evangelization**.

Teaching

The Apostles also had primary responsibility for ensuring that the message of Jesus was not distorted. When there were disputes, early Christians went to

evangelization The bringing of the Good News of Jesus Christ to others through words and actions.

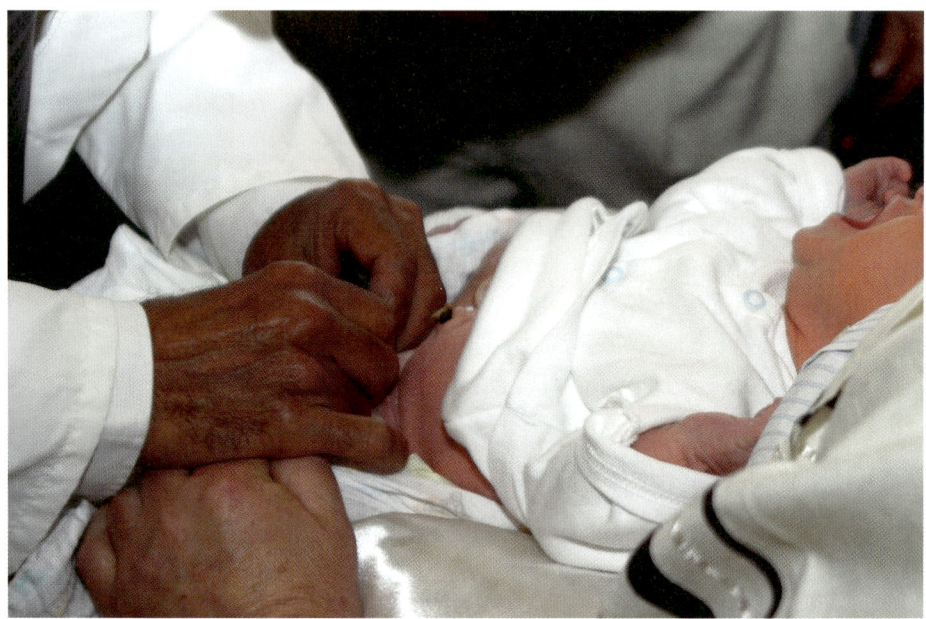

A bris *is the Jewish ceremony in which a baby boy is circumcised. Traditionally, this takes place on the eighth day of the baby's life and is held in a synagogue during the morning services. The ritual is performed by a* mohel *(rhymes with "boil"). Some mohels work full time in this profession, but many are also physicians, rabbis, cantors, or nurse-midwives. A mohel is trained in the Jewish laws concerning circumcision, as well as in modern surgical hygiene.*

the Apostles to sort them out. This marks the difference between their role as preachers and their role as teachers.

An early dispute involved the participation of Gentiles in the Church. When God spoke to Peter in a vision, Peter became convinced that the offer of salvation in Jesus Christ was available for Gentiles as well as Jews (see Acts 10:9–49), but subsequent questions arose about what elements of Judaism were essential to Christianity. For example:

- What parts of Mosaic Law did the Gentile Christians need to follow?

- Did they have to follow Jewish dietary laws?

- Was it necessary for Gentile Christians to worship in the Jewish Temple?

- Did male Gentiles who converted to Christianity need to be circumcised? (Circumcision was the sign of the covenant between Abraham and his descendants.)

To resolve these matters, Paul, his traveling companion Barnabas, and others went to Jerusalem to consult with the leaders of the Church there. "After much debate had taken place" (Acts 15:7), Peter announced their decision: the Gentiles would not need to be circumcised or follow the other Mosaic laws, for Jesus had taught that it wasn't the Law that brought salvation. "On the contrary, we believe that we are saved through the grace of the Lord Jesus" (Acts 15:11).

This event, known as the Council of Jerusalem, exhibits key principles by which the early Church was governed and by which the structures of the Church would develop over the ensuing centuries:

1. Unity. It was essential for Christians to be unified in their beliefs and practices. Instead of each local group doing its own thing, they sought guidance from authorities in the Church regarding matters of importance.

2. *Apostolic authority.* When early Christians couldn't agree on something, they knew where to go with their question: to the Apostles. The Twelve had been chosen by Jesus himself, had followed him, and had listened at his feet. Other followers of Christ trusted that the Apostles would faithfully interpret and apply the Gospel message.

3. *Petrine primacy.* The Apostles themselves recognized their own leader. Peter had been singled out by Jesus for leadership, and the early Church recognized his authority. At the Council of Jerusalem, the **presbyters** and Apostles discussed the question and arrived at a consensus, but it was Peter who approved the decision and announced it to the world.

These principles have continued to guide the Church throughout her history. The unity of the Church is rooted in common beliefs and practices. These have their ultimate source in the life and teachings of Jesus, but the Church relies on the successors of the Apostles, the bishops, to ensure that

presbyters The Greek name (meaning "elders") for priests, that is, members of the order of priesthood. Presbyters, or priests, are coworkers with their bishops and assist them in priestly service to the Church.

this teaching is interpreted and applied accurately. The pope, as the successor of Peter, fills his role as head of the Apostles; he is the "perpetual and visible principle and foundation of unity of both the bishops and . . . the faithful" (*Lumen Gentium*, 23).

Witness

In all ages, people have rejected the Gospel because they perceive that it will challenge their cherished beliefs or interfere with their way of life. Richard Dawkins, a scientist and well-known contemporary atheist, argues that Christianity promotes ignorance, intolerance, and other abuses.[5] Abigail Favale, a twenty-first-century feminist who later embraced the Catholic faith, wrote before her conversion, "I don't like the Bible. It is teeming with things that completely contradict my most deeply held beliefs and ethics."[6] Some oppose Christianity because it threatens their positions of power and wealth. Joseph Stalin, who ruled the Soviet Union during the imprisonment of Fr. Ciszek, feared that religious freedom would undermine his communist regime. Whatever the reasons motivating hostility toward the faith, Christians have frequently endured persecution. It was true in the earliest years of the Church, it is true today, and it has been true in every era in between.

Catholics today all around the world are persecuted for their faith and sometimes die for their faith.

The lives—and deaths—of the Apostles are therefore a witness to the life-transforming power of the Gospel. The teaching of Jesus is not merely a pleasant set of ideas that can help us live a more satisfying life. To follow Jesus is to commit our lives completely to his service and to the truths he taught about humanity and God. These truths make some people uncomfortable. Sometimes, they so upset people that they react violently. The Apostles experienced this firsthand. Remember that all the Apostles except John gave their lives for the faith, that is, they were *martyrs*.

The Apostles knew that they were literally risking their lives when they preached the Gospel, but they did it anyway because Christ had commanded them to bring the Good News to the entire world. The first Apostle to be killed for his belief in Jesus was James, who died in a persecution launched by Herod, the king who ruled Jerusalem and the surrounding area under the authority of the Roman Empire: "King Herod laid hands upon some members of the church to harm them. He had James, the brother of John, killed by the sword" (Acts 12:1–2).

Christian martyrdom continues. Christianity is the most persecuted religion in the world today. According to the *Religious Freedom Report* by the foundation Aid to the Church in Need, Christianity is threatened in thirty-eight countries, twenty-one of which are places of persecution. "It might be hard for us to believe, but there are more martyrs today than in the first centuries," said Pope Francis, because "they speak the truth and proclaim Jesus Christ." This is true also in countries that in theory support religious freedom.[7]

Although we might not be killed for our faith, all Catholics will face persecutions as they strive to follow Jesus. Have you witnessed pushback among your peers for those who take Catholic pro-life positions, support traditional marriage, refrain from sex before marriage, or take a Catholic position on any other hot-button issues? All of us will find ourselves in situations where it is uncomfortable or controversial to be Catholic. We are called to be witnesses ("martyrs") in those situations: to speak and act with charity rather than hostility, but also to speak and act in a way that clearly identifies us as Catholic. When we stand up for our faith even when it is hard to do so, we are following the example of the Apostles. We are being "apostolic."

SECTION Assessment

Comprehension

1. What happened to the Apostles on Pentecost?

2. What was remarkable about Peter's speech to the Jews gathered in Jerusalem for Pentecost?

3. What is the Great Commission?

4. Name the three ways that the Church's apostolic nature originates with the Apostles.

5. What is the difference between the Apostles' preaching and their teaching?

6. What was the decision reached at the Council of Jerusalem regarding Gentiles?

Vocabulary

7. Define *Magisterium*.

8. When were the *four marks of the Church* added to the creed? When was the creed formalized?

Reflection

9. Choose two gifts of the Holy Spirit and explain how one is manifested in your life and how the other can be more visible in your actions.

10. What does finding the remains of St. Peter under the basilica at the Vatican have to do with Petrine primacy?

11. Have you been persecuted for taking a stand on an issue? Have you ever persecuted someone for taking a stand on an issue? Explain.

ST. PAUL: FROM PERSECUTOR TO APOSTLE

The first Christian martyr was not an Apostle, but rather Stephen, who had been chosen by the Apostles to be a deacon in the Church. Some Jewish authorities were threatened by his preaching about Jesus with "wisdom and the spirit," and they "instigated some men to say, 'We have heard him speaking blasphemous words against Moses and God'" (Acts 6:10, 11). Recognizing his accusers' lack of faith, Stephen responded by presenting a summary of the history of the Old Covenant and the failures of the Chosen People to be faithful to God. "You always oppose the holy Spirit," he concluded. "You are just like your ancestors. Which of the prophets did your ancestors not persecute? They put to death those who foretold the coming of the righteous one, whose betrayers and murderers you have now become. You received the law as transmitted by angels, but you did not observe it" (Acts 7:51–53).

Stephen then had a vision of Jesus standing at the right hand of God in heaven: "Behold, I see the heavens opened and the Son of Man standing at the right hand of God" (Acts 7:56). His accusers saw this as blasphemy and were furious. "They cried out in a loud voice, covered their ears, and rushed upon him together. They threw him out of the city, and began to stone him" (Acts 7:57–58). Death by stoning was the punishment dictated in the **Pentateuch** for a variety of serious sins, including blasphemy. Stephen's Jewish listeners were thus reacting in the way they believed was consistent with the faith of Abraham, Isaac, and Jacob. Normally, a witness to the crime would begin by casting the first stone, and then others would join, implying the community's approval of the judgment. (In the rocky terrain of Palestine, the projectiles used were easy to come by.) The victim might be rendered unconscious by an

Pentateuch Meaning "five books" in Greek, the first five books of the Old Testament: Genesis, Exodus, Leviticus, Numbers, and Deuteronomy.

early blow, or death might be drawn out as he or she was pelted repeatedly, eventually dying of blunt force trauma. It was a harsh and painful death, but capital punishment by excruciating methods (for example, crucifixion) was common in this period in history.

In the face of this cruelty, Stephen's reaction is even more remarkable. Just before he died, Stephen set an example for all Christian martyrs to follow. First, he commended his soul to God by saying, "Lord Jesus, receive my spirit." Then he offered forgiveness for those who persecuted him, even as he was being battered by the rocks they hurled: "He fell to his knees and cried out in a loud voice, 'Lord, do not hold this sin against them'" (Acts 7:59–60). In both of his dying statements, Stephen was following the example of Jesus on the Cross; Jesus had also commended his spirit to God and asked his Father to forgive those who killed him.

The martyrdom of St. Stephen.

As Stephen died, a young man stood nearby who watched the cloaks of Stephen's killers as they went about their bloody business. His name was Saul, and he fiercely supported the effort to wipe out the new Christian faith. Saul also had a Roman name: Paul.

Who was Saul? We learn much of the information about him from the letters of St. Paul and the Acts of the Apostles. He was born of the Jewish tribe of Benjamin in Tarsus in approximately AD 10 during the reign of the Roman emperor Augustus. Tarsus was a city in Cilicia (present-day south-central Turkey). Like many Jews of his time living outside of Palestine, he had both a Jewish name and a Roman name. His Jewish name, Saul, was the name of the first king of Israel, also from the tribe of Benjamin; his Roman name, Paul, or Paulus, was a well-known family name.

Saul received an excellent Greek education in Tarsus. He also learned the trade of tent making there, which allowed him to support himself during his later missionary activities (it is possible that he evangelized many of his customers, using the sales of his tents as a way to begin conversations). Because he was a Roman citizen, Saul was later guaranteed a Roman trial. His upbringing in Tarsus also familiarized him with Gentile religions, philosophies, and customs. Saul studied to be a rabbi under the famous teacher Gamaliel (see Acts 22:3). Saul was a strict Pharisee and willing to persecute anyone he thought was deviating from true Jewish practices. This is what led him to be present at and participate in the martyrdom of Stephen.

In one of the most surprising and dramatic religious conversions in all of history, Saul would become the greatest missionary in the Church. Although St. Paul was not one of the Twelve Apostles called personally by Jesus in the Gospels, the Risen Christ appeared to him on the road to Damascus and brought about his conversion. This is why St. Paul is called an Apostle. His missionary zeal and his prominent role in the newborn Church meant that he shared closely in the apostolic ministry of the Twelve. He profoundly influenced the early Church in two ways: he spread the faith by *preaching*, and he taught the faith by *writing*.

The Preaching of St. Paul

Over the course of about ten years during the 40s and 50s, Paul traveled across much of the Roman Empire, preaching the Gospel in places that are today in the countries of Syria, Turkey, Greece, and Italy. This extensive travel was

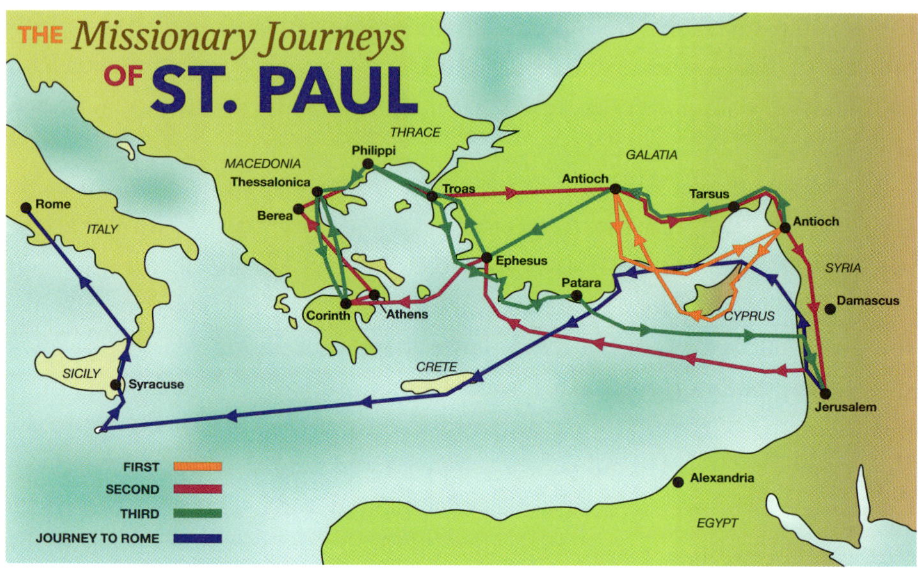

enabled by the impressive system of roads that had been constructed and the commercial shipping routes that had developed in the Mediterranean world under the Roman Empire. The unity and peace generated by the strength of the Roman legal system and the stability of Roman rule during the first two hundred years of the Christian era—often called the *Pax Romana*, or Roman Peace—also aided the spread of Christianity, including Paul's ministry. Biblical scholar William Ramsay concluded that "the Roman roads were probably at their best during the first century after Augustus had put an end to war and disorder. . . . Thus St. Paul traveled in the best and safest period."[8]

Paul shared about Jesus Christ with anyone who would listen. As a Jew, he enjoyed access to synagogues in the cities he visited, and he would initially preach to his fellow Jews, making the case that the Messiah they had been awaiting had arrived. Although some Jews believed and became followers of Jesus, many resisted Paul's message, just as he for a time had resisted the same message.

So, Paul began preaching in public squares or wherever he could find an audience. Most of Paul's listeners were not Jews, and many of these Gentiles believed the message Paul conveyed. Although they had not been awaiting

epistles From the Greek word for "letters," books in the New Testament in the form of letters. Some of the epistles attributed to St. Paul and others are known as catholic, or universal, epistles.

the Messiah foretold by the prophets as the Jewish people had, they recognized the truth and attractiveness of Jesus's message of love, forgiveness, and freedom from sin and death. Some of the Gentiles were already associated with *Hellenists*—Jews who were more open to Greek and Roman influences and willing to allow their faith and religious practice to be shaped to some extent by the culture around them. Paul made it clear that Jesus had intended his message of salvation for the whole world, not just for Jews. Paul enjoyed immense success among the non-Jews of the empire, and hence he is called the "Apostle to the Gentiles."

The Writing of St. Paul

Out of twenty-seven books in the New Testament, St. Paul wrote thirteen—far more than any other author. Paul's writings supplement the content of the Gospels in important ways, and the beliefs of Christianity owe much to Paul's articulation of the character and message of Jesus. Paul's creative mind provided some of the powerful images that have been used to depict the Church ever since.

Paul's **epistles**, or letters, are addressed to Christian communities across the Roman Empire, groups of believers that had been established by Paul or other evangelists in the earliest days of the Church. The titles of the letters tell us where those communities were located. For example, the Letter to the Ephesians spoke to Christians in Ephesus, an important Roman port city on the Mediterranean coast of what is now Turkey and home to one of the Seven Wonders of the Ancient World, the Temple of Artemis. It was in this letter that Paul likened the Church to a building, a temple of God that would long outlast the awe-inspiring Temple of Artemis. Writing to the Gentiles who made up the Ephesian Christian community, Paul insisted that they were now part of the Chosen People: "So then you are no longer strangers and sojourners, but you are fellow citizens with the holy ones and members of the household of God." This household, Paul continued, is "built upon the foundation of the apostles and prophets, with Christ Jesus himself as the capstone." Through Christ, "the whole structure is held together and grows into a temple sacred in the Lord; in him you also are being built together into a dwelling place of God in the Spirit" (Eph 2:19–22). In the image of the house of God, Paul captures essential features of the Church: that without Christ the Church is nothing;

Modern-day Ephesus, now known as Selcuk, Turkey.

that the Apostles are also indispensable to the life of the Church; that all her members grow in holiness by remaining within its protecting walls.

Paul also wrote two letters to the Christians in Corinth, a gritty port city in what is now Greece. In the First Letter to the Corinthians (12:12–26), he offered the most evocative metaphor for the Church, an image that theologians, saints, and popes have elaborated on ever since: the Body of Christ. Using the image of a body, Paul conveys the idea of combining flourishing diversity and essential unity. "Now the body is not a single part, but many," he writes. "If a foot should say, 'Because I am not a hand I do not belong to the body,' it does not for this reason belong any less to the body." Not every part of the body looks the same, acts the same, or has the same function within the body, but every part is nonetheless equally a part of the body. Even more, this diversity is precisely what makes the body's overall effectiveness possible. "If the whole body were an eye," Paul asks, "where would the hearing be? If the whole body were hearing, where would the sense of smell be?"

Even as the body needs different parts to make up a marvelous whole, so the Church needs people of different talents, backgrounds, cultures, and interests to do God's work. "But as it is, God placed the parts, each one of them, in

Rio Antirio Bridge on the Gulf of Corinth, Greece.

the body as he intended," Paul says. "There are many parts, yet one body. The eye cannot say to the hand, 'I do not need you,' nor again the head to the feet, 'I do not need you.'" Every part of the body is integrally connected to every other part. "If [one] part suffers, all the parts suffer with it; if one part is honored, all the parts share its joy."

Then Paul takes the analogy one step further. Not only is the Church a body, he says, but "now you are Christ's body, and individually parts of it." The Church is the Body of Christ. To do the work of Christ, that body needs many parts. "Some people God has designated in the church to be, first, apostles; second, prophets; third, teachers; then, mighty deeds; then, gifts of healing, assistance, administration, and varieties of tongues" (1 Cor 12:27–28).

Today, the Church is made up of about 1.3 billion people worldwide from a vast variety of nations and backgrounds. This diversity is an asset to the Church, because her members put their different perspectives and talents at the service of God. They are all united because they recognize the head of the Church, Jesus Christ. Like the Apostles, all Catholics have access to the Holy Spirit through their connection to Christ. "It is Christ who, as head of the Body, pours out the Spirit among his members to nourish, heal, and organize them in their mutual functions, to give them life, send them to bear witness, and associate them to his self-offering to the Father and to his intercession for the whole world" (*CCC*, 739).

SECTION Assessment

Comprehension

1. What was Stephen accused of?

2. How did Stephen's martyrdom resemble the Crucifixion of Jesus?

3. What is the significance of St. Paul's names?

4. How did the *Pax Romana* aid Paul's missionary work?

5. According to Paul, how is the household of the Church held together?

Vocabulary

6. How many *epistles* did St. Paul write?

Reflection

7. Describe an example of how you can use everyday conversation as a lead-in to share the Gospel with someone.

8. Explain the analogy of a body that Paul used to describe the Church in your own words.

A CHURCH OF MARTYRS

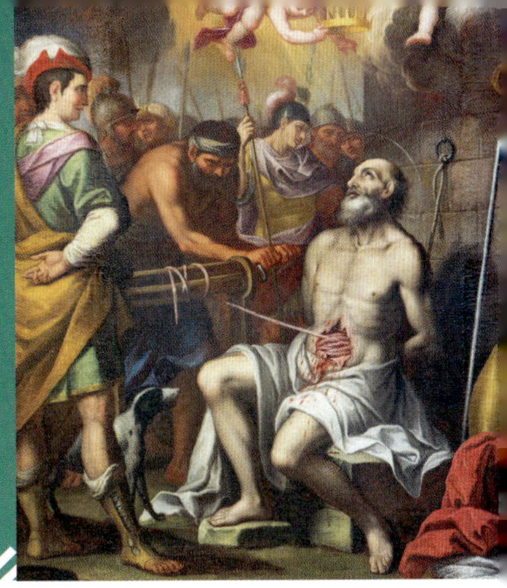

Akash Bashir was an average young man looking forward to a full life. Raised in a humble family, he attended a Catholic school in the city of Lahore, Pakistan. He spent time studying, socializing with friends, and playing sports. After graduation, he started working at a clothing factory.

There was one thing that distinguished Akash from the crowd: his Catholic faith. Catholics were a tiny minority in the largely Muslim nation of Pakistan. For the most part, Catholics and Muslims lived peaceably together, but there were also radical Islamic groups that were hostile toward Catholics and other Christians. In 2013, terrorists attacked a church in Pakistan, killing more than eighty people. Churches began using volunteer security guards from their congregations to try to prevent further violence. In 2014, twenty-year-old Akash volunteered for the job at his parish church.

On a Sunday morning in March of 2015, Akash noticed a man with explosives hidden under his clothing trying to enter the church. Akash blocked his way, saying, "I may die, but I will not let you in." The attacker detonated his bomb, killing himself, Akash, and fifteen bystanders, but sparing the nearly one thousand people inside the church.

The priest who was saying the Mass credited Akash with saving his life. He observed that Akash's witness created greater devotion among the parishioners. "It is a blessing for our local church," he said. "It will strengthen our faith. Ours is a Church of martyrs."

Akash's family was deeply saddened to lose their beloved son and brother. He was "part of my heart," his mother said. "But our happiness is greater than our grief," she continued. "He was a simple boy who died in the path of the Lord and saved the priest and worshippers." Akash's brother took his place as a volunteer guard. Akash's cause for canonization has been opened, meaning that he may one day be officially declared a saint by the Church. To his mother, however, "Akash is already our saint."[9]

"Ours is a Church of martyrs." This is an accurate description of the Church at many times and in many places, never more so than in the early centuries of the Church's existence. From the very beginning of the Church down to the present, persecution has been a reality for many believers. Whether it is religious authorities, angry mobs, or government officials, there have always been those who feel threatened by Christian believers in one way or another. Members of the Church have faced discrimination, imprisonment, torture, and even death. Like Catholics in Pakistan in the twenty-first century, Christians in the Roman Empire in the first through third centuries were a small, vulnerable minority. Deciding to follow Christ in the early days of the Church came with a risk.

Akash Bashir

On March 15, 2015, outside St. John's Catholic Church in the Youhanabad area of Lahore, Pakistan, twenty-year-old Akash Bashir stepped in front of a suicide bomber who attempted to enter the church as Mass was taking place. Bashir was one of at least fifteen people who died in the attack. Seventy others were wounded. A nearby Protestant church was attacked at the same time.

After Akash was named Pakistan's first Servant of God in February of 2022, Archbishop Sebastian Francis Shaw of Lahore began the process of Akash's beatification, the following month reporting to the **papal nuncio** to Pakistan: "Akash Bashir, a young man, sacrificed his life for his brothers and sisters who prayed in church. He discovered something much greater than this earthly life. And he understood it without studying theology or philosophy. He lived a simple life, following Jesus every day, every moment, even when it was not expected."

papal nuncio A formal representative of the pope who has both political and ecclesial power. He is an ambassador to local governments and reports on the conditions of the Church in the nation where he has been assigned by the pope.

The Courage of Early Christians

Stephen, Paul, and all of the Apostles but John were killed because they preached the Gospel and refused to deny their commitment to Christ. In fact, each of their examples fits the requirements of martyrdom that the Church later crafted. Martyrdom must have three elements:

1. The person must be put to death. Suffering, no matter how intense, is not a qualifier for martyrdom. Real martyrs do not seek death but accept it when it comes.

2. The person must die for Christ and the faith. For example, he or she must proclaim faith in Christ or refuse to renounce faith in him before being put to death.

3. The person does not die out of hatred for the enemy, but in joy out of love for Christ and the truth of the faith.

Many successors of the Apostles in the early centuries of the Church—bishops such as Polycarp of Smyrna and Ignatius of Antioch—also suffered martyrdom. In the hundred years after St. Peter's death, all nine of his successors as bishop of Rome (pope) were killed. Many other Christians lost their lives in subsequent persecutions through the end of the third century.

Some of these witnesses to the faith are familiar to Mass-going Catholics because their names are mentioned in the **Roman Canon**. Among these are Sts. Perpetua and Felicity, who died in 203 in a persecution during the reign of Emperor Septimius Severus. Perpetua was a newly married young mother, born into privilege in Carthage, in the Roman province of Africa. She willingly sacrificed her wealth and status when she decided to follow the Christian way. During her imprisonment, Perpetua kept a diary, which was preserved by her fellow Christians and added to by witnesses of her martyrdom. In it, she tells of her father's heartfelt pleas to her to save her life by giving up her resolve to be Christian.

Perpetua also tells of meeting Felicity, a young slave who was pregnant at the time of her arrest and gave birth to her child in prison. When she cried

Roman Canon The name for Eucharistic Prayer I in the Mass of Paul VI, which came into existence after the Second Vatican Council. The Roman Canon, or Canon, has its origins in the sixth century during the pontificate of St. Gregory the Great.

Sts. Perpetua and Felicity

out in pain during childbirth, one of her jailers asked her what she would do when she faced wild beasts in the arena. Felicity answered, "Now it is I who suffer; then, there will be Another in me who will suffer for me, because it is for him that I will be suffering then." After a terrifying attack by a beast in the Roman arena in Carthage, Perpetua and Felicity were both killed by the sword. Perpetua's last recorded words were an encouragement to her companions: "Stand fast in the faith, and love one another, all of you, and be not offended at my sufferings."[10]

Although much of our information regarding the early Church comes from Christian sources, there are also written records from Roman historians. The Roman governor Pliny, for example, wrote to the emperor Trajan in the early second century about the problems that followers of Jesus were causing. Pliny described Christians testifying that "they met on a stated day before it was light, and addressed a form of prayer to Christ, as to a divinity." Pliny saw the new faith as a "contagious superstition" that "is not confined to the cities only, but has spread its infection among the neighboring villages and country." Although the purpose of his letter is to determine when and how Christians should be punished, Pliny indirectly provides evidence of the Gospel's spread and the firmness of Christians' belief in the divinity of Jesus.[11]

The environment of persecution that surrounded the early Church shaped the character of Christianity during these years. As adherents of an illegal religion, Christians could not build churches or worship in public, so they gathered to pray and celebrate the Eucharist in private homes. Accepting the faith was not a pathway to influence, riches, or popularity; rather, it often led to rejection by society and sometimes to rejection by one's own family. It meant trying to live up to difficult teachings that exhorted believers to love

THE AGE OF
Christian Persecution

Focus Question: How did the Church grow and prosper in spite of persecutions?

One reason that the Roman authorities persecuted Christians was that they believed that the Roman gods were angered as more and more Roman citizens abandoned faith in them and became Christians. Many of the worst and most systemized persecutions of Christians were rooted in the belief that Christianity was nothing short of treason. Christians were blamed for all of the misfortunes of the Roman Empire, ranging from floods and epidemics to military invasions. Although Christians tried to demonstrate that they were good citizens, they refused to offer sacrifices to the Roman "gods" because they knew that they were not gods at all.

The severity of the persecutions varied from decade to decade and from region to region. The persecution of Christians in the city of Rome under the emperor Nero (64–68) was particularly cruel. Christians were not just killed; they were tortured in a variety of ways to provide entertainment to the populace. On the other hand, through most of the second century, although Christianity remained outlawed, Christians were not sought out for persecution. They were only punished if someone specifically brought them before the

Emperor Nero with his royal court after the fire of Rome in the year AD 64.

courts. In the first half of the third century, Christians were rarely persecuted for their faith, but then Decius came to power in 249.

Decius held strongly to the belief that many of Rome's problems arose because the Roman gods were angry at the conversion of so many to Christianity. Decius enacted a law that required everyone to offer sacrifices to the gods of the empire. Those who did not have a certificate to prove they had offered the necessary sacrifices were to be shunned and treated as criminals with no rights. Decius did not want to kill Christians outright because he believed, correctly, that martyrs only attracted more people to Christianity.

By the end of the third century, Christians were barely being threatened, but then a controversy erupted involving the military. Church leaders began to teach that Christians should not be part of the military. In 295, a number of Christians were killed for refusing to join or attempting to leave the Roman army. The emperor became convinced that Christians were a threat to Roman security and ordered that all Christians should be expelled from Roman legions. Rather than see their ranks dwindle, many Roman officers tried to force Christians to abandon their faith. Those Christians who refused were executed.

In 303, an order was issued that all Christians be removed from positions of responsibility and that all Christian buildings and writings be destroyed. Some Christians were tortured and killed when they refused to hand over their copies of the Scriptures. When a fire broke out in the imperial palace, Christians were accused of setting it. Finally a decree was issued ordering the arrest of all Church leaders. A second decree ordered all Christians to offer sacrifice to Roman gods under penalty of death.

Despite the verbal and physical hostility aimed at Christians in these early centuries, converted new Christians were not only religious but in many places quite open about their Christian identity. One example of this was in the second century in Asia Minor. When a local governor began to persecute Christians from the poor and lower classes, *all* of the Christians of the region, including those in positions of wealth and power, paraded in front of his home. They wanted to make it clear that the Christian faith was not limited to a small group of social outcasts.

Further Study and Reflection

- Share three ways Catholics today are countercultural among peers, neighbors, and society at large.
- Were Christians really "thrown to the lions"? Research and determine whether this common statement is true or false.

and forgive others, even enemies, to be faithful to spouses and avoid sexual sin, and to give possessions to and care for the poor and sick. As we have seen, it sometimes meant death. Christianity was not a faith for those who wanted an easy life.

The courage of martyrs such as Perpetua and Felicity inspired other Christians to stand firm in their belief. It also caused non-Christian Romans who witnessed these martyrdoms to begin to wonder about the source of such strength and perseverance. Some of them opened their hearts to the message of the Gospel and began following the way of Jesus. So, despite the persecution, the Church steadily grew and spread.

The Necessity of the Church

The prevalence of persecution in the early Church raises a question: Why were the early Christians so committed to their faith that they would cling to it even in the face of death?

The account of Polycarp's martyrdom, written by witnesses in the second century, provides insight into the answer. When the elderly bishop was ordered to renounce Christ and denounce Christianity, he replied, "Eighty and six years have I served him, and he never did me any injury: how then can I blaspheme my King and my Savior?"[12] For Polycarp, Jesus was "King," which meant that the commands of Christ superseded the authority of the state. If the government demanded that he do something contrary to Christian principles, such as declare the falsity of the Gospel, then he could not obey.

Jesus was also "Savior," which meant that it was through following Christ that Polycarp would be brought to eternal life. When the Roman official described the manner in which Polycarp would be killed, he answered, "You threaten me with fire which burns for an hour, and is then extinguished, but you know nothing of the fire of the coming judgment and eternal punishment, reserved for the ungodly."[13] For Polycarp as for the other early Christians, it was imperative to follow Christ, even in the face of persecution, because through following him—through being members of his Church—they would find salvation.

This is why the sin of *apostasy*, renouncing Christ and his Church, was taken so seriously by the early Christians. Some even argued that a former Christian who had committed apostasy should never be forgiven or permitted to return to the community of believers. The Church condemned this view and decided that a repentant sinner could *always* be forgiven and return to the Church, but the importance of belonging to the Church was beyond question.∞ To understand that following Jesus was the way to salvation and then to abandon that way was in essence to reject the gift of salvation.

∞ Note

Those who committed apostasy were called *lapsi* (lapsed). Many bishops and confessors of the time argued that the *lapsi* should undergo a long penitential process before being welcomed back to the Church. This included Christians who had offered sacrifices to Roman idols or renounced their faith to avoid punishment and death.

As he was put to death, Polycarp said, "Eighty and six years have I served him, and he never did me any injury: how then can I blaspheme my King and my Savior?"

In today's world, there are many people who have never accepted Christianity or who have left the Church. In the United States, almost 30 percent of adults are religious "nones," meaning that they describe themselves as atheists, agnostics, or "nothing in particular." Additionally, 13 percent of all American adults are ex-Catholics.[14] At the same time, there are nearly four and a half million adult converts to Catholicism in America, and millions more return to the Church after leaving for a time (they often call themselves "reverts," and a high number of them are young adults aged twenty-five to thirty-four).[15] These facts highlight the importance of reaching out to non-Catholics and Catholics who have stopped practicing their faith, of witnessing to the graces available in the Church, and of assuring them of a welcome reception into the Body of Christ.

Following Christ through being faithful to his Church remains the normative way to receive the salvation that God offers to everyone. "It is in the Church that Christ fulfills and reveals his own mystery as the purpose of God's plan" (*CCC*, 772). Presenting an image of the Church as a vineyard, Jesus said, "I am the vine, you are the branches. Whoever remains in me and I in him will bear much fruit, because without me you can do nothing" (Jn 15:5). Catholics understand this to mean that to separate from the Church is to separate from Jesus himself. Being disconnected from Christ, the source of spiritual life, means spiritual death. "Anyone who does not remain in me will be thrown out like a branch and wither; people will gather them and throw them into a fire and they will be burned" (Jn 15:6). The early Christians understood that it was only through the community of believers, the Church, that they could unite themselves to the saving actions of Jesus.

The *Catechism of the Catholic Church* teaches that the "Church's first purpose is to be the sacrament of the *inner union of men with God*" (*CCC*, 775). This unity of our souls with God is the path to true unity with others. And because our communion with one another is rooted in union with God, "the Church is also the sacrament of the *unity of the human race*" (*CCC*, 775). This is why the Church teaches that Baptism is "necessary for salvation for those to whom the Gospel has been proclaimed and who have had the possibility of asking for this sacrament" (*CCC*, 1257).

It is possible for God to grant the gift of salvation not only to non-Catholics but also to non-Christians: "*God has bound salvation to the sacrament of Baptism, but he himself is not bound by his sacraments*" (*CCC*, 1257). Yet all people who are saved, both those inside and those outside the visible boundaries of the Church, attain salvation through the ministry of Jesus, who works through his Church. It is possible for someone who is not visibly a member of the Church to be spiritually united with the Church nonetheless.

As St. Paul wrote to the Corinthians, the Church is the Body of Christ. We are thus united with Christ and each other in this one Body, and we grow in unity by receiving the sacraments, which are available only through the ministry of the Church. God preserves the integrity of the truth of the Gospel by guiding the pope and bishops, the successors of the Apostles. Christ instituted the sacraments of the Church so that his followers would have a constant source of *grace*—access to union with him. It is thus only in the Church that we find the fullness of truth and the totality of the means of salvation. The early Christians knew that it is vitally important to remain connected to Christ through his Church.

SECTION Assessment

Comprehension

1. How did Akash Bashir meet the Church's requirements for martyrdom?

2. What did Felicity mean by "Another in me who will suffer for me" in her answer to the prison guard?

3. Describe the environment of persecution that the early Church faced.

4. How did Polycarp explain the early Christians' commitment to their faith and willingness to accept death?

5. How did the early Church respond to those who committed the sin of apostasy?

6. How can the Church be the "sacrament of the unity of the human race"?

Vocabulary

7. Which Eucharistic Prayer is the *Roman Canon*?

Reflection

8. What argument could you use to convince a "none" to become Catholic or an ex-Catholic to return to the faith?

9. How far would you go to witness to your faith? Share an example.

FOUNDATIONS OF BELIEF AND PRACTICE

In 1873, an Eastern Orthodox bishop was searching through some old documents in the archives of a monastery in the ancient city of Istanbul, Turkey. Amid the dusty and neglected stacks of texts, he made a stunning discovery: a manuscript from the eleventh century—a collection of early Christian writings—that apparently no one knew was there. Among those writings was a copy of the *Didache*, also known as the "The Teaching of the Apostles." The *Didache* dates from the late first century and describes early Christian belief and practice.∞ Many Christian writers had mentioned this important document down through the centuries, but it was believed that no copy had survived. With the discovery of this text, historians now had strong evidence concerning the nature of the early Church.[16]

It is striking how much Catholics today share in common with those early Christians. The *Didache* says that Christians should use water to baptize, and that Baptism should be done "in the name of the Father and of the Son and of the Holy Spirit." It encourages Christians to pray and fast. It talks about "the Eucharist," instructing Christians to "give thanks" for the "cup" and the "broken bread." It says that only the baptized should participate in the Eucharist. It tells Christians to "come together" on "the Lord's Day," to "break bread and give thanks,

---

∞ Note

A primary purpose of the *Didache* was to aid *catechumens*—that is, those undergoing a period of study and spiritual preparation before receiving the Sacrament of Baptism—to learn about the faith. Because of persecutions, the catechumens had to prepare in secret. The *Didache* mentions the Trinitarian formula, lays out moral teachings, and explains the rites of Baptism and the Eucharist.

having first confessed your sins, so that your sacrifice may be pure." It describes the exemplary behavior of the Christian: "Your prayers, your giving to the poor and all your deeds, should be done in accordance with the Gospel of the Lord."[17]

The *Didache* is a short text and doesn't provide a full picture of early Christian life, but what it does say is surprisingly familiar. Of course, there have been changes in the many centuries since its writing, but this ancient document proves that the essential elements of Christianity have remained the same from the beginning. Essential elements to which the *Didache* attests include how early Christians prayed, the importance of communal life, and how sharing in the presence of the Lord in the "breaking of the bread," that is, in the Sacrament of the Eucharist, was most essential.

How Early Christians Prayed

As Church Father St. John Damascene put it, "Prayer is the raising of one's mind and heart to God or the requesting of good things from God" (*CCC*, 2559, quoting *De Fide Orthodoxa*, 3, 24). Through prayer, the Christian creates and maintains "a vital and personal relationship with the living and true God" (*CCC*, 2558). Without prayer, there is no recognition of God, no relationship with his Son, no conduit for the Spirit. Obviously, prayer is an essential element in the life of a Catholic.

As with everything else in the Christian life, we follow the example of Jesus as a model for prayer. Jesus prepared for key events in his ministry by praying. He prayed for his disciples. He prayed for God's will to be done. And he taught us how to pray by giving us a model of prayer in the Our Father.

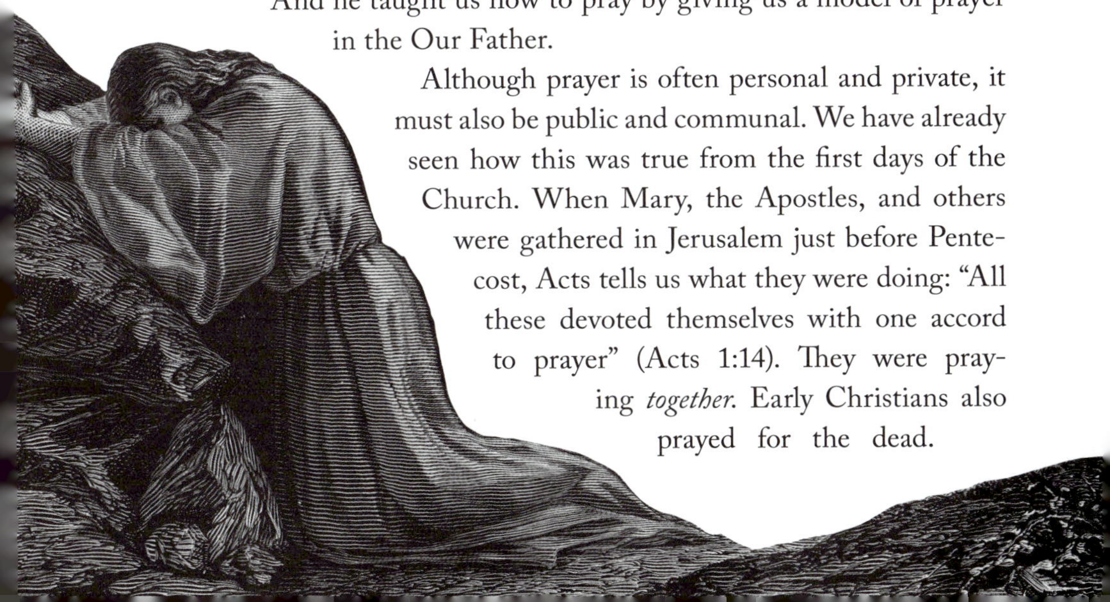

Although prayer is often personal and private, it must also be public and communal. We have already seen how this was true from the first days of the Church. When Mary, the Apostles, and others were gathered in Jerusalem just before Pentecost, Acts tells us what they were doing: "All these devoted themselves with one accord to prayer" (Acts 1:14). They were praying *together*. Early Christians also prayed for the dead.

Church Father Tertullian wrote: "We offer sacrifices for the dead on their birthday anniversaries" (*De Corona Militis*, 3, 3). He meant anniversaries of the day they died and were born into heaven. They also prayed to God through the intercession of Mary and the saints. St. Cyprian of Carthage wrote: "Let us on both sides [of death] always pray for one another" (*Letters*, 56, 5). Early Christian icons reveal a posture of Christian prayer: Christians often stood with their hands extended. This posture, called *orans*, was popular even among pagan religions. When Christians began to pray in this way, the posture's resemblance to the posture of Jesus on the Cross added to its significance.

How Early Christians Gathered Communally

Living in community with others was a powerful reality of the early Church that is highlighted in the Acts of the Apostles following the experience of Pentecost: "All who believed were together and had all things in common" (Acts 2:44). What did they do together? "They devoted themselves to the teaching of the apostles and to the communal life, to the breaking of the bread and to the prayers" (Acts 2:42).

This prayer life did not remain private but poured forth into acts of charity toward others. The early Christians were so concerned with caring for each other that "they would sell their property and possessions and divide them among all according to each one's need" (Acts 2:45). The way that Christians cared for each other was a powerful example to those who observed them, and this example drew many new converts to the faith. In a letter to the Roman emperor, an early-second-century Christian writer named Aristides described the way of life the followers of Christ practiced:

> And when they see a stranger, they take him in to their homes and rejoice over him as a very brother. . . . And whenever one of their poor passes from the world, each one of them according to his ability gives heed to him and carefully sees to his burial. And if they hear that one of their number is imprisoned or afflicted on account of the name of their Messiah, all of them anxiously minister to his necessity, and if it is possible to redeem him they set him free. And

---

orans A Latin word meaning "praying or pleading"; commonly refers to the posture of prayer with one's hands extended. Traditionally, this is a posture reserved for the priest at Mass.

if there is among them any that is poor and needy, and if they have no spare food, they fast two or three days in order to supply to the needy their lack of food.[18]

The community of the early Church was also multicultural and multiracial. The description of the local church in Antioch in Acts (13:1) mentions members from different locations, races, and cultures from around the Roman Empire.

How Early Christians Celebrated the Eucharist

The communal prayer life of the Church revolved around the Eucharist, the celebration of the Body and Blood of Christ. It is clear from the *Didache*, the New Testament, and the writings of the early Church Fathers that the Eucharist was, as later Church teaching would put it, "the source and summit of the Christian life" (*CCC*, 1324, quoting *Lumen Gentium*, 11). Church historian Mike Aquilina notes that "the historical record is clear about this: Wherever Christianity spread, the Church immediately established the **liturgy**—'the breaking of the bread and the prayers'—on the 'Lord's day' (Rev 1:10), which was Sunday.∞ Indeed, every generation of the Church's history has left us evidence of its eucharistic life."[19]

From the very beginning of the Church, gathering to "break bread," the earliest description of the Eucharistic celebration, was at the heart of the daily life of Christians: "Every day they devoted themselves to meeting together in the temple area and to breaking bread in their homes" (Acts 2:46). In these gatherings, Christians would reenact what Jesus himself did at the Last Supper, when he offered himself, through the Passion and Death he was about

---

liturgy The public worship of the Church, which includes the celebration of the Eucharist and the other sacraments, as well as the Liturgy of the Hours, or Divine Office, the official prayer of the Church. The word *liturgy* literally means "public work." In Catholic tradition, *liturgy* means the participation of the People of God in the work of God.

∞ Note

Whereas for Jews, the Sabbath is Saturday, a "day of grace," the seventh day that closes out the week (from Genesis 2:2), for Christians the Lord's Day is Sunday because Sunday commemorates Easter, the day Christ rose from the dead.

to suffer, to the Father for the sake of our salvation. In the First Letter to the Corinthians, written in approximately AD 56, St. Paul provides the earliest record of the words of institution used by bishops and priests to consecrate ordinary bread and wine into the Body and Blood of Christ: "The Lord Jesus . . . took bread, and after he had given thanks, broke it and said, 'This is my body that is for you. Do this in remembrance of me.' In the same way also the cup, after supper, saying, 'This cup is the new covenant in my blood. Do this, as often as you drink it, in remembrance of me.' For as often as you eat this bread and drink the cup, you proclaim the death of the Lord until he comes" (1 Cor 11:23–26).

In light of its connection to the Last Supper, this Christian meal-gathering was often called "the Lord's Supper" or simply "Eucharist," which is Greek for "thanksgiving." As the Eucharistic meal's origin at the Last Supper indicates, sharing a meal for religious purposes had precedent in the Jewish feast of Passover, as well as in other ancient religions. It's impossible to know exactly how the earliest Christians celebrated the Eucharistic meal, and there was likely some variation in the days before the liturgical rites of the Church had been standardized, but the New Testament and other documents provide some evidence for what the Lord's Supper involved.[∞]

The sacramental nature of the Eucharist as instituted by Christ at the Last Supper has always been the responsibility of the successors of the Apostles, those who hold the office of bishop in the Church. Local bishops ordain priests for ministry, and the sacred orders of the bishop and priest have

∞ Note

Besides the sources already cited (Paul's epistles, *Didache*), the writings of St. Justin Martyr in the mid-second century provide a valuable if slightly later description of the Eucharist. See also Eugene LaVerdiere, SSS, *The Eucharist in the New Testament and the Early Church* (Collegeville, MN: Liturgical Press, 1996).

The altar in Karongi Genocide Memorial Church, Kibuye, Rwanda, depicting the Last Supper.

always been responsible for offering the sacrifice of the Mass, just as the Levitical priesthood of the Old Covenant had been responsible for offering sacrifice on behalf of all the Jews.

The Eucharistic gathering would usually take place at a believer's house, but don't imagine a small, one-room shelter. Rather, houses were usually sizable, with a central courtyard and one large room for the gathering. The Christians did not sit; they stood and faced east, or in the direction of Jerusalem. The bishop or presbyter leading the liturgy also faced east, and the altar was set up against the east wall. There was a chair reserved for the bishop or presbyter. Deacons usually stood either near the bread and wine or outside the door watching and welcoming those who entered.

As the phrase "breaking of the bread" indicates, these Eucharistic meals always included at least one key ingredient: bread. Bread was the primary staple of the diet in Palestine in the first century AD, and so was important both literally and figuratively as a symbol of the nourishment and sustaining of life more generally, as is evident in Jesus's famous prayer, "Give us this day our daily bread," and in his use at the Last Supper of bread (and wine) that he changed into his Body and Blood. After the prayers, the Body and Blood of Christ would be distributed, probably by deacons.

The early Christians also shared other food in common on these occasions, apart from the liturgy. Sometimes abuses occurred in this practice, as some people brought food, others didn't, and a few people went hungry. Also, some people drank to excess and became intoxicated. St. Paul condemned this practice: "Do you not have houses in which you can eat and drink? Or do you show contempt for the church of God and make those who have nothing feel ashamed? What can I say to you? Shall I praise you? In this matter I do not praise you" (1 Cor 11:22).

Over the centuries, the "breaking of bread" liturgy came to be called "the Mass," from the Latin *missa*, which means "dismissal." The full sending at the end of the liturgy is *Ite, missa est*, or "Go, it is the dismissal." The Mass provides an opportunity for the community of believers to gather to hear God's Word, to join in the priest's offering of Jesus to the Father, and to receive the Body and Blood of Christ in Holy Communion. Although the liturgy that surrounds the Eucharist may look somewhat different now than it did at the time of the Apostles, what has not changed is the importance of the Body of Christ in the life of the Church. "The Eucharist is at the center of the life" of the universal and the local Church (*CCC*, 893).

Through Baptism, all Catholics are enabled and committed to "serve God by a vital participation in the holy liturgy of the Church" (*CCC*, 1273). Membership in the Church implies a duty to worship God at Mass. The importance of worship and the centrality of the Eucharist to the life of the Christian are the reasons we are obligated to attend Mass at least once a week, on Sunday, as well as on **holy days of obligation**. Catholics are to receive Holy Communion at least once per year, during the Easter season, and are strongly encouraged to receive Holy Communion every Sunday or even more frequently as long as they are free from **mortal sin**.

How the Early Church Grew

The zeal of Apostles and evangelists such as Peter and Paul, the witness of martyrs such as Perpetua and Felicity, and the edifying example of ordinary

---

holy days of obligation The days in the Church Year when all Catholics are obliged to participate in Mass. In the United States, the holy days of obligation are January 1, the Solemnity of Mary, the Holy Mother of God; Thursday of the Sixth Week of Easter, the Solemnity of the Ascension of the Lord; August 15, the Solemnity of the Assumption of the Blessed Virgin Mary; November 1, the Solemnity of All Saints; December 8, the Solemnity of the Immaculate Conception of the Blessed Virgin Mary; and December 25, the Solemnity of the Nativity of the Lord.

mortal sin A serious violation of God's law of love that results in the loss of God's life (sanctifying grace) in the soul of the sinner. For a sin to be mortal, it must concern grave matter, there must be full knowledge of the evil done, and there must be full consent of the will.

Christians who shared their possessions, lived in peace, and cared for each other—all of these led to extraordinary growth in the number of Christians even as the Church was being persecuted. Exact numbers are impossible to know, but scholars estimate that from fewer than ten thousand followers of Christ in the year 100, the Church grew to about six million members by the year 300, when the age of Roman persecution was drawing to a close.[20]

These Christians were a diverse group. Men and women from a variety of socioeconomic backgrounds embraced the faith. Christian teaching insisted that groups that had been treated poorly in ancient Greek and Roman civilizations—foreigners, slaves, women, and children—were to be accorded the respect due to them as children of God and brothers and sisters in Christ. St. Paul had written memorably to the local church in Galatia that "through faith you are all children of God in Christ Jesus," and as such, "there is neither Jew nor Greek, there is neither slave nor free person, there is not male and female; for you are all one in Christ Jesus" (Gal 3:26–28).

Jesus had women disciples. Besides his own mother, Mary, and Mary Magdalene—out of whom Jesus exorcised a demon and who stood by at his Crucifixion and discovered his empty tomb—Jesus had women traveling

Christ at the Home of Martha and Mary, *by Eugène Buland.*

companions, like Susanna and Joanna, who helped support his ministry (see Luke 8:1–3); friends Mary and Martha (see Luke 10:38–42), and the "daughters of Jerusalem" who mourned his impending Death (see Luke 23:27–28). Women took on important roles in the Church, whereby they served the community in various ways. In certain places and during limited periods in the history of the Church, some women served as "deaconesses."∞ Widows and orphans, groups that had been neglected and shunned in many societies, were given special attention by Christians. The message that all people are to be treated with justice and compassion was revolutionary in the Roman Empire in the opening centuries of the first millennium AD, but it was a message that gradually won the day.

Early Christians did not put these ideals into practice perfectly. As with any other era of Church history, they struggled to live up to the teachings of Jesus. However, their example did set them apart from the dominant culture of the time, and the goodness they exhibited had a strong appeal to non-Christians who were looking for a better way. Under the leadership of the Apostles and their successors, the early Church preached the Good News throughout the Roman Empire and beyond, making an impressive beginning toward fulfilling the Great Commission, Christ's command to spread the faith to "all nations."

SECTION Assessment

Comprehension

1. What was the primary purpose of the *Didache*?

2. Name two ways that early Christians prayed.

3. What is the source of the earliest text for the institution of the Eucharist?

4. Why did the first Christians and the bishop face east during the "breaking of the bread"?

5. What was an abuse that took place at the Eucharistic gathering, and how did St. Paul condemn it?

6. Who were Susanna and Joanna?

Vocabulary

7. What is the literal meaning of the word *liturgy*?

8. What does *mortal sin* have to do with reception of Holy Communion?

Reflection

9. How do Catholics today imitate the way of life of early Christians that Aristides described? Share one example. In what area do Catholics need to improve?

10. On a scale of 1 to 10, how important do you rate Sunday Mass attendance? Explain.

11. Where else does the Church need to expand in today's world in order to fulfill the Great Commission?

∞ Note

While historical analysis of this aspect of the early Church continues, these "deaconesses" have been understood by the Church to be distinct from the ordained diaconate that is reserved for men. See Congregation for the Doctrine of the Faith, International Theological Commission, *From the Diakonia of Christ to the Diakonia of the Apostles* (2002), esp. chap. 2, sec. 4.

Section Reviews

Focus Question

How did the Church grow and prosper in spite of persecutions?
Complete one of the following:

- Look up one area in the world where Catholics are being persecuted today and report one quotation from a persecuted Catholic in that area.

- Explain the different kinds of persecution you would face from family members and Roman citizens if you were a Jewish convert to Christianity in the first century. Which would you find most difficult to endure? Explain.

- Research and report numbers of Christians at the end of the first century, the end of the second century, and the end of the third century.

Introduction

Love Is the Source of the Church

Review

God is the source of love. God loves in relationship between the Three Divine Persons, Father (Creator), Son (Savior), and Holy Spirit (Advocate). The Church was founded on God's love. On Pentecost, the Holy Spirit came in a special way to the Apostles, and the Church was first revealed to the world. After Pentecost, the Apostles led the proclamation of the Gospel throughout the Roman Empire. They also modeled the Christian life by praying together and living according to the moral teaching of Jesus. They did all of this in spite of facing persecution.

Assignment

Explain why it is important to distinguish between how people understand the Three Divine Persons of the Holy Trinity and how God understands himself in Three Divine Persons.

Section 1
The Holy Spirit Is Present in the Church

Review

The biblical account of the early history of the Church is told in the Acts of the Apostles, whose authorship is credited to St. Luke. After the Holy Spirit descended on the Apostles on Pentecost, a Jewish harvest feast on the fiftieth day after both Passover and the Resurrection, they were emboldened with faith and began to follow Jesus's Great Commission to spread the Gospel. The apostolic nature of the Church was established in the early Church. The Apostles built up the Church through their preaching, teaching, and witness. The Holy Spirit continues to guide the Church through the Magisterium.

Assignment

Imagine you live in Jerusalem at the time of Jesus but haven't heard of him before Pentecost. What are two questions you would have for Peter after hearing his speech?

Section 2
St. Paul: From Persecutor to Apostle

Review

St. Paul, also known by his Jewish name, Saul, was well educated and a tent maker by trade. A strict Pharisee who persecuted Christians, he had studied under the famous teacher Gamaliel to be a rabbi. He watched over the cloaks for those who stoned St. Stephen to death. After Paul's surprising conversion, he traveled extensively, founded local Christian communities, and preached especially to the Gentiles. He is known as the "Apostle to the Gentiles." Paul was also a prolific writer. He wrote thirteen of the epistles in the New Testament, explaining the faith with striking images.

Assignment

Read 1 Corinthians 9:19–27. What does it mean to be "free in regard to all"? How can this type of freedom work well in sharing the Gospel with different kinds of people?

Section 3
A Church of Martyrs

Review

Many Christians in the first three centuries were martyrs. To be a martyr, a person must be put to death, die for Christ and the faith, and accept death voluntarily. The severity of the persecutions and the number of martyrs varied from decade to decade and region to region. The courage of martyrs inspired other Christians to stand firm in their belief and attracted non-Christian Romans to the faith. Following Christ through being faithful to his Church remains the normative way that God offers salvation to all. The Church is the "sacrament of the inner union of men with God" and the "sacrament of the unity of the human race."

Assignment

What kind of life would you have to live in order to be recognized by the Church as a saint? Be specific.

Section 4
Foundations of Belief and Practice

Review

A first-century text called the *Didache* describes the practices of the early Church, which were similar to Catholic practices today. The Lord's Supper, the name for the early Eucharistic liturgy, was held in the houses of Christians, where those gathered would reenact what Jesus himself did at the Last Supper, offering himself to the Father for our salvation. The Apostles and their successors had the responsibility for the sacramental nature of the Eucharist. The Church grew in membership despite challenges of living under an oppressive government. The Church was a diverse group of men and women from many socioeconomic backgrounds and cultures.

Assignment

Describe how being part of a group helped you to accomplish something you would not have been able to do on your own. How does the Church fulfill a similar role?

Chapter Projects

Choose and complete at least one of the following projects to assess your understanding of the material in this chapter.

⚙ 1. Compare the Work toward Ecumenism of the Subjects of Sieger Köder's Pentecost

On the second floor of Sieger Köder's 2007 *Pentecost (I Will Pour Out My Spirit)* painting are three recognizable twentieth-century historical figures who each had an important role in ecumenism. Find the painting online and research and write a short biographical profile of each person depicted, making sure to describe each person's key role in the ecumenical movement. For extra credit, find out if, when, and where any of the three people met in person:

- Dietrich Bonhoeffer
- Athenagoras I of Constantinople
- Pope John XXIII

⚙ 2. Illustrate the Poem "Marble Floor"

The following poem, "Marble Floor," describes the mystical meaning of the papacy and was written by Bishop Karol Wojtyla (later Pope John Paul II) in 1962 around the opening of the Second Vatican Council. Draw an illustration to represent the meaning of the poem using any art medium of your choice. Include a written description of your illustration that explains its meaning and its connection with the poem:

> Our feet meet the earth in this place;
> there are so many walls, so many colonnades,
> yet we are not lost. If we find
> meaning and oneness,
> it is the floor that guides us. It joins the spaces
> of this great edifice, and joins
> the spaces within us,
> who walk aware of our weakness and defeat.
> Peter, you are the floor, that others

may walk over you (not knowing
where they go). You guide their steps
so that spaces can be one in their eyes,
and from them thought is born.
You want to serve their feet that pass
as rock serves the hooves of sheep.
The rock is a gigantic temple floor,
the cross a pasture.

⚙ *3. Write an Essay to Reach Out to the "Spiritual but Not Religious"*

Cardinal Timothy Dolan of New York once told a large group of high school students: "We are living in an era where people believe in Christ, but not his Church. They want the king, but not the kingdom; they want to believe without belonging; they want the faith but not the faithful. But for the committed Catholic, the answer to that is 'no can do.' Jesus and the Church are one." Cardinal Dolan went on to suggest three ways to address this problem:

1. Focus on the Church as a "spiritual family."
2. Discover a "noncombative apologetics" which can "credibly, convincingly, and compellingly articulate our Catholic faith" both to those inside the Church and to those who are hostile to the Church.
3. Fess up to the sinful side of the Church.

Write an essay that focuses on how you can, both individually and with your Catholic peers, enact these three suggestions with the objective of encouraging those who have left the Catholic Church to return.

⚙ *4. Role-Play the Council of Jerusalem*

The Council of Jerusalem (see Acts 15:1–21) was convened to deal with a crucial issue facing the early Church. The first in a long line of councils, it set historical precedent for dealing with conflict and controversy in the Church. Work with your classmates to develop a role-play for the Council of Jerusalem. Choose a cast for the following roles:

- Paul

- Barnabas
- Peter
- James
- a group of Jewish Christians
- members of the council

Work together to write a script for each part. Structure the drama as a debate, giving both sides an opportunity to speak before a verdict is given by Peter and the council.

Optional: Choose an issue facing the Church today and hold a council using the same format as above.

⚙ *5. Depict Several Images of the Church from* Lumen Gentium

Lumen Gentium (Dogmatic Constitution on the Church) is a Second Vatican Council document that describes the mystery of the Church using many different images. Read Chapter 1, Paragraphs 1 through 8, of the document, and make a list of five different images you notice there. In an art notebook, illustrate on separate pages each of the images you chose using your choice of medium. Include a title below each drawing.

Faithful Disciple
St. Clement of Rome

St. Clement of Rome was pope in the first century. In most second-century lists of popes, he is named the fourth pope, behind St. Linus and St. Anacletus, also known as Cletus. However, according to the second-century defender of the faith Tertullian and St. Jerome (347–420), Clement was Peter's immediate successor and was consecrated by St. Peter himself.

Clement may have grown up as a slave in the household of the cousin of the Roman emperor Domitian. It is also possible that he was associated with Peter and the Apostles. In Philippians 4:3, a reference is made to a Clement who was Paul's "true yokemate" and who "struggled at my side promoting the gospel." These elements, like other parts of the life of St. Clement, cannot be proven for sure.

One of the more attested facts of Clement's life is that he was the author of the *First Letter of Clement*, a long document written between AD 95 and 98 that survives in complete form today. Beyond the New Testament and the *Didache*, it was one of the most influential and most-read documents of the time.

The *First Letter of Clement* was addressed to the Church in Corinth. The main subject involves how *presbyters*, or priests, were being treated poorly there and actually being deposed from their positions. It does not appear that the Corinthian church explicitly sought out Clement's opinion on what was occurring, but as the bishop of Rome occupying the seat of St. Peter, he took the initiative to provide it. He wrote of both the authenticity of apostolic succession and the injustice being done to priests in Corinth:

Our Apostles, too, were given to understand by our Lord Jesus Christ that the office of the bishop would give rise to intrigues. For this reason, equipped as they were with perfect foreknowledge, they appointed the men mentioned before, and afterward laid down a rule once for all to this effect: when these men die, other approved men shall succeed to their sacred ministry. Consequently, we deem it an injustice to eject from the sacred ministry the persons who were appointed either by them, or later, with the consent of the whole Church, by other men in high repute and [who] have ministered to the flock of Christ faultlessly, humbly, quietly and unselfishly, and [who] have moreover, over a long period of time, earned the esteem of all. (*First Letter of Clement*, 44)

The *First Letter of Clement* was read frequently in the early Church.

A legend surrounding the end of Clement's life is that he was exiled to Crimea, where he worked in the mines before eventually being killed by being thrown into the sea with an anchor around his neck. The legend also says that the angels made him a grave in the sea, which was discovered once the tides ran low.

St. Clement of Rome should be remembered for his devotion to the Church and his prayers for her leadership. The following is a prayer for bishops and attributed to him:

Grant to them, Lord, health, peace, concord, and stability, so that they may exercise without offense the sovereignty that you have given them. Master, heavenly King of the ages, you give glory, honor, and power over the things of the earth to the sons of men. Direct, Lord, their counsel, following what is pleasing and acceptable in your sight, so that by exercising with devotion and in peace and gentleness the power that you have given to them, they may find favor with you.

Comprehension

1. What is one attested fact about the life of St. Clement?
2. Who was the audience for the *First Letter of Clement*?
3. What was the letter's main subject?

Reflection

Write about a priest who exhibited kindness and care to you or your family.

Prayer

This ancient prayer has its roots in both Sacred Scripture and Sacred Tradition. With phrases taken from Psalm 104, the opening line of the prayer echoes the *sequence*—a liturgical prayer that is either sung or read just before the Gospel on certain high feast days—prayed on Pentecost Sunday. "Send forth your Spirit and renew the face of the earth" is also part of the responsorial psalm on Pentecost Sunday.

Come, Holy Spirit

Come, Holy Spirit, fill the hearts of your faithful and kindle in them the fire of your love.

Send forth your Spirit and they shall be created, and you shall renew the face of the earth.

O God, who have taught the hearts of the faithful by the light of the Holy Spirit, grant that in the same Spirit we may be truly wise and ever rejoice in his consolation.

Through Christ Our Lord. Amen.

The Church Grows and Defines Herself

St. Kateri Tekakwitha

➤ Fr. Claude Chauchetière

There are many saints who were converts to the faith, but perhaps none as noteworthy as St. Kateri Tekakwitha. Born in 1656 to a Mohawk warrior father and an Algonquin Christian mother, Kateri was orphaned at a young age before she could be baptized. She converted to Christianity as a teenager after recovering from the smallpox that killed her parents and left her face permanently scarred. She also decided to commit herself to perpetual virginity, to the disdain of her tribe, which expected her to accept an arranged marriage. Kateri died in 1680 at the age of twenty-three or twenty-four. Witnesses to her death said that about fifteen minutes after she died, her face became clear and the smallpox scars disappeared.

This painting of St. Kateri was the first to be composed, just one year after her death. The artist was Fr. Claude Chauchetière, SJ, her confessor at the time of her death. Fr. Chauchetière had become disillusioned since being sent from France to the New World, but Kateri's childlike faith reinvigorated him. He wrote a small book to accompany his painting of her.

This portrait was painted with sepia ink, a brown pigment prepared from the secretions of cuttlefish. A year later Fr. Chauchetière made a copy of the painting using oil paints that is still on display at the Mission of St. Francis Xavier in Kahnawake, a Mohawk territory on the banks of the St. Lawrence River across from Montreal.

The painting contains many symbols to represent Kateri's life. The red lilies on her white vest represent her virginity and purity. The canoe shows Kateri and those who accompanied her on the voyage to the Mission of St. Francis Xavier. There was actually room for only three people in the canoe, but Chauchetière added the character of Divine Providence behind Kateri because God had guided her on her journey.

Kateri is painted in red, representing the red blanket that she had at the time she arrived at the Mission. Her vest is white, also representing her purity. Her face has Algonquin features, which perhaps came from her mother's side. The color of her face is rosy, representing how it was transfigured after her death. Her left moccasin is painted differently than her right, recalling that she walked with a limp on her left foot. She was small in stature, probably about four feet five inches in height. The dark blue blanket in the portrait is the one she wore around herself on the days she received Holy Communion. The shrub on her right side is meant to represent the thorn branches she slept on as a form of penance.

If you would like to collect other images of St. Kateri Tekakwitha and create your own artistic rendition of her, see Chapter 3 Review, Chapter Project 1.

How did the early Church respond to theological and doctrinal debates?

Introduction

The Church Gains the Freedom to Flourish

Section 1

The Church Spreads the Gospel

Section 2

The Church Teaches the Truth

Section 3

Church and Government Coexist

Section 4

The Church Establishes the Canon of Scripture

Constantine was nervous as he pondered what the next day would bring. He and his army were camped just outside the imperial capital of Rome, preparing to cross the Milvian Bridge to enter the city and take full control of the mighty Roman Empire. In their way stood the army of Constantine's rival, Maxentius. As he fretted on the eve of the battle that would determine the future of the empire, Constantine wondered whether the heavens would bless him with a victory.[∞] Accounts of what happened next vary, but according to two early Church historians who knew Constantine, the emperor beheld a

Milvian Bridge today.

∞ Note

Following the death of Galerius in 311, the Roman Empire was divided among Licinius, Maximinus Daza, Maxentius, and Constantine. Constantine began a campaign to take control of the empire. He marched on Rome, Maxentius's capital city, in a surprise attack. Although Constantine's forces were inferior, Maxentius at first fell back into Rome with his troops. Once he regrouped, Maxentius prepared to go out and meet Constantine.

vision that depicted the Chi-Rho symbol, meaning Jesus Christ, accompanied by the words "In this sign you will conquer." Constantine instructed his men to adopt the symbol as their standard and enter battle under the sign of Christianity.∞

Whatever occurred that day, what followed afterward is certain. Constantine gained a decisive victory over Maxentius in October of 312 and went on to rule the Roman Empire until his death in 337. He attributed his victory to the God of the Christians. The historian Eusebius wrote: "Thus the pious emperor, glorying in the confession of the victorious cross, proclaimed the Son of God to the Romans with great boldness of testimony."[1] While Constantine's story has been embroidered by later Christian admirers, secular historians agree that Constantine's rule marks a decisive shift in the Roman Empire's attitude toward Christianity.[2] From the year 312 onward, Constantine the Great would favor Christianity as no previous emperor had. He decreed the removal of legal restrictions on the Christian faith in 313 in the Edict of Milan and returned confiscated property. The age of persecution was over, and the Church enjoyed the freedom to grow and prosper.

Changing the Culture

Constantine enacted many reforms that helped to transform the pagan culture of the empire into the Christian culture that took its place. Christians already recognized Sunday as a feast day celebrating the Resurrection, but Constantine added the authority of the state to this custom by prohibiting commercial activity on Sunday. While slavery was virtually universal at the time and Constantine did not outlaw it, his reforms lessened its severity. For example, he forbade the previously common practice of branding slaves' faces, on the grounds that the face reflected the image of God. Constantine also increased the public visibility of the Church by donating prominent buildings, some of which were former pagan temples, to the Church. He built the first St. Peter's Basilica on the site of Peter's grave (recall the story of Margherita Guarducci from the

∞ Note

In Greek, *chi* and *rho* are the first two letters of *Christ*. According to Christian historian Eusebius, Constantine saw the vision in the sky. Lactantius, another historian who also knew Constantine, said the vision of the Chi-Rho came to Constantine in a dream.

St. Helena *and the* Cross of Christ

Around the time that Constantine became emperor, his mother, St. Helena, became a Christian. She devoutly promoted the faith and encouraged her son to favor the Christian religion. In the late 320s, Helena visited Palestine to honor the sites of Jesus's life while also hoping to locate the true Cross of Christ.

Several traditions have developed around St. Helena's visit to Jerusalem. One story, recounted in a medieval Christian **hagiography** called the *Golden Legend*, holds that the Cross of Christ was hidden under stones in a ditch near a pagan shrine to the goddess Venus and that Christians came to the site to venerate the Cross. Because of the persecutions, Christians shared the location of the Cross by word of mouth, and a Christian from the area reportedly shared this information with St. Helena. According to the *Golden Legend*, a man named Judas dug up the site and found three crosses. Not knowing which one was the authentic Cross, he laid each on the corpse of a young man about to be buried. When he laid the third cross on the man, the dead man came to life.

Contemporary Christian historians verified that St. Helena came into possession of the Cross of Christ. For example, in his letter to the emperor Constantius II (Constantine's son and successor), St. Cyril of Jerusalem wrote: "The saving wood of the cross was found at Jerusalem at the time of Constantine."

---

hagiography A Greek term for the biography of a saint; *hagio* comes from a term that means "holy" or "saintly," and *graphy* means "to write."

feature "St. Peter and a Startling Discovery" in Chapter 2, Section 1). Eventually, Constantine became a Christian himself due in great part to the encouragement of his mother, **St. Helena**. He was baptized shortly before his death.

During Constantine's reign, the fundamental orientation of society changed. Judea, once considered by the Romans a troublesome province to be repressed by force, was now a holy land, revered for being the home of Christ. Rome, once prominent as the capital of the vast empire, was now honored for being the site of St. Peter's martyrdom and the home of his successors, the popes. Church leaders—bishops, priests, and deacons—who had for centuries been targets of persecution and lived furtively and simply, were now important public figures who presided over grand churches. The foundation was being laid for a European civilization that for a thousand years would be closely identified with the Catholic Church.

The Challenges of Growth

As the followers of Jesus continued to spread the Gospel across the empire and beyond, new difficulties arose. The Church's newfound wealth and influence increased the faith's public profile, but they also tempted some Christians, including some popes and bishops, to greed and pride. Relieved of the constant threat of persecution, Christians began to squabble among themselves about the correct way to understand the identity and teachings of Jesus. The Church was

compelled to debate and define *orthodox* ("right belief") doctrine. Some believers did not accept these decisions, creating confusion and division in the Church.

The Church also deliberated the nature of the documents that formed the written foundation of Christianity, Sacred Scripture. They determined the canon of the Bible (see Section 4) that would from then on be considered the inspired Word of God. In the continued growth and development of these early centuries of the Church's existence, the Church Fathers played a major role. Figures such as St. John Chrysostom, St. Basil, and St. Augustine of Hippo interpreted and elaborated on the Bible and the teaching tradition. They also criticized the problems they noticed among fellow Christians, including sexual immorality, jealousy, and vanity. The Church Fathers thus guided the Church's growth and furnished a rich and extensive set of theological and spiritual writings that would challenge and edify Christian believers in the centuries that followed.

SECTION Assessment

Comprehension

1. What do the two accounts of Constantine's vision of the Chi-Rho agree on?

2. Name two ways that Constantine was accommodating to Christians.

Vocabulary

3. How does the *Golden Legend* fit the definition of a *hagiography*?

Reflection

4. Why do you think that the Cross of Christ was hidden under stones?

5. What is your experience of how greed and pride can cause damage to a group that you have participated in?

THE CHURCH SPREADS THE GOSPEL

If you are a Christian, have you ever wondered how that happened?

It is possible that you personally chose Catholicism or another form of Christianity. If so, you learned about your new faith from *someone*. Maybe that someone was a friend who shared his or her own faith with you, or perhaps you did your own research and read articles or books or listened to podcasts created by someone who was broadcasting his or her faith story to others.

Or you may have "inherited" Catholicism from your parents, being baptized as an infant. In that case, your parents shared their faith with you. But how did your parents receive this faith? Someone shared it with them: either their own parents or someone else.

The point is that the Catholic faith is passed on by *sharing*. Through words or actions, one person proclaims the Gospel to another. That person then does the same and so on until the faith spreads to every corner of the world. The word *gospel* means "good news." The word *evangelist* equates with "bringer of good news." The Apostles and their collaborators, such as St. Paul, dedicated their entire lives to spreading the Gospel, but it hasn't only been the "big names" of the New Testament who evangelized then and in the years since.

All Catholics are called to be evangelists: to share the Gospel, the Good News of salvation, to everyone we encounter. There are times when we are asked to testify publicly about our belief in Jesus Christ. There are more times—actually, each waking day—when we are to represent Christ and the Gospel through our actions and the way we live our lives.

Christians Stand Apart from the Dominant Culture

Jesus described his disciples this way: "You are the salt of the earth. But if salt loses its taste, with what can it be seasoned? It is no longer good for anything but to be thrown out and trampled underfoot" (Mt 5:13). Christian behavior is not and has never been intended to be on autopilot. In other words, Christians are not to just go through the motions and follow current and accepted trends. Christians stand out in radical ways from the rest of society, much as meat that is salted and seasoned stands out from meat that is not. Early Christians acted in ways that set them apart from the dominant Roman culture and drew attention to the Gospel.

The metaphor of salt was an easy one for first-century inhabitants of Palestine to understand. Salt was essential not only for flavoring, but as a preservative for first-century Mediterranean staples like fish and olives. The Jews of Palestine had a massive source of salt nearby in the briny Dead Sea. However, there is a negative aspect to the Dead Sea as well: the high levels of magnesium chloride in its salt give off a noticeable, nauseous odor.[3] Jesus's listeners would have had experience with poor-quality salt due to primitive purification techniques or dishonest salt merchants who laced sodium chloride with additives so as to increase the volume of this valuable commodity. Such salt, having "lost its taste," would have been worthless for flavoring food and would instead have kept food bland. Jesus's metaphor reminded his disciples to be different and to reflect the true value of salt, that is, to be bold in their words and actions, speaking out against injustice and mistreatment of all people, especially the poor and vulnerable, at every turn.

Jesus added another metaphor to describe Christians: **"You are the light of the world."** He went on to explain that people do not "light a lamp and then put it under a bushel basket; it is set on a lampstand, where it gives light to all in the house. Just so, your light must shine before others, that they may see your good deeds and glorify your heavenly Father" (Mt 5:14–16).

Following Jesus's exhortations, the early Christians gradually shared their faith across the Roman world. By the time Constantine ended the great persecutions, the Gospel had already spread through much of the Roman Empire, with substantial communities of believers in the regions that are now North Africa, Greece, Italy, southern Spain, and France.

The Egyptian city of Alexandria, for example, was an important early center of Christian life. Founded by the Greek conqueror Alexander the Great in the fourth century BC, Alexandria used its position at the Nile River's outlet into the Mediterranean Sea to grow into one of the largest cities in the Roman Empire, a hub of trade and education. At the time of Christ, it also housed the largest Jewish community outside Palestine, so it was a natural location for the

The Greek general Alexander the Great lived three centuries before the time of Christ, but he never-theless had a great influence on Christianity. Alexander was taught by the philosopher Aristotle and respected the Jewish religion. His greatest influence, however, was uniting the Middle East with the classical Greek and later Roman culture in which Jews, Greeks, and Romans lived in the same society. The entire ancient world spoke Greek, which made it possible for the spreading of the Gospel in one language, first in spoken form and then in written form.

early Church to spread. Although historical evidence is inconclusive, Christian tradition holds that the Gospel writer St. Mark brought the faith to Alexandria and became its first bishop. In the second and third centuries, Alexandria would be home to several major Christian thinkers, including Clement of Alexandria and Origen. Alexandria's Christians experienced the persecution that affected many followers of Christ in this period. In 248, a mob incited by Christians' refusal to offer sacrifice to pagan gods attacked believers, looting and destroying their property, forcing some to worship the Roman gods, and killing others,[4] but the Christian community survived and continued to thrive. In the time of the emperor Constantine, Alexandria's bishop, St. Athanasius, rose to become a towering figure in Christian theology.

Over the course of the three hundred years after the legalization of Christianity, virtually all of the old Roman Empire became predominantly

Literally the
Light of the World

University of Notre Dame history professor Fr. William Miscamble, CSC, shared a memory of a recent visit to communist Ho Chi Minh City (Saigon). Catholics were permitted to attend Mass and practice their religion in Vietnam, but they remained under the watchful eye of government officials and the police. Fr. Miscamble noted that parishioners at a Saturday evening vigil Mass kept their motor scooters locked up behind the parish gates so they wouldn't be stolen. After the dismissal—"Go in peace, glorifying the Lord by your life"—the parishioners jumped on their scooters and spewed out in various directions in a literal mass exodus into the somewhat hostile streets of the city with their bright headlights lighting the way. Fr. Miscamble commented: "The scene was remarkable. They were bringing the light of the world to their neighbors."

All Christians are to be the light of the world (and salt for the world) in similar bold ways in imitation of Christ. The *Catechism of the Catholic Church* teaches: "In all of his life Jesus presents himself as *our model*. He is 'the perfect man,' who invites us to become his disciples and follow him. By humbling himself, he has given us an example to imitate, through his prayer he draws us to pray, and by his poverty he calls us to accept freely the privation and persecutions that may come our way" (*CCC*, 520).

Christian. The Catholic faith had rooted itself especially in Europe, where it would remain a powerful force and from where Catholic missionaries would eventually launch into the rest of the world.

Who Were the New Believers?

For new converts to Christianity in the early Church, accepting the faith meant more than merely saying, "I believe in Jesus." It meant learning the doctrines of the Church and training to live according to her precepts. Those who were "in training" to become Christian were known as **catechumens**. In the age of persecution, catechumens took on the same risks that full-fledged Christians faced. Sts. Perpetua and Felicity, martyrs in Carthage (see subsection "The Courage of Early Christians" in Chapter 2, Section 3), were catechumens and not yet baptized when they were arrested and sentenced to death for being Christians.

Although details of the reasons why early catechumens chose to prepare for Baptism are scarce,∞ the Acts of the Apostles recounts a number of conversions. In some cases, miracles performed by the Apostles and other Christians attracted observers to the faith the wonderworkers professed (see Acts 5:12–16). On another occasion, an entire household (parents, children, and servants) was baptized at once, implying that dependents might have followed their elders into the faith as a matter of loyalty or necessity rather than of personal choice (see Acts 18:8).≈

In another case of conversion, Acts recounts the story of the well-to-do merchant Lydia, "a worshiper of God," who was persuaded by the preaching of Paul because "the Lord opened her heart" (Acts 16:14). This suggests that

---

catechumens People who are undergoing a period of study and spiritual preparation before receiving the Sacrament of Baptism.

> ### ∞ Note
>
> St. Augustine is one early Christian the details of whose conversion have been preserved. Of the pivotal moment of his conversion (see Chapter 1, Section 1), Augustine explained he had no wish to read further from the biblical verse he had randomly opened to: "Nor was there need. No sooner had I reached the end of the verse than the light of certainty flooded my heart and all dark shades of doubt fled away." He was baptized shortly afterward.

Lydia was already a religious person, predisposed to hear the message of the Gospel. Similarly, in Philip's encounter with the Ethiopian, the man is reading the Hebrew Scriptures but not understanding it, and Philip explains how the prophecies of the Old Testament were fulfilled in Jesus (see Acts 8:26–39). There is evidence that many Romans had grown skeptical of the religion of the pagan gods and were searching for a more convincing answer to deep questions like "What is the meaning of life?" and "What happens after I die?" The extraordinary Gospel of Jesus Christ could fill that longing.

Those who decided to become Christian were sometimes convinced by intellectual arguments. Even more converts were attracted to the charity and fellowship they saw among Christians. The Acts of the Apostles and the

≈ Note

This example from the Acts of the Apostles supports the Church's practice of infant Baptism. The Baptisms of entire households undoubtedly included children of all ages, including newborns. Also consider that when Peter spoke from the upper room window on Pentecost, he said, "Repent and be baptized, every one of you, in the name of Jesus Christ for the forgiveness of your sins; and you will receive the gift of the holy Spirit. For the promise is made to you and to your children and to . . . whomever the Lord our God will call" (Acts 2:38–39).

Epistles of St. Paul testify to the generosity of believers in assisting the needy among them. Christians distinguished themselves by their care for the sick and diseased, who were often shunned in Roman culture. Tertullian noted that it was the love Christians shared that most attracted others: "It is mainly the deeds of a love so noble that lead many to put a brand on us and say, 'See how they love one another.'"[5] Women, slaves, and members of other marginalized groups were no doubt drawn to the message of God's acceptance of all without regard to social status (see Galatians 3:28).[6] Teachings about salvation and eternal life surely were important to many, while the moral code offered by the Gospel may have been the primary attraction to others. The available historical evidence suggests that people of all kinds—Jews and Gentiles, men and women, the rich and the poor—sought entrance into the Church for many different reasons.

Whatever drove the conversions, the decision to become Christian was the beginning, not the end, of what could be a lengthy initiation process. The method of forming catechumens in the faith and of bringing them into the Church has varied from place to place and across the Church's history, but the process has usually lasted from a few months to a few years. Traditionally, the most rigorous period of preparation was during the season of Lent, at the conclusion of which new Christians were brought into full membership in the Church.

We still find this general approach in the Church today. In most parishes, catechumens (the unbaptized) as well as candidates (non-Catholic Christians) who wish to become Catholic go through a period of education and preparation typically known as the **Order of Christian Initiation of Adults (OCIA)**. Commonly, they are baptized or profess their faith as Catholics, and then receive their First Holy Communion, during the Easter Vigil Mass, held the night before Easter Sunday.

The catechumenate aims at bringing the conversion and faith of catechumens to maturity, in response to God taking initiative in their lives in union with the universal Church and the local parish community. The catechumenate is to be "a training period in the whole Christian life . . . during which

---

Order of Christian Initiation of Adults (OCIA) The process through which non-Catholic adults learn about and join in full communion with the Catholic Church by receiving the sacraments of Baptism (if they have not already received Christian Baptism), Confirmation, and Eucharist.

disciples are joined to Christ their Teacher. Therefore, catechumens should be properly instructed in the mystery of salvation and in the practice of Gospel morality, and by sacred rites which are to be held at successive intervals, they should be introduced into the life of faith, of liturgy, and of love, which is led by the People of God" (*Ad Gentes Divinitus*, 14).

All of the earliest Christians were "converts"—people who had been raised in a faith other than Christianity or in no faith at all. Catholic converts have played an incalculably important role in the Church ever since. In every age, there have been great convert saints, hailing from widely different backgrounds and cultures. St. Kateri Tekakwitha (see the feature "St. Kateri Tekakwitha" in this chapter) was an indigenous American, a member of the Mohawk people, who became Catholic in the late seventeenth century. In Africa in the late nineteenth century, the Ugandan saint Charles Lwanga joined the Church at the age of twenty. St. Teresa Benedicta of the Cross (also known as St. Edith Stein) was a German Jew and a brilliant philosopher who became a Catholic in 1922 (see subsection "The Rise of Totalitarianism" in Chapter 7, Section 3). The Catholic Church welcomes and benefits from the new perspectives and enthusiasm that converts contribute to the community of believers.

Pope Francis has renewed the call for evangelization in our own time, affirming that the task of sharing the Good News is at the heart of the mission of the Church: "Christians have the duty to proclaim the Gospel without excluding anyone. Instead of seeming to impose new obligations, they should appear as people who wish to share their joy, who point to a horizon of beauty and who invite others to a delicious banquet." This sharing of our joy applies to all members of the Church: "In all the baptized, from first to last, the sanctifying power of the Spirit is at work, impelling us to evangelization" (*Evangelii Gaudium*, 14, 119).

SECTION Assessment

Comprehension

1. Why were Jesus's listeners familiar with salt that would lose flavor?

2. How did the city of Alexandria become an important local Christian Church?

3. How do we know that the Church has baptized infants since her earliest days?

4. Why might pagan Roman citizens have been attracted to Christianity?

Vocabulary

5. Who are *catechumens*?

6. What is the purpose of the *Order of Christian Initiation of Adults (OCIA)*?

Reflection

7. Who is someone who personally shared the Gospel with you? Explain why this is memorable to you.

8. What is an action that you can take to be light of the world to others?

THE CHURCH TEACHES THE TRUTH

Recall that the Apostles, St. Paul, and others gathered at the Council of Jerusalem (see sub-subsection "Teaching" in Chapter 2, Section 1) and deliberated over who can belong to the Church and what should be required of Gentile Christians upon Baptism. After a debate, Peter issued the council's decision. The Council of Jerusalem was a blueprint of sorts for other councils that would follow. There have been twenty-three **ecumenical councils** in the Church's history, the most recent being the Second Vatican Council, which was held between 1962 and 1965. A succession of ecumenical councils began after the great persecutions ended and bishops were free to gather publicly and debate Catholic teaching. These councils of the early centuries formulated essential doctrine concerning the Divine Person at the center of the Church: Jesus Christ.

Like the Council of Jerusalem, ecumenical councils were often called in response to differences of opinion. Sometimes these debates were vigorous, even violent. At the first ecumenical council—held in 325 in the city of Nicaea, in what is now northwestern Turkey—the bishops determined that the testimony of the Gospels and the **apostolic tradition** clearly taught that Jesus is both wholly God and wholly man at the same time. Succeeding councils defined more precisely what this means. Building on the tradition of Greek philosophy articulated by Plato and Aristotle, the council fathers also discussed and ultimately defined other foundational truths of Christianity,

ecumenical councils Gatherings of all Catholic bishops of the world under the authority of the pope to discuss and make decisions about teachings and practices that apply to all local churches (dioceses).

apostolic tradition Another name for Sacred Tradition; refers to Church teachings that have been passed down by the popes and bishops, the successors of the Apostles.

some of which are difficult to understand. For example, three councils in the fourth and fifth centuries addressed questions about the Holy Trinity—the understanding of the one God as a Trinity of Three Divine *Persons* in one *being*—which is perhaps the most essential theological Church teaching.

Ecumenical Councils Address Heresies

The First Council of Nicaea took on the topic of the Trinity in connection with the Church's understanding of the Incarnation of Christ, who would be defined as the Second Person of the Trinity. Because Jesus was obviously a man and understood to also be God, it meant that he was one Divine Person with two natures (divine and human). One simple way of understanding the difference between these terms is that *person* refers to that which makes someone individual—the aspects that make you "who" you are. The *nature* is that which makes a being "what" it is—the package of attributes and capacities that are attached to a kind of thing. All human beings possess a human nature. We have bodies, and we are able to think and communicate and love, but how we go about these things expresses our personality, our *individual* expression of that common nature. The "who" of Jesus is the Second Divine Person of the Trinity, while the "what" of Jesus is twofold: God and man.

Opposition to the teachings of the First Council of Nicaea was fueled by *Arianism*, named for Arius, a priest from Alexandria who denied the divinity

First Council of Nicaea.

of Christ. He claimed that God the Father existed for all time and that Jesus was created by God and not divine. At the Council, the Church formulated the understanding that Jesus is "begotten, not made, and one in being with the Father." The First Council of Nicaea became so embroiled in this debate that a physical fight broke out between Arius and St. Nicholas of Myra.

Although this kind of violence in the name of religion cannot be justified, it does point to the intensity of religious belief during this time. The reason that people were so passionate about these questions is that they understood the importance of getting them right. If Jesus wasn't *really* God, what did that make of his claims to be the "Son of God"? Or if he never really made those claims, what did that mean for the reliability and truth of the Gospel accounts? If Jesus wasn't *really* a man, how could he have suffered and died and thereby offered himself as a sacrifice for our salvation? The very identity of the Church—what it means to be Christian—hinged on the answers to these questions. The First Council of Nicaea condemned Arianism and declared the divinity of Christ. However, the teaching of Christ's divinity only led to more questions about how the Three Divine Persons function together.

The First Council of Constantinople convened in 381. This council affirmed the Nicene Creed (see subsection "The Apostolic Nature of the Church" in Chapter 2, Section 1) and additionally defined the divinity of the Holy Spirit, the Third Person of the Trinity, in response to a heresy of the Macedonians, who denied this teaching. The Church also condemned *Apollinarianism*, a heresy that claimed that Jesus was divine but not human (the opposite of Arianism) and that Jesus did not have a human soul.

Fifty years later, at the Council of Ephesus in 431, the Church refuted *Nestorianism*, a heresy that taught that Jesus was a human person joined to the Divine Person of the Son. Nestorians also believed that Mary was the mother only of the human person Jesus, not of the Divine Person. The Council of Ephesus stated that Christ has two natures, divine and human, but is one Divine Person. Therefore, Mary should be called the Mother of God.

Another heresy arose after the Church ruled against Nestorianism. Some theologians argued that Jesus could not be separated into two natures at all. Not only was Jesus one person, they surmised, but he also possessed a single divine nature, under which his human appearance was subsumed. This heresy is called *Monophysitism*, meaning "one nature." The Council of Chalcedon in 451 addressed Monophysitism by reiterating and expanding on the Nicene

Creed. Jesus is one Divine Person with two natures, they declared; he is at once the human son of Mary and the divine Son of God, with those two natures united without confusion, change, division, or separation.

Although the decisions of these councils were clear and the majority of Christians have accepted them in the centuries since, there were groups of believers who did not accept the councils' texts, which led to misunderstanding and disunity. For example, some Christian communities in the vicinity of present-day Syria and Iran rejected the council's theology, split from the rest of the Church, and became a distinct religious group known as the Nestorian Church or the Church of the East. It thrived for a time, expanding into India and China, but later declined as other religions came to dominate those regions.

Similarly, several local churches, including in Egypt and Ethiopia, rejected the Council of Chalcedon. These communities survive to this day and have collectively come to be known as the Oriental Orthodox churches, including among others the Coptic Orthodox (Egypt), the Ethiopian Orthodox, and the Armenian Apostolic. Some of these churches are sizable. Although Egypt is a predominantly Muslim country, its Coptic Christians constitute around 10 percent of the nation's population, and their church predates the arrival of Islam by at least five hundred years. Over the centuries, certain groups within many of these churches did reunite with the Roman Catholic Church, creating "Eastern Catholic" Churches within the worldwide Catholic Church. Chapter 4 offers more information on Eastern Catholic Churches.

Recently, the errors of the ancient heresies have reappeared under slightly different guise. For example, in 2006 the Congregation for the Doctrine of the Faith, a Vatican agency tasked with defending and promoting the Catholic faith, examined a contemporary theologian's writings and found a failure "to affirm Jesus' divinity with sufficient clarity."[7] The same could have been said of Arius 1,700 years ago.

The Magisterium: Teaching Office of the Church

Trusting in Jesus's promise to be "with you always" (Mt 28:20), the Church holds that Jesus did not leave his people without a way to definitively know the truths of the faith. Instead, he bestowed on the Apostles the authority to teach sound doctrine. The Catholic Church continues to believe that the Apostles, in the form of their successors, the pope and bishops, guide the Church in this way. The Magisterium is the teaching authority of the Church.

The Magisterium's responsibility is "to preserve God's people from deviations and defections and to guarantee them the objective possibility of professing the true faith without error" (*CCC*, 890). This preservation from error assures the **indefectibility** of the Church, that is, the principle that the Church herself, in her teaching office, will be reliable, even as members of the Church individually will sin, make mistakes, and hold faulty views.

To this end, "Christ endowed the Church's shepherds with the charism of infallibility in matters of faith and morals" (*CCC*, 890). This "charism of infallibility" means that the Holy Spirit guides the leaders of the Church so that they will not err when teaching about what has been revealed by God through the life and preaching of Jesus. This is why Catholics are obligated to accept such teaching "with the submission of faith" (*Lumen Gentium*, 25).

The Church's infallibility can be exercised in two ways. First, the pope—the successor of Peter, the head of the Apostles—teaches without error when

Pope Pius XII during the Assumption of Mary to Heaven ceremony in 1950.

indefectibility Regarding Church teaching and the Church herself, a term meaning that the Church and her teachings are incapable of failure and decay to the end of time.

he declares a doctrine in a manner known as *ex cathedra* ("from the chair"—a reference to the Chair of St. Peter, a symbol of the pope's authority). Pope Pius IX used this method to teach infallibly the **dogma** concerning Mary's Immaculate Conception. On December 8, 1854, accompanied by a retinue of two hundred bishops and cardinals, the pope processed into St. Peter's Basilica in Rome and began Mass. Following the Gospel reading, the pope stood and read aloud the words of the apostolic constitution he had written for the occasion. After introductory passages explaining the history and reasons behind his declaration, he solemnly pronounced the words of definition:

> We declare, pronounce, and define that the doctrine which holds that the most Blessed Virgin Mary, in the first instance of her conception, by a singular grace and privilege granted by Almighty God, in view of the merits of Jesus Christ, the Savior of the human race, was preserved free from all stain of original sin, is a doctrine revealed by God and therefore to be believed firmly and constantly by all the faithful.[8]

By using these definitive words, the pope made it clear that he intended to invoke the charism of infallibility in this teaching on Mary. The dogma of the Immaculate Conception was to be accepted by all Catholics as an indisputable part of their faith. In 1950, Pope Pius XII made a similar infallible statement concerning the Assumption of Mary into heaven. Since that time, no pope has issued a doctrine *ex cathedra*.

The second way the Church's infallibility can be exercised is when the bishops, together with the pope, teach as a group the truths of the Catholic faith in a definitive manner. This is what happens at ecumenical councils, but it can also occur when bishops teach individually in their own local churches but do so in unity of doctrine with each other and with the pope.[9]

The Magisterium of the Church was at work in the early councils, in which their decisions set the standard for Christian belief. In the Councils of Nicaea, Constantinople, and Ephesus, the Magisterium proclaimed the essential Christian belief in the Blessed Trinity:

---

dogma The name for truths that the Church teaches that have been specifically revealed by God. Acceptance of dogma is essential for complete faith and the deepest possible relationship with God. Denial of dogma is heresy.

 **the First Divine Person**—the almighty and eternal God the Father—and his work of creation;

 **the Second Divine Person**—Jesus Christ, God the Son—and his work of redemption;

 **the Third Divine Person**—God the Holy Spirit—who is the origin and source of the sanctification that comes to us through Christ's one, holy, catholic, and apostolic Church (see *CCC*, 190).

Acceptance of the tenets of the Apostles' Creed, Nicene Creed, and other Church dogmas is essential for Catholics to have a complete faith and the deepest possible relationship with God. There are two things to keep in mind about Church dogmas:

1. They are infallible and irreformable.

2. They cannot change in their essence because the truth, which has been revealed by God, remains for all eternity.

This does not mean that human language to express dogmas cannot change. Different expressions of dogma evolve over time.

∞ Note

Non-Catholics and Catholics alike often misunderstand the meaning of infallibility related to Church teaching. First, infallibility is not a magic wand that the pope and bishops get to wave over their teachings to make them inviolable and true. Rather, infallibility is God's promise to the Church that when it comes to matters pertaining to faith and morals and salvation, Catholics can be confident that Church teaching will be a definitive guide. This gift does not apply to other statements the pope or bishops make. The pope cannot declare, for example, that all people from Cleveland must root for the Pittsburgh Steelers and expect that Catholics will comply. Such a statement is not a matter of faith and morals and salvation.

SECTION Assessment

Comprehension

1. How did the First Council of Nicaea explain that Jesus was both God and man?

2. Besides affirming the Nicene Creed, which topic did the First Council of Constantinople address?

3. Explain the heresy of Monophysitism and how the Church responded.

4. What is the responsibility of the Magisterium?

5. What are the two ways that the Church can exercise the charism of infallibility?

Vocabulary

6. Define *apostolic tradition*.

7. Which *dogma* did Pope Pius XII declare infallible in 1950?

Reflection

8. How would you explain the doctrine of the Holy Trinity to a third-grader?

CHURCH AND GOVERNMENT COEXIST

After the Roman Empire ended its persecution and legalized Christianity in the early fourth century, the Church herself soon became the dominant force within the empire. The Church was permitted to own property and construct church buildings. She could establish hospitals for the care of the poor and the sick. Her bishops became influential figures in the political realm. These developments set the stage for a different kind of conflict between the government and the Church.

When the emperor Constantine legalized Christianity, he may well have been motivated by genuine belief in the truth of the Gospel. But other motives were also in the mix. As faith in the traditional gods of Rome—including faith in the emperor, who was counted as a god—declined, Constantine saw that something needed to take its place. For a vibrant, united empire composed of a variety of nations to be maintained, it was necessary for citizens of various races and cultures to have a common bond. A religion that invited all people to join its ranks and made no distinctions by race, class, or sex was perfect for this purpose.

The Church didn't see herself primarily in this role, however. The Church did not need or necessarily want to be identified with the Roman Empire. The Church had already spread beyond the empire's boundaries and, inspired by the promise of Jesus, was confident that she would outlast mighty Rome. So while Constantine and succeeding emperors sought to nudge the Church toward their own interests, the pope, bishops, and laity were more concerned with following the Gospel's lead and did not always cooperate with the government. The *Church Fathers*, the theologians of the first eight centuries of Christianity whose teachings made a lasting mark on the Church, often found themselves debating religious beliefs that impacted the Church's relationship with the government.

Who Were the Church Fathers?

As one historian puts it, the story of the early Church "was the story of a family, and of how the 'fathers' of that family strove to keep their household together, to preserve the family's patrimony, to teach and discipline their children, and to protect the family from danger."[9]

There is no single, authoritative list of Church Fathers, but there is a general, imperfect consensus about who belongs in the group and who doesn't. The fifth-century monk and writer St. Vincent of Lérins proposed a set of criteria that have been followed ever since. A Church Father must have

1. held orthodox doctrine;

2. exhibited holiness of life;

3. been approved by the Church; and

4. lived in the early centuries of the Church.[10]

Those designated Church Fathers stretch from first-century figures such as St. Clement of Rome and St. Ignatius of Antioch, also referred to as "Apostolic Fathers" because they personally knew the Apostles, to St. John Damascene, who died in 749. There are also other designations like "Greek Fathers" (those who wrote in the languages of the eastern Mediterranean), including

The Five Fathers of the Eastern Church with the Five Fathers of the Western Church.

St. Cyril of Jerusalem and St. John Chrysostom of Constantinople, and "Latin Fathers" (those who lived in the West), including St. Hilary of Poitiers and St. Ambrose of Milan. Most Church Fathers are recognized by the Church as saints, but some are not. A few Church Fathers were popes, many were bishops, and some were monks.

Whatever their differences in background, all of the Church Fathers had a key role in cultivating the Church as a world-changing institution. In the words of one historian, "These teachers helped bring Christianity out of its diapers into adulthood. No one can ever again play the role that they played

∞ Note

Even these criteria must be taken with a grain of salt. Some widely recognized Fathers do not fulfill all four requirements. It is actually the judgment of Church historians that decides who is a "Church Father" and who isn't.

POST-NICENE CHURCH FATHERS

Focus Question: How did the early Church respond to theological and doctrinal debates?

Church Fathers are also categorized by the eras in which they lived. The Apostolic Fathers were those whose lifetime overlapped the Apostles; the Ante-Nicene Fathers lived during the period after the Apostolic Fathers but before the First Council of Nicaea in 325 and during the worst age of Christian persecutions; and the Post-Nicene Fathers lived after the First Council of Nicaea. Three Post-Nicene Fathers are described here, all known for their ability to practice their faith publicly but also to hold public discourses regarding important matters of the faith.

St. John Chrysostom Calls Out Sinners

St. John Chrysostom (ca. 347–407) was *patriarch*, or bishop, of Constantinople, the Roman Empire's capital, which was constructed by and named after the emperor who legalized Christianity. John Chrysostom was one of the greatest preachers the Church has ever known, hence his appellation *Chrysostom*, "golden-mouthed." Hundreds of his homilies have survived, and they provide a clear window into the preaching of this influential Father.

John Chrysostom used his considerable oratorical skills to call attention to the sins of fellow Christians, and he did not spare the rich and powerful. Although he was not opposed to wealth per se, he was keenly aware of the corrupting influence of the love of money and material goods, and he stridently attacked those evils. He was especially incensed when the rich refused to use their bounty to assist those who were in need.

He could be quite specific and earthy in his criticisms. In one homily, he attacked the apparently fashionable practice of using fancy chamber pots (urinals). "Ashamed indeed I am," he admitted of the delicate topic, "but it is necessary to speak it. . . . It is ye should be ashamed, that are the makers of these things. When Christ is famishing, do you so revel in luxury?" Using silver dishes was extravagant enough, John fumed, "but the making unclean vessels also of silver, is this then luxury? Nay, I will not call it luxury, but senselessness; nay, nor yet this, but madness."[10]

Fearlessly committed to speaking the truth of the Gospel, John did not defer to anyone, including the most powerful figures in the empire. The empress Eudoxia felt herself targeted in John's condemnations of opulence and vanity, and he was twice exiled from Constantinople at her behest. However, the people of Constantinople were devoted to their archbishop, recognizing that he was genuinely concerned about both their material and their spiritual welfare. St. John Chrysostom is an example of the Church's obligation to defend the poor and downtrodden, even if it means arousing the animosity of the wealthy and powerful.

St. Ambrose of Milan and the Emperor Theodosius

The Church's role in standing up to political authority is also evident in a dispute between Bishop Ambrose of Milan and Emperor Theodosius. St. Ambrose (ca. 338–397), who had been born into an important Roman family and served as a political official before becoming bishop, admired the Roman Empire but was also convinced that the Church was superior to it, in the sense that the Church was primarily concerned with spiritual matters whose importance was eternal. He understood that if the interests of the state and the interests of the Church came into conflict, he must defend the interests of the Church.

Ambrose represented the dramatic transformation of the empire brought about by Christianity. He was "the first Latin Church Father to be born, reared, and educated not as a pagan, but as a Christian. He was likewise the first descendant of the Roman high aristocracy to stand up publicly for the Church, and to have found in it his life-work." To this work he brought considerable talents: "Of superior intelligence, energetic, a born diplomat and where necessary an extremely adroit tactician, he seems never to have faltered in his real purpose and in his religious and ethical convictions."[11]

In 390, a rebellion in the Greek city of Thessalonica provoked retaliation by Roman soldiers, who massacred thousands of citizens. Whether Theodosius directly ordered the killing is disputed, but he was in any case held responsible, including by Ambrose. The great northern Italian city of Milan was at the time the capital of the region, and Theodosius was a Christian, so Ambrose was the emperor's bishop as well as his friend and so felt compelled to call Theodosius to repentance. This was a delicate matter. For centuries, Roman emperors had been considered divine, and to call into question their decisions was to risk severe punishment. The situation began to change when Constantine legalized Christianity, but it was still an act of courage for a Church leader to presume himself worthy of judging the actions of an emperor.∞

St. Ambrose's letter to Theodosius, which has been preserved, provides a model of episcopal leadership in calling a Christian ruler to a higher standard. Ambrose begins by expressing regard for their friendship and praising the emperor's "zeal for the faith." But he then laments the violence in Thessalonica and, comparing Theodosius to King David, who also made terrible mistakes, urges the emperor to repent and to say, like David, "I have sinned against the Lord" (2 Sm 12:13). By this repentance, Ambrose wrote, David "became more acceptable to God, for it is no matter of wonder that a man should sin, but this is reprehensible, if he does not recognize that he has erred, and humble himself before God." Ambrose did not wish to condemn Theodosius but rather to encourage him to restore his relationship with God by admitting his sin. "I have written this, not in order to confound you, but that the examples of these kings may stir you up to put away this sin from your kingdom, for you will do it away by humbling your soul before God."[12]

Theodosius initially stood on the dignity of his office and refused to repent. Ambrose then denied him admittance to the cathedral in Milan and access to Holy Communion. But in time, after Ambrose had repeatedly implored him, Theodosius voluntarily submitted, demonstrated his regret, and was welcomed back into church on Christmas Day of 390. Ambrose and Theodosius were also personally reconciled, and they remained friends until the emperor's death five years later.

The episode of Ambrose and Theodosius proclaimed a truth that sent shock waves across the centuries: All people, even emperors, are subject to the laws of God. Every Christian, no matter how powerful, stands within, not above, the Church. Time and again, kings, queens, and other political officials would seek to influence, use, or even destroy the Church for the purpose of political gain. Time and again, their dynasties and empires fell, while the Church has remained, secure in Jesus's promise to be with her until the end of time.

Thus it was with the Roman Empire. One of the greatest empires the world has ever seen, the political regime in whose shadow the Church had grown for four hundred years, eventually faltered. In 476, an invading Germanic king deposed the Roman emperor, bringing the Roman Empire in Italy to an end. (The empire would survive in the East, based in Constantinople, for another thousand years.) Yet in the old lands of the Western empire—Italy, Spain, France, and England—the Church endured, and her mission to spread the Gospel and lead her members to holiness persisted.

St. Augustine of Hippo's *The City of God*

When St. Ambrose preached in his cathedral in Milan, one of his listeners was St. Augustine of Hippo (see Chapter 1, Section 1), who was searching for the truth and had many questions answered by the brilliant bishop of Milan. The decline of the Roman Empire led St. Augustine to reflect on the Church and her relationship with human governments and nations. His reflection has profoundly shaped the Church's understanding of herself and her relation to the secular world ever since.

St. Augustine (354–430) was not alive at the official end of the Roman Empire in 476, but he lived through the sack of Rome by the Visigoths in 410 and died during the siege of his city of Hippo, in what is now Algeria, by another Germanic tribe. In his detailed, philosophical book *The City of God*, disseminated in 426, Augustine responded to arguments circulating in the declining empire that Christianity was the cause of Rome's demise and that because the Church's fortunes were closely tied to the empire's, Rome's fall would also damage the Church. Following the example of his mentor St. Ambrose, Augustine insisted that an important distinction be made between the Church and the empire and noted especially their differences. He pointed out that while Christians were citizens of Rome or some other political entity ("the earthly city"), they are more importantly citizens of the "city of God." Christianity was not the cause of Rome's decline, St. Augustine argued, for the teachings of Christ encouraged Christians to be exemplary citizens: virtuous, faithful, truthful. Augustine also pointed out that the demise of the Roman Empire had begun historically well before the time of Christ and before his name had been "blazoned among the nations with that glory which they vainly grudge."[13]

St. Augustine's lasting point is that it is inevitable that secular kingdoms will decline and fall; this is the pattern of history. Yet this should be no cause for undue distress among Christians, who recognize that spiritual realities are more important than temporal, earthly realities. The earthly city is passing, while the city of God is eternal. "In that city," Augustine writes, "all the citizens shall be immortal, men now for the first time enjoying what the holy angels have never lost. And this shall be accomplished by God, the most almighty Founder of the city. For he has promised it, and cannot lie, and has already performed many of His promises, and has done many unpromised kindnesses to those whom He now asks to believe that he will do this also."[14]

St. Augustine reminds us contemporary citizens of the city of God that our perspective must extend beyond this world. Members of the Church should be confident in God's promise that, no matter what happens to earthly kingdoms, they will enjoy happiness forever in God's heavenly kingdom.

Further Study and Reflection

- St. John Chrysostom was known as a *Christian apologist*. Explain what that means in relation to his life.
- How did St. Ambrose become a bishop? Describe the scene.
- Read St. Augustine's *Confessions*, VIII, 12. Summarize his conversion to Christianity from that reading.

during those exciting, formative years when the Church was young."[15] One important way the Church Fathers shaped the Church was to define her relationship to the world around her, and in particular to the secular rulers who throughout history had claimed authority over religion. **St. John Chrysostom**, **St. Ambrose of Milan**, and **St. Augustine of Hippo** exemplify the Church's position as a counterpoint to the state during this time.

SECTION Assessment

Comprehension

1. Name two of Constantine's motivations to legalize Christianity in the Roman Empire.

2. Why did the Church not necessarily want to align itself with the Roman government?

3. What are the four qualifications to be considered a Church Father?

4. In what period did the Ante-Nicene Fathers live?

Reflection

5. In which period do you think it would have been the most challenging to be a Church Father? Why?

THE CHURCH ESTABLISHES THE CANON OF SCRIPTURE

Henry Graham (1874–1959) was born in Scotland. His father was a Presbyterian minister who harbored the hope that his son would follow in his footsteps. For a time, Henry shared this dream. He had had little exposure to Catholicism, for in his part of the country "**papists** were as rare as snakes in Ireland." He learned the Bible thoroughly, studied divinity at the university, and was on the verge of joining his father in the Presbyterian ministry. But doubts crept in as he began to learn more about the Catholic Church, and about the history of the composition of the Bible that he knew and loved so well. When he realized how strongly he was attracted to Catholicism, he became fearful, knowing how devastating his conversion would be to his family and friends. He even burned all of his Catholic reading material and other belongings, including a picture of the pope.

However, as Henry put it later, "the fire that burned the books could not burn the love and longing for Catholic doctrine and ritual out of my heart." Eventually, he joined the Catholic Church. Henry's conversion to Catholicism was difficult for his father, who was at first "shocked and saddened," but he soon came to recognize that his son must follow his conscience, even to the Church of Rome. For his part, after he became Catholic Henry experienced "ever-increasing delight and wonder at the new world of beauty and sanctity that gradually opened out before me."[16] Three years after his conversion, in 1906, Henry was ordained a Catholic priest. In 1917, he was ordained and named auxiliary bishop of St. Andrews and Edinburgh, Scotland.

Bishop Henry Graham noted that it was his evolving understanding of Sacred Scripture that first led him to the Church. He wrote about his findings

---

papists A name, sometimes used in a derogatory way, for Catholics that express their loyalty to the pope.

concerning the Church and Scripture in a book titled *Where We Got the Bible*, in which he summarizes four key points about the relationship between the Church and Sacred Scripture:

1. The Church existed before the writings of the New Testament did. The Apostles passed on the faith for decades before the books of the New Testament were written or collected, and most of the Apostles didn't write anything that has survived. Wrote Graham: "Thousands of people became Christians through the work of the Apostles and missionaries of Christ in various lands, and believed the whole truth of God as we believe it now, and became saints, before ever they saw or read, or could possibly see or read, a single sentence of inspired Scripture of the New Testament, for the simple reason that such Scripture did not then exist."

2. The New Testament was not composed by a single author as a single source. The New Testament is made up of twenty-seven books by at least eight different authors, written at different times over the course of approximately fifty years.

3. There were many writings circulating in the early centuries of the Church. There was no automatic consensus about which writings were truly the inspired Word of God, which were sound but not inspired, and which were to be rejected by serious Christians. It was left to the Church to decide, according to a set of criteria established by the Church, which writings were inspired.

4. Following the first three points to their logical conclusion, the canon of Scripture did not appear at once directly from God, whole and complete. Instead, it was important figures in the Church—Matthew, Mark, Luke, John, Paul, Peter, and so on—who wrote the material in the New Testament; and it was authority figures in the early Church, mostly successors of the Apostles (bishops), who evaluated the array of writings and determined which ones should be included in the canon.

It was through a series of councils, in conjunction with the approval of the pope, that the Church established the canon of the Bible. These councils took place at cities in Asia Minor (Turkey) and North Africa in the final decades of the fourth century. The twenty-seven books of the New Testament that were accepted by these Church authorities have been recognized as the **canon** of Scripture by virtually all Christians ever since. The forty-six books of the Old Testament identified by these councils were accepted by all Christians for many centuries and still match the Old Testament canon approved for use in the Catholic Church.

Sacred Scripture Is Only Part of the Deposit of Faith

The *Catechism of the Catholic Church* reminds us that "the Christian faith is not a 'religion of the book'" (*CCC*, 108). Rather, the Bible is the "book of the Church." There is a close and mutually supportive relationship between the Church and the Bible: "In Sacred Scripture, the Church constantly finds her nourishment and her strength" (*CCC*, 104). Through the Bible, Christians hear the words of God himself. "In the sacred books, the Father who is in heaven meets His children with great love and speaks with them" (*Dei Verbum*, 21). Holding a special place because of their focus on the life and teaching of Jesus, "the *Gospels* are the heart of all the Scriptures" (*CCC*, 125).

The Catholic Church recognizes that Divine Revelation—God's revealing of himself to the world—takes places through the twofold movement of Sacred Scripture and **Sacred Tradition**.∞ The Gospel of Jesus Christ has been transmitted through both channels, which work in conjunction with one

---

canon A name for those books of the Bible that have been accepted as normative for the faith.

Sacred Tradition The living transmission of the Church's Gospel message found in the Church's teaching, life, and worship. It is faithfully preserved, handed on, and interpreted by the Church's Magisterium.

∞ Note

Sacred Tradition began with the Apostles, under the inspiration of the Holy Spirit. They, in turn, passed on this gift to the succeeding pope and bishops. Sacred Tradition is contained in the Church's teaching, life, and worship. Some concrete examples of Sacred Tradition include creeds, doctrines, hierarchical structure, liturgy, types of prayer, and social teaching and practice.

another. This task of conveying the message of the Gospel was "faithfully fulfilled by the Apostles who, by their oral preaching, by example, and by observances handed on what they had received from the lips of Christ, from living with Him, and from what He did, or what they had learned through the prompting of the Holy Spirit." The task of transmitting revelation was also fulfilled "by those Apostles and apostolic men who under the inspiration of the same Holy Spirit committed the message of salvation to writing" (*Dei Verbum*, 7). There is therefore a "close connection and communication between sacred tradition and Sacred Scripture. For both of them, flowing from the same divine wellspring, in a certain way merge into a unity and tend toward the same end" (*DV*, 9).

Given this common source and common purpose, "Sacred Tradition and Sacred Scripture form one sacred deposit of the word of God, committed to the Church" (*DV*, 10).∞ This is why "both Sacred Tradition and Sacred Scripture are to be accepted and venerated with the same sense of loyalty and reverence" (*DV*, 9). Finally, the whole of revelation—contained in both Sacred Tradition and Sacred Scripture—is entrusted to the teaching office of the Church (the Magisterium), which "is not above the word of God, but serves it, teaching only what has been handed on, listening to it devoutly, guarding it scrupulously and explaining it faithfully in accord with a divine commission and with the help of the Holy Spirit" (*DV*, 10).

When we put all these pieces together, we see that "sacred tradition, Sacred Scripture, and the teaching authority of the Church, in accord with God's most wise design, are so linked and joined together

Four Englishmen opposed to the Church in the seventeenth century are shown fighting over the Bible.

that one cannot stand without the others" (*DV*, 10; see also *CCC*, 75–83). In other words, the Church and the Bible are indissolubly united, and together they teach us the truth about God, humanity, and the way to salvation.

It is also important to recognize that some non-Catholic Christians indeed belong to a "church of the book." Some of these denominations do not assign equal weight to Sacred Scripture and Sacred Tradition. For some Christians, the Bible is God's final revelation to the world. According to this view, answers to every human question can be found in the pages of Scripture. In these denominations, the Bible is the primary focus for instruction, worship, and prayer. Catholics, on the other hand, hold that the Bible is not a "dead letter." Rather, Christ, through the ongoing inspiration of the Holy Spirit in every generation, must continue to open the minds of Catholics to understand the meaning of Sacred Scripture.

How the Church Understands Sacred Scripture

Aided by the teachings of the Church Fathers, Catholics have a unique method for reading, praying with, and understanding Sacred Scripture that is known as the *fourfold senses of Scripture*. This method, which you may already have learned in an introductory Scripture course, examines the writings of the Bible according to four "senses," or ways of interpreting the text: literal, allegorical, moral, and anagogical.[∞] The Church Fathers pioneered, practiced, and built upon these ways of approaching the Bible, bestowing on the Church a vast body of research, insight, and reflection on the meaning of the Word of God and its importance for the Christian life.

St. Jerome (ca. 345–420), instrumental in producing the Latin edition of the Bible known as the **Vulgate**, contributed to understanding the literal sense of Scripture by insisting on accuracy in translation from Scripture's original

---

∞ Note

The *literal* sense is what the words themselves plainly mean, without further elaboration. The other three senses are *spiritual*, pointing to truths beyond the literal sense of the words. The *allegorical* sense (including typology) is the meaning as it relates to Jesus Christ and the New Covenant. The *moral* sense is the meaning for the life of the Christian—how we should act as followers of Christ. The *anagogical* sense has to do with the ultimate end of humankind in eternity.

languages of Hebrew and Greek. St. Clement of Alexandria (ca. 150–ca. 215) invoked Scripture in teaching about morality. He cited many passages to show that the Christian, no matter his or her age, is a "child of God" and supported his exhortations with many analogies from the Psalms and other Old Testament works. For Clement, the writings of the Old Testament were not merely descriptions of the past; they also contained guidance for living as a Christian.

Origen (ca. 185–ca. 253) was another Alexandrian, born somewhat later than Clement. He was the most prolific writer of the Church Fathers, publishing hundreds of commentaries on various books of the Bible. One of these commentaries, on the Song of Songs from the Old Testament, interprets its romantic poetry as a metaphor for the soul's relationship to God. Countless commentators ever since have followed Origen's example, most notably St. Bernard of Clairvaux (1090–1153), who wrote that the author of the Song of Songs "expressed the longing of the holy soul, its wedding song."[17]

By the time of John Cassian (ca. 360–ca. 435), a monk and theologian, the Church's spiritual interpretations of the Bible were well established. Cassian is credited with naming the four senses of Scripture, invoking, for example, how Jerusalem can be understood in four different ways: "in the historical sense as the city of the Jews, in allegory as the Church of Christ, in anagogy as the heavenly city of God 'which is the mother of us all' (Gal 4:26), and in the [moral]

St. Bernard of Clairvaux preaching the Second Crusade in 1146.

Vulgate The name for St. Jerome's fifth-century AD translation of the Bible into Latin, the common language of the people of his day.

sense as the human soul."[18] St. Augustine similarly described the fourfold interpretation: "In all the sacred books, we should consider eternal truths that are taught, the facts that are narrated, the future events that are predicted, and the precepts or counsels that are given."[19]

By drawing on the Bible so profusely and incorporating its words into their thinking about God and Christian conduct, the Church Fathers created a lasting bond between the Bible and the Church. For the Church Fathers, to be Catholic was to be rooted in Scripture, and that is the way the Church has seen the connection ever since.

SECTION Assessment

Comprehension

1. Why did Henry Graham think that he was going to disappoint his father?

2. What did Origen teach about the Song of Songs?

3. What are the four senses of Scripture?

Vocabulary

4. Explain the metaphor of *papists* being "as rare as snakes in Ireland" in Graham's part of the country.

5. How was the *canon* of Scripture determined?

6. How do Sacred Scripture and *Sacred Tradition* work together?

Reflection

7. What is the difference between being a Christian who understands the Church as a "church of the book" and being one who sees the Bible as the "book of the church"?

Section Reviews

Focus Question

How did the early Church respond to theological and doctrinal debates?
Complete one of the following:

- Write definitions of *Apostolic Church Fathers*, *Latin Church Fathers*, and *Greek Church Fathers*, and list the names of those who are classified in each category.
- List the first seven ecumenical councils and their main subject matter.
- Read the *Catechism of the Catholic Church*, 128. What does "typology" refer to in this paragraph?

Introduction
The Church Gains the Freedom to Flourish

Review

The emperor Constantine was at the forefront of the change in culture surrounding Christianity from one that suffered persecution to one that enjoyed preferred status. With the preferred status, internal squabbles arose in the Church. Church Fathers were among those helping to resolve some of the issues, including around Sacred Scripture.

Assignment

Research and describe the Edict of Milan. Write down three ways that Christianity changed after the Edict of Milan was issued.

Section 1
The Church Spreads the Gospel

Review

With Christianity legalized, the Church spread even beyond the boundaries of the Roman Empire. Pagans were attracted to intellectual arguments of Christianity, the Church's moral teachings, and particularly her charitable example. The *catechumenate* is the name for the initiation process for new Christians. Catechumens sometimes had years of preparation before being baptized, although they were aligned with the Church throughout the process. All members of the Church continue to be called to evangelize others and share the Gospel with those who have not yet heard it.

Assignment

Research information about the Order of Christian Initiation of Adults (OCIA) process at your parish or a nearby parish. How long is the catechumenate? How many adults were baptized at the last Easter Vigil? What are some ways that the entire parish participates in the OCIA process?

Section 2
The Church Teaches the Truth

Review

The first several ecumenical councils addressed understandings of the identity and nature of Christ as well as of the Blessed Trinity, usually in response to heresies that had cropped up. It was and remains the task of the Magisterium to "preserve God's people from deviations and defections and to guarantee them the objective possibility of professing the true faith without error" (*CCC*, 890). The Church's infallibility functions in two ways: when the pope teaches in statements he declares *ex cathedra* and when the body of bishops, together with the pope, definitively teach the truths of the Catholic faith.

Assignment

Research Church dogmas and choose one. Explain how it is significant to your everyday faith.

Section 3
Church and Government Coexist

Review

Constantine understood that Christianity helped facilitate unity in the Roman Empire. The Church, however, did not feel the need to align herself closely with the government. *Church Fathers* is the name for men in the early centuries of the Church approved by the Church for holding and explaining orthodox Christian doctrine and living lives of holiness They are classified based on the periods and places they lived in.

Assignment

Research the difference between a Church Father and a Doctor of the Church. Define *Doctor of the Church*, and name at least three of those who have been given that title.

Section 4
The Church Establishes the Canon of Scripture

Review

The Church determined the canon of the Bible through a series of councils. The canon did not appear at once from God, whole and complete. Sacred Scripture and Sacred Tradition together form the one Deposit of Faith. The Church understands the Bible as a living document that the Holy Spirit uses to inspire Catholics in every generation.

Assignment

Interpret this statement: "Catholicism is a faith of the living Word of God."

Chapter Projects

Choose and complete at least one of the following projects to assess your understanding of the material in this chapter.

⚙ 1. *Create Your Own Image of St. Kateri Tekakwitha*

Make a printed or digital album that includes five artistic renditions of St. Kateri Tekakwitha other than the one shown at the beginning of this chapter. These can be paintings, statues, murals, or any other type of image of St. Kateri. Include a detailed caption for each image you choose, with information about its artist, location, and year created. Create a sixth image of St. Kateri on your own. Use any art medium of your choosing (e.g., pencil, chalk, paint), including computer generated. Place your image on the final page or slide of your album.

⚙ 2. *Correct Major Heresies That Plagued the Church*

The chart below lists many of the heresies the Church faced from the third to the ninth centuries. Complete the elements of the chart. In the second column, summarize the heretical teachings. In the third column, summarize the orthodox teachings of the Church, and quote one or more of the sources listed.

HERESY	HERETICAL TEACHING	ORTHODOX CHURCH TEACHING
Gnosticism		Quote: St. Irenaeus, *Against Heresies*
Arianism		Quote: St. Athanasius, First Council of Nicaea
Apollinarianism		Quote: First Council of Constantinople
Nestorianism		Quote: Council of Ephesus, St. Cyril of Alexandria
Monophysitism		Quote: Council of Chalcedon, Pope Leo I in Tome of Leo

Name at least three heresies in today's world that threaten Catholicism from the outside. Answer this question: How can the Church combat these heresies?

⚙ *3. Formulate a Plan for Making Disciples*

By virtue of their Baptism, all Catholics are called to share faith with others. Jesus's instruction to "go, therefore, and make disciples of all nations" (Mt 28:19) applies to everyone. The Office for Formation of the Laity of the Archdiocese of Philadelphia identified several ideas for evangelization in a short summary, "Everyday Evangelizing for Everyday Catholics." Here are some of them:

Before You Can Evangelize (Pre-evangelization)

- Pray daily.
- Carry a cross in your pocket.
- Read the Bible.
- Receive the sacraments.
- Communicate with those who inspire you.

Evangelizing in All Situations

- Respond "Thank God" when someone shares good news with you.
- Share a story of how God works in your life.
- Ask people to pray for your intentions.
- Make the Sign of the Cross when dining out.
- Invite someone who is not Catholic to Mass.

Develop a further list of ideas for sharing the faith with your peers, either Catholics who need a refresher in their faith or those who have no experience of Catholicism. With these groups specifically in mind, write up an evangelization plan that focuses on what you can do

- this week;
- this month; and
- this year.

For each part of the plan, include answers to the five *W*s and *H* questions:

- Who is to be evangelized? (And *who* is to do the evangelization?)

- What is the desired result?
- Where will this take place?
- When (during which week, month, and year) will this happen?
- Why is this an important task?
- How will this take place?

For reference, note ideas from the USCCB Committee on Evangelization and Catechesis. See www.usccb.org.

⚙ *4. Create and Analyze an Online Survey on Church Issues*

Create several surveys addressing Church issues introduced in this chapter and put them online on one or more social media platforms. You should have at least ten separate survey questions, each with three or four answer options. For example:

Is Mary the Mother of God?
   a. Yes

   b. No

   c. Only the mother of the human Jesus

Jesus is
   a. Human only

   b. Divine only

   c. Human and divine

Who wrote the Bible?
   a. God on his own

   b. Human beings on their own

   c. Human beings inspired by God

Create a chart listing the results of each survey question (number of responses and percentages). Write a one-page essay summarizing what you learned about what people believe about the Catholic Church.

⚙ *5. Share a Dramatic Reading and the Meaning of a Poem*

As Cardinal Karol Wojtyla, Pope John Paul II wrote the poem "Marble Floor" in 1962 near the start of the Second Vatican Council. The poem represents the mystical meaning of the papacy. Practice reading the poem, found in Chapter 2 Review, Chapter Project 2. When you feel ready, videotape yourself reading the poem in a setting of your choice. You may wish to add background music to the reading. Also, answer the following questions regarding the content of the poem in writing:

- What is it that guides us as we walk amid the walls and colonnades of a church?

- Which Apostle does the floor represent?

- One of the titles of the pope is "Servant of the servants of God." What portion of the poem represents this title of the pope?

- The poem states that in the Church there are "so many walls, so many colonnades." What does this mean? What is the danger for a Catholic who sees only one wall or one colonnade?

Turn in your video to your teacher in an approved format along with your written responses to the questions.

Faithful Disciple
St. Monica

It's impossible to appreciate the life of St. Augustine of Hippo (see Chapter 1, Section 1) without likewise knowing about his mother, St. Monica (ca. 333–387), a North African saint born in Tagaste, which is in present-day Algeria. Monica was born into a Christian family and married at a young age to Patricius, a pagan who held some type of official position in the local government. Patricius had a violent temper, and his wife's practice of her faith, including prayer and almsgiving to the poor, is said to have bothered him.

Monica had two other children who survived infancy besides her oldest, Augustine. She desired Baptism for all three, but her efforts were repulsed, first by her husband and later by her children themselves. When Augustine became ill, she became especially concerned that he would die unbaptized. When he recovered, her worry took on a new strain. Augustine

St. Monica

began to follow *Manicheism*, a heresy that claimed that the body was evil while the soul alone was good. He also lived out of wedlock with his girlfriend and their son. Although Monica was so disgusted with Augustine that she would not let him eat or sleep in her home, she had a dream of some kind in which she was told not to abandon him.

Around this time, Monica went to visit an unnamed bishop, who shared consoling words with her: "At present the heart of the young man is too stubborn, but God's time will come. The child of your tears will not perish." More motivated than ever, Monica followed Augustine to Rome, only to discover that he had already left for Milan. She followed him there as well. These efforts have given her the title of "The Persistent Mother." In Milan, Augustine had connected with St. Ambrose, and the window to his conversion had been opened. Ambrose advised Monica to temper the direct nature of imposing her wishes on her son. "Talk more to God about Augustine than to Augustine about God," he told her.

Finally, at the Easter Vigil in 387, Augustine and several of his friends were baptized by St. Ambrose. St. Monica had lived with her son in the six months before his Baptism, enjoying the least tumultuous days with him that she had ever experienced. Augustine planned to return to North Africa with his mother and live out a Christian life in his native place. But on their way home, Monica became ill. She told her son not to worry: "Nothing in this world now affords me delight. I do not know what there is now left for me to do or why I am still here. All my hopes in this world have now been fulfilled."

Monica also had little care about where she would be buried. Originally, she was buried in Ostia, a small village on the coast of Italy near Rome. In the sixth century her remains were moved to a hidden crypt at Saint Aurea Church in Ostia. In 1430, Pope Martin V moved her relics to the high altar of the Basilica di Sant'Agostino, named for her son, in Rome. Many miracles were credited to Monica along the way to Rome. She was acclaimed a saint in the era of the Church before there was a formal canonization process. She is the patron of alcoholics, of women who have been abused, and particularly of parents whose children have left the faith. Her feast day is on August 27, one day before the feast day of her son, St. Augustine. St. Monica was a female saint in the era of Church Fathers.

Comprehension

1. When did Monica become a Christian?
2. What did the unnamed bishop tell Monica?
3. What did Monica tell Augustine as she approached death?

Reflection

Explain the advice of St. Ambrose to Monica to "talk more to God about Augustine than to Augustine about God." What is a specific way that you can apply this advice to your own life?

Prayer

This prayer by St. Augustine of Hippo, an excerpt from his *Confessions* (book 10), is prayed on his feast day, August 28. In this prayer, besides lamenting the later stage of life when he came to be baptized and know the Lord, St. Augustine also confronts the problem of suffering that he and all other human beings must face. A reading from Job 7:1–21 accompanies this prayer on his feast day.

Prayer of St. Augustine

Late have I loved Thee, O Beauty so ancient and so new; late have I loved Thee! For behold Thou were within me, and I outside; and I sought Thee outside and in my unloveliness fell upon those lovely things that Thou hast made. Thou were with me and I was not with Thee. I was kept from Thee by those things, yet had they not been in Thee, they would not have been at all. Thou didst call and cry to me and break open my deafness: and Thou didst send forth Thy beams and shine upon me and chase away my blindness: Thou didst breathe fragrance upon me, and I drew in my breath and do not pant for Thee: I tasted Thee, and now hunger and thirst for Thee: Thou didst touch me, and I have burned for Thy peace.

4

The Church Rises to Prominence

The Duomo of Milan and Organ

The organ at the Duomo (Italian for "church" or "cathedral") of Milan, Italy, is itself a piece of art. The history of this cathedral, the largest in Italy (see subsection "Cathedrals of the Middle Ages" in Chapter 4, Section 4), has been linked to its organ since the first organ was built there in 1394 shortly after construction on the cathedral began. The current great organ at the cathedral wasn't assembled until 1938. It was restored in 1986 and repositioned in the cathedral's **presbytery**. This organ is the largest in Italy and one of the fifteen largest in the world. With 15,800 pipes, the longest nearly thirty feet high and the smallest only a couple of inches, it is second in Europe in total number of pipes to the organ in St. Stephen's Cathedral in Passau, Germany.

What makes an organ a piece of art, however, is its sound, not its size. The organ's placement on the right side of the presbytery, where it is at the same distance from all the sound sections, was intended to improve the acoustics. The original organ created in 1939 in reality had seven organs positioned at different points throughout the cathedral. For example, a great organ was placed in two artistic cases on both sides of the high altar and a choir organ was installed on a platform at the end of a choir stall. The renovated organ has five organs and five consoles. A secondary console with three manuals is positioned at ground level on the left side of the altar and is linked to the organ both electronically and manually. The restored organ was introduced on September 8, 1986, with a concert by the cathedral's organist, Luigi Benedetti. It continues to be played at all important liturgies throughout the Church Year.

The Duomo of Milan in its entire scope is a magnificent work of art. Built in a Gothic style that had reached its peak around the beginning of construction in 1386, the cathedral took over six centuries to complete. This long history makes it difficult to connect the cathedral with any one architect. At the end of the fifteenth century, Leonardo da Vinci, one of the greatest architects and artists of all time, was commissioned to design the cathedral's *tiburium*, or tower. Da Vinci designed a buttress that would hold the tower and strengthen the infrastructure of the entire cathedral. The style of the tower is Gothic like the rest of the cathedral, but he used Renaissance methods in its design, including a more octagonal layout for its base.

---

presbytery The part of the cathedral with raised steps that is reserved for the clergy during the celebration of Mass. Today, especially in Catholic churches, the presbytery is known as the *sanctuary*.

How was the Catholic Church important to human progress during the Middle Ages?

AN ERA OF GREAT ACHIEVEMENTS

It is first worth exploring the meaning of the term *Middle Ages*. Taken from two Latin words—*medium* (middle) and *aevum* (age), which have also been combined into *medieval*—the period has been labeled as anywhere from a long one thousand years from about 500 to 1500 to a more precise dating from the fall of the Western Roman Empire in 476 to the beginning of what is known as the Western Schism in 1378, when there were multiple claimants to the papal throne (see subsection "Spiritual Challenges to the Papacy" in Section 3 of this chapter). The first half of the Middle Ages (ca. 500 to 1000) is often called the "Dark Ages."

The ways that historical eras are classified by modern historians can often project an unfair or misleading understanding of both why certain periods have been arbitrarily defined by years and also why they are labeled with certain names. Clearly, calling a period the "Dark Ages" was intended to indicate that not much of worth took place during that time. Even calling the period the "Middle Ages" is an attempt by historians to indicate that this was an era that took a back seat to the more prominent ancient times (prior to 500) and the Renaissance and Reformation period that overlapped and followed (ca. 1450–1650). Twentieth-century Catholic writer **G. K. Chesterton** reminds us "that Parliaments are medieval, that all our Universities are mediaeval, that city corporations are mediaeval, that gunpowder and printing are mediaeval, that half the things by which we now live, and to which we look for progress, are mediaeval."[1]

Historian Steve Weidenkopf has called attention to the use of the term *medieval* for this period as a way to disparage the Church's accomplishments among both Protestant and later **Enlightenment** authors who "solidified the modern understanding of the word as a synonym for barbaric, bloody,

G. K. Chesterton

Gilbert Keith Chesterton (1874–1936) was one of the best writers of the twentieth century. He wrote hundreds of books, poems, plays, and short stories. He was also a journalist, writing over four thousand essays and columns primarily for the *Illustrated London News*. Chesterton converted from Anglicanism to Catholicism and wrote several books of **apologetics**. When asked to explain why he had become a Catholic, he replied: "The difficulty in explaining 'why I am a Catholic' is that there are ten thousand reasons all amounting to one reason: that Catholicism is true."

superstitious, primitive, bigoted, and intolerant, among others."[2] In fact, Chesterton was right: There were exceptional achievements in the Middle Ages. Most of these are connected with the Church.

The Fall of Rome

As the Roman Empire faltered in the fifth century, bands of people from the east (sometimes called *barbarians*) moved in to occupy its domains. This was a centuries-long process, sometimes peaceful and sometimes brutally violent. Prominent among the leaders of the barbarian tribes was Attila, king of the

---

Enlightenment Name for a period in Europe that began in the late seventeenth century that was also known as the *Age of Reason*. The term *Enlightenment* implies that religious people of the Middle Ages were in the dark and that only human reason separated from religious beliefs could bring them into the light.

apologetics The defense and explanation of the teachings, beliefs, and practices of the Catholic faith. Its purpose is to remove objections to the faith, explain different principles, and win people over to Christ and the Church.

Huns, a people from Central Asia who conquered formerly Roman domains in western Asia and eastern and central Europe. In the 450s, Attila's forces ravaged what is now northern Italy and threatened the capital city Rome itself in 452. A weakened Rome was incapable of defending itself, so the citizens elected to beg for mercy, hoping to avoid the death and destruction that Attila usually left in his wake.

Pope St. Leo I led a delegation to negotiate with Attila. To their surprise, the Hun leader agreed to spare Rome. The city was saved. Legends developed around the incident, including a claim that Attila was cowed by a vision of Sts. Peter and Paul, who stood beside the pope when Attila and Leo encountered each other. Whether there was divine intervention or not, the episode highlights the character of the new world dawning in the fifth century. The

The Meeting of Pope Leo I and Attila the Hun, *a fresco by Raphael and Giulio Romano.*

pope was now a leading figure not only in the Church but also in the state. The Church was no longer on the margins of society; she was at the center of the Mediterranean world.

Although Pope Leo's efforts won Rome a temporary reprieve, the empire's days were numbered. Historians generally date the end of the empire in the West to 476, the year that the barbarian king Odoacer took control of the city of Rome and deposed Emperor Romulus Augustus. This is also the approximate beginning of the so-called Middle Ages, or medieval period. When the Roman Empire in the West collapsed, Christians found themselves in a new situation. Without a strong government to organize social and educational institutions, it fell to the Church to provide the structure of society. In the process, the Church herself attained a more concrete and elaborate structure. The Middle Ages saw the emergence of many of the features that we associate with the Catholic Church today.

In the Middle Ages abbesses often were in charge of more than one monastic community, occasionally those of both women and men. Not all of the women in a convent were eligible to be abbess; usually, for example, a woman had to be at least forty years old, a professed nun for ten years or more, and not a widow.

The Rise of Monasticism and Devotions to Saints

Foremost among new religious institutions of the Middle Ages was *monasticism*. Almost from the beginning of Christianity, some believers separated themselves from the world and devoted themselves to penance and prayer. Initially, they sought radical solitude (the word *monk* derives from the Greek *monos*, meaning "single" or "alone").[3] What began as individuals alone in the desert wilderness (hermits), however, gradually grew into communities of men and women. As numbers increased and rules were applied, large and small houses formed—monasteries for men and convents for women—and these became important institutions in the life of Europe. Monks and nuns consecrated themselves to Christ and committed themselves to prayer and work. In the process, they established charitable services such as helping the poor and caring for the sick; they gathered, learned, and passed on scientific and theological knowledge; and they contributed to the technological and economic development of Europe.

Monasteries, in particular, also served many practical purposes. In many places during the medieval period, law enforcement was weak or nonexistent. Monasteries, often walled structures with a large population, provided some security against armed marauders causing destruction wherever they went. As they accumulated land, monasteries also became centers of economic and political power, and their **abbots**, like bishops, became important political figures. Because of this, heads of aristocratic families would encourage at least one son or daughter to enter religious life in the hope that they would rise to a position of prominence in the Church. The rules in the monasteries and convents were often lax, and the monks and nuns were able to pursue a life of ease with little religious devotion.

However, monastic communities also gave the Church many saints. There have been saints in every age of the Church, but the Middle Ages saw the proliferation of devotions to them and the creation of a formal process for

---

abbot The title given to the leader of a community of twelve or more monks. *Abbot* derives from *Abba*, the Hebrew word meaning "Father." The equivalent for female leaders is *abbess*.

recognizing people of extraordinary sanctity in the Church called *canonization*.∞ Devotion to the saints gave rise to important practices in the Church's spiritual life, such as feast days and pilgrimages. Saints represent a wildly diverse array of models of holiness for Catholics to admire and emulate.

The Romanesque Cathedral of Angoulême, France.

∞ Note

During the Middle Ages, relics of martyrs were divided and shared with many local churches, and these relics were venerated by Christians. Soon Christians beyond the local area traveled to venerate the relics of these martyrs. There was a growing concern that Christians might be honoring or asking intercession from fictional characters. It was originally left to the bishops of a particular area to recognize and approve a saint as worthy of veneration. Bishops received the biographies and evidence of miracles associated with those who had been known for their holiness. Eventually the pope became involved in offering final approval for a person's sainthood. The first saint to be officially canonized by a pope was St. Ulrich of Augsburg, a bishop canonized by Pope John XV in 993.

New Roles for the Pope

The bishop of Rome (the pope) increased in power during the Middle Ages, not only in spiritual affairs but in secular affairs as well. As we saw with Pope Leo and Attila the Hun, the pope had become an important figure in the political realm, where his decisions affected the fortunes of the kings and queens of Europe. Three years after the incident with Attila, Pope Leo negotiated with the Vandals and kept their army from burning the city.

In the sixth century, it was the Lombards who were united and poised to conquer Rome. At the time, floods had destroyed much of the Roman food supply, and an epidemic had broken out in the city itself. St. Gregory the Great, a monk, worked with Pope Pelagius II to organize sanitation and food for those in need. Later, reluctantly named pope himself, Gregory organized food distribution within Rome and oversaw the rebuilding of the city's aqueducts and defenses. He also negotiated a lasting peace with the Lombards.

Popes of the Middle Ages were religious leaders and, by default, the secular leader of Rome as well. This gave the Church unprecedented power, but it also carried with it temptations and pitfalls.

Rise of Cathedrals and Universities

The growth of Catholic institutions, the wealth of the Church, and the devotion of the faithful combined with improving technology to create one of the wonders of the Middle Ages and a powerful expression of Catholic faith: cathedrals. As with saints, there have been cathedrals throughout Church history, but the medieval period was unique in its extraordinary production of awe-inspiring, spiritually uplifting, and enduring church structures.

Gothic-style Chartres Cathedral in Chartres, France.

Early in the Middle Ages, cathedrals featured the Romanesque style, with thick walls and small openings for windows, similar to a fortress. In the twelfth century, the Gothic style of cathedrals appeared in northern France, with high, thick walls, ribbed vaulting, and flying buttresses to distribute the weight of the ceilings. Gothic cathedrals are well known for their stained-glass windows featuring scriptural scenes and lives of the saints and letting in colorful light.

Cathedrals of both styles were designed to be settings fit for the worship of God and to point to qualities that the Church aspires to reflect: beauty, transcendence, and eternity. The cathedrals were centers of civic life, including education. From cathedral schools grew the great universities of Europe, which have shaped the Church and Western civilization in profound ways ever since.

The following sections unpack more details of lessons of the faith that resulted from these elements of the Middle Ages.

SECTION Assessment

Comprehension

1. Differentiate between the terms *Middle Ages*, *Dark Ages*, and *medieval*.

2. What is the difference between a monastery and a convent?

3. What was the significance of the high walls around monasteries in the Middle Ages?

4. Why did a canonization process for saints become necessary?

5. How did Romanesque and Gothic cathedrals differ in structure?

Vocabulary

6. Compare the role of the *abbot* in a monastery to that of the pope for the entire Church.

Reflection

7. What have you previously learned about the Middle Ages?

8. Name a saint you are devoted or attracted to and explain why.

THE RHYTHM OF MONASTIC LIFE

"The girl other girls will hate." That's how magazines described Dolores Hart in the months leading up to the release of the 1957 film *Loving You*, starring the "King of Rock and Roll," Elvis Presley. Dolores would be the recipient of the first-ever on-screen kiss bestowed by the heartthrob Presley, and girls across America would be green with envy.

Things were looking up at the time for Dolores. Born Dolores Hicks in 1938 to young parents struggling through a stormy marriage, Dolores had spent much of her childhood with her grandparents, to escape the ugly environment created by her abusive father and alcoholic mother. She wasn't raised in religion, but she did attend Catholic schools, where she was taught by Catholic sisters and began to be attracted to the faith. She felt God's presence especially in the school chapel. During a time of critical illness, she began praying sincerely for the first time. "Out of that moment," she remembered later, "I found the gift of faith." With her parents' permission, she was baptized a Catholic at the age of ten. She called it "the greatest moment of joy in my ten years of life."

Although she admired the sisters who educated her and inspired her faith, Dolores had very different plans for her future. She was going to be a movie star. With the help of determined friends, a pretty face, and a winning personality, Dolores turned this seemingly unrealistic dream into a reality. After her successful debut with Elvis, the Hollywood tabloids listed her as one of the industry's future stars. She was receiving ten to fifteen fan letters per week. She made another movie with Elvis, then one with another big star, Montgomery Clift. She appeared in a Broadway production of *The Pleasure of His Company* in 1958, for which she was nominated for a Tony Award for Best Featured Actress. She dated several young men and thought that she would marry one of them.

174

"Many people don't understand the difference between a vocation and your own idea about something. A vocation is a call—one you don't necessarily want. The only thing I ever wanted to be was an actress. But I was called by God."
—Dolores Hart

But then, like so many before her, Dolores heard a call.

She was looking for relaxation, a break from her hectic Hollywood life, and a friend recommended a monastery in Connecticut. "I told her that I had had my fill of nuns and declined. But the idea of that kind of retreat kept creeping back into my thoughts," she recalled. In the fall of 1958, she finally visited. She returned several times over the next few years, witnessing the rhythm of monastic life: a combination of prayer, especially the Liturgy of the Hours, and labor, such as cooking, cleaning, sewing, and gardening. She was also struck by the first words of the *Rule of St. Benedict,* a guide to monastic life: "Listen, O son, to the precepts of thy master, and incline the ear of thy heart."

She returned to life as an actress, but she was not at peace. While working on the set of her next film, she "experienced the first in what became a frequent 'where-am-I-going-what-am-I-doing' sense of desperation." She was combing her hair in her dressing room, staring at the mirror, when she "distinctly heard these words in [her] head: 'You know this is not what you want.'"

She heard that voice with the same message repeatedly over the next couple of years, and eventually she answered it. In the spring of 1963, she broke up with her fiancé, left California, and entered the Abbey of Regina Laudis in Connecticut. The former movie star would be a nun.

Mother Dolores Hart has been asked countless times over the years, "How could I throw away a promising acting career for the monastic life of a cloistered nun?" She says, "I left the world I knew in order to reenter it on a more profound level." She says that "a vocation is a call—one you don't necessarily want. The only thing I ever wanted to be was an actress. But I was called by God."

Hollywood journalists were flabbergasted. The starlet's decision seemed to come out of nowhere, and some predicted that the beautiful young woman who had tasted the success of the world wouldn't last very long in a monastery far removed from those pleasures, but they were wrong. More than sixty years later, Dolores is still a nun at the Abbey of Regina Laudis in Connecticut. Like many monks and nuns before her, she has been able to use her talents in her religious vocation, organizing a community theater at the abbey. Of course, monastery life, like any other life, has had its challenges, one being dealing with other nuns. As one of Dolores's sisters quipped, "They used to throw Christians to the lions. Now they make us live together."[4]

God knew better than Dolores what would satisfy the deepest longings of her heart, what would make her truly happy. Dolores heard that call and answered it. Many of us are called to "normal" lives, characterized by marriage, children, and regular jobs. But some are called to more "unusual" vocations: life as a consecrated religious person—a priest, sister, brother, monk, or nun. Millions of Catholics throughout the history of the Church have been called to religious life, so we shouldn't be surprised when God calls us in ways we may not ever have considered.

Foundations of Monasticism

The reasons that Mother Dolores Hart sought out the monastic life in a convent are similar to why Christians beginning in the years before Constantine and the legalization of Christianity chose to separate themselves from the world. Just as it is today, in all times the practice of Christian morality in the world has been difficult. Before the third century, Christian men and women were practicing **asceticism**, in most cases without even leaving their homes. When Christianity became legal and part of the societal mainstream, widespread martyrdom—thought to be the highest Christian witness—for the most part ceased. Asceticism and eventually monasticism became the highest forms of Christian expression for serious-minded Christians.

St. Anthony of Egypt

St. Anthony of Egypt (251–356), also known as St. Anthony of the Desert, was the founder of Christian monasticism. Motivated by the Gospel story of the rich young man who was instructed by Jesus to sell everything and give to the poor (see Matthew 19:16–30), Anthony disposed of all of his possessions and went off into the Egyptian desert to learn ascetic discipline from an old hermit who was already living there. Even though he was far from "civilization," Anthony was constantly beset by visitors who wanted to converse and pray with him and to learn about God. Anthony eventually understood that God was calling him to teach others. He made a deal with visitors: They could live near him and he would visit them periodically; in exchange, they would leave him to his solitude for the majority of the time.

When the hermits of the eastern Mediterranean began attracting followers and forming communities, it became necessary to formulate and record some principles of organization, some statutes that would guide those who were striving to grow in holiness as they lived together.∞ These guides became known

---

asceticism Strict self-denial as a means of spiritual discipline. Christian ascetics imitate Christ's life of self-sacrifice in order to live the Gospel more faithfully.

∞ Note

The movement from individual to communal monasticism improved safety and survival. Men and women who lived together were better protected than those who lived alone. Also, by sharing jobs like farming, preparing food, and repairing shelter, monks and nuns could devote more of their time to prayer.

The Montecassino Abbey was founded as the first house of the Benedictine Order in 529 by St. Benedict. It was there that he wrote the Rule for his order. The monastery has been plundered and destroyed in war throughout its history, most recently in the Battle of Monte Casino in World War II when it was destroyed by Allied bombing.

as *rules*. In the east, the *Rule of St. Basil* was the most popular manual for monasteries. St. Augustine also composed a rule, which was adopted by many religious orders that formed later in the medieval period. But the most influential document for religious life in the Catholic Church is the *Rule of St. Benedict.*

St. Benedict of Nursia (480–547) was born just after the Roman Empire in the West fell. Like the Desert Fathers in the East, Benedict initially fled the world by himself, seeking the life of a hermit in the hills of Italy, but others were attracted to his holiness, and he eventually helped to organize many monasteries. At the same time, his sister St. Scholastica (see Faithful Disciple profile "St. Scholastica" in this chapter) organized a convent for women. Communities of Benedictine monks and nuns around the world today—including Mother Dolores Hart's Abbey of Regina Laudis—still trace their origins to Benedict and Scholastica 1,500 years ago.

To give order and direction to the monks' lives, Benedict composed his rule. He drew on the previous Rules of Augustine and Basil but also added his own elements to craft a guide that would be practical and flexible and could be used for centuries to come by many different people in many different places.

The Montecassino Abbey was rebuilt after the war. After the Second Vatican Council, the abbey was one of the few territorial abbeys within the Catholic Church, controlling several nearby parishes. Pope Francis removed the jurisdiction of the parishes by the abbey in 2014. As of 2015, there were thirteen monks living at Montecassino.

This rule would serve as the basis for the constitutions of most of the religious orders, including nonmonastic orders like the Jesuits, Franciscans, and Dominicans, that have been founded in the centuries since.[5]

In his rule, Benedict outlined the responsibilities of the head of the monastery, the abbot (or abbess for convents), exhorting him to treat the brothers differently based on the needs of their souls: "One with gentleness, another with rebukes, another with persuasion, so let him, according to the character and intelligence of each, mould and adapt himself." He urged monks to make major decisions "in council," that is, as a community, with the input of all the monks. He offered a long list of spiritual disciplines necessary to the monastic life, including:

- to follow the commandments;

- to do charitable works;

- to listen with goodwill to holy reading; and

- to be frequently occupied in prayer.

Much of the rule concerned the requirements of praying the Liturgy of the Hours, a devotion still practiced in most religious orders. Benedict also gave practical advice concerning how to deal with rebellious monks, how to manage the tools of the monastery, and how the monks should dress.

Benedict stressed the virtues of poverty, chastity, and obedience, which have been the vows taken by members of most religious orders ever since. He also encouraged hospitality in the monasteries, the welcoming of travelers and others in need. From this foundation, monasteries and convents became houses of charity, especially care for the sick.

Finally, Benedict argued for the importance of work. "Idleness is inimical to the soul," he wrote. With many monks toiling diligently, monasteries became centers of industry, growing agricultural products, raising livestock, producing cloth from wool, mining and manufacturing metal goods, and publishing written materials.

Another kind of work was scholarship. Some monks taught reading, writing, math, and other subjects to fellow monks and other students. Others were tasked with copying manuscripts, including the Sacred Scriptures. In the centuries before mechanized printing, this was the only way to pass down the sacred texts. "Day by day, year after year," monks and nuns "would persevere in their holy labors, copying with loving care every letter of the sacred text from some old manuscript of the Bible."[6] They would often illustrate these texts with lovely designs and images, creating "illuminated" manuscripts. A famous example is the **Book of Kells**, a decorated manuscript of the Gospels dating to the ninth century, which is on display at Trinity College in Dublin, Ireland.

During a period when weak and unstable governments could not sponsor schools, monks and nuns preserved the literary and philosophical legacy of the ancient world and the Church Fathers. The work of monasteries and convents was thus vital to feeding, clothing, and educating Europeans throughout the

---

Book of Kells An illuminated manuscript of the four Gospels that was produced by the monks of St. Columba in Iona, Scotland, before being brought to Kells, Ireland, in about 795 to keep it safe from Viking marauders. It is believed that the priests who read from the Book of Kells had the passages memorized and would hold the images facing the congregation so that they could learn from the beauty of the work.

Middle Ages. In these ways, the *Rule of St. Benedict* provided a firm foundation on which to build the medieval structures of Church and society.

The Universality of Monastic Practices

During the Middle Ages, monasteries and convents were prominent. The figures of the friar, monk, abbot, nun, and abbess were also familiar in literature. Most Europeans of that period would have had contact with monasticism, yet many Catholics today do not have that same experience. Over the centuries following the Middle Ages, a variety of forces combined to bring about the eclipse of the monastic tradition: declining numbers of men and women entering monasteries; corruption and laxity among monks and nuns, provoking opposition from the laity and from Church authorities; and anti-Catholic measures by political regimes that confiscated monastic property and dissolved monastic institutions. Monasteries are clearly not as prominent in Catholic life today as they were during the medieval period.

However, monastic life is still present in many ways.

First, as the presence of Mother Dolores Hart and the Abbey of Regina Laudis indicates, there remain many places where monasticism is practiced

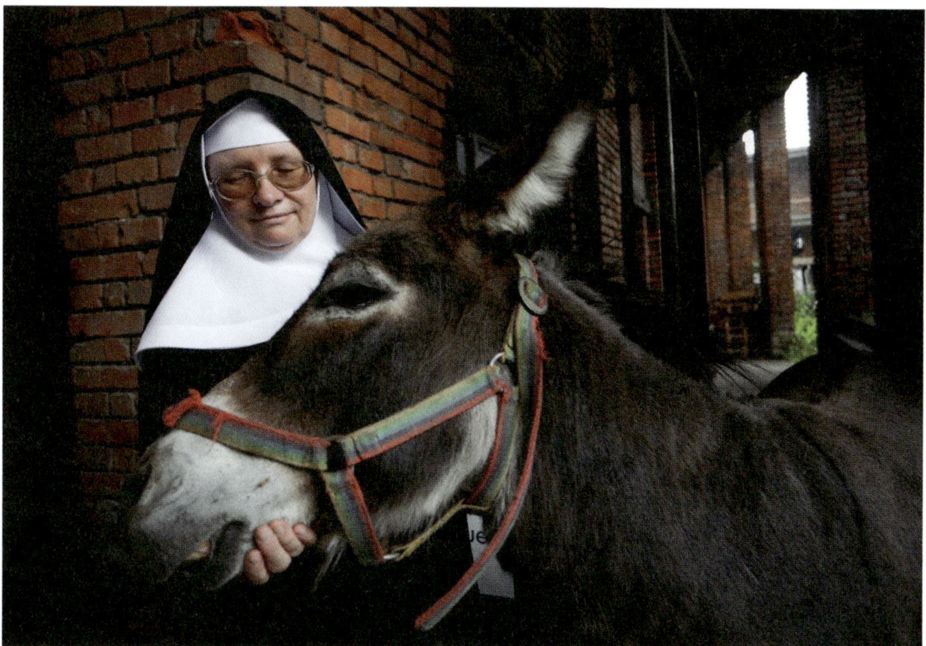

Mother Superior Stefania Polkowska cares for a donkey at the Monastery of Benedictine Nuns in Staniatki, Poland.

throughout the world. The first Benedictine monastery in the United States, St. Vincent Archabbey in Latrobe, Pennsylvania, was established in 1846. It is still there, with an affiliated college, and other monasteries (and colleges) sprang from it and still exist in places such as North Carolina, Minnesota, and Kansas. Monasteries still support themselves by selling things they produce through their work; some well-known items are beer, coffee, fudge, and caskets.

Second, although there are fewer monasteries, the congregations of consecrated religious that developed out of monasticism remain common and continue to play a large role in Catholic life. Dominicans, Franciscans, Jesuits, Sisters of Mercy, Sisters of Charity, and many other religious orders are active in many places in education, health care, social justice ministries, and parish life.

Third, monastic ideals have embedded themselves in the spiritual life of the Church. The Liturgy of the Hours, which gained traction through monastic practice, has taken on an important place in Catholic devotion as the official prayer of the Church. Monastic emphasis on spiritual disciplines such as abstinence and fasting helped to promote and maintain these as Catholic practices. In a broad sense, the monastic model is applicable to all believers. To be a monk is to "take one's spiritual formation seriously, hoping, in the end, to be in 'sweet communion' with God." A life devoted to prayer and work is a worthy aim for anyone. In this sense, in the words of one contemporary writer, "All Christians are monks," or at least capable of being so.[7]

SECTION Assessment

Comprehension

1. What led St. Anthony of Egypt to monasticism?

2. What were some elements that St. Benedict of Nursia added to the monastic Rules of St. Augustine and St. Basil?

3. Name two spiritual disciplines that St. Benedict deemed necessary for monastic life.

4. What are three ways that monastic life is still present today?

Vocabulary

5. Describe a basic difference between *asceticism* and monasticism.

Reflection

6. How do you imagine the rhythm of monastic life that was first attractive to Mother Dolores Hart?

THE CALL TO HOLINESS

You may have realized by now that the early Christians were very serious about their faith. First, there were Christians in the age of the martyrs who willingly gave up their lives in imitation of Christ. After Christianity was legalized and the opportunities to witness to belief in Christ by dying for him diminished, some sought out an extreme lifestyle by separating themselves from the world. At the core of their choices was the desire to be a saint, from the Latin word *sanctus*, meaning "holy."

God wants us all to be saints. In fact, all who are in heaven are called saints. We should all want to go to heaven. Even in heaven, as on earth, there will be those who achieve different degrees of holiness. St. Thérèse of Lisieux once had a vision of heaven in which she saw "that one could be a saint in varying degrees, for we are free to respond to our Lord's invitation by doing much or little in our love for him." When she reflected on this, St. Thérèse prayed, "My God, I don't want to be a saint by halves." This is the same motivation that leads Christians to accept martyrdom or to choose a life of monasticism.

Are these options—martyrdom or monasticism—the only route to sainthood? No! We can each live lives of holiness (remember, holiness is equivalent to sainthood) by rooting ourselves in God, who is himself holiness. Holiness is God's innermost essence. Holiness expresses the perfection of God and refers to his majesty, power, and transcendence. God does not intend his holiness to distance us from him, as if we were unworthy to share in his holiness. In fact, in becoming incarnate in the Divine Person of his Son, Jesus, God's holiness came close enough to us that we can be made holy through our imitation of that Son.

Leah Libresco Sargent is a popular Catholic writer and speaker who has worked in lay ministry with students at Princeton University, but she took an unusual path to begin her journey to holiness. Leah grew up as an atheist in New York. Through high school and college, she studied in the fields of physics and mathematics, hoping to find answers to the meaning of life. She was troubled, however, by her inability to conceive a solid ground in scientific truth for ethical behavior. She wondered: How do we know the right way to act? Through a process of study, debate, and reflection, she finally concluded that there must be a loving being at the heart of the universe. She embraced the reality of a personal God and eventually converted to Catholicism.

Leah Libresco Sargent

However, adapting to the ways of faith wasn't always easy. For one thing, she had to learn to pray. One dimension of Catholic prayer that she found helpful was the intercession of the saints: "Just learning that there's a particular patron saint for my struggle does a lot to break the power of my unhappiness to isolate me. It means that my misfortune is not unique. Not only is the saint herself at least one proof-of-concept person who faced the same hardship, but . . . [e]nough of us are united by our need that someone was chosen specifically to watch over us."[8]

Leah discovered that God not only draws us to his life of holiness with himself as the model; he also provides us with others who have imitated the life of Christ well and returned to God in heaven. These are the saints who provide us concrete examples of how to be holy.

The Holiness of the Church

Holiness is one of the four marks of the Church: one, holy, catholic, and apostolic. (We learned about the apostolic mark in Chapter 2.) Holiness is defined as "a separation from all that is evil and attachment to what is good." As such, holiness is closely related to sainthood or **sanctification**—being freed from sin and united with God. Because the Church is united with Christ, who is perfectly holy, she too is spotless, pure, and in perfect communion with God.

You may want to pause at this point and consider how the Church can be perfectly holy and spotless when you are aware of many times when the Church has not seemed to be so. There have been **Crusades** championed by popes who gave indulgences to soldiers for killing so-called infidels. There was the **Inquisition** that led to heretics being tortured. In recent times, there has been a sexual abuse crisis among the clergy. So how, then, can the Church be holy? The truth is that in the history of the Church, *all* Catholics, including many Church leaders, have sinned. All people are sinners. This is true, but the Church has been responsible for far more examples of holiness than of sin.

The Church has always been, in the words of St. Augustine, a *corpus permixtum*—a "mixed body" of saints and sinners. This understanding comes straight from Jesus, who told a parable about the Kingdom of Heaven where sinners (weeds) intermingled among the righteous (wheat). Jesus explained that "if you pull up the weeds you might uproot the wheat along with them" (Mt 13:29).

It is incorrect, then, to think that the holiness of the Church depends on the holiness of her members. One of the images of the Church used by Jesus himself is the *Bride of Christ*. John the Baptist spoke of Jesus as "the bridegroom" (Jn 3:29), and Jesus referred to himself the same way (Mk 2:19). St. Paul reinforces the image in his Letters to the Corinthians, referring to the Christian community as "betrothed" to Christ (2 Cor 11:2). The image of the Bride of Christ mirrors the image of the Church as the Body of Christ because

---

sanctification Means "being made holy." The first sanctification of a person takes place at Baptism. The second sanctification takes place from how the person lives his or her life in growing in the likeness of God. The third sanctification takes place when the person enters heaven and is fully united with God for all eternity.

Crusades A series of military expeditions in the eleventh, twelfth, and thirteenth centuries made according to a solemn vow by Christians to return the possession of the Holy Land from the Muslims to the Church.

Inquisition A Church tribunal established in the early thirteenth century that was designed to curb heretical teachings and beliefs. In collaboration with secular authorities, papal representatives employed the Inquisition to judge the guilt of suspected heretics with the aim of getting them to repent. Unfortunately, many abuses crept into the process.

Christ as Bridegroom.

Scripture and Church teaching hold that marriage unites two persons, who thereby become "one body." Paul writes: "Husbands, love your wives, even as Christ loved the church and handed himself over for her to sanctify her, cleansing her by the bath of water with the word, that he might present to himself the church in splendor, without spot or wrinkle or any such thing, that she might be holy and without blemish" (Eph 5:25–27; see also *CCC*, 823). The Church's holiness is thus dependent on the holiness of Christ. The Church, the bride, is holy because of Christ, her spouse.

The Church has been founded by Christ, who is both God and man. Since she is united with God in Christ, the Church is pure and holy. However, although her members on earth are sanctified by God's grace, they remain subject to temptation and often commit sin. We all experience something like this in our own existence as a combination of body and soul. You may have a strong desire to dunk a basketball, or run a four-minute mile, or throw a ninety-mile-per-hour fastball, but your body is unable to do these things. There is a disconnect between what your soul or spirit aspires to and what your physical limitations permit. In the moral life, too, you might want to be a more respectful son or daughter, a more caring friend, a more diligent student—but when the time comes to make it happen, temptations to do otherwise feel too strong. This experience led St. Paul to make his famous lament, "I do not do the good I want, but I do the evil I do not want" (Rom 7:19). Jesus explained more clearly: "The spirit is willing, but the flesh is weak" (Mt 26:41).

Many find it challenging and even scandalous that even though the Church's members on earth are sanctified by God's grace, they remain subject to temptation and frequently commit sins. Catholics are obligated to embrace and defend the Church's moral teachings, yet often fail to follow the teachings themselves. This seems to open Catholics, especially Catholic leaders who teach the faith publicly, to the charge of hypocrisy.∞ In reality, Catholics recognize that, as sinners, we can achieve holiness only through the grace made available through Christ and his Church: "All members of the Church, including her ministers, must acknowledge that they are sinners. In everyone, the weeds of sin will still be mixed with the good wheat of the Gospel until the end of time. Hence the Church gathers sinners already caught up in Christ's salvation but still on the way to holiness" (*CCC*, 827).

Thus appears the paradox we see now and throughout history: an imperfect Church preaching a message of perfection. The Church claims to be holy not because her members possess the power to be holy, but because Jesus is holy, and he has taken the Church—us—as his bride.

The Holiness of the Saints

While perfect holiness is impossible for human beings in this world, the saints are those who achieved an extraordinary degree of holiness and are therefore held up as examples for us to follow. Saints exhibit the qualities of holiness brilliantly. The "number-one trait of these heroes and heroines of holiness," according to one reflection on sainthood, is "being head over heels in love with God." Saints are consumed by a love "so mighty, so burning, and so pure that it overflows into a love for neighbor that the worldly world does not even dream of."[9]

How does this love transform a saint's life and, concurrently, the lives of those the saint serves? St. Teresa of Calcutta, also known as Mother Teresa, is a dramatic example from the twentieth century. Mother Teresa perceived a call from God to serve those who were neglected by everyone else, the "poorest of the poor," and she dedicated her life to that purpose. In the slums of Calcutta, she found devastating poverty, but she recognized that the more painful

It is important to be clear about what hypocrisy is. A hypocrite is someone who says one thing but *actually believes and acts otherwise*. If I truly believe that lying is wrong and yet I lie when I find myself in a difficult situation, I am not a hypocrite; I'm merely a weak, sinful human being. Doubtless there are hypocrites in the Church (and throughout society), people who don't honestly believe what they teach concerning faith and morality. But falling into sin is not the equivalent of hypocrisy. Hopefully this analogy helps you to appreciate the position of the Church.

ailment experienced by those who lived in poverty was neglect, the feeling that no one cared about them. Mother Teresa founded a religious order, the Missionaries of Charity, to help, and she and her sisters (and later brothers) began by going into the worst areas of the city, finding people who were sick and dying in the streets, and bringing them into houses where the sisters tended and accompanied them during their final days.

Mother Teresa was rightly honored during her life. She won the Nobel Peace Prize in 1979, but after her death came a shocking disclosure. Her personal letters revealed that Mother Teresa had spent decades in profound spiritual pain, deprived of the comfort of feeling God's presence and uncertain about the goodness of her soul and her work. Her sense of abandonment even led her to call into question the existence of the God to whom she had dedicated her life. "In my soul I feel just that terrible pain of loss," she wrote to her spiritual director, "of God not wanting me—of God not being God—of God not really existing."[10]

Eventually, Mother Teresa learned to embrace the darkness and the seeming absence of God from her prayer life as a share in the darkness experienced by Christ in his own suffering and death. With perseverance, she continued to remain committed to prayer and the sacraments. She insisted that her Missionaries of Charity spend several hours a day in prayer before the Blessed Sacrament. In response to some who questioned whether this was a good use of

Mother Teresa ministering to the poor on the streets of Calcutta.

their time when there was so much demand for their services, Mother Teresa replied, "If my sisters did not spend so much time in prayer, they could not serve the sick and the poor at all."[11] She closely identified the sacraments of the Church with her charitable work. "As Missionaries of Charity," she wrote, "we are especially called upon to see Christ in the appearance of bread and to touch him in the broken bodies of the poor."∞

Nourished by the grace of prayer and sacraments, Mother Teresa radiated holiness to the world despite her interior struggles. People of all faiths and no faiths were inspired by her example, and many of them traveled to Calcutta and asked to help in her ministry. In her speech accepting the Nobel Prize, she cited Jesus's admonition in Matthew 25:40: "Whatever you did for one of these least brothers of mine, you did for me." She also said that to practice Christ-like love is holiness: "Holiness is not a luxury of the few, it is a simple duty for each one of us, and through this love we can become holy."[12] By persevering in love of God and neighbor, Mother Teresa became a saint and a model of holiness.

How the Church "Makes" Saints

To the extent that we achieve holiness, we already are saints. This is why Paul used the word *saints* to refer to all members of the Church.[13] However, St. Teresa of Calcutta, St. Paul, and many others are saints in another sense as well. Throughout the Church's history, certain men and women have been honored as models of the Christian life and exemplars of holiness. In the early centuries of Christianity, the martyrs, such as Sts. Felicity and Perpetua, were especially honored as saints for obvious reasons. Their love for Christ was so strong that they were willing to sacrifice their lives rather than deny him. As the era of persecution ended, other ways of demonstrating exemplary holiness

∞ Note

Mother Teresa compared her reception of Jesus followed by service to the poor in the same way that Mary, after the Annunciation, immediately went "in haste" (Lk 1:39) to help her pregnant relative, Elizabeth. Similarly, Mother Teresa told her sisters: "As soon as we receive Jesus in Holy Communion, let us go in haste to give him to our sisters, to our poor, to the sick, to the dying, to the lepers, to the unwanted, and to the unloved. By this we make Jesus present in the world today."

began to be recognized as well. For example, St. Augustine of Hippo and St. Benedict of Nursia were admired for their service to the Church, their devout prayer life, and their charity toward those in need. Saints were often associated with miracles, which were seen as a sign of God's favor.

For many centuries, the process of selecting a Christian for special honor was unsystematic. A *cult*, or devotion to a saint, would develop in a certain region, usually with the approval of the bishop. The cult might remain local, or it might spread to other parts of the Church. Thus, individual communities might have their own saints who were not known beyond a small geographic area. They might possess relics of their saints, usually skeletal remains of the body, but also clothing or other items associated with their lives. They might celebrate feast days in remembrance of their saints, often on the day of death, when the saint passed on to his or her eternal reward.

As the centuries passed, the number of saints recognized in this way increased, and eventually there were thousands. During the Middle Ages, the Church tried to bring more order to the situation. Local saints were not prohibited, but the Church selected certain saints to be honored by all Catholics everywhere. These were given feast days on the universal **liturgical calendar**.

The Church also brought order to the method by which a holy person was approved for veneration. Increasingly, the process of *canonization*—recognition as a saint—was centralized in the hands of the pope, who delegated most of the work to other officials in the Vatican. Today, this office is called the Dicastery for the Causes of Saints. Over time, the process became increasingly complicated and lengthy. Today, canonization proceeds through four main phases, each linked with different titles:

1 When a prospective saint is formally proposed for sainthood, the sponsoring diocese or other organization submits a set of documents to the dicastery in Rome. The person's "cause" for canonization has been introduced, and he or she is now known as a "Servant of God."

2 After a thorough investigation, the dicastery may confirm that the person demonstrated "heroic virtue" during his or her life, which bestows the title "Venerable."

3 A further period of examination and the confirmation of at least one certifiable miracle permit the person to proceed to the next stage, "Blessed."

4 Finally, when all research is complete, the person's holiness is beyond doubt, and two miracles have been confirmed, a joyous ceremony of canonization takes place. The Church has a new "Saint."

The canonization process can be long and involved (and expensive∞). This is because the Church recognizes that she has a duty to be careful about determining who she presents as worthy of emulation, but the pope can also dispense with certain requirements and expedite the process when he believes the situation demands it. This was the case for Mother Teresa, for example, for whom Pope John Paul II waived the normal five-year waiting period after death before a cause can begin.

Over the centuries, the popularity of various saints has waxed and waned, and the status of their feast days in the Church's liturgical calendar has changed. After the Second Vatican Council (more information in Chapter 8), as part of her effort to simplify a liturgical calendar that had grown complicated and confusing, the Church removed about ninety saints' days from the calendar. Those removed were mainly saints from the early centuries of the Church—from long before the formal canonization process was in place—about whom there was little solid historical evidence, although many legends may have grown up around them. Some of the more popular included St. Christopher, St. Ursula, and St. Philomena. This did not mean that the Church officially declared that these men and women had never existed or that they were not saints. It only meant that they no longer had public liturgical recognition in the Church.

It is important to understand that the Church does not "make" saints in the sense of "deciding" who gets the title. The process of canonization is

∞ Note

One reason that only about 5 percent of the over ten thousand canonized saints have been married people is that religious communities usually have more resources, both financial and in terms of know-how, to present one of their members' causes to sainthood than those who might advocate for a married couple or other laypeople.

intended to identify at least some holy people who have lived in extraordinary union with God. God has already made them saints; the Church is simply recognizing the fact and recommending their example to her members. The purpose of this system is to assist and encourage Catholics now and in the future to pursue holiness themselves: "By canonizing some of the faithful, i.e., by solemnly proclaiming that they practiced heroic virtue and lived in fidelity to God's grace, the Church recognizes the power of the Spirit of holiness within her and sustains the hope of believers by proposing the saints to them as models and intercessors" (*CCC*, 828).

As Leah Libresco Sargent can attest, the Church's hope of inspiring others with the lives of the saints "as models and intercessors" has been realized repeatedly in the lives of Catholics through the ages. Many saints drew those around them on to holiness during their lifetimes, but the power of saintly example stretches across time and place. In the twentieth century, the German Jewish philosopher Edith Stein came across the autobiography of St. Teresa of Ávila, a sixteenth-century Spanish Carmelite nun. Edith read through the night and declared, "This is the truth!"[14] She became Catholic, joined the Carmelites, took the name Teresa, lived a holy life, and was canonized by Pope John Paul II as St. Teresa Benedicta of the Cross.

After two thousand years that have seen the Church spread to every corner of the earth, the roster of the saints presents a splendid array of diversity, examples of innumerable different paths to holiness. Pope John Paul II, "the first great canonizing pope of the modern age," expanded the number of saints dramatically, naming 483 during his long pontificate.[15] Later, he was himself canonized by Pope Francis. We have already met martyr saints who

St. Christopher carrying the Christ Child.

were married women (Perpetua and Felicity) as well as bishop saints who were scholars and Church Fathers (Augustine and Ambrose). The medieval period saw many monk and nun saints who devoted their lives to prayer and work: Benedict, Scholastica, Bernard of Clairvaux, and Hildegard of Bingen. Some saints were notorious sinners who repented (Mary Magdalene and Augustine), while others were devout from youth (Dominic Savio and Bernadette Soubirous). Saints who suffered martyrdom have sometimes been canonized as groups (the North American Martyrs, the Uganda Martyrs, the Martyrs of Japan), and so was a married couple: Louis and Zélie Martin, the parents of St. Thérèse of Lisieux.

The saints are indispensable to the life of the Church for the reasons already laid out, but there is one more reason: their love of God and neighbor entails love for the Church, which leads them to work for her good. They recognize that the Church is the font of grace—that their own union with Christ comes through the Church, and that the good of the world depends on the Church's ministry. Not only does the saints' love for the Church make them the most stalwart defenders of the Church; it also makes them the most determined reformers of the Church.

Everyone and everything needs reform. At the individual level, we grow lazy and need a "kick in the pants" or get burned out and need a vacation. We fall into bad habits and need to break them. We sin and need to repent. The same holds true for groups of people—for institutions, including the Church. The dynamism, energy, and dedication that built the institution fade, and its members rest on the laurels of the past, growing complacent. Complacency enables corruption. Reform—a return to the ideals of the founding—is necessary.

Since her founding by Christ, the Church has continually needed reform, and the saints are the reformers par excellence. St. Benedict renewed monastic life in Italy. Five hundred years later,

Reliquary of St. Ursula, circa 1489. A carved and gilded wooden reliquary in the shape of a Gothic chapel, containing oil-on-panel inserts of scenes of the life and martyrdom of St. Ursula.

The Liturgical Calendar

The cycle of seasons and feasts that Catholics celebrate is called the Church Year or liturgical year. The Church Year is divided into six main parts:

1. Advent
2. Christmas
3. Lent
4. Triduum (the three days from Holy Thursday evening to the Easter Vigil)
5. Easter
6. Ordinary Time

Easter, the celebration of Jesus's Resurrection, is the apex of the liturgical year. Its importance is so monumental that every Sunday is a celebration of Easter, a "Lord's Day" set apart as "the pre-eminent day for the liturgical assembly, when the faithful gather 'to listen to the word of God and take part in the Eucharist, thus calling to mind the Passion, Resurrection, and glory of the Lord Jesus, and giving thanks to God'" (*CCC*, 1167, quoting *Sacrosanctum Concilium*, 106). Other feast days are reserved for saints important in the formation of the Church, such as Peter and Paul; martyrs, such as Agnes and Ignatius of Antioch; holy popes, such as Gregory the Great and Leo the Great; and monks and nuns, such as Benedict and Scholastica. By filling her calendar with observances relating to the lives of Jesus, Mary, and the saints, "in the course of the year," the Church "unfolds the whole mystery of Christ" (*CCC*, 1163).

the Benedictine order that Benedict founded needed reform, and a collection of saints—Bruno, Bernard of Clairvaux, Robert of Molesme, Stephen Harding—reinvigorated monasticism by founding new Benedictine orders, the Cistercians and the Carthusians. "The saints have always been the source and origin of renewal in the most difficult moments in the Church's history" (*CCC*, 828). In our own time, the Church still needs reform, and saints must step forward to provide it.

Our Individual Path to Sainthood

It is true that Catholics are sinners, but we are freed from sin and sanctified through uniting ourselves with Christ and receiving his Holy Spirit. This happens in the fullest way through participation in the Church. Beginning with Baptism, the sacraments are consistent sources of **grace**, and availing ourselves frequently of those sacraments that we can receive repeatedly—Confession and Holy Communion—is a sure path to sanctification. As good nutrition, strenuous workouts, and technical instruction contribute to our body's ability to jump higher, run faster, and throw harder, so the grace available through the Church strengthens our spiritual capacity.

We also grow in holiness through:

- charity (loving God and our neighbor);

- prayer (talking with God); and

- service (meeting the needs of the poor and vulnerable)

These actions are essential to the Christian life. Charity, or love, is the most essential. It "is the soul of the holiness to which all are called" (*CCC*, 826). Charity is wanting and acting toward the good of others. In our quest for holiness, we are strengthened by the wider Christian community, including those who have gone before us and belong to the **communion of saints**—the community of all those who have followed, are following, or will follow Christ and attain salvation. The communion of saints is what Leah Libresco Sargent

grace A free and unearned favor from God, infused into our souls at Baptism, that adopts us into God's family and helps us to live as his children.

communion of saints The unity of all people who have been redeemed by Christ, both the living and the dead.

experienced when she felt the comfort of knowing that there were others who sympathized with her problems and interceded for her with God.

SECTION Assessment

Comprehension

1. Does the holiness of the Church depend on her members? Explain.

2. Where did the Church's understanding of herself being a *corpus permixtum* arise?

3. How did Mother Teresa show that she was consumed by the love of God?

4. Why did Mother Teresa consider prayer before the Blessed Sacrament time well spent?

5. What are the six seasons on the Church's liturgical calendar?

6. Name the four steps of canonization.

Vocabulary

7. Define *sanctification*.

8. Differentiate between what occurred during the *Crusades* and what occurred during the *Inquisition*.

9. How does a person qualify for membership in the *communion of saints*?

Reflection

10. How do you imagine the "varying degrees" of sainthood as they exist in heaven?

11. Of the three ways mentioned for growing in holiness, which do you find most difficult? Why?

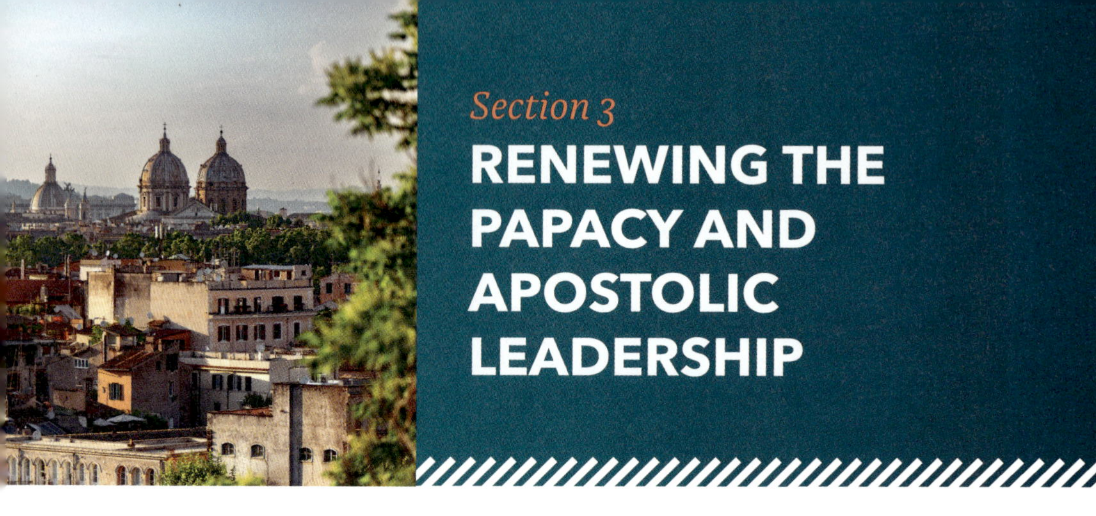

RENEWING THE PAPACY AND APOSTOLIC LEADERSHIP

In the same eleventh century that St. Bruno and St. Bernard were reforming the Benedictines, Pope St. Gregory VII (1073–1085) was elected to lead the Church. Many priests and bishops at the time flouted the Church's requirement of celibacy and were involved in illicit sexual relationships. Some bishops also obtained their positions by bribery and were more concerned with maximizing their income than with serving the people of their diocese. Pope Gregory was distressed by this greed and immorality among the clergy and officials of the Church, and he dedicated his papacy to eradicating it.

In Gregory VII's case, the papacy proved to be a force for reform. In succeeding years, the papacy itself was not immune to corruption. Like saints, the popes were a diverse array of personalities, and this diversity was on display throughout the Middle Ages. In fact, much of the Middle Ages featured varying examples of "good popes" and "bad popes." Recall that a different good Pope Gregory, **Pope St. Gregory the Great** in earlier medieval times, embodied a link between the two great Church institutions that existed side by side: monasticism and the papacy.

Once again, no man or woman on earth (other than Jesus and Mary) exists without sin. A pope's power in the Church is not dependent on his personality or whether he is "good" or "bad." A pope exercises authority in the Church because he occupies the office of bishop of Rome and is thereby the successor of St. Peter, Prince of the Apostles. Peter was designated by Jesus as the Church's foundational first leader: "And so I say to you, you are Peter, and upon this rock I will build my church" (Mt 16:18). Jesus's words were the origin of the papacy and the basis for its theology, but the practice of the papacy has nonetheless evolved over the course of time, prominently in the Church's first thousand years and through to the end of the Middle Ages.

Pope St. Gregory the Great

Born into a prominent Roman family in 540, St. Gregory the Great had been a government official before entering a Benedictine monastery. Gregory's vivid account of St. Benedict of Nursia's life (*The Dialogues*) and spirited promotion of the *Rule of St. Benedict* are in large measure the reason it remains in practice today in monastic life.[16] In 590, Gregory was elected pope, and his pontificate extended until his death in 604. Under his direction, non-Christian regions were evangelized (Great Britain in particular), the monastic life was fostered throughout the Church, and liturgical music, a style of music known today as **Gregorian chant**, was organized and promoted.

Gregorian chant A monophonic, sacred form of song sung in Latin that arose in the ninth and tenth centuries and was named for St. Gregory the Great.

Tracing the Primacy of the Holy See

If you are trying to understand or explain the role of the pope in the Catholic Church, remember one thing: **Rome is the key**. In the Church, Rome is sometimes called the Holy See. The term *see* in this case means "seat." The Holy See (also called the Roman See or Apostolic See) holds jurisdiction over the Diocese of Rome and the Catholic Church worldwide, and also exercises sovereignty over the city-state known as Vatican City. The pope is the head of the Holy See and of the Catholic Church because he is the bishop of Rome. If Pope Francis (or any other pope) were the bishop of Spokane, Washington, instead of Rome, he would not be the pope. Rome is the key.

Why? Rome became the heart of the Church and the seat of the papacy because the city was the site of the death and burial of the early Church's two great Apostles, Peter and Paul. From the time of Peter's first successor (Linus) onward, the bishop of the church in Rome was recognized as Peter's heir and the leader of the entire Church. The second-century Church Father St. Irenaeus of Lyon articulated the principle of *apostolic succession*, the passing on of the teaching and authority of the Apostles. In his work *Against Heresies*, Irenaeus listed the names of the twelve men who had held the office of bishop of Rome after Peter up to the time of his writing. "In this order, and by this succession," he insisted, "the ecclesiastical tradition from the Apostles, and the preaching of the truth, have come down to us. And this is most abundant proof that there is one and the same vivifying faith, which has been preserved in the Church from the Apostles until now, and handed down in truth."[17]

While St. Irenaeus and other Christians recognized the primacy of the bishop of Rome in the Church, they also identified apostolic succession in the bishops of other local churches. This concept of the community of Apostles with Peter at their head provided the Church's essential structure, which would further develop and expand during the Middle Ages and beyond. This structure is known as the *governing office* of the Church. Like the *teaching office*, or *Magisterium*, we discussed in Chapter 3, the governing office is composed of the bishops under the leadership of the pope. Each bishop governs the local church assigned to him (known today as a *diocese*), making decisions regarding all aspects of the life of the Church in that area. The bishop possesses much freedom and responsibility within his diocese, but the exercise of his authority is still subject to the higher authority of the pope, just as the Apostles deferred to Peter. "Their authority must be exercised in communion with the whole

What's the Difference between Eastern Orthodox *and* Eastern Catholic?

Focus Question: How was the Catholic Church import-ant to human progress during the Middle Ages?

One reason that the *Rule of St. Benedict* rather than the *Rule of St. Basil* came to dominate Roman Catholic religious life is that Christianity gradually split in two, breaking down roughly into "Eastern" and "Western" sections. Eastern monasteries have tended to follow St. Basil, while west-ern monasteries followed St. Benedict.

As we saw in Chapter 3, division in the Church has unfortunately been a part of Christian experience from the beginning. The early Christological disputes led to divisions between the Catholic Church and the Assyrian Church of the East and the Oriental Orthodox churches (including the Coptic Orthodox Church) in the fifth century. But the largest body of believers remained intact for hundreds of years, encompassing the lands evangelized by Paul (Asia Minor, Greece, Italy) as well as North Africa and much of Europe. This unity came to an end in 1054.

Tension had been building between East and West for a long time. One piece of the story is simply the march of world history. The unity of the Roman Empire itself weakened, and its Western side withered, culminating, as we have seen, in the fall of the Western empire in 476, while the empire endured in the East. This separation led

St. Benedict

St. Basil

to diverging political, cultural, and religious tendencies. The Latin language gradually became dominant in the West, while Greek continued to be used in the East. As bishops and theologians used different languages, their capacity to communicate—and to agree—declined. In the West, Church authorities introduced a clarification into the Nicene Creed (see the Appendix), specifying that the Holy Spirit "proceeds from the Father *and the Son*." It may seem like a small point, but for Eastern theologians, the *filioque* ("and from the Son") clause was a radical innovation that they could not accept. Their understanding was that the Holy Spirit proceeds from the Father *through* the Son. Moreover, they questioned the authority of the Church to alter the wording of the ancient creed that had been formulated by ecumenical councils. Thus, the creed from the Council of Nicaea—a major point of unity for all Christians— now became a source of controversy.

Another traditional source of unity was the pope himself, his primacy emanating from the office of the bishop of Rome as the successor of St. Peter, who was the acknowledged head of the Apostles. After the fall of Rome, Constantinople, the capital of the Eastern Roman Empire, assumed increased importance. The bishop (or **patriarch**) in Constantinople demanded a larger share of Church authority. While all agreed that the pope, as successor of Peter, deserved *some kind* of primacy, not all agreed on the exact nature of that primacy. Did the pope have the sole authority to appoint or depose the

Orthodox churches have distinctive gold domes and drums that symbolize God's interaction with people on earth.

The architecture of the Maronite Catholic Cathedral (next to the mosque) in Beirut resembles many of the other Catholic rite churches.

patriarch of Constantinople, for example, or was the bishop of Rome "first among equals" and thus required to consult the heads of other important sees (Constantinople, Alexandria, Antioch, Jerusalem) before making major decisions?

These differences and others came to a boil in 1054, when Pope Leo IX sent representatives to Constantinople to try to deal with various religious and political matters. The papal delegation ended up in an escalating dispute with the patriarch of Constantinople, and both sides ended up excommunicating (expelling from communion with the Church) the other. The churches that followed Constantinople became known as "Greek" or "Eastern Orthodox," while those that followed Rome were "Latin" or "Roman Catholic."

patriarch The name for bishops of one of five *episcopal sees*, the name for the places of residence of bishops: the Eastern patriarchates of Jerusalem, Antioch, Constantinople, and Alexandria, and the Latin patriarchate of Rome. From the time of St. Peter, the bishop of Rome (the pope) was acknowledged as the principal patriarch.

Over the centuries, efforts were made to bring these two wings of the Church back into communion, but to no avail. Eastern Orthodoxy continues to exist today, represented in various segments under the patriarchs of major sees such as Constantinople (Istanbul), Moscow, and Alexandria. In 1965, Pope Paul VI and Patriarch Athenagoras I mutually nullified the thousand-year-old excommunications, a sign of progress in dialogue between the Eastern and Western Churches, but the fundamental divide between the two religious bodies remained.

Various groups within the Orthodox churches have reunited with the Catholic Church, however, creating the twenty-one Eastern Catholic Churches. These churches retain the customs and liturgical practices of their own traditions but recognize the authority of the pope and are in full communion with Roman Catholicism. For example, the Ukrainian Catholic Church was formed in 1595, when seven bishops in Ukraine agreed to join the Catholic Church on the condition that they could continue to conduct their own Divine Liturgy (the Byzantine liturgy that developed in the East) rather than use the Roman Rite. Today, there are about five million Ukrainian Catholics, a large number of them in the United States.

Coptic Orthodox pope Tawadros II of Alexandria, Egypt, prays together with Pope Francis at the Vatican's Redemptoris Mater Chapel in May 2023.

The Eastern Catholic Churches are an example of the "unity in diversity" that characterizes the Catholic Church. "The rich variety of ecclesiastical disciplines, liturgical rites, and theological and spiritual heritages proper to the local churches 'unified in a common effort, shows all the more resplendently the catholicity of the undivided Church'" (*CCC*, 835, quoting *Lumen Gentium*, 23). Even though Eastern liturgies may look and sound different from the Mass that Western Catholics are accustomed to, the purpose and essence of all Catholic liturgies are the same. Variations according to local cultures are a natural expression of the different ways that the Gospel has been proclaimed in different places. "Through the liturgical life of a local church, Christ, the light and salvation of all peoples, is made manifest to the particular people and culture to which that Church is sent and in which she is rooted" (*CCC*, 1202). Because Eastern Catholics partake of communion in the Body of Christ, share a belief in the essential tenets of Catholicism, and recognize the pope as head of the Church, they are fully in union with the universal Catholic Church. "The great richness of such diversity is not opposed to the Church's unity" (*CCC*, 814).

To answer the question posed in the title of this feature—"What's the difference between Eastern Orthodox and Eastern Catholic?"—if the name has *Orthodox* in it, the community is not in full communion with Rome and does not recognize the primacy of the pope. Eastern *Catholic* Churches are in full communion with the pope and the Catholic Church.

Further Study and Reflection

- How did the papal delegation "end up in an escalating dispute with the patriarch of Constantinople" upon their visit in 1054?
- Research and share a recent development in unification between the Catholic Church and Eastern Orthodox Churches.
- Why should the term *catholic* be associated with unity? Review the derivation of the term before answering.

Church under the guidance of the Pope" (*CCC*, 895). The pope's authority and jurisdiction extend to the entire Church, while each bishop's authority applies only in his own diocese.

Over time, this basic framework developed into the Church structure we see today. At the local level, Catholics participate in the life of the Church through worship and other activities in their own parish, which is led by a *pastor*, an ordained priest who is assigned by the bishop. Parishes are grouped together in a diocese (or archdiocese, normally located in a larger city), which is under the authority of a bishop (or archbishop). These local dioceses are united through their bishop to the pope, who, two thousand years after the martyrdom of St. Peter, still presides over the universal Church from the Holy or Roman See: "The individual bishops . . . are the visible principle and foundation of unity in their particular churches," while the pope is "the perpetual and visible principle and foundation of unity of both the bishops and . . . the faithful" (*Lumen Gentium*, 23).

In their exercise of authority and leadership, the pastors of the Church, including popes and bishops, take as their model Jesus Christ, who said, "I am the good shepherd. A good shepherd lays down his life for the sheep" (Jn 10:11). The Church's pastors are to guide and guard their people from error, as a shepherd protects his flock.[18] They are to treat with compassion those who have strayed from the fold and call them back to life in the Church just as the shepherd in the parable of the lost sheep left his ninety-nine sheep to find the one that was lost (see Luke 15:1–7). Multiple recent studies have revealed that upward of one-third of Catholics born after 1982 have left the Church. A pastoral role for both ordained leaders and all Catholics is to reach out and search for those who have left the Church and welcome them home.

Spiritual Challenges to the Papacy

While Popes St. Gregory the Great and Gregory VII displayed holiness of life and strove to lead the Church closer to Christ, other medieval popes were exhibits of mediocrity, or even sources of scandal. To reiterate the point already made at the beginning of this section, although the members of the Church on earth are sanctified by God's grace, they are subject to temptation and frequently commit sin. In its humanity, the papacy can look ugly, and never did it look uglier than during the period of vice and chaos in the fourteenth and fifteenth centuries.

In 1305, the cardinals of the Church elected a French archbishop to be the next pope, and he took the name Clement V. France was already a powerful nation, and it aspired to greater power. France's king, Philip IV, saw that one path to power was to control the Catholic Church. In the very unassertive Pope Clement V, the king saw his opportunity. Encouraged by the French government and using the legitimate excuse that there was political instability in Rome, Pope Clement V never left France to take up residence in Rome. Instead, he settled in the city of Avignon, which was technically an independent city but was located within French territory.

This was scandalous because Rome, as the place of the martyrdom of Peter and Paul and of Peter as bishop, is the place in the Church with primacy. Additionally, Pope Clement's tendency to defer to King Philip compromised the independence of the Church from the state, after this issue had been so ably addressed by early Church leaders such as St. Ambrose of Milan (see the feature "Post-Nicene Church Fathers" in Chapter 3, Section 3). Finally, Clement and his successors built a luxurious palace to house themselves and their assistants in Avignon. Faithful Catholics justifiably believed that the head of the Church was no longer acting as a good shepherd for the welfare of the Church but was instead living for his own comfort and catering to the interests of the French state.

Palace of the Popes in Avignon, France.

One of those concerned Catholics was St. Catherine of Siena. "Up, Father! Put into effect the resolution you have made." Catherine wrote these words in 1376 to Pope Gregory XI in Avignon. The popes had been in Avignon for Catherine's entire life, but she knew it wasn't right. Catherine had gained a reputation for her intense spiritual life and boundless charity, and she believed God intended to use her as an instrument to reform the papacy. So she traveled to Avignon and personally entreated Pope Gregory XI to stand up to evil forces in the Church and to return to Rome. Persuaded by her heartfelt pleas and his own conscience, Gregory agreed to make the city of Peter once again the seat of the papacy.

But then Catherine heard rumors that Gregory was vacillating. Opposed by powerful cardinals and worried about his reception in the unsettled city of Rome, Gregory procrastinated. Months passed with no action. Catherine responded by writing vigorous letters to him, remaining respectful but firm. "I long to see you the sort of true gentle shepherd who takes an example from the shepherd Christ, whose place you hold," she wrote. "So come, come! Delay no longer," she exhorted the cautious pope.[19] In January of 1377, Gregory finally brought the papal court back to Rome.

The "Avignon papacy" thus came to an end, but the papal crisis did not. When Pope Gregory XI's successor quickly alienated some of the cardinals, they elected another candidate to be pope, creating two claimants to the papal throne: the valid pope and an "antipope." Thus began the Western Schism. When a council was called to try to resolve the problem by appointing a different pope, the other two refused to resign, so now there were three popes! This created rampant division and confusion within the Church. Each claimant had a following of devout Catholics who believed that their man was the true pope. Each pope appointed his own bishops. The structure of the Church, so important for unity and harmony, was broken.

The situation improved at last when, meeting from 1414 to 1418, a Church council urged the other claimants to resign and elected a new pope, Martin V. Pope Martin's election was recognized as valid because the legitimate pope, Gregory XII, approved the acts of the council and voluntarily submitted his resignation for the purpose of healing the schism. The Catholic faithful coalesced around Martin as the true pope, but the reputation of the papacy had been badly damaged. Over the next hundred years, a period known as the "Renaissance papacy," most popes would do nothing to repair the serious

St. Catherine of Siena before the pope in Avignon.

harm that had been done. For example, Pope Alexander VI (reigned 1492–1503) was a member of the powerful Borgia family. He was accused of bribery in obtaining the papacy, although the charge has not been historically proven. According to the papal historian Eamon Duffy, Alexander was "a worldly and ruthless man, and at the time of his election, was already the father of eight children, by at least three women. That such a man should have seemed a fit successor to Peter speaks volumes about the degradation of the papacy."[20]

The Renaissance popes did do much to build up the material aspect of the Church, accumulating wealth, building churches, and sponsoring great works of art, and this tangible flourishing was not without spiritual benefit. The art and architecture of the period still inspire Christian devotion today, but the spiritual welfare of the Church was much neglected by her leaders during this time. The spectacle of popes living in luxury and consorting with mistresses undermined the role of the papacy as a sign of the Church's holy and apostolic character. Church leaders distracted by wealth, political quarrels, and personal gratification were incapable of recognizing and promoting necessary reforms.

Yet even after the most troublesome periods of Church history, because of her establishment by Christ and aided by other reformers, the papacy has remained an institution that draws us into a unity that goes beyond national or cultural boundaries. As the successor of St. Peter and the head of the **college of bishops**, the pope is the pastor who watches over the whole Church and each of her members throughout the world.

SECTION Assessment

Comprehension

1. How does a pope derive his authority?

2. Where does the Holy See's jurisdiction extend?

3. What list did St. Irenaeus include in *Against Heresies* that supports apostolic succession?

4. Explain the framework of the governing office of the Church from the pope to local parishes.

5. What was the *filioque*? What did it have to do with the division of the Church between West and East?

6. What is the difference between Eastern Orthodox and Eastern Catholic Churches?

---

college of bishops Also known as the Ordo (Order) of Bishops; a term to denote the bishops who are in communion with the pope. Just as the Apostles with St. Peter made up one apostolic college, so do the bishops and the pope.

7. How did popes come to live in Avignon?

8. How was the situation of the "three popes" finally resolved?

Vocabulary

9. What is a characteristic of *Gregorian chant*?

10. What role in the Roman Catholic Church does the role of the *patriarch* correspond to?

Reflection

11. What might be a starting point to encourage a Catholic who has left the Church to return? Explain how you might aid a person's return.

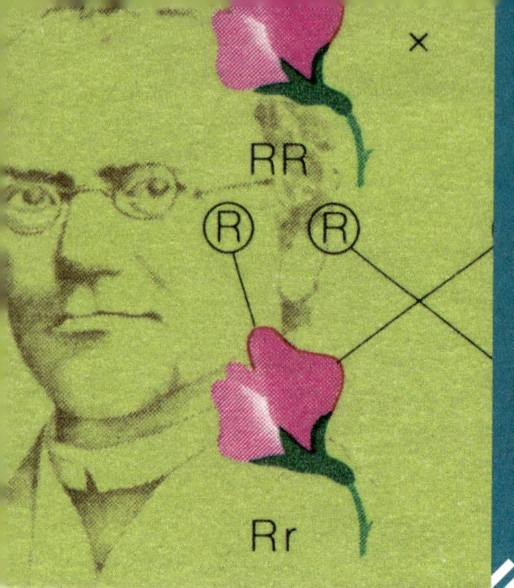

BUILDING LASTING STRUCTURES AND INSTITUTIONS

The Seine River flows through the heart of Paris, one of the world's most storied cities. At the center of the metropolis, in the middle of the river, is the Île de la Cité (City Island). The island is filled with historic buildings, but overshadowing them all is the famous Cathedral of Notre Dame. It is a national landmark, figuring prominently in Europe's history and culture. The French novelist Victor Hugo chose it as the backdrop for his classic *The Hunchback of Notre Dame*, which Disney turned into an animated film in 1996. Not just Catholics, not just French citizens, but millions of people around the world were saddened when the magnificent church was severely damaged by a fire in 2019.

Notre Dame is just one of the stunning churches erected during the Middle Ages, many of which still stand today. Across Europe, from Durham in northern England to Córdoba in southern Spain, from Lisbon to Cologne to Prague, massive cathedrals constructed during the medieval period witness to the importance of the Catholic faith in these nations and have provided inspiration to worshippers for centuries. As venues for architecture, painting,

The French National Forestry Office Wood and Services Department's head sits near a trunk of an oak tree selected to be used in the reconstruction of Notre-Dame de Paris Cathedral. A total of one thousand oaks were needed to rebuild the spire and roof of the cathedral. Oaks from every region of France were used to rebuild the national monument, around half from state land and the rest from private donations.

The spire of the Cathedral of Notre Dame collapsed in a devastating fire in 2019. Since that time restoration has proceeded with nearly a thousand workers from around the world present each day. The spire is being carefully rebuilt with cataloged wood from forests and the absence of nails, primarily to recapture the acoustics that were present in the cathedral from before the fire.

and sculpture, they are also displays of human creativity. In the words of the British historian Paul Johnson, "The medieval cathedrals of Europe . . . are the greatest accomplishment of humanity in the whole theatre of art."[21]

Built along with most of the medieval cathedrals were "cathedral schools," which evolved into universities. In contrast to the monastic schools which preceded them, cathedral schools had as teachers educated laymen hired by the cathedrals. In monastic schools, the teachers were the monks. Likewise, while most of the students in monastic schools did enter the monastery and continue in vowed religious life, students in cathedral schools, for the most part, began to seek careers outside of Church life. The University of Paris, also known as the Sorbonne, is the second oldest university in the world and was originally attached to the Cathedral of Notre Dame as a cathedral school.

Cathedrals of the Middle Ages

Most of the grandest Catholic churches in Europe (and elsewhere) are *cathedrals*. The word comes from the Latin *cathedra*, meaning "chair" (recall the *ex cathedra* teaching of a pope in our discussion of infallibility in Chapter 3). A cathedral is located in a city that is the headquarters of a diocese, and it contains a ceremonial chair, the chair of the bishop.

To reflect the importance of their city, region, and the bishop himself, the home churches of bishops became status symbols. Cities vied with each other to win for their churches the titles of tallest, largest, or most ornate. Builders pushed the limits of medieval technology and financial resources to raise soaring towers above high walls filled with stained glass windows.

The cathedral, or Duomo, in Milan, Italy, illustrates the nature of the cathedral as a community project. In 1386, its foundations were laid, funded by a large donation from the Duke of Milan. But the people of the city did their part. "In a record of donations," writes historian Barbara Tuchman, "the whole of society appears."[22] Organizations worked as groups: the Guild of Armorers, the Drapers, the College of Notaries. Neighborhoods banded together to raise funds. Aristocrats, merchants, laborers, and even prostitutes contributed money to build the cathedral. The medieval workers made a

Milan Cathedral

Cathedral of Our Lady of the Angels, Los Angeles, California.

promising start, but as with many of these monumental cathedrals, construction would continue for centuries afterward. The structure begun in the fourteenth century was not completely finished for another six centuries, in 1965. Officially known as the Cathedral-Basilica of the Nativity of Saint Mary, the Duomo of Milan still serves the Archdiocese of Milan today, its spectacular forest of spires and pinnacles awing worshippers and tourists alike. In fact, this cathedral is the largest cathedral in Italy—larger than St. Peter's Basilica in Rome—and one of the largest cathedrals in the world.

Why does the Church devote so many resources to creating inanimate objects like church walls, altars, tabernacles, and artwork? One important reason for the Catholic emphasis on the church building itself is the symbolism evoked by these items—that is, the spiritual realities to which the physical structure points. Like a human person, the Church has both a body and a soul. It is both physical and spiritual. There are aspects of the Church that we can see: church buildings, Catholic people, the Eucharist, and there are aspects that we cannot see: the saints in heaven, the grace given to us through sacraments, God's love for us.

The physical elements of the church building make concrete the spiritual realities of the faith. The expense and beauty of the materials used to fashion the tabernacle and sacred vessels point to the Real Presence of Jesus in the Eucharist. The soaring ceilings and towers draw the eyes and mind heavenward, reminding us of our final destination. The sun streaming through stained glass windows and the candles on the altar symbolize Christ's brilliance as the light of the world, chasing away the darkness of falsehood and sin.

Countless people throughout history have testified to the impact of beautiful houses of worship. Henry Graham, the Presbyterian studying for the ministry who converted to Catholicism (see Chapter 3, Section 4), described his attraction to the Catholic churches he encountered: "The very buildings themselves were holy and edifying and true 'houses of prayer,' and, where the Catholics could afford it, they were obviously meant to be as worthy of the majesty of God as poor mortals could make them."[23]

The magnificent medieval cathedrals are lasting testaments to Catholic efforts to create structures "worthy of the majesty of God." However, the central purpose of a Catholic church is to bring the People of God together to worship—to participate in the sacrifice of the Mass to seek communion with God, who is present in the Sacrament of the Eucharist. Even the plainest and most humble church can serve this purpose, and the Real Presence of Jesus housed in the tabernacle and indicated by the red tabernacle light is present in every Catholic church. Henry Graham noticed it when he was searching for a spiritual home. "Of the Real Presence," he recalled of his pre-Catholic days, "I then and for long afterward knew absolutely nothing, yet I always experienced in a Catholic church a strange feeling of awe and mystery which I never felt in any other."[24]

Universities of the Time

The University of Paris, located south of the Cathedral of Notre Dame, just across a bridge connecting her island to the "Left Bank" of the Seine River, is another institution that grew up during the Middle Ages and the years following. It remains today one of the world's most prestigious universities. Some of the most brilliant minds of the medieval period, including St. Thomas Aquinas, were associated with the University of Paris.

Other early universities emerged in Oxford, England; Salamanca, Spain; and Bologna, Italy. Bologna in particular became known for its courses in **canon law**. Canon law gradually developed over hundreds of years in order to aid the Magisterium in articulating the life and structure of the Church to Catholics and non-Catholics alike. The law of the Church consists of pastoral norms, directives for living the faith and the moral life, as well as instructions regarding the structure of the Church and how her various elements should interact. This body of law includes, for example, the **precepts of the Church**, a basic set of duties that all Catholics must fulfill. Other laws of the Church govern how the sacraments are conducted; stipulations regarding Catholic marriage, for example, include the requirement that the wedding ceremony take place within a church.

Georgetown University in Washington DC is the oldest Catholic university in the United States, founded in 1789 by Archbishop John Carroll near the time of the founding of the nation.

canon law The official body of rules (canons) that provide good order in the Catholic Church. It was the first modern Western legal system. Canon law has been revised several times, most recently in the Latin Church in 1983 and in the Eastern Church in 1991.

precepts of the Church Five key Church laws that Catholics are required to keep: (1) you shall attend Mass on Sundays and on holy days of obligation and rest from servile labor, (2) you shall confess your sins at least once a year, (3) you shall receive the Sacrament of the Eucharist at least during the Easter season, (4) you shall observe the days of fasting and abstinence established by the Church, and (5) you shall help to provide for the needs of the Church.

While Church laws are related to the unchanging moral law given by God, they also contain *disciplines*, or directives that can be changed by legitimate authority according to new circumstances over time. For example, the Church used to require Catholics to fast—to refrain from all food and drink—from midnight until the person received Communion the next day, whenever that might be. If Mass was in the evening of the following day, the priest and the people were not allowed to eat for upwards of eighteen hours. In the twentieth century, this requirement was eased several times. Currently the Church asks us to fast from everything but water for one hour before receiving Communion. The doctrine on the Real Presence of Jesus in the Eucharist remains constant, but the specific way in which we honor Christ's Real Presence in the Eucharist can change over time.

The life of the university and the life of the Church were closely entwined in other ways besides the formation and study of canon law. Most of Europe's universities sought and received formal approval by the pope, and many of the age's greatest scholars were churchmen. Several of the great discoveries of the Middle Ages took place at Church-sponsored universities and were credited to Catholics. For example:

English friar **Roger Bacon** (ca. 1220–1292), who taught at the Universities of Paris and Oxford, was a pioneer in the use of the scientific method.

Nicholas Copernicus (1473–1543), who attended a cathedral school and the University of Kraków in Poland as well as the University of Bologna (to study canon law), famously concluded that the earth revolved around the sun, introducing the "Copernican Revolution" in astronomy.

Augustinian friar and abbot **Gregor Mendel** (1822–1884), who studied at the University of Vienna and experimented with plants at his monastery, helped to establish the field of genetics.

The Church's commitment to learning and to scientific inquiry helped to lay the foundations of the modern educational system and its academic disciplines. This is yet another lasting legacy of the Middle Ages, a period that seems far away but was, in fact, crucial in shaping both the Church and the broader society that we inhabit today. Calling part of this period the "Dark Ages" turns out to be very misleading, if not downright inaccurate.

SECTION Assessment

Comprehension

1. What were two differences between cathedral schools and monastic schools in the Middle Ages?

2. What is the name of the largest cathedral in Italy?

3. What is the central purpose of a Catholic church?

4. Name one discovery that took place at a Catholic university during the Middle Ages and the person who made it.

Vocabulary

5. List the *precepts of the Church*.

Reflection

6. Share a brief argument against building ornate cathedrals. What is the counterargument to your points?

Section Reviews

Focus Question

How was the Catholic Church important to human progress during the Middle Ages?

Complete one of the following:

- Research and create a spreadsheet listing five popes from a particular age (e.g., the early Church or recent times) by length of time in the papacy, by chosen names, by national origin, by age at the time of election, and by any other category you find interesting.

- Read Chapter 3, "On the Hierarchical Structure of the Church and in Particular on the Episcopate," from the Second Vatican Council document *Lumen Gentium*. Imagine you have been commissioned to write an abridged version of this chapter. Write a one-sentence summary for each paragraph, 18 to 29. Write a concluding one-paragraph summary of the entire chapter.

- Look up two canonization processes that are currently underway. Explain for each how long it has been going on, its current status, and something about the person under consideration.

Introduction

An Era of Great Achievements

Review

The ways that historians have written about the Middle Ages have dismissed the many achievements of the period, roughly from 500 to 1500. The Church herself was a pillar of the period, strengthening the governmental, social, educational, and artistic foundations that kept European society going after the fall of the Roman Empire and that have carried on to succeeding eras.

Assignment

Research and name one famous scientist, one famous architect, one famous artist, and one famous saint who lived between 500 and 1500.

Section 1
The Rhythm of Monastic Life

Review

After the age of martyrs ended, Christians considered asceticism and eventually monasticism to be the highest forms of Christian achievement. St. Anthony of Egypt is considered the founder of monasticism, and St. Benedict of Nursia formalized a rule that continues to be followed in monasteries in the Western Church. The rule is detailed and includes directions to welcome visitors from the outside and for the monks to not remain idle but to do work to support the monastery. Although monasteries have diminished, monastic life is still present in the Church today, some monastic spiritual practices now extended to lay Catholics.

Assignment

Where is the nearest monastery or convent to you? What is the name of the religious community that sponsors it? How many members does it currently have? List one other unique fact about the place.

Section 2
The Call to Holiness

Review

Holiness is the essence of God. In human terms, it is "a separation from all that is evil and attachment to what is good." We are all called to be saints, that is, holy. The Church herself is holy because of her attachment to Christ. Nevertheless, her members on earth are subject to temptation and frequently commit sin. These sinners in no way diminish the holiness of the Church. Canonized saints are examples of holiness whom we are called to emulate. Our own individual path to sainthood involves prayer, charity, and service to others.

Assignment

Why is it incorrect to think that the holiness of the Church depends on the holiness of her members?

Section 3
Renewing the Papacy and Apostolic Leadership

Review

A pope's authority is not dependent on whether he is "good" or "bad." His authority comes from his office of bishop of Rome. The Church's structure is called the governing office of the Church and is composed of bishops under the leadership of the pope. In 1054, a split in the Church occurred in the division between East and West. Some Eastern churches returned to union with Rome and are called Eastern Catholic Churches. Despite a dark period in the papacy in which the pope lived outside of Rome in Avignon and then there were multiple claimants to the papacy, reforms encouraged by St. Catherine of Siena and the apostolic institution of the papacy itself guaranteed its lasting role in Church governance.

Assignment

Read John 10:2–4. How does this image of the sheepfold describe one intended role of the pope?

Section 4
Building Lasting Structures and Institutions

Review

Many majestic and lasting cathedrals were constructed during the Middle Ages. The physical aspects of these cathedrals emphasize the importance of the spiritual realities they are meant to express. They are lasting testaments to the majesty of God. Cathedral schools connected with the cathedrals evolved into the world's first universities. One point of emphasis of these schools was to teach Church law and disciplines. Universities were also centers of scientific inquiry and the source of discoveries of lasting value.

Assignment

Describe an occasion when you were personally taught by a bishop or one lesson you have read from a bishop. What was the lesson?

Chapter Projects

Choose and complete at least one of the following projects to assess your understanding of the material in this chapter.

⚙ 1. Outline the History of the Organ in Catholic Liturgy

The Second Vatican Council offered special praise for the pipe organ, leading many to categorize the organ as a "sacred instrument": "In the Latin Church the pipe organ is to be held in high esteem, for it is the traditional musical instrument which adds a wonderful splendor to the Church's ceremonies and powerfully lifts up man's mind to God and to higher things" (*Sacrosanctum Concilium*, 120). This statement and the general sentiment about the organ and its use in Catholic liturgy introduce several related questions. Answer each of the following questions with a written statement. Cite references for each answer.

- Is the organ a sacred instrument?
- Can an instrument be sacred?
- Who invented the first organ?
- When were organs first used in the liturgy?
- Where was the first Catholic church with an organ?
- What are three prominent organs in Catholic churches in the world today?
- Why did organ use become popular in the Church?
- Are there some instruments that are not approved for use in the liturgy?
- Can an organ accompany Gregorian chant? Why or why not?
- Share a link with a favorite organ recital held in a Catholic church. What do you like about it?

⚙ 2. Sketch a Church Sanctuary Using Charcoal

Charcoal is a perfect medium for beginning artists. It allows you to work with geometric shapes, lines, and contours while also being able to "smudge" the edges and even erase as you go. Check out a tutorial on charcoal art for beginners to see if you would like to attempt a charcoal drawing. There are many types of charcoal utensils to consider. Nitram charcoal is very durable, and it is soft enough to create smooth blends while also allowing for detailed drawing. You will also need a durable type of paper with texture so that it will not tear when you are drawing.

Your project is to draw a view of a Catholic church sanctuary that includes at least a tabernacle and a sanctuary lamp. To work from a location outside of a church, take a photo of a favorite sanctuary and use it for a model. *Optional*: Add red to the drawing for the sanctuary lamp using colored pencil, a colored sponge, or another medium that you research and find workable.

⚙ 3. Write a Report on the Liturgy of the Hours

Besides being arranged around the seasons of the Church Year, the liturgical calendar also is connected with daily prayer. Today, monks, nuns, priests, and laypeople pray throughout the day on a schedule based on the Church's Liturgy of the Hours. Examine the names of the daily prayers. Do the following: (1) write a definition for each name; (2) explain the significance of each hour of prayer; (3) write a report summarizing the history and organization of the entire Liturgy of the Hours.

- Matins
- Lauds
- Terce
- Sext
- None
- Vespers
- Compline

⚙ 4. Make a Mind Map of Facts about the Avignon Papacy

A mind map is an organized or free-flowing diagram that organizes several points around a central theme. It uses words and pictures to help explain a complex topic more clearly but with as much detail as necessary. Some mind maps are sequential and ordered branch by branch or level by level. Others are free flowing, meaning that you can add information as it comes to you.

Develop a mind map around the era of the Avignon papacy. You may use that title as your central theme or choose another related title (e.g., St. Catherine of Siena, Three Popes, Western Schism). Include at least twenty-five facts in your mind map.

⚙ *5. Compare Early Forms of Monasticism*

St. Basil the Great in the East and St. Benedict of Nursia in the West are considered founders of the rules of communal monasticism. However, they were both heavily influenced by St. Pachomius (292–348), who eventually founded nine monasteries with hundreds of monks each. Make a chart, graph, or flow chart that compares St. Pachomius, St. Basil, and St. Benedict, focusing on these and other elements of your choice:

- origins and biography
- rules of monastic life
- monasteries founded
- unique contributions to monastic life
- death and canonization

Faithful Disciple
St. Scholastica

St. Scholastica

St. Scholastica was born into a wealthy Italian family in 480. Her twin brother was St. Benedict of Nursia, the founder of the Benedictine order. Most of the information we have about Scholastica comes from another saint, the famous reformer St. Gregory the Great, who wrote about her in his *Dialogues*. St. Gregory tells that Scholastica was dedicated to God from a young age. She was a nun who founded and led a community of women a few miles away from her brother's abbey at Monte Cassino.

St. Scholastica visited her brother near his abbey once every year; during the visit, they would spend time praying together and discussing sacred writings and topics. One year, sensing that her death was near, Scholastica asked Benedict to stay the night so that they might continue their conversations, but Benedict resisted because his own rule said that he must stay in his room (known as a *cell*) each night. Scholastica bowed her head in prayer, and immediately a tremendous storm began outside of the place where they were, preventing Benedict from returning to the abbey. When Benedict asked Scholastica what she had done, she replied, "I asked a favor of you and you refused. I asked it of God and he granted it."

Scholastica died several days later. According to St. Gregory, three days later, Benedict was in his cell. Looking up to the sky, he saw his sister's soul leave her body in the form of a dove and fly up to the secret places of heaven.

Rejoicing in her great glory, he thanked almighty God with hymns and words of praise. He then sent his brethren to bring her body to the monastery and lay it in the tomb he had prepared for himself. Benedict passed away shortly afterward.

St. Scholastica is the patron saint of nuns and convulsive children, and people ask her intercession against storms and rain.

Comprehension

1. Where did St. Scholastica live?
2. How was St. Scholastica able to change her brother's mind about staying longer to speak with her?

Reflection

Why might siblings from the same family each choose the religious life? Why might they choose different vocations from each other?

CHAPTER 4 REVIEW

Prayer

St. Gregory the Great, also known as Pope Gregory I, received his spiritual formation as a monk under the direction of St. Benedict of Nursia. He is known as "Great" because he was canonized by popular acclaim after his death. He is also a Doctor of the Church and one of the greatest popes to ever sit in the Chair of St. Peter. Among his accomplishments are the reforms he made to the liturgy. The following prayer was written by St. Gregory the Great himself.

Prayer of St. Gregory the Great

It is only right, with all the powers of our heart and mind, to praise you, Father, and your only-begotten Son, our Lord Jesus Christ: Dear Father, by your wondrous condescension of loving-kindness toward us, your servants, you gave up your Son. Dear Jesus, you paid the debt of Adam for us to the Eternal Father by your blood poured forth in loving-kindness. You cleared away the darkness of sin by your magnificent and radiant Resurrection. You broke the bonds of death and rose from the grave as a Conqueror. You reconciled heaven and earth. Our life had no hope of eternal happiness before you redeemed us. Your Resurrection has washed away our sins, restored our innocence, and brought us joy. How inestimable is the tenderness of your love! Amen.

The Church Readdresses Her Unity

Miracles of St. Francis Xavier
Peter Paul Rubens

This large altarpiece, *The Miracles of St. Francis Xavier*, was painted by Flemish artist Peter Paul Rubens (1577–1640) in 1617 or 1618. It was commissioned by the Jesuit order to celebrate the missionary work of St. Francis Xavier in Asia during the first half of the sixteenth century. The depiction in the painting of many miracles by St. Francis led many people to believe in and discuss these occurrences. Note St. Francis standing on a large altar on the right side of the painting. On the left, a mother holding a baby with water coming from his mouth represents a time when St. Francis saved a baby from drowning in India. In the middle of the painting, the men in the Korean outfits represent initial doubters of the miracles of St. Francis who were eventually convinced of his actions. The blind man on the right side points to another of Francis's miracles: healing the man and giving him his sight.

The Jesuits' missionary efforts were robust in the sixteenth and seventeenth centuries (see subsection "Jesuit Missionaries of the Sixteenth and Seventeenth Centuries" in Section 4 of this chapter). During this period after the Protestant Reformation, Rubens intended to show that the miracles by this Catholic missionary were part of the restoration of the prominence of the Church.

The artist himself had a remarkable life. Born in Germany, Rubens studied in Antwerp and Italy before eventually settling in Antwerp, Belgium, where he was appointed court painter for the Habsburg rulers of the region. He had a disciplined routine for painting, rising at four o'clock in the morning and working straight through until five in the evening. He would have someone read classical literature to him while he painted. In the evening he would go out riding on his horse. He was an avid collector of coins and ancient sculptures, including an Egyptian mummy.

The altarpiece shown here was commissioned by the Jesuits in Antwerp for their church in that city, now known as St. Charles Borromeo Church. It was completed before St. Francis Xavier became a saint in 1622 and was part of the Jesuits' campaign for his canonization. It is now housed in the Kunsthistorisches Museum in Vienna.

If you would like to create a journal with sketches of other Jesuit missionaries of the sixteenth and seventeenth centuries, see Chapter 5 Review, Chapter Project 1.

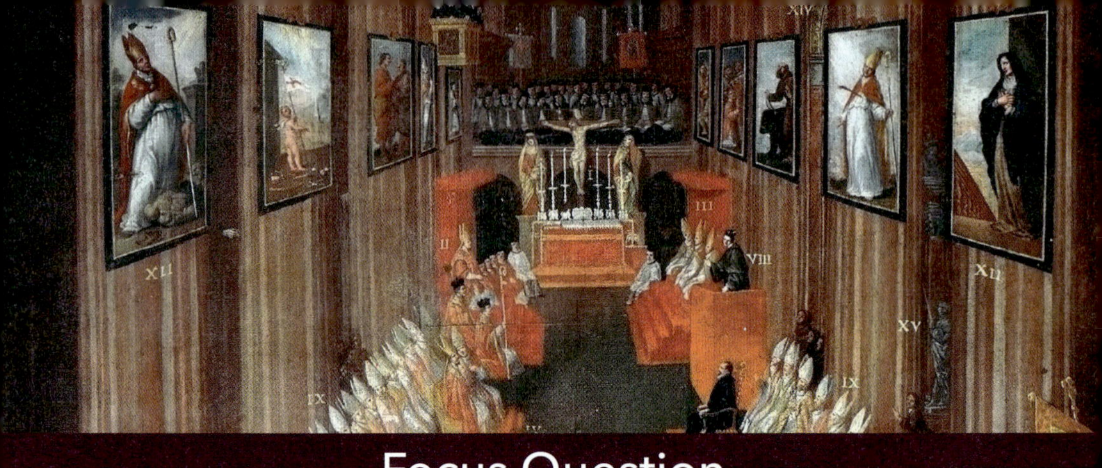

How do the marks of unity and catholicity support the Church's missionary efforts?

RENEWING WITHIN AND EXPANDING WORLDWIDE

By the early sixteenth century, the old basilica built by Constantine over the grave of St. Peter (see subsection "Changing the Culture" in Chapter 3, Introduction) was in poor condition. Pope Julius II decided to replace it with a grand new edifice, a monument to the glory of God and a tribute to the great Apostle Peter, and also a reflection of the wealth and power of the Catholic Church. The result is St. Peter's Basilica in Rome, one of the largest and most magnificent churches in the world.∞

To build such a church required massive funding. One way the pope could raise funds was by soliciting donations in return for spiritual favors. He sent preachers out across Europe promising *indulgences*—forgiveness for the punishment due to sin—in return for a contribution toward the pope's building project.

The theology of the indulgence was sound. Christians can atone for sins by acts of prayer or charity, but the indulgence preachers of the sixteenth century weren't always careful to explain that theology correctly. The possibility of misunderstanding and corruption increased when the good deed involved money rather than spiritual activities.

One notoriously careless preacher, the Dominican friar Johann Tetzel, preached about indulgences in eastern Germany. A Catholic priest in the area, Martin Luther, heard about Tetzel from people who took the papal preacher

∞ Note

Some of the most prominent and lasting art in history is displayed at St. Peter's Basilica. Pope Julius II commissioned Michelangelo to paint the ceiling of the Sistine Chapel in 1508. It was a grueling four-year project. The Sistine frescoes by Michelangelo include the prominent *Creation of Adam* scene on the ceiling and the *Last Judgment*, painted many years later on the end wall of the chapel.

to be saying that a monetary donation to the Church was essentially an easy ticket into heaven. Luther was incensed. He believed that salvation was a gift from God and couldn't be "bought" by tossing a few coins into a collection basket. He challenged Tetzel to a public debate.

Such theological debates were common. Dissatisfaction with the preaching of indulgences was common, but the fallout from this event was uncommon. Thanks to a combination of misunderstanding and inflexibility on both sides, the disagreement spun quickly out of control. Luther's critique expanded into doubts about the authority of the pope and the perennial teachings of the

Sample of an indulgence certificate for donating alms to build a Catholic church.

Church. The pope excommunicated Luther, hoping to change his mind, or at least to prevent the further spread of his ideas, but his action only aggravated the conflict. In the end, a large number of Catholics followed Luther rather than the pope, and what is now known as the Protestant Reformation began.

Repentance and Conversion

Our study of Church history so far has demonstrated that the Church is always in need of reform. The Church is composed of sinful human beings, and so sin is always present, always threatening to undermine the mission of the Church as Christ's presence on earth. Jesus himself recognized the constant threat that sin posed to those who would follow him. At the beginning of his public ministry, he called on his listeners to turn away from sin as a prerequisite for accepting the Good News: "Repent, and believe in the gospel" (Mk 1:15). As individuals, we are in constant need of *repentance* and *conversion*. To repent is to "regret"—to regret committing sin; and to convert is to "turn"—to turn away from sin and toward God. As a family of believers, we are collectively in need of repentance and conversion as well. The sins of the members of the

Church bring corruption and decay into the Church. The virtue of the members of the Church is required to drive the corruption out and bring holiness in its place. As we have seen, saints—those who practice virtue heroically—are often in the forefront of reform movements.

Recall also from Chapter 4 that the leadership of the Church, including the papacy, was suffering from corruption in the fifteenth century. The efforts of saints such as St. Catherine of Siena had helped, but not enough. There were still many abuses that needed attention. The failure to address these abuses was part of the reason Martin Luther attacked the Church, and part of the reason so many believers were sympathetic to his views.

Even as the Protestant movement divided the Church, there were forces of reform at work within her. The Catholic Reformation (or Counter-Reformation), which also took place during the sixteenth century, renewed the papacy, the clergy, the religious orders, and the broader Church in lasting ways that have been preserved to this day.

Missionary Efforts

Whenever and wherever the Church is healthy and vibrant, Catholics are impelled to share their faith with others. The interior renewal of the sixteenth-century Church coincided with European exploration and colonization

In the 1930s, three lay brothers carry buckets and other farming equipment as part of their farming training for foreign missionary work at St. Josephs College, Mill Hill.

of vast stretches of the world to the west, south, and east. Just a few years before the new St. Peter's Basilica was begun, Christopher Columbus made contact with the Americas, bringing to the attention of the Church millions of people who had never heard the Gospel.

While new Catholic missions to the Americas, Africa, and Asia were exciting, they also presented certain challenges. European missionaries struggled to communicate effectively with native populations who spoke different languages, practiced different religions, and had deeply ingrained habits that might not conform to Christian morality. European colonists and soldiers often had priorities, such as increasing political power or acquiring wealth, that collided with the missionaries' aim of inculcating the faith. Missionaries themselves caused scandal by failing to live up to the moral codes they taught or by treating indigenous people harshly.

Despite these difficulties, the missionaries' often heroic efforts paid off. The faith spread and the Church's expansion across the world helped to highlight her universal character. During this period, it appeared for the first time in history that Christianity really would extend across the entire world—that the Great Commission (see subsection "Make Disciples of All Nations" in Chapter 2, Section 1) to preach the Gospel to "all nations" was being fulfilled.

Santa Barbara Mission in Santa Barbara, California.

The Gospel brought to the Americas by Christian missionaries was intended to unite new cultures through God's saving message, not cause division. Likewise, divisions that occurred in the Church due to the Protestant Reformation and its aftermath run counter to the intention of Jesus that his followers remain united.

SECTION Assessment

Comprehension

1. What was sound about the theology of indulgences?

2. What was faulty about the practice of indulgences?

3. How did the goals of the explorers sometimes conflict with those of the missionaries?

4. What did the Church accomplish through the missionaries' efforts?

Reflection

5. Which do you consider to be a more difficult task: reformation of one's personal life or reformation of an institution? Explain.

UNITY THREATENED BY ABUSES

When Jesus bade farewell to the disciples he was sending out into the world, he said, "I pray not only for them, but also for those who will believe in me through their word, so that they may all be one, as you, Father, are in me and I in you" (Jn 17:20–21). Taking to heart the prayer of Jesus, we believe the Church is to be *one*. Unity, or oneness, is a mark of the Church. The Church's unity emanates from the unity of God, Three Divine Persons living in community with one another. The Second Person of the Trinity, Jesus Christ, came to earth to heal division; he "reconciled all men to God by the cross, . . . restoring the unity of all in one people and one body" (*Gaudium et Spes*, 78). It is the Church's "soul," the Holy Spirit, who is a force for unity, bringing about a "wonderful communion of the faithful" (*CCC*, 813).

The unity of the Church is realized above all through love—the love between the Divine Persons of the Trinity, the love of Christians for God, and the love of Christians for one another. St. Paul teaches that love is the "bond of perfection" (Col 3:14). If you have experienced a loving family life or deep friendships, you have a good idea of how love functions to bring about unity. When people truly love one another, they want what is best for the other. They are willing to sacrifice their own preferences for the sake of the other. They derive satisfaction and joy from seeing the happiness of the other. When people relate to each other this way, they feel a strong connection. They tend to work together toward common aims, and they understand that their own well-being is closely tied to the well-being of others.

The same thing happens in the Church, which is the "family of God." The unity created by the bond of love is evident in three "visible bonds of communion" (*CCC*, 815)—ways of showing that the Church is genuinely and concretely one. First, we are united by professing the faith taught by the Apostles. Second, unity is achieved through celebrating together the liturgies of the Mass and other sacraments. Third, unity is maintained by the unbroken line of apostolic succession, as the pope and bishops preserve the teaching of Jesus and provide a solid structure for the Church (see subsection "Tracing the Primacy of the Holy See" in Chapter 4, Section 3).

There is only *one* Church. The Church that Jesus founded, that he entrusted to the Apostles, and that continues in the present world "subsists in . . . the Catholic Church, which is governed by the successor of Peter and by the Bishops in communion with him" (*Lumen Gentium*, 8).∞ Because the Holy Spirit guides the Church and not because of any intrinsic merit or superiority of the Church's members, the Church is the means to communion with Christ and therefore the way to salvation. "It is only through Christ's Catholic Church, which is 'the all-embracing means of salvation,' that they can benefit fully from the means of salvation" (*Unitatis Redintegratio*, 3).

This mark of unity or oneness of doctrine and spirit does not mean that the Church is not diverse. A wide variety of people can and do share belief in the creed of Catholicism, communion in its sacraments, and the bonds of love in service and care for each other. As we have seen, the diversity of the one Church is manifested in her saints. Brothers and Apostles St. Peter and St. Andrew were working-class fishermen from Palestine. St. Augustine from North Africa and St. Gregory the Great from Italy were members of

---

∞ Note

The use of the phrase *subsists in* in the Second Vatican Council document does not mean that the Catholic Church is only a "part" of the Church of Christ and that other parts exist elsewhere. Rather, it means "exists as a substance." There is only one substance, which is the Catholic Church. Then why didn't the Council just plainly say that the Church of Christ *is* the Catholic Church? Pope Benedict XVI explained that the use of *subsists in* was meant to show that in other church communities not in full communion with the Catholic Church, "many elements of sanctification and truth" (*LG*, 8) can be found. But he added that in those communities, these elements are derived from and entrusted to the Catholic Church.

One Catholic Convert

Julie Swenson was raised in a strong Protestant Christian family in the twentieth-century United States. "My mother and father were good and loving parents who nurtured me in a solid Christian environment," she remembers, "inculcating in me a deep love for Jesus and for the Bible." She did not suspect at the time that she "might not know the whole story of the Christian Church." Through a long process of experience, research, and reflection, she gradually came to believe, despite having been taught to despise Catholicism as unbiblical, that the "whole story" was reflected in the Catholic Church.

Prompted by a **Calvinist** minister's sermon, she read and meditated on 1 Timothy 3:15, where Paul speaks of the "household of God, which is the church of the living God, the pillar and foundation of truth." The passage, she writes, "jangled a warning bell deep within me" because "my instincts told me that the Lord's household must be one of harmony and unity." Even though she was at the time "a committed Evangelical," she was troubled that the many Protestant denominations were "fraught with division and doctrinal disagreements."

Her quest for unity around true doctrine opened Julie to learning more about the Catholic Church. Through physical suffering, she came to a Catholic view of grace and sanctification: that "God had created me a responsible, rational person who must continually reach out for his grace and, aided by that grace, turn away from sin in order to be saved." As she continued to read more about Catholic doctrine, she found her soul "nourished and fortified by the Church's rich, mature, and time-tested system of faith and morals. It was like finding the pearl of great price." For a time Julie and her husband participated in an **Anglican** parish, but in the end they could not accept Anglican theories of the church that saw Anglicanism as a "branch" of Catholicism or as a "middle way" between Protestant and Catholic. This was not the unity that Julie believed was necessary for the household of God. Finally, Julie and her family entered the Catholic Church, finding in it "the fulfillment of the faith that had been mine all along."[1]

Calvinist Follower of John Calvin, who denied the Catholic understanding of the sacraments and condemned the papacy, monasticism, and clerical celibacy. Calvinists believe in double predestination, which falsely teaches that God wills that some people go to hell in advance of any wrongdoing on their part.

the Roman Empire's upper-class elite. St. Elizabeth of Hungary (d. 1231) was a wealthy queen, while St. Bernadette Soubirous was a peasant. St. Thomas Aquinas was one of history's most brilliant minds, while St. Joseph of Cupertino (d. 1663), the patron saint of those with learning disabilities, struggled through school. And in recent years, while it is true that Mass attendance has decreased worldwide, the actual number of Catholics worldwide has *increased*, fueled by the initiation and reception into the Church of new members.∞ There are as many stories of why people seek out the Catholic Church as there are new Catholics. When you have the opportunity, read the story of **one Catholic convert** and why this person chose to enter the Church.

St. Joseph of Cupertino

St. Elizabeth of Hungary

Although the unity of the Church comprises amazing cultural, ethnic, and socioeconomic diversity, there are wounds to that unity. From the beginning, some Christians have not been in full communion with the Church. Recall the major divisions in the Church in her early centuries brought about by heretical beliefs and the Church's response to those at the Councils of Nicaea, Ephesus, and Chalcedon. The Church sees such divisions as "ruptures that wound the unity of Christ's Body" and understands that these wounds "do not occur without human sin" (*CCC*, 817). Divisions in the Church

Anglican The name for the Church of England established by King Henry VIII. Although their clergy and liturgical practices appear similar to those of Catholics in many respects, Anglicans do not validly celebrate the Sacrament of the Eucharist or Holy Orders.

∞ Note

By the start of the 2020s, the worldwide Catholic population exceeded 1.34 billion, which continued to be about 17.7 percent of the world's population, according to the Vatican newspaper, *L'Osservatore Romano*. This marked an increase of 16 million Catholics—a 1.12 percent increase—compared to 2018, while the world's population grew by 1.08 percent.

in the aftermath of the Protestant Reformation led to ongoing differences on issues like legitimate apostolic authority and understanding and practice of the sacraments.

Abuses That Threatened Unity

Various abuses that had troubled the Church through much of the Middle Ages were widespread and seemingly condoned through the end of that period. One perennial problem was *nepotism*, that is, the appointment of relatives to positions of leadership. Although there could be good reasons for a pope, for example, to designate his nephew to be a bishop or cardinal, the practice created at least the appearance of corruption, of basing decisions on personal whim or favoritism rather than on the good of the Church. In many cases, it was clear to all observers that the appointment had nothing to do with the holiness of the beneficiary. Imagine if the government or business leaders today appointed primarily sons and daughters, nieces and nephews, to fill important positions, even though they had little or no expertise in those positions or job requirements. Something like this was happening in the Church in the fifteenth century.

The scandal caused by the practice of nepotism was increased by the fact that many such appointments carried with them substantial financial rewards, which created an incentive for another abuse, *simony*, whereby a potential appointee would bribe the official who had the power to appoint. Sometimes, an arrangement would be worked out so that a portion of the new office-holder's income would be skimmed off by the official who appointed him—in essence, a kickback.

An appointment that entailed income was known as a *benefice*. The connection between money and Church offices led to another abuse: *pluralism*, or the holding of multiple benefices. As we have seen, the model for a bishop is supposed to be Christ himself, especially under the image of the Good Shepherd. A bishop is supposed to be attached to his flock—the people of his diocese—and to put their spiritual needs above all else. During the Middle Ages, it became common for individual clergy to hold multiple offices such as bishop or abbot. For example, as actually happened in England in the eleventh century, one man might be simultaneously archbishop of Canterbury, bishop of Winchester, and abbot of Gloucester. The three offices provided a large amount of income, but it was impossible for a single person to fulfill all those duties adequately. Such pluralism gave rise to yet another abuse: *absenteeism*. A bishop who led two different dioceses might choose to live full-time in only one of them, or even neither, receiving the income from both benefices but exhibiting no personal interest in the priests or people of one or both dioceses.

These corruptions in the leadership of the Church rippled out into innumerable other problems. Where bishops showed little concern for the quality of their clergy, unqualified men could enter the priesthood. Priests could be insufficiently educated. They might seek the priesthood for the wrong motives, such as desire for power or money, or they might be unsuited to the priesthood due to lack of spiritual commitment to prayer, service, and chastity. When such men became priests, they introduced more corruption into the leadership of the Church, continuing a vicious cycle. This was the environment that encouraged abuses such as Johann Tetzel's preaching of indulgences, which provoked Martin Luther to rebellion against the Church herself.

Reform within Reform

All people have a responsibility to work toward unity in the Body of Christ by reforming their own lives, reaching out in charity and deference toward others, praying for peace and unity, and submitting to the teaching and disciplines of the Church. "Christ always gives his Church the gift of unity, but the Church must always pray and work to maintain, reinforce, and perfect the unity that Christ wills for her" (*CCC*, 820). This "reform within reform" is a function for the institutional Church herself, institutions within the Church, and individuals.

We learned earlier that the father of Western monasticism, St. Benedict, was a reformer. Distressed by the state of the Church and society, he tried to bring greater order to religious life and ensure that monasteries would be places of holiness. Yet, as previously noted, by the twelfth century many monks had abandoned the zeal and ideals of Benedict (see subsection "How the Church 'Makes' Saints" in Chapter 4, Section 2). Monk-saints such as Robert of Molesmes, Stephen Harding, and Bernard of Clairvaux saw the need for reform and founded new monasteries where the Benedictine commitment to prayer and work would be lived more faithfully. Members of their reformed order of Benedictines were known as *Cistercians*. By the seventeenth century, however, the Cistercians themselves needed reform.

Aerial view of the Abbey of La Trappe. (Right) Jean de Rancé.

Jean de Rancé (1626–1700), the abbot at the Abbey of La Trappe in northwestern France, noticed that many of his fellow abbots led comfortable lives, were waited on by servants, and traveled away from their monasteries frequently. He also saw that most monks in general failed to follow the Cistercian rule on many points, such as fasting, praying the Divine Office regularly as a community, and refraining from frivolous conversation. Abbot de Rancé gradually introduced more discipline at La Trappe, beginning with spiritual reading during the time the monks ate their meals. The monks also returned to the practices of diligent labor and generous giving to the poor. While de Rancé recognized that the penitential life of the monk was not for everyone, he thought it served an important purpose for those who were called to it. "I believe it is our particular call," he wrote, "to show to the Christian world that, as every worldly good, without God, is empty, so God, without any worldly good, is . . . all-sufficient."[2]

The reforms at La Trappe spread throughout the world, forming a new branch of the Cistercian order, the "Trappists." The Trappists still exist; in the twentieth century, their monastery in Kentucky was the home of the well-known spiritual writer Thomas Merton (see Faithful Disciple profile "Thomas

Merton" in Chapter 7). The history of Benedictine monasticism shows how the temptation to sin is not a problem that can be dealt with once and for all; the need for reform is persistent. The Church is constantly in need of reformation.

SECTION Assessment

Comprehension

1. From where does the Church's unity emanate?

2. How is the Church's unity realized?

3. What are the three visible bonds of the Church's unity?

4. What does it mean to say that the Church of Christ subsists in the Catholic Church?

5. Explain how nepotism can lead to simony.

6. Differentiate between the abuse of pluralism and the abuse of absenteeism in the Church of the Middle Ages.

7. What abuses among the Cistercians did Jean de Rancé seek to correct?

Vocabulary

8. How are *Calvinists* different from *Anglicans*?

Reflection

9. Who is a Catholic convert that you know? Why did this person choose to enter the Catholic Church?

THE PROTESTANT REFORMATION

When Martin Luther challenged the Church's practice of indulgences, neither he nor anyone else realized how far-reaching the consequences would be. His act of defiance of the pope tapped into widespread dissatisfaction among Catholics concerning abuses such as nepotism, simony, and pluralism. It provided an opening for clergy and theologians who disagreed with various Church teachings to make those disagreements public and to build movements that took Christian theology in different directions. It also offered an opportunity for politicians, operating from more selfish motives, who saw that they might benefit from division in the Church.

Luther's movement at first spread mainly in Germany, which was a region divided into many different *principalities* (areas ruled by princes) and *duchies* (areas ruled by dukes). These areas were all part of the overarching Holy Roman Empire, whose emperor at the time was Charles V, a Spanish king. Charles V was a devout Catholic, and the Holy Roman Empire was closely associated with the papacy. Some of the German princes who sought greater independence from the empire therefore saw an opportunity in Luther's rebellion. If they could weaken their subjects' attachment to the Catholic faith, or at least to the pope as the leader of their faith, then their attachment to the empire would also weaken, and the local rulers' power would increase. One German ruler whose support of Luther was critical was Frederick III of Saxony. Whether Frederick was motivated by political reasons, sympathy for Luther's theological views, or simply concern for what he saw as the injustice of the condemnation of the reformer is unclear, but Frederick provided Luther with protection from arrest by imperial authorities.

At the same time that Luther's questioning of Church authority was spreading through Germany, a similar movement was afoot in France and

Switzerland. Other reformers, such as John Calvin and Ulrich Zwingli, interpreted the Bible in ways opposed to Catholicism and concluded that a different theology and liturgy were necessary to return to the true meaning of the Scriptures. They did not see the Magisterium as having authority to define the meaning and use of the biblical texts; instead, they held that scholars trained in biblical languages and attuned to Christian history and tradition could discern the proper meaning of Scripture for themselves. For example, although the Catholic approach to Luke 22:19—"This is my body"—was to take Jesus's words at the Last Supper literally, Calvin asserted that Jesus meant this reference to his body only to be symbolic. This interpretation led to a completely different view of the Eucharist. Calvin's ideas gave rise to the "Reformed" tradition within Protestantism, which gradually spread through much of Western Europe and beyond. For example, the Puritans who arrived at Plymouth Rock in 1620 and settled in New England were Calvinists.

Meanwhile, yet another stream of the Reformation was gaining strength in England. There, King Henry VIII desired a male heir, which his wife, Catherine of Aragon, had (from his perspective) failed to deliver. He was attracted to another woman, Anne Boleyn, with whom he hoped he could have a son. Standing in the way was the Church's prohibition of divorce and remarriage. For their son to be a legitimate heir, his union with Anne would have to be approved by the Church. The pope refused to grant the exemption Henry

St. Thomas More visited by his wife and daughter before his execution and St. John Fisher just prior to his execution as ordered by King Henry VIII.

sought, but the king decided to move ahead anyway. He coerced the bishops of England to cooperate and in the process launched a full-scale rebellion against the Catholic Church and the pope. Two prominent figures, the chancellor of the realm, St. Thomas More, and the bishop of Rochester, St. John Fisher, refused to approve Henry's new marriage; they were both beheaded and are recognized by the Church as martyr-saints.

In this way, almost the entire English church separated from the Catholic Church in the early sixteenth century, even as Luther, Calvin, and others were drawing thousands of others out of communion with the pope. Christian unity, as tenuous and imperfect as it had been for many centuries, was now completely breaking down in Europe. Over the succeeding hundred years or so, Protestantism would come to predominate in large parts of the continent. Much of Germany, especially in the north and east, as well as all of Scandinavia (Denmark, Norway, Sweden, and Finland) became Lutheran. Most of Switzerland became Calvinist, and there were pockets of Calvinists throughout much of France. Calvinism spread to the Netherlands and Scotland, where it gave rise to the Presbyterian ecclesial community. Protestantism also made inroads into Eastern Europe, in places such as Poland, the Czech Republic, and Hungary.

The religious landscape of Europe thus changed dramatically over the course of the sixteenth century. What exactly were the new ideas and practices that the Protestant reformers made popular? A look at the theology of the Reformation helps to answer that question.

The Theology of the Protestant Reformation

It is first important to understand that Protestant Christians are a diverse group with a variety of beliefs and liturgical practices. This is even more true today than it was in the sixteenth century. So any summary of "Protestant" tenets is going to be a generalization that will gloss over many details and variations. With that qualification in mind, we can identify certain issues that were at the heart of the Reformation movements and that have largely persisted up to the present day as key differences between Protestant ecclesial communities and the Catholic Church.

Reformation theology can be summarized in the **three solas**. First, there is **sola sciptura (Scripture alone)**. Luther and others believed that the Bible is "the sole source of divine revelation, the only inspired, infallible, final, and authoritative norm of faith and practice."[3] In contrast, Catholics believe that

The Council of Trent (fourth session) responded to Luther's translation of the Bible by reaffirming that Scripture has been "dictated, either by Christ's own word of mouth, or by the Holy Ghost, and preserved in the Catholic Church by a continuous succession."

Divine Revelation is contained in both Sacred Scripture and Sacred Tradition. The Church teaches that Scripture cannot be separated from Tradition. In fact, it was the Church, guided by the Holy Spirit, that came to decide what was Scripture.

The other two *solas* can be grouped together: **sola gratia (grace alone)** and **sola fide (faith alone)**. These principles hold that **justification** "is an act of God's free grace unto sinners, in which he pardons all their sins, accepts and accounts their persons righteous in his sight; not for anything wrought in them, or done by them, but only for the perfect obedience and full satisfaction of Christ, by God imputed to them, and received by faith alone."[4] Catholic teaching emphasizes that Baptism, the sacrament of faith, is the means by which God justifies a person. Through this gift, God makes us inwardly righteous and pours faith, hope, and charity into our souls.

As they applied these ideas to the life of the Church, the reformers modified or abandoned many Catholic practices. As they saw it, there was no mandate in Scripture for many Catholic beliefs, and so those false ideas needed to be purged. The sacraments of Holy Orders, Matrimony, Anointing of the

justification Describes the state of cleansing from sin through faith in Jesus Christ and Baptism and by the grace of the Holy Spirit and being made right with God. Justification not only frees us from sin but sanctifies us in the depth of our being.

The Catholic Mass *versus*

Focus Question: How do the marks of unity and catholicity support the Church's missionary efforts?

Catholic apologist Brandon Vogt points out in his book *What to Say and How to Say It, Volume 3: Even More Ways to Discuss Your Faith with Clarity and Confidence* that many people believe that all Christian worship services are the same, often grouping the Catholic Mass into that category. In fact, there are significant differences between the Catholic Mass and Protestant worship services. Vogt points out four key differences:

Difference 1: Sacrifice versus Teaching

The Mass is fundamentally a sacrifice. It involves a re-presentation of Christ's self-offering on Calvary in the Eucharist—a sacrifice we participate in by joining with Christ as he offers himself to the Father. On the other hand, most Protestant worship services do not involve a liturgical sacrifice. They include times of praise and worship, fellowship, and community activities. But at core the services are about teaching. Most of the time is devoted to people listening to a minister speak about the Scriptures.

Mass is based on sacrifice and communion (thus the altar), while most Protestant services are based on teaching (thus the prominent lectern).

Protestant
Worship Services

Difference 2: Universal versus Local

A Catholic Mass includes the same prayers, creed, readings, responses, canon, Communion, and dismissal worldwide. On the other hand, almost every Protestant community is unique and provincial. Many Protestant communities design their own services to accommodate the unique demographics and personal circumstances of their congregations. They sometimes even change the order of the service every week, trying to avoid being stale.

Catholic liturgy remains consistent and recognizable, wherever you are in the world. This contributes to the Church's universality. The Mass serves as a source of unity, drawing people together across ethnic and geographic lines. It solidifies the reality of our participating in one Church, the Body of Christ.

Difference 3: Communal versus Individual

At Mass, we participate in the re-presentation of Christ's sacrifice. We come together as the Body of Christ, united by the Sacrament of the Eucharist. So, for Catholics, there's no such thing as "worshipping by yourself," at least liturgically. Even a priest saying Mass by himself is united spiritually to all believers across the world, along with the angels and saints in heaven.

For most Protestants, however, worship is centered on the relationship between the individual Christian and Jesus. The presence of people like the pastor or worship leader might uplift them with preaching, teaching, and praiseful song, but the service is meant to cultivate the individual's connection to God. Of course, Catholics also place a high value on developing a personal relationship with Jesus, but the Mass never prioritizes this individual experience; the Mass is fundamentally communal, pulling us out of ourselves and into the full Body of Christ.

Difference 4: Initiated versus Seekers

Many Protestant and nondenominational churches aim at drawing people not fully committed to the Lord, who are typically called "seekers" or the "uninitiated." They create a welcoming atmosphere for their services with lively music, no dress code, coffee bars, and engaging greeters. They want to make their church as attractive as possible to non-Christians since their Sunday service is the main entry point to faith.

However, the Catholic Mass does not aim to attract seekers or the uninitiated. Mass is not the starting point for Catholic evangelization. It's the finish line where you want someone to end up. The Church does not usually encourage us to bring to Mass people who have no religious background, as they are unlikely to understand or appreciate what is going on (and, of course, they aren't able to receive Communion, which can seem off-putting to some). A parish event, an information session, or the OCIA process are typically much better opportunities for inviting family, friends, and neighbors to church. They function as better points of entry into the Catholic Church.[5]

Further Study and Reflection

- Record a five- to seven-minute conversation with a Protestant classmate in which the two of you describe what happens at Catholic Mass and Protestant worship service and why each part is meaningful to you.
- What are the basic elements of Jewish and Muslim worship? Write a brief description of each.
- Research why the relics of saints are often placed in Catholic altars. Find out if the relics of a saint are placed in the altar at a local parish. If so, which saint?

Sick, Confirmation, and Penance would no longer be sacraments or would be done away with completely. There would be no ordained, celibate priesthood separate from the laity. The bread and wine were not truly transformed into the Body and Blood of Jesus in the Eucharist, and so the liturgy was not a renewal of Christ's sacrifice on Calvary but instead a communal meal and an opportunity to hear the Word of God. Many practices associated with Catholicism that were believed to not have roots in Scripture were shunned or at least diminished in importance, for example, the use of sacramentals such as rosaries, crucifixes, holy water, and statues; veneration of Mary and other saints; prayers for the dead (the souls in Purgatory); and the hierarchical structure of the Church (bishops and the pope).

While this schema describes the main points of difference between Protestants and Catholics, there are variations among Protestant traditions on many of these matters. Protestants in the Reformed (Calvinist) stream reject the Catholic doctrine of **transubstantiation**, which holds that the bread and wine are transformed into the Body and Blood of Christ; for them, the bread and wine were merely symbols of Christ's presence. However, Lutherans believe that Jesus did become present in the bread and wine in some sense, though leave open exactly how to define that presence. Some varieties of Angli-

cans (who are known as "High Church" or "Anglo-Catholic") hold to "consubstantiation," whereby Jesus became truly present in the elements of the Eucharist, but the bread and wine were still present as well.

Most Protestants continued to see Baptism as a sacrament and to practice it in a way that was largely consistent with the Catholic rite. The Catholic Church defines the essential elements of Baptism as the use of water and the Trinitarian formula (in the Latin Church: "I baptize you in the name of the Father and of the Son and of the Holy

---

transubstantiation Church teaching that holds that the substance of the bread and wine is changed into the substance of the Body and Blood of Christ at the consecration at Mass.

Spirit"), with the minister's intention to "do what the Church does when she baptizes" (*CCC*, 1256). While Protestant ecclesial communities differ in the timing and details of Baptism, most of them use this same basic formula. Because of this, the Catholic Church does not "rebaptize" Christians who have already received that sacrament in their non-Catholic community. Instead, if they choose to become Catholic, they make a profession of faith in Catholicism and then receive additional sacraments as necessary (Confirmation and First Holy Communion). Faith traditions that identify as Christian but do not practice Baptism according to this norm are exceptions to this rule. Two examples are the Church of Jesus Christ of Latter-Day Saints (Mormons) and the Religious Society of Friends (Quakers).

While Protestant reformers were trying to solve the Church's problems by introducing changes to Catholic doctrine and liturgy, other reformers sought to change the bad practices that had developed in Catholicism while remaining faithful to the tradition and authority of the Church.

SECTION Assessment

Comprehension

1. What was likely Frederick III's motivation for siding with Martin Luther?

2. Which Protestant tradition did the Puritans who settled in America descend from?

3. What incident led to Henry VIII's starting his own church in England?

4. Differentiate between the three *solas*: *sola scriptura*, *sola gratia*, and *sola fide*.

5. Why doesn't the Church rebaptize most Christians who wish to become Catholic?

Vocabulary

6. How is the Church's understanding of *transubstantia-tion* different from the Church of England's definition of consubstantiation?

Reflection

7. Think about someone you know who left the Catholic Church. Why did he or she do so? Next, think of someone you know who entered the Catholic Church as an adult. Why did he or she do so?

THE CHURCH REAFFIRMS HER UNITY AT THE COUNCIL OF TRENT

Section 1 painted a pretty grim picture of the Church at the time of the Protestant Reformation, but the good news is that the Church had the resources to solve her problems. As the story of the renewal and reformation of the Benedictine order demonstrates, it is possible to call fellow Catholics to turn away from sin and recommit to holiness. Another religious who inspired the Church to reform was St. Teresa of Ávila, who helped reinvigorate the Carmelite order. These focused reforms of religious communities helped to model larger reforms that would take place in the Church as a whole.

The Church never wavers as the Bride of Christ, and the key to her reform is to return in faith to the Bridegroom. The first step of reform for either the Church as a whole or her individual members is to recognize our weakness. "All members of the Church, including her ministers, must acknowledge that they are sinners" (*CCC*, 827). Spurred by the challenges posed by Luther, Calvin, and Henry VIII, the Church convoked an ecumenical council that would address abuses but more importantly would clarify the meaning of authentic Church teachings.

The obstacles to such a council were significant. When Pope Paul III initially proposed a council in 1537, he intended for Protestant reformers to participate, but they refused. Political and military conflicts in some nations made it impossible for some bishops to attend. Then there was disagreement about where the gathering should take place, as various cities vied for the income and influence that would accrue from hosting the event. Finally, a sufficient number of prelates came together in the northern Italian city of Trent on December 13, 1545, and the council could be opened. Even so, the council was interrupted and moved on several occasions due to outbreaks of disease, deaths of popes, and conflicts between popes and secular rulers, but it persevered and eventually accomplished its intended business. For a period of eighteen years (1545–1563), meeting off and on over the course of twenty-five sessions, bishops and other council fathers clarified Catholic doctrine, outlawed corrupt practices, and exhorted clergy and laity to genuine faith and devotion.

The Council of Trent had an immediate and lasting impact on the character of the Catholic Church and her relationship with the world. On doctrinal matters, the council clearly articulated the Catholic position in contrast to the Protestant *solas*. Against *sola scriptura*, it taught that both Sacred Scripture *and* Sacred Tradition were sources of Divine Revelation. Sacred Tradition, the truths of the faith handed down through the oral or written teachings of the Church outside the Bible, was a sure source of truth, just like Sacred Scripture.

> *In this universe, shaped by open and intercommunicating systems, we can discern countless forms of relationship and participation. This leads us to think of the whole as open to God's transcendence, within which it develops.* **Faith allows us to interpret the meaning and the mysterious beauty of what is unfolding.** *We are free to apply our intelligence towards things evolving positively, or towards adding new ills, new causes of suffering and real setbacks.* **This is what makes for the excitement and drama of human history, in which freedom, growth, salvation and love can blossom, or lead towards decadence and mutual destruction.**
>
> **Pope Francis (Laudato Si', 79)**

As Henry Graham (see Chapter 3, Section 4) pointed out, this position makes sense because the Church predated the writing of the New Testament. The teachings of Christ had to be passed on through some means other than the Scriptures in the early years of the Church, so there had to be some authority independent of the Bible that could interpret the Bible and settle disputes about its meaning. In recent times, Pope Francis explained that Sacred Tradition is, like a tree, deeply rooted but also growing. The teaching of the Church must always be in accord with the truths of the Gospel, but that doesn't mean it is stagnant. "Christianity," Pope Francis said, "in fidelity to its own identity and the rich deposit of truth which it has received from Jesus Christ, continues to reflect [on issues] in fruitful dialogue with changing historical situations. In doing so, it reveals its eternal newness" (*Laudato Si'*, 121).

Against *sola gratia* and *sola fide*, the council affirmed that *both* faith and works are necessary in the life of the Christian. The bishops found this view to be consistent with Scripture, citing the assertion in the Letter of James that "faith without works is useless" (Jas 2:20). While the grace of God is indispensable, the believer must willingly cooperate with it. Salvation *is* dependent on God's grace, but human beings have free will and can reject or accept the gift of salvation. Similarly, justification and sanctification come about through the power of the Holy Spirit, but we participate in the process by taking actions that express and reinforce our faith: prayer, acts of charity toward others, and fulfilling our daily duties in work and family life.

The Council of Trent also reaffirmed sacramental theology, enumerating the Seven Sacraments and defending them against Protestant critiques. It formalized the definition of transubstantiation.[∞] It reiterated that Holy Orders

∞ Note

Chapter 4, Session 13 states: "And because that Christ, our Redeemer, declared that which He offered under the species of bread to be truly His own body, therefore has it ever been a firm belief in the Church of God, and this holy Synod doth now declare it anew, that, by the consecration of the bread and of the wine, a conversion is made of the whole substance of the bread into the substance of the body of Christ our Lord, and of the whole substance of the wine into the substance of His blood; which conversion is, by the holy Catholic Church, suitably and properly called Transubstantiation" (https://history.hanover.edu/texts/trent/ct13.html).

St. Teresa
OF ÁVILA

Teresa was a pretty and popular young woman from a wealthy Spanish family, the de Cepedas. Born in 1515, she wanted to follow God's will and pursued the life of a consecrated religious, but she was not fully committed to giving up her own comforts for the sake of true holiness. The Carmelite convent she entered was lax, and most sisters participated more energetically in the social life it provided than in the prayer life that was supposed to be at the center of their day. According to one description of religious communities in Teresa's sixteenth-century Spain, "Those who wanted an easy and sheltered life without responsibilities could find it in a convent."[6] Teresa figured that all her needs would be provided for, and she could enjoy fine food, comfortable lodging, and the pleasant companionship of her sisters—without the hassles of marriage and children.

Gradually, however, Teresa's spiritual life grew more intense. In intimate conversations with God in prayer, Teresa came to see herself truly as his bride and recognized that seeking perfection meant more than an easy, pleasant life. She began practicing various kinds of penance, including *fasting* (refraining from food for long periods) and depriving herself of material comforts, such as a soft bed. She also devoted herself to prayer, sometimes spending hours at a time contemplating the goodness and love of God. With her spiritual life in order, she brought her renewed love for Christ to bear on the world by undertaking the reform of her religious order.

St. Teresa of Ávila is recognized today as one of the great figures of the Catholic Reformation. To reform the genuine purpose of the Carmelite order, Teresa founded a new convent of Carmelite nuns that enforced the rules of the order more strictly. She inspired others, including Carmelite men such as St. John of the Cross, to reform their own religious houses as well. Teresa faced severe opposition at times, often from fellow Carmelites and others in the Church, but she forged ahead with confidence that the reform she championed was the way God was calling her to be faithful to and serve the Church. She also hoped that the reform of the Carmelites would serve as a model of reform in the Church at large.

St. Teresa of Ávila also inspired individuals in her time and through today to reform their personal lives. In her classic text on contemplative prayer, *The Interior Castle*, she used the image of a castle with seven levels to describe the journey of a soul ever deeper into God's presence. For a person who pursues a relationship with God to the utmost and who is given the grace to achieve it, the result is "spiritual marriage," a complete union with God. For Teresa, as for all the saints, love was the central message and goal of the Christian life. "The Lord doesn't look so much at the greatness of our works," she declared, "as at the love with which they are done."[7] For her insights into prayer and the mystical life of the soul, Teresa has been named a *Doctor of the Church*, a designation bestowed by the pope on saints who have made major contributions to theological understanding.

confers an indelible mark on the soul of the priest, creating a sacred priesthood that is distinct from the analogous priesthood of all believers. In response to the contrary claims of the Protestant reformers, the council held that Matrimony, like all the other sacraments, was, in fact, instituted by Christ and rooted in Scripture. It defined marriage between Christians as a sacred covenant, an indissoluble bond that is to be exclusive and lifelong. It identified the origin of marriage as a natural institution in the account of Adam and Eve in the Book of Genesis, which states that "a man leaves his father and mother and clings to his wife, and the two of them become one body" (Gn 2:24). Jesus reinforced this idea and affirmed the sanctity of marriage in the New Covenant when he said of husbands and wives that "they are no longer two, but one flesh. Therefore, what God has joined together, no human being must separate" (Mt 19:6). On the strength of the testimony of Scripture and Tradition, the council concluded that Matrimony "is to be numbered amongst the sacraments of the new law."[8]

On matters of Church discipline, the council attacked the widespread practices that led to corruption. It prohibited the selling of indulgences. It did away with pluralism and absenteeism, restricting a bishop to a single diocese and ordering him to reside there. It condemned simony and nepotism. Moving beyond prohibitions, it sought to foster the conditions for well-trained and holy priests by mandating that all dioceses create seminaries for the proper formation of candidates for the priesthood. It also required that all priests report directly to a bishop or other superior. These reforms were designed to ensure that the scandals of immorality (such as living with concubines) and faulty theology (such as Johann Tetzel's preaching on indulgences) would be eliminated as much as possible from among the Catholic clergy.

Being made up of sinners, the Church will always be in need of reform. The Church, "at the same time holy and always in need of being purified, always follows the way of penance and renewal" (*Lumen Gentium*, 8). Conversion away from sin and back toward Christ is "an uninterrupted task for the whole Church" (*CCC*, 1428). The Council of Trent was one important example of Church reformers blazing a "way of penance and renewal" during the difficult period of the Protestant Reformation.

The Aftermath of the Reformation

At the Council of Trent, many Church leaders still hoped that unity could be restored. As the Protestant communities grew and spread over the course of the sixteenth and seventeenth centuries, however, it became clear that Protestantism was here to stay and that the Catholic Church would need to come to an understanding of how non-Catholic Christians could be part of the *one* Church, the Body of Christ.

The Church's dedication to unity explains why the Protestant Reformation was seen as a threat to the mission of the Church and why it quickly gave rise to a terrible political conflict. As Lutherans, Calvinists, and Anglicans grew in membership throughout Europe, Protestant rulers vied with Catholic rulers for supremacy across the continent. In many places, religious loyalty and political loyalty became inextricably bound together, that is, to be a "good Spaniard" was to be Catholic, while to be a "good Englishman" was to be Anglican.

This situation ignited numerous wars of religion for over a century following the Reformation. Religion became the excuse for violence that really stemmed from other causes. Atrocities occurred on both sides. In France, Catholic mobs attacked and killed thousands of Protestants in what became known as the St. Bartholomew's Day Massacre (1572).[∞] In England, under Queen Elizabeth I (ruled 1558–1603) and subsequent monarchs, the public practice of Catholicism was outlawed, and priests were hunted down and killed. One such priest was St. Ambrose Barlow, whose execution gave rise to the legend of Wardley Hall.

Eventually, Protestants and Catholics both recognized that unending conflict was not a satisfactory solution to religious differences. After an initial but

∞ Note

The violence began in Paris early on the feast day of St. Bartholomew (August 24) with the assassination of Protestant leaders who were gathered—ironically—for the marriage of a Protestant nobleman with the king's Catholic sister, which was intended to promote peace between Protestants and Catholics in France. Catholics in Paris and then throughout France began attacking non-Catholics, and killings continued for several months. The violence stemmed from a variety of political, cultural, and religious factors, and historians continue to debate many of the details of the event, such as whether it was deliberately orchestrated and how many people died. It is nonetheless widely agreed to be "the most notorious episode in sixteenth-century Europe's civil and religious wars." See Barbara B. Diefendorf, *The Saint Bartholomew's Day Massacre: A Brief History with Documents* (Boston: Bedford/St. Martin's, 2009).

The Legend of WARDLEY HALL

Wardley Hall is a historic manor house in northwestern England. In 1745, while it was undergoing renovation, its owner found what appeared to be a treasure chest hidden in the walls. He broke it open and discovered a human skull.

In the early seventeenth century, the owners of Wardley Hall had been the Downes family, who were related to the family of St. Ambrose Barlow and at whose home Fr. Barlow sometimes said Mass. During the time when Catholicism was prohibited, priests would sneak from one Catholic household to another, offering sacraments and, when necessary, hiding in *priest holes*, secret places constructed in many English homes of the period.∞

Persecution of Catholics had eased during the reign of King Charles I, but in the 1640s tension between Anglicans and Catholics again worsened. On Easter Sunday of 1641, a mob led by an Anglican pastor accosted Fr. Barlow

The skull of martyred Benedictine St. Ambrose Barlow is kept in a special through-wall casing, that it may be seen from the stairs and from the hall reception room in Wardley Hall.

∞ Note

A Jesuit brother, Nicholas Owen, was a specialist in constructing priest holes; some of his ingenious hiding places can still be seen today in old English manor houses.

after he had finished saying Mass at a nearby estate. Barlow was convicted of treason and executed, and his head was displayed on a pike as a public warning to other Catholics.

The Downes family obtained this relic of Fr. Barlow and hid it in their house. Over the next hundred years the property changed hands, and the skull was forgotten, until it was rediscovered during the renovation of 1745. Speculation on the skull's origin and eerie stories about happenings surrounding it continued into the late twentieth century, at which time scientific and historical research concluded with reasonable certainty that the skull was in fact that of St. Ambrose Barlow, who was canonized by Pope Paul VI in 1970 as one of the Forty Martyrs of England and Wales. Wardley Hall is now the residence of the bishop of the Roman Catholic Diocese of Salford, and the "Skull of Wardley Hall" remains on display there, a testament to the bitter religious conflict that roiled Europe in the post-Reformation period.[9]

short-lived attempt at a truce in the **Peace of Augsburg**, the **Peace of Westphalia** settled on a compromise that would minimize conflict. It established the principle of "his reign, his religion," meaning that the ruler of a given territory would decide on the religion of that territory. Citizens of that country could either accept the faith of the ruler or move elsewhere. The idea of religious pluralism—that people of different faiths could live together in the same place—was not yet comprehensible to most people. National and religious loyalty were too closely tied to allow for a distinction between the two. The notion that both a Catholic and a Lutheran could be loyal Germans at the same time seemed unimaginable.

Remember, however, that discord in the Church was not new: the Church had long understood Eastern Churches (Orthodox, Coptic, etc.) to be in "imperfect communion" with the Church of Rome, but the Protestant movement presented a greater challenge. The Eastern Churches had preserved many of the essential elements of Christian unity: belief in the Real Presence in the Eucharist, an ordained priesthood, and apostolic succession (bishops). As Reformation belief and practice evolved, most Protestants came to reject most of these elements, even as they preserved other essential beliefs, such as the Trinity, the Incarnation, and the saving action of Jesus's Death and Resurrection.

All Who Are Saved Are Connected with the Church

At the Council of Trent and afterward, the Catholic Church gradually developed concepts and language to deal with the spread of Protestantism and to promote the unity, in varying degrees, of all people with the Church. The Church continues to affirm the fullness of Christ's presence and the means of salvation *in the Catholic Church*. All people are called to belong to the Church of Christ; it is not an exclusive club open to a privileged few.

Peace of Augsburg A treaty between the Catholic Holy Roman emperor and an alliance of Lutheran princes that the leader (whether a prince or a king) of each region of Germany could choose either the Catholic faith or the Lutheran faith as the one official religion for his area of political control. A Catholic bishop who converted to Lutheranism had to give up his property. Those who did not want to participate in the religion of the region were expected to migrate to an area where their religion was practiced.

Peace of Westphalia A series of treaties that ended the Thirty Years' War between Catholics and Protestants in Germany, legalized Calvinism in Germany, and gave Protestantism equal status with Catholicism.

In the reality of a large, diverse, and sometimes messy world, however, not all accept or even hear that call in the same way. The Second Vatican Council, held from 1962 to 1965, declared that "those also can attain to salvation who through no fault of their own do not know the Gospel of Christ or His Church, yet sincerely seek God and moved by grace strive by their deeds to do His will as it is known to them through the dictates of their conscience" (*Lumen Gentium*, 16). Thus, all those who are saved are saved *through the Church and through the saving action of Jesus Christ*, but not all the saved are *visibly* members of the Church. In accord with his plan and in ways often mysterious to us, God offers everyone the possibility of salvation.

There are therefore various degrees of communion with the Church. Some believers are "fully incorporated in the society of the Church"; they are those who "accept her entire system and all the means of salvation given to her, and are united with her as part of her visible bodily structure and through her with Christ, who rules her through the Supreme Pontiff and the bishops. The bonds which bind men to the Church in a visible way are profession of faith, the sacraments, and ecclesiastical government and communion" (*Lumen Gentium*, 14). If you are a baptized and "practicing" Catholic—one who goes to church and receives the sacraments regularly and recognizes the authority of the Magisterium—then you fit into this category.

However, the Church is also "joined in many ways to the baptized who are honored by the name of Christian, but do not profess the Catholic faith in its entirety or have not preserved unity or communion under the successor of Peter" (*LG*, 15; *CCC*, 838). Those "who believe in Christ and have been properly baptized are put in a certain, although imperfect, communion with the Catholic Church" (*UR*, 3; *CCC*, 838). Non-Catholic Christians such as Episcopalians, Presbyterians, Lutherans, Baptists, Methodists, and nondenominational evangelicals are in this kind of relationship with the Church. This understanding also allows for the vast diversity of the Protestant traditions: the more closely a Christian's belief and practice align with what the Catholic Church holds, the more intimate is the communion of that believer with the Church.

Although tension between Catholics and Protestants has persisted in various ways ever since the Reformation, the violent conflict that characterized the sixteenth century has largely disappeared. In an increasingly secular world, Christians of various traditions—Catholic, Protestant, and Orthodox—have increasingly come to see each other as allies rather than enemies. The doctrinal and liturgical differences among the Christian groups are still important, but all have agreed to debate and resolve those disagreements by peaceful means. Within this environment of mutual respect, the unity of the Church remains a priority, and Catholics continue to work toward unity and to pray, in the words of Christ, "that they may all be one" (Jn 17:21).

SECTION Assessment

Comprehension

1. What is the first step of reform for the Church and her individual members?

2. Why did it take so long for the Council of Trent to begin?

3. How did the Council of Trent respond to *sola scriptura*?

4. How did the Council of Trent respond to *sola gratia* and *sola fide*?

5. What is evidence that Matrimony is one of the sacraments?

6. Why did the council create diocesan seminaries?

7. What was a "priest hole"?

8. Explain the image of a castle in St. Teresa of Ávila's *The Interior Castle*.

Vocabulary

9. Differentiate between the *Peace of Augsburg* and the *Peace of Westphalia*.

Reflection

10. In your own words, explain how the Church holds that all people who are saved are part of the unity of the Catholic Church.

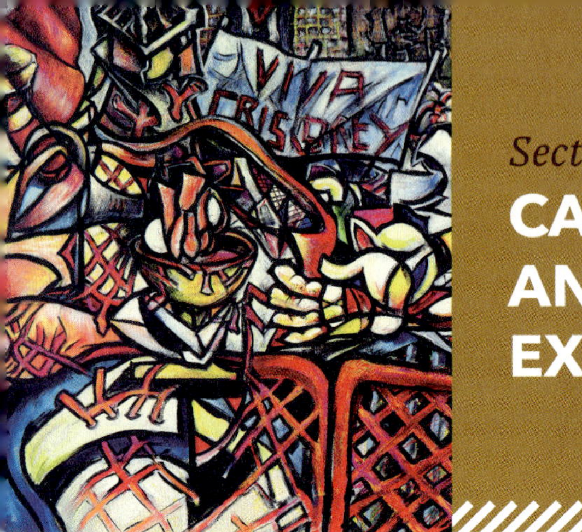

Section 4
CATHOLICITY AND THE AGE OF EXPLORATION

The desire to extend the boundaries of the Church to people in new lands can be seen as a manifestation of the third mark of the Church: *catholic*. The word *catholic* means "universal" as well as "total" or "whole." The Church is catholic in both of these senses. The Church is whole because she possesses the "fullness of the means of salvation" (*Unitatis Redintegratio*, 3). Because the Church is the Bride of Christ, totally united to him, there is nothing lacking in the Church's spiritual life. As noted earlier, the marks of the Church are closely related; the catholicity and the unity of the Church are as two sides of the same coin. "In the beginning God made human nature one and decreed that all His children, scattered as they were, would finally be gathered together as one" (*Lumen Gentium*, 13).

The Church is also catholic in the sense of universal: "sent out by Christ on a mission to the whole of the human race" (*CCC*, 831). While this catholicity has been present throughout the Church's existence, in the sixteenth and seventeenth centuries the Church began truly to realize its potential as a *catholic* Church, extending herself across the entire world and encompassing "all nations." The "character of universality [catholicity] which adorns the People of God is a gift from the Lord himself whereby the Catholic Church ceaselessly and efficaciously seeks for the return of all humanity and all its goods, under Christ the Head in the unity of his Spirit" (*LG*, 13; *CCC*, 831). The spread of the Church around the world in the Age of Exploration was truly a project of evangelization.

Jesuit Missionaries of the Sixteenth and Seventeenth Centuries

Twenty-five years before Martin Luther posted his challenge to Johann Tetzel, the Spanish Empire sponsored the expedition of Christopher Columbus to explore the far western reaches of the Atlantic Ocean. Soon European explorers, conquerors, and colonists would be traversing the "new worlds" of the Americas, Africa, and Asia, generating cultural encounters that would too often be characterized by misunderstanding and violence, but that also sometimes showed the potential for fruitful cooperation in the creation of new cultures and new nations. It was also an opportunity to preach the Gospel in regions previously untouched by the message of Jesus. Through her missionaries, the Church was an important part of this age of exploration. The new Society of Jesus, also known as the Jesuits, was at the forefront of this period's missionary efforts.∞

St. Francis Xavier, one of the first Jesuits, arrived in India in 1542. Although there were a few Christians there—a community that traced its origins to the preaching of the Apostle St. Thomas in the first century—the large and populous Indian subcontinent was dominated by Muslim and Hindu influence. St. Francis began working in the Portuguese colony of Goa, then ventured further into southern India, converting and baptizing thousands of native Indians into the Catholic faith. Francis went on to southeast Asia, evangelizing the people of the Malay Peninsula and various islands near Indonesia. In 1549, he entered Japan, a kingdom that had resisted European influence. Overcoming many obstacles and risking his life, he was finally granted permission by the emperor to present the teachings of Jesus to the Japanese people. The Japanese church that Francis established would endure through centuries of persecution.

In the 1550s, another Jesuit, St. José de Anchieta, was sent to the Portuguese colony of Brazil. Like many other Jesuits, he was a talented student. Despite chronic back pain, he labored for forty-four years among the native

∞ Note

St. Ignatius of Loyola, a Basque knight whose career was ended by a leg wound, read and meditated on the life of Jesus and the lives of the saints during a lengthy period of recovery. From this experience, he composed in 1523 the *Spiritual Exercises*, a classic work on Christian reflection. Then, during a ten-year period of schooling at the University of Paris, Ignatius gathered around him a "company" or "society" of six companions, including St. Francis Xavier and St. Peter Faber, who took the traditional vows of poverty, chastity, and obedience along with a fourth vow—loyalty to the pope—as a sign of their commitment to fight against Protestantism. This Society of Jesus became the Jesuits. Known today for their educational efforts, the Jesuits began as a vigorous missionary order that brought the faith to the New World and to the Far East.

people of Brazil, learning their language and teaching them about the faith, often through poems he wrote. He also wrote and directed many religious plays, which were performed in the Brazilian jungle. Using his knowledge of medicine, he tended the people's wounds and illnesses, and learned about the medicinal benefits of several native plants. Anchieta is also counted among the founders of Brazil's two largest cities, São Paulo and Rio de Janeiro.

Statue of José de Anchieta in Santos City, Brazil.

In 1601, a third Jesuit, Matteo Ricci, became the first European to enter the "Forbidden City" of Beijing, the capital of the mighty but isolated Chinese Empire. Ricci gained the emperor's favor by sharing the insights of European intellectual and technological advances. Ricci was highly trained in geography and astronomy, and he impressed the Chinese with his knowledge, not to mention his navigational and astronomical devices. By taking on local customs such as dressing as a member of the Chinese elite rather than as an Italian priest and by expressing Christian concepts in terminology that was more familiar in Eastern religion and philosophy, he was able to gain a sympathetic hearing. Ricci thereby laid the groundwork for other missionaries who would gradually build a small Chinese Catholic community.

In 1636, St. Isaac Jogues, inspired by the stories recounted by Jesuit missionaries returning to France from their work among the indigenous peoples of North America, decided to dedicate his life to preaching the Gospel in what is now the Great Lakes region of Canada and upstate New York. While learning native culture and language among the friendly Hurons, Jogues was captured by a band of hostile Mohawks, who savagely beat and tortured him and other prisoners. One of Jogues's Jesuit colleagues was killed. Jogues survived, escaped, and returned to France, but he was now determined to bring Christianity to the Mohawk people. He returned to North America, where

The tapestry of St. Kateri Tekakwitha hung on St. Peter's Basilica during a special Mass to name seven new saints in St. Peter's Square on October 21, 2012. Four Apache women from New Mexico attended the canonization.

he was initially well received by his former captors and was able to negotiate a peace between the French and the Iroquois, the confederation to which the Mohawks belonged. When he visited the same village again a while later, however, the Mohawks blamed the priest for the disease and famine that had afflicted them. They beheaded him and his companion, but Jogues and other missionaries had planted seeds of faith. Ten years after the Jesuits' martyrdoms, Kateri Tekakwitha was born in the same village where they had been killed. Known as the "Lily of the Mohawks," St. Kateri became the first Native American canonized saint in the Catholic Church.

In China, Japan, India, Brazil, Canada, and many other places, Catholic missionaries in the sixteenth and seventeenth centuries faced physical and mental hardship, learned difficult new languages and customs, and suffered material deprivation, imprisonment, and sometimes death in order to fulfill Christ's Great Commission to "go, . . . make disciples of all nations" (Mt 28:19).

The Mission of Evangelization

Making disciples of all nations is the goal of the Church's mission of evangelization, and those who dedicate themselves to this goal are *missionaries* or *evangelists*. To evangelize, in the literal meaning of its Greek roots, is to "announce good news." Those who evangelize are sharing the Good News of salvation through Jesus Christ with those they encounter. The task of evangelization falls in a particular way to the successors of the Apostles, the bishops, along with priests and deacons, to whom was entrusted the "duty of completing and consolidating the work [the Apostles] had begun" (*LG*, 20; *CCC*, 861) and also falls under the apostolic mark of the Church. Yet all Catholics are called to participate in the Church's mission of evangelization, "the proclamation of Christ by word and the testimony of life" (*LG*, 35; *CCC*, 905).

In fact, recent popes have spoken of the *new evangelization* or *re-evangelization*, sharing the faith with those who have stopped practicing it, either by their own choice or by being prohibited to do so by an authoritative government, as required of all Catholics. In 2010, Pope Benedict XVI extended the charge for the new evangelization by creating the Pontifical Council for Promoting the New Evangelization. This council's task was to teach and promote ways to evangelize

Two volunteers with a Catholic Charities Disaster Relief Team give aid to arriving refugees at the reception hall of Sacred Heart Catholic Church in McAllen, Texas.

in a world that is openly hostile to the Gospel of Jesus Christ, the Church, and religion itself. Indeed, when nations easily choose war as the preferred means for addressing conflicts, when they ignore the plight of the poor in their midst, when they shuffle the elderly and disabled into the margins of society, and when they treat pregnancies as inconveniences easily snuffed out through abortion, it is the entire culture that is in need of evangelization. "In the deserts of the secularized world, man's soul thirsts for God, for the living God," Pope Benedict said, shortly before he announced the establishment of the council.

Pope Francis has also spoken about those leaving the Catholic Church—in Latin America and elsewhere—and how the Church can help them find their way back to the faith: "Instead of being just a church that welcomes and receives by keeping the doors open, let us try also to be a church that finds new roads, that is able to step outside itself and go to those who do not attend Mass, to those who have quit or are indifferent. The ones who quit sometimes do it for reasons that, if properly understood and assessed, can lead to a return. But that takes audacity and courage."[10] In other words, re-evangelization requires more than a welcoming spirit; it requires action. It requires evangelizers who will go to those who have wandered away from the Church and minister to them with warmth and mercy.

The Catholic Church in the United States has not been immune to a decline among those who actively participate in the sacraments and Church life, but recent years have brought some positive trends. For example, not only has the influx of immigrants from Latin America offset the loss of Catholics who have fallen away, but in many parts of the country their participation has reinvigorated the Church. Archdioceses and dioceses in the United States with large Latin American and other immigrant populations have focused more attention on these new Americans through such initiatives as

> offering comprehensive social services and referrals to the proper local agencies;

> advocating politically for immigrant rights; and

> recruiting seminarians from among the immigrants.

However, even the once hopeful prospect of the US Church's maintaining membership through the influx of new Latinos is now at risk. A 2023 Pew Research study found that while 43 percent of Latino adults in the United States identify as Catholics, this number is down from 67 percent in 2010.[11]

Pope John Paul II also spoke and wrote often of evangelization as a task of ongoing missionary work with a diversity of actions and audiences. The first type of evangelization, he explained in his pastoral letter *Redemptoris Missio* (*Mission of the Redeemer*), occurs in situations where the Gospel is not known at all. In those instances, the Gospel must be preached and the Church must set up local churches to accompany the preaching. The second kind of evangelization occurs in those local communities where the Church is already established and practiced. Missionary and evangelization efforts to these Catholics demand pastoral care with training to teach them to be evangelists themselves. Third are places where the "baptized have lost a living sense of the faith, or even no longer consider themselves members of the Church, and live a life far removed from Christ and his Gospel. In this case what is needed is a 'new evangelization' or a 're-evangelization'" (*Redemptoris Missio*, 33).

The Church's missionary efforts springing from Jesus's charge to "make disciples of all nations" (Mt 28:19) require that the Gospel be preached to all people in all lands and in all times. This requires that evangelization involve preaching to non-Catholics, non-Christians, and people with no religion at all. However, in some ways "preach" is a misnomer. The Church's best efforts at evangelization of people who have not heard or have not accepted the Gospel are through *dialogue*.

Pope Paul VI explained in his first encyclical, *Ecclesiam Suam* (*His Church*), that "the Church must enter into dialogue with the world in which it lives. It has something to say, a message to give, a communication to make" (65). The work of evangelization does center on dialogue, but as the Congregation of the Faith noted in its 2000 declaration *Dominus Iesus* (*The Lord Jesus*), it must at the same time recognize that "*objectively speaking*, they [followers of other religions] are in a gravely deficient situation in comparison with those who, in the Church, have the fullness of the means of salvation" (22). This situation demands a much deeper level of dialogue, a level the Pontifical Council for Inter-Religious Dialogue in 1991 explained reaches deep into a person's spirit (see *Dialogue and Proclamation*, 40).

Refugees from Ukraine take shelter with Dominican friars in Krakow, Poland.

In the work of evangelization, other potential dialogue partners with the Church include politicians, artists, and intellectuals from other religious faiths. The Catholic side of the dialogue represents the Church as both a human and a divine institution. When the Church speaks, she speaks out for truth and against sinfulness. Dialogue is never understood as fulfilling the Church's obligation to evangelize by sharing the conviction that salvation comes through Jesus Christ and in the Church he established.

Improving on the sixteenth and seventeenth centuries' missionary and evangelization efforts into new worlds, the Church's extension today into every part of the world does not eliminate diversity of language, custom, and culture but instead incorporates that diversity into the Body of Christ. "In the mind of the Lord the Church is universal by vocation and mission, but when she puts down her roots in a variety of cultural, social and human terrains, she takes on different external expressions and appearances in each part of the world" (*Evangelii Nuntiandi*, 62). Catholicity does not suppress legitimate difference, but is instead intended to bring unity that includes the diversity.

SECTION *Assessment*

Comprehension

1. How are the marks of Church unity and catholicity related?

2. What are the origins of the Society of Jesus?

3. Why might St. Francis Xavier have found a Christian community that already existed upon his arrival in India?

4. What were two ways that Matteo Ricci achieved success in his missionary work in China?

5. What motivated St. Isaac Jogues to evangelize the Mohawk tribe?

6. What is the literal meaning of *evangelize*?

7. What does re-evangelization require?

8. What are three types of audiences for evangelization that Pope John Paul II wrote of?

9. How is the influx of Latino immigrants who maintain membership in the Catholic Church in the United States now at risk?

Reflection

10. On a scale of 1 to 10, with 10 being "very interested," how interested are you in becoming a Catholic/Christian missionary? Explain.

11. Write a three-paragraph testimony of your faith.

Section Reviews

Focus Question

How do the marks of unity and catholicity support the Church's missionary efforts? Complete one of the following:

- Research and write down one quotation from Pope Paul III's 1537 apostolic letter *Sublimis Deus* (*On the Enslavement and Evangelization of Indians*) that speaks to the pope's condemnation of the insensitive and often exploitative treatment of the native peoples by Church missionaries.

- Research and write about how the Church would respond to *religious indifferentism*, the opinion that all religions and all ways of expressing one's faith are basically equal or essentially the same. Use the term *subsist* in your answer.

- For non-Catholics: arrange to attend a parish event with one of your classmates (e.g., Sunday Mass, youth group, bazaar). Write a short reflection on the experience, and rate how welcome you felt.

Introduction
Renewing Within and Expanding Worldwide

Review

The sixteenth and seventeenth centuries were times of public renewal and reform for the Church, precipitated in part by the protests of Martin Luther and others against both long-held Church teachings and more recent corruptions. Also, the Church was able to extend her footprint to new areas through the efforts of missionaries who were among a long line of faithful disciples who responded to Christ's Great Commission to preach the Gospel to all people.

Assignment

Write a definition of *indulgence* in your own words based on the *Catechism of the Catholic Church*, 1471.

Section 1
Unity Threatened by Abuses

Review

Unity, one of the four marks of the Church, emanates from the love between the Divine Persons of the Trinity. The Church is modeled on this love as the "family of God." Although the bonds of unity have been tried and tested, there remains only one Church, the way to salvation. This fact does not influence the Church's diversity. She is made up of all kinds of people. Over the centuries the threats to the Church's unity have been dealt with, leading to reforms and "reform within reform," especially modeled by religious communities who effect their own renewals.

Assignment

Read the *Catechism of the Catholic Church*, 813. What does it mean to say that "the Church is one because of her source"?

Section 2
The Protestant Reformation

Review

Luther's protest against the Church branched out to others, and several Protestant ecclesial communities emerged around leaders like John Calvin and Ulrich Zwingli. In England, a large majority of the Church split with King Henry the VIII after his request for divorce and remarriage was denied by the pope. The basic differences between Protestants and the Church can be grouped around the three *solas*: *sola scriptura* (Scripture alone), *sola gratia* (grace alone), and *sola fide* (faith alone), which rejected Sacred Tradition and denied the necessity of a person doing good works to cooperate with God's grace as taught by the Church.

Assignment

Answer the following questions: Who founded the following Protestant communities: Amish, Baptists, Moravian Church? When? Where? Why?

Section 3
The Church Reaffirms Her Unity at the Council of Trent

Review

The Council of Trent had two primary goals: (1) acknowledging and reforming problems related to the clergy and religious life that had been broached in part by the Protestant reformers and (2) clearly stating Church doctrine, especially on matters that had been challenged by the reformers. With history proving that Protestants were not returning to the Church, the Church grappled with understanding and explaining how all people remain part of or subsist in the Catholic Church as a means for their salvation.

Assignment

Locate and cite a reference from the Council of Trent included in the *Catechism of the Catholic Church*. Explain its context in the *Catechism* and what teaching it addresses.

Section 4
Catholicity and the Age of Exploration

Review

The mark of catholicity is represented in two main senses: The Church is whole in that she possesses the "fullness of the means of salvation." The Church is universal in that she is sent by Christ to spread the Gospel to the ends of the earth. Both of these aspects of catholicity were represented in the Age of Exploration as missionaries travelled to bring the fullness of salvation to people who had not previously heard the Gospel. The Jesuits were the most prominent missionaries of the sixteenth and seventeenth centuries. The mark of catholicity is also related to the mark of unity, as the preaching of the Gospel is meant to bind all people together, and to the mark of apostolicity, as evangelization is the Great Commission.

Assignment

Name an example of how the Church currently fulfills her universal mission.

Chapter Projects

Choose and complete at least one of the following projects to assess your understanding of the material in this chapter.

⚙ 1. Sketch Three Catholic Missionaries from Existing Images

In a sketchbook, draw the faces of three Jesuit missionaries who were active from 1500 to 1700. These might include Francis Xavier, Isaac Jogues, Jacques Marquette, Matteo Ricci, Alessandro Valignano, Alexandre de Rhodes, Roberto de Nobili, Jean de Brébeuf, Fermín de Lasuén, Francisco Álvarez, António Vieira, Eusebio Kino, José de Anchieta, or Peter Claver. Use an image of each explorer to model your drawing. Make a sketch in pencil using different leads (e.g., ebony, 2H, 4B) before adding color. On the page facing each sketch, include a one-page biography of the missionary.

⚙ 2. Write and Share a Quiz on the Sixth Session of the Council of Trent

Read the text of the sixth session of the Council of Trent. Write down five teachings of the council related to what is necessary for the justification of the soul. Rework these statements into questions and answers, and print them on flash cards. Give the flash cards to a classmate to study and review. After allowing a sufficient amount of time, video record yourself quizzing the student using the same questions but without the flash cards. Turn in the recording to your teacher.

⚙ 3. Analyze a Decision Based on the Spiritual Exercises of St. Ignatius of Loyola

You can use the *Spiritual Exercises* of St. Ignatius of Loyola to help you make a number of important decisions, such as to drink alcohol or not, to follow your parents' rules or break them, to keep the same group of friends or hang out with a new group, to choose a college prep course of study or a vocational track, to go to Sunday Mass or not, and many more. Choose two important decisions and apply them to a chart like the one below. Follow the directions and complete each box for both decisions.

DECISION	*Name two choices for the decision (as in the examples given above).*
PRAY	*Write a personal prayer for making the right choice.*
LOOK AT ALL SIDES OF THE ISSUE	*Make a list of the pros and cons for each choice. Weigh each side. Consider what people you respect would say about this choice. Also consider what the Church has to say.*
IMAGINE YOUR FINAL CHOICE	*Think about the consequences if you choose the way you think you will. What would your parents say? What would a younger brother or sister think about your choice? If you are uncomfortable with the answer to either of these questions, you may be about to make a wrong choice.*
MAKE YOUR CHOICE AND ACT	*Tell what your choice is and why you made it. If you haven't made the choice, tell what it* will *be.*
EVALUATE YOUR CHOICE	*Does or would this choice bring a feeling of satisfaction or one of regret? Explain why.*

⚙ *4. Note Trends in the Church in America*

Research and summarize trends in diversity in the Catholic Church in America. For example, view the 2016 CARA report "Cultural Diversity in the Catholic Church in the United States" that is available at the United States Conference of Catholic Bishops website (www.usccb.org). Do the following:

- Organize what you consider to be five important categories into a graph, chart, or table. Write one sentence summarizing the data for each category.

- Provide several different ratios that compare information in two columns. For example, priests/parish; high school students/school; Sunday

Mass goers/Catholics; Catholic population/total US population. Compare the ratios over different years.

- Make two columns: Negative Trends and Positive Trends. Include at least three summary points supported by current statistics in each column.

⚙ *5. Analyze and Use Social Media for Evangelization*

How effective is social media for evangelization? Complete the following assignment and answer the questions in a written report:

- Over the course of three days, how many Scripture passages and faith-centered messages are posted on your social media feed?

- Print one of the messages on your feed. Why do you think the person posted this message? How many comments did the message have? How many positive comments? Negative comments?

- What would make you engage with a Scripture passage or faith-centered post? Would it have to be inspirational? Pondering? Related to a current event?

- How does the identity of the person who posted a Scripture passage or faith-centered message impact whether or not you would read and engage with the post?

- Copy and paste what you consider an effective or inspiring social media post on God, faith, or religion. Explain why you find it so.

- Write and post a one-paragraph social media post on faith that you believe would be effective or inspiring for your peer group. Summarize the comments you received about this post.

Faithful Disciple
St. Margaret Mary Alacoque

Living after the Council of Trent and during the time of the Age of Exploration was a seventeenth-century nun of the Visitation order named St. Margaret Mary Alacoque. She is known to this day because of her devotion to the Sacred Heart of Jesus.

Jesus appearing to St. Margaret Mary Alacoque.

Margaret Mary was born in Burgundy, France, the fifth of seven children of a prosperous public servant and his wife. She developed a case of rheumatic fever at the age of ten that kept her confined to bed for about four years, during which she developed a devotion to the *Blessed Sacrament*, that is, to Jesus in the Eucharist, reserved in the tabernacle after Mass. When she vowed that she would enter a convent, she immediately returned to health. Margaret Mary entered the Visitation Convent at Paray-le-Monial. She experienced visions of Christ from the age of twenty. On December 27, 1673, she began to receive a series of visions that lasted over a year.

In these visions, Christ told her that she was his chosen instrument to spread devotion to his Sacred Heart, but not everyone believed she was telling the truth. Her confessor, St. Claude de la Colombière, did believe that her visions were authentic. Margaret Mary finally won her superior over, but she could not convince theologians that the visions were true. When Margaret Mary became the assistant superior of her community, the convent finally began to observe the feast of the Sacred Heart, a devotion that spread to other Visitation convents.

What does devotion to the Sacred Heart of Jesus entail? It is a devotion to the love that God has for us, emblematized by the symbol of the heart. The Sacred Heart of Jesus is a symbol of his divine love, which he shares with the Father and the Holy Spirit. It is also a symbol of the burning love that is infused into Jesus's soul and enriches his human will. St. John, the beloved disciple, reclined at Jesus's side at the Last Supper (see John 13:23) near to his heart. Devotion to the Sacred Heart is practiced in many ways, for example, through attending Mass and receiving Holy Communion on the first Friday of each month, spending time in Eucharistic Adoration, making a **novena** to the Sacred Heart of Jesus, and meditating on images of the Sacred Heart. The Solemnity of the Sacred Heart became a feast on the Church's liturgical calendar in 1856. It is celebrated on the Friday after Corpus Christi Sunday, usually in June.

After Margaret Mary's death in 1690, the Jesuits helped preserve the devotion to the Sacred Heart of Jesus, but it was not officially recognized by the Church until seventy-five years later. In March of 1824, Pope Leo XII pronounced Margaret Mary venerable. When her tomb was opened in 1830, it was discovered that her body was incorrupt (it had not decayed). Pope Pius IX declared her Blessed in 1864. Pope Benedict XV canonized Margaret Mary Alacoque in 1920. Her body now lies in a chapel at Visitation Convent that attracts many pilgrims from around the world.

Comprehension

1. What led to Margaret Mary's devotion to the Blessed Sacrament?
2. What was the relationship between Margaret Mary's illness and her decision to enter the convent?
3. What devotion did Christ want Margaret Mary to promote?

Reflection

Which option for devotion to the Sacred Heart resonates with you the most? Why?

---

novena A set form of prayers for nine consecutive days in preparation for a feast and in petition of a favor from God.

Prayer

St. Ignatius of Loyola wrote this prayer, known as the *Suscipe* (Receive), and suggested it to those who were seeking to follow the will of God. He thought of it as a petition for our ability to love God rather than for God's love for us. It is part of his *Spiritual Exercises*, originally in the fourth week.

Prayer of St. Ignatius

Take, Lord, receive all my liberty, my memory, my understanding, my whole will, all that I have and all that I possess. You gave it all to me, Lord; I give it all back to you. Do with it as you will, according to your good pleasure. Give me your love and your grace; for with this I have all that I need. Amen.

The Church Enters the Modern World

Our Lady of Guadalupe

▶ Alejandro Romero

The image of Our Lady of Guadalupe, revealed on the *tilma* (cloak) of an indigenous man named Juan Diego near Mexico City in 1531, has never been more popular. It is reprinted on candleholders, blankets, and T-shirts. Today, a person might even be able to buy an item marked with the Virgin of Guadalupe at the corner gas station. In Los Angeles, Palestinian and Indian business owners have taken to putting the Virgin of Guadalupe on their walls. One man explained that he does this "to show people that I'm with them . . . that I'm not some foreigner guy." George Valerio, part owner of a barbershop in East Los Angeles, has a spray-painted image of Mary on the side of his store because, he said, it pays homage to his family's Catholic faith and to growing up in the Mexican area of the city.[1]

There are hundreds of wall murals of Our Lady of Guadalupe in the United States, including one on 16th Street in the Pilsen neighborhood of Chicago. This mural was painted by local artist Alejandro Romero when he first arrived in Chicago from Mexico in 1998. Romero went on to become a famous Chicago artist, hosting an art gallery in Pilsen and sponsoring Chicago's only museum of Latin American art. His paintings and murals have a broad reach across the city, including being featured at O'Hare International Airport. He said he painted the mural of Our Lady of Guadalupe to represent his Mexican "culture and roots."

In 2018, with the mural already needing repair, someone spray painted graffiti across it. A local resident, Nancy Quintana, said she was sad and angry when she saw the defacement. Her emotions turned to advocacy, and she contacted Romero, who agreed to do the repair once he was released from the hospital from an illness. Before that could happen, a man Nancy Quintana could only identify as "Tom" had begun the repairs himself. He told her, "Ma'am, I am Catholic, and until you get ahold of the original muralist, I mean no disrespect, but I am going to fix her face until he can get to her." Nancy Quintana pulled a rosary out of her pocket and gave it to the man.[2]

Romero finished the repairs soon after, and the Virgin of Guadalupe mural remains an important part of Pilsen, Chicago, and all of the Americas. Our Lady of Guadalupe is the patron of North, South, and Central America.

If you would like to research the history of the original image of Our Lady of Guadalupe that was given to St. Juan Diego and answer other questions about the apparitions, see Chapter 6 Review, Chapter Project 1.

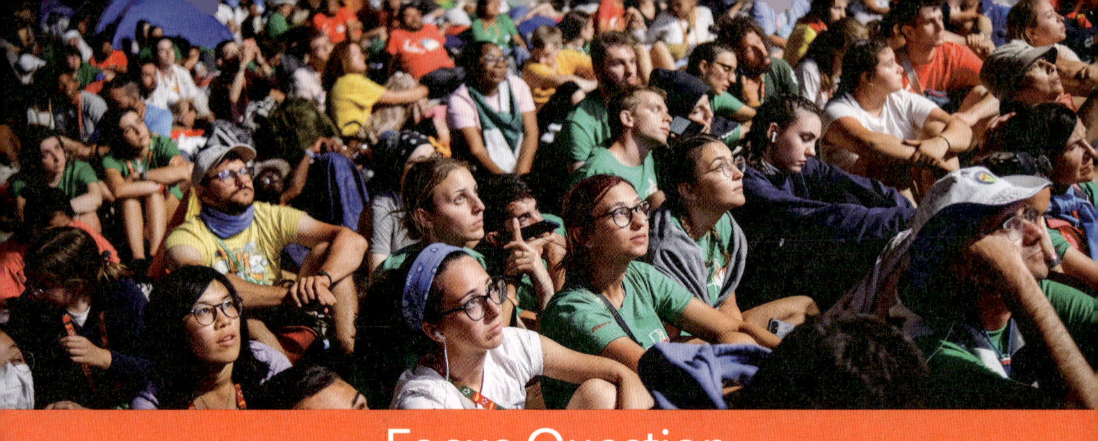

What are common challenges to practicing one's faith in a society hostile to religion?

Introduction
Turmoil and Opportunity Coincide

Section 1
Enlightenment and Revolution

Section 2
Mary: Beacon of Renewal in the Church

Section 3
The Church Balances Individualism and Communion

Section 4
The Church and Religious Freedom

TURMOIL AND OPPORTUNITY COINCIDE

On July 17, 1794, sixteen women were hauled into a public square in Paris. Ranging in age from late teens to mid-eighties, they were Carmelite nuns—members of St. Teresa of Ávila's order—from Compiègne, fifty miles north of the capital. They had been condemned to death for refusing to abandon the religious life that they had vowed to observe. They were interviewed by members of the revolutionary party and allowed to remain in their convent. But when the revolutionaries returned and found letters written by the nuns in support of the monarchy and against the revolution, their fate was sealed.

As the wagon made its way to the site of execution, the nuns sang hymns of praise. While the youngest nun was led to her death, she chanted the opening verses of Psalm 117:

> Praise the LORD, all you nations!
>> Extol him, all you peoples!
> His mercy for us is strong;
>> the faithfulness of the LORD is forever.
> Hallelujah!

When her voice was silenced by the blade of the guillotine, the other nuns took up the song. One by one they were beheaded, until at last the singing ceased. All was silent. The crowd of onlookers, usually boisterous and bloodthirsty, was stunned by the cruelty and senselessness of the murder of this peaceful, harmless group of women. Eleven days later,

At the guillotine the Martyrs of the Carmelites of Compiègne face execution on July 17, 1794.

Maximilien Robespierre, the architect of the **Reign of Terror** that brought the Compiègne Carmelite martyrs and so many other French people to their deaths, would find his own neck submitted to the guillotine.[3]

The French Revolution and the Church

Paris, with its famous university and magnificent Cathedral of Notre Dame (see Chapter 4), became in the late eighteenth century the site of terrible violence. France, the nursery of countless saints, monasteries, popes, and religious orders over the centuries, turned against the Church, confiscated her property, and killed its own native Catholics. The French Revolution began in a spirit of hope with the belief that the abuses of power perpetrated by the aristocratic classes against the common people could be ended and that the rights of all people could be respected. Many priests and bishops originally supported its goals and mission, but the revolution soon took a dark turn as radical, anti-Christian forces gained control of its direction. Instead of establishing justice and equality for all, the revolutionaries used power to perpetuate abuse and violence against targets who were perceived to be the oppressive forces of the past: the royal family, the titled nobility, and the Catholic Church.

The French Revolution was the culmination of rapid changes in the world. After the Middle Ages, the modern nations of Europe gradually took shape and grew powerful. Expansive, militant empires such as Spain, Britain, France, and Austria-Hungary were ruled by monarchs who claimed that they had been appointed by God to exercise absolute power within their realms and to extend their nations across the world. As we have seen from earlier eras, whenever the Church exercised political influence, internal problems such as corruption and lust for power usually followed. But this new situation caused new problems for the Church. As the influence of the Church weakened in the face of increased government power, there were fewer checks on the actions of political officials. Undaunted by the opposition of the Church, monarchs often

---

Reign of Terror A horrific time of persecutions in France that began in September of 1793. Before it ended in July 1794, the king and queen had been beheaded, and thousands of nobles, priests, nuns, and brothers had been executed. Other clergy had to sign a pledge of allegiance to the radical government. Also, the government attempted to set up a state religion, the Christian calendar was replaced by a secular calendar, and Catholic churches were seized and converted into "Temples of Reason" with religious statues replaced with statues of revolutionary philosophers.

In 1793 Notre Dame de Paris was rededicated to the Cult of Reason, and then to the Cult of the Supreme Being. During this time the cathedral was occupied by a mob, who beheaded statues and plundered the treasures of the cathedral.

acted with impunity, which diminished the independence of the institutional Church and the freedom of individual Catholics. Many people felt that they lacked a voice in their own countries, dissatisfaction spread, and revolutions broke out across Europe, beginning with France in 1789.

Eventually, democracy, the political system whereby people have the opportunity to participate in their own governance, spread throughout Europe and across most of the world. By the end of the nineteenth century, most nations were no longer ruled by kings and queens but politicians put into power by popular elections.

The Catholic Church was caught in the midst of this turmoil. At times, as exemplified in France, the Church was seen as part of the *Ancien Régime*, the "old rule" that needed to be thrown off. The state saw the Church as its enemy, or at least as a threat to its aim of securing the complete loyalty of its people. But for the most part, for the common people, the Church, which provided education and charity to the poor, remained a friend and an ally.

Although these political transitions were often painful both for individual Catholics and for the institutional Church, the Church endured and even

The French Revolution

Christianity had a long history in France dating back to the days of the Church Fathers, including St. Irenaeus, who was bishop of Lyon in the second century. King Clovis of the Franks had been baptized by St. Remy of Reims in 496, leading to the Christianization of the whole kingdom. For around eight hundred years, the kings of France were crowned by a French archbishop in the cathedral at Reims. One of those kings, Louis IX, is recognized by the Church as a saint (and is the namesake of the American city of St. Louis). Another saint, St. Joan of Arc, helped preserve French independence from England during the Hundred Years' War. The Catholic faith and French identity were entwined.

However, many revolutionaries saw this close relationship between the French government and the Catholic Church as the source of the nation's troubles and believed that genuine freedom could only be achieved when people were liberated from the oppression of the rulers of the state (the king) and the Church (priests and bishops). As the revolution developed, these anti-Catholic leaders took control of the French government. Laws were passed to confiscate Church property, to destroy religious houses such as monasteries (and outlaw the existence of religious orders altogether), and to force all priests to swear allegiance to the French nation over any allegiance to the pope or the Church. Some priests and other consecrated religious complied, some went into hiding or exile outside of France, and some, such as the Carmelite

Massacre of priests in the Carmes Church in Paris in 1792.

Martyrs of Compiègne, resisted and were imprisoned or executed. The anti-religious frenzy released by the revolution extended to physical churches as well: vandals stole or destroyed countless works of art such as statues, altars, and stained-glass windows in the magnificent cathedrals that had beautified the French landscape.

The excesses of the French Revolution and its Reign of Terror eventually gave way to moderation. Napoleon Bonaparte came to power in 1799 and restored order to the country. Napoleon was no great friend of the Church, but he did recognize that most French citizens still considered themselves Catholic and that some kind of compromise with the Church was preferable to outright persecution. Although the relationship between the Church and the French government under Napoleon continued to be fraught with conflict (Napoleon's forces captured and exiled two successive popes, Pius VI and Pius VII), the situation of the Church in France gradually improved, setting the stage for eventual renewal of Catholic life in that nation.

The departure of the clergy during the French Revolution.

thrived in the new world that was forming. The Church is not attached to any particular form of government or any particular national regime. Remember, as described in St. Augustine's *The City of God* (see the feature "Post-Nicene Church Fathers" in Chapter 3, Section 3), Catholics are to remain focused on heavenly, not earthly goals. However, the Church does ask for the freedom to be herself: to worship, to teach, to serve. Where government permits these activities, the Church is at home. Whenever government restricts the Church's freedom, there will be conflict.

Opportunities for Renewal and Growth

In every age, the Church has faced the challenge of being part of history while also transcending it. Catholics participate in the events of the secular world in which they live, but they must also judge which aspects of their environment are compatible with the faith and which are not. The Church offers a reliable standard, provided by the Creator himself, by which to judge human action. Around the French Revolution, the Church *supported* the exploration of creation through science, the extension of political rights, and economic progress that reinforced the dignity of the human person, while she at the same time *condemned* corruptions of science, politics, and economics that undermined the truth about humanity and its relationship to God.

Even where the Church struggled, as in revolutionary France, the ground for renewal was being prepared. In the nineteenth century, the French Church that had been pounded to her knees during the revolution rose with renewed vigor. Within France itself, several powerful witnesses to faith and truth emerged. For example,

St. John Vianney provided a model for the priesthood, dedicating his life not to gaining power and enjoying comfort but to caring for his parishioners.

St. Bernadette Soubirous saw visions of the Blessed Virgin Mary, reigniting Marian devotion and laying the foundation for a Marian shrine at Lourdes that became famous for miracles of healing.

Blessed Frédéric Ozanam renewed the Church's dedication to the poor by devoting himself to caring for the neglected people of Paris and in the process founding one of the world's largest charitable organizations, the Society of St. Vincent de Paul.

As noted in Chapter 5, a vibrant Church is a missionary Church. Nineteenth-century French missionaries shared the Gospel across the world to the Americas, Africa, and Asia. They were supported by the French people through organizations such as the Society for the Propagation of the Faith.∞ One beneficiary of French commitment to evangelization was the United States, where a high percentage of the earliest missionaries and bishops were from France. St. Isaac Jogues (see subsection "Jesuit Missionaries of the Sixteenth and Seventeenth Centuries" in Chapter 5, Section 4) and Fr. Jacques Marquette both explored and evangelized along the Mississippi River. There was also Fr. Stephen Badin, who rode horseback throughout Indiana, Ohio, and Kentucky, providing sacraments to scattered Catholics and buying the land on which future parishes would be built. A unique religious community that sought to combine the work of priests, brothers, and sisters under one charism—devotion to hope in the Cross of Christ—became known as the Congregation of Holy Cross. Some of its missionaries settled in Indiana and later founded the University of Notre Dame, along with many parishes and schools.

Elsewhere in the Americas, Spanish and Portuguese missionaries continued building a thriving Church. Devotion to Mary was a strong factor in Spanish North America as well. A native Mexican convert, St. Juan Diego, saw a vision of Mary near Mexico City in 1531, and Our Lady of Guadalupe has been a central figure in Mexican Catholicism ever since. While French

∞ Note

The Society for the Propagation of the Faith was founded by a Frenchwoman, Pauline Jaricot, in 1822 in order to support missionary priests, brothers, and sisters in mission areas. The first collection of the society went to the large dioceses of Louisiana and to two in Florida. The territory of these dioceses stretched to Canada. The society's gifts to missions would cease as soon as the mission churches could support themselves.

missionaries worked in the Great Lakes region and in New England, Spanish missionaries established the faith in Florida and the southwestern United States. The Church in the United States grew rapidly in the nineteenth century as Catholic immigrants flocked to the land of freedom and opportunity.

The effort to spread the Gospel across the world continued as the Church reached places she had never been. Missionaries reached the interior of Africa, where native converts such as St. Charles Lwanga in Uganda demonstrated heroic commitment to their newfound faith, even to the point of martyrdom.

The Church faced many new challenges, but her central mission remained what it always had been: to continue the work of Christ on earth.

SECTION Assessment

Comprehension

1. How did the Church initially feel about the French Revolution?

2. What happened to change the Church's response to the revolution?

3. What was the mission of the Society for the Propagation of the Faith?

Vocabulary

4. Identify the *Reign of Terror*.

Reflection

5. How does the reminder to search for the city of God apply to your own life and times?

ENLIGHTENMENT AND REVOLUTION

While the Catholic Church had dominated Europe in religion, governance, and culture through the Middle Ages, the *modern period*, approximately the sixteenth through the nineteenth centuries, saw a decline in belief and religious unity across much of the continent. New ideas spread, and some of them called into question the bedrock tenets of Christianity. By the end of the modern period, the Church faced a world where many governments were hostile to religion and many people were skeptical about the truths of Christianity.

The Protestant-Catholic strife of the Reformation period played a role in this development. Christianity professed to be a faith based on the teachings of Jesus, including "love your enemies." It exhorted its adherents to practice charity, justice, and forgiveness. Yet society witnessed (or participated in) factions of Christians persecuting and killing other factions of Christians. The Thirty Years' War (1618–1648) between the Catholic Holy Roman Empire and various Protestant states devastated large swaths of Europe. Although it's clear in retrospect that the war was not exclusively or perhaps even primarily about theology (it had as much to do with European states jockeying for power), the religious divisions of the Reformation did play a role in fomenting

Battlefield scene from the Thirty Years' War.

conflict between Catholics and Protestants. The English Civil Wars (1642–1651), which pitted one religious group (Anglicans, who were by and large loyal to the king) against another (Calvinists, who wanted different rulers), had a similar effect in England.

In France and elsewhere, intellectuals such as Voltaire (d. 1778)∞ began to question whether the faith that had permeated European society for 1,500 years was a beneficial influence on humanity after all. Was religion making people intolerant of each other and causing violence and wars? Christianity, according to Voltaire, was "assuredly the most ridiculous, the most absurd and the most bloody religion which has ever infected this world."[4] If people abandoned their commitment to religion, Voltaire believed, then they could base their lives on reason rather than on irrational faith, and the world would be a better, more peaceful place. Such ideas were spreading throughout Europe, weakening both support for the Catholic Church as an institution and adherence to the Christian faith (Catholic or Protestant) in general.

Voltaire

This Enlightenment mentality (see subsection "The Church and the Enlightenment" in this section) ran against the plan for creation that God had revealed throughout salvation history. When Enlightenment thinkers sought to understand the world apart from God's revelation, they misunderstood its purpose and the nature of true progress, which was this: "God created the world for the sake of communion with his divine life, a communion brought about by the 'convocation' of men in Christ, and this 'convocation' is the Church" (*CCC*, 760). The purpose of history, in the Christian view, is not technological, scientific, or economic progress, even if those are desirable in themselves. The chief aim of human effort should be the salvation of all people. "Just as God's will is creation and

∞ Note

François-Marie Arouet was a French Enlightenment writer, historian, and philosopher who went by the pen name "Voltaire." A staunch critic of the Church, he once implored the French king to "do the human race an eternal service by extirpating this infamous superstition."

is called 'the world,' so his intention is the salvation of men, and it is called 'the Church'" (*CCC*, 760, quoting Clement of Alexandria).

Emphasis on material achievement and neglect of spiritual matters is a characteristic tendency of **modernity**. The spread of democratic governments, scientific and technological advances, and an increase in economic prosperity are all positive developments that came with modernity. Yet these developments were often accompanied by the disintegration of traditional communities, the breakdown of family life, and a decreasing concern for the spiritual well-being of the human person. These negative developments gave rise to the paradox of modernity: unprecedented material wealth and technology combined with spiritual confusion and disillusionment.

The Church offers the solution to this paradox, because she understands that true happiness and freedom cannot be found in material possessions, political influence, or worldly success. Simply put:

- **The Church firmly believes** that Christ, who died and was raised up for all, offers to every human person through the Holy Spirit the light and the strength necessary to measure up to his or her destiny.

- **The Church likewise holds** that in her most benign Lord and Master can be found the key, the focal point, and the goal of humanity, as well as of all human history.

- **The Church also maintains** that beneath all changes there are many realities that do not change and have their ultimate foundation in Christ, who is the same yesterday and today, yes and forever (*Gaudium et Spes*, 10).

In other words, in the midst of rapid change and increasing complexity, the Church continues to proclaim the simple, unchanging truth of salvation in Christ.

The Church Is a Pioneer of Science, Not an Enemy of Science

When Voltaire and other intellectuals touted the benefits of abandoning religious belief, one prominent idea they had was to substitute it with science. The Scottish philosopher David Hume (d. 1776) insisted that religion and science

modernity A movement of the late modern period that began in the late eighteenth century and lasted through the twentieth century that attempted to reduce or limit Church teaching to modern advances in history, science, and biblical research.

were entirely separate enterprises because the Church was based on faith while science was based on reason. By the eighteenth century, the promotion of faith as apart from reason led to a strong current of thought that viewed Christianity, and the Catholic Church in particular, as hostile to science.

The belief that "faith" or "the Church" is an enemy of science does not withstand historical scrutiny. In fact, it is completely wrong. From the beginning of modern science, countless scientists have also been devout Catholics. As noted in Chapter 4, monasteries were hotbeds of scientific and technological investigation and advance in the Middle Ages and beyond. Many of the pioneers in modern fields of science were consecrated religious—priests, monks, or other Church officials. Nicholas Copernicus (d. 1543), who inaugurated the "Copernican Revolution" in astronomy by advocating the theory of *heliocentrism*—the revolving of the planets around the sun—was a cleric assigned to a Catholic cathedral in Germany.

Jesuit priests in particular were especially prominent in the field of astronomy. Even proponents of the Enlightenment conceded that "one cannot talk about mathematics in the sixteenth and seventeenth centuries without seeing a Jesuit at every corner."[5] For example, a Jesuit astronomer, Christopher Clavius (d. 1612), was responsible (along with Aloysius Lilus) for an astronomical discovery that removed ten days from the year 1582 and created the Gregorian calendar. His story is connected to that of St. Teresa of Ávila (see the feature "St. Teresa of Ávila" in Chapter 5, Section 3). Teresa died on October 4, 1582, and her funeral was held the following day, October 15. That is not a typo. Ten days were subtracted from the calendar as a result of the Catholic Church's dedication to astronomy, which persists to this day. The current Vatican Observatory, created by Pope Leo XIII in 1891, is a well-known research organization, with stations in Italy and Arizona. And in the 1920s, a Belgian diocesan priest, Georges

Christopher Clavius was partially responsible for an astronomical discovery that removed ten days from the year 1582 and created the Gregorian calendar.

Lemaître, formulated a theory of the universe's origins (later called the "Big Bang") that is widely accepted among contemporary cosmologists.

Catholic contributions to science in the modern period and beyond have not been limited to astronomy. Consider:

Blessed Nicholas Steno (d. 1686), a Catholic convert who became a priest and bishop, was a major figure in the founding of the science of geology.

Alessandro Volta (d. 1827), an Italian physicist, invented the electric battery. The unit of electrical potential, the *volt*, is named after him. He saw no conflict between his scientific research and his Catholicism, as he testified in a personal letter: "I have never, as far as I know, wavered in my faith."[6]

Gregor Mendel (d. 1884) was an Augustinian friar whose studies of the plants at his monastery in what is today the Czech Republic are credited with creating the field of genetics.

Julius Nieuwland (d. 1936), a Holy Cross priest, aided in the creation of synthetic rubber through his research into a colorless gas called acetylene.

Mary Kenneth Keller (d. 1985), a Sister of Charity of the Blessed Virgin Mary, was a pioneer in the field of computer science and perhaps the first American to earn a doctorate in the field.[7]

Notwithstanding this evidence of the Church's support for science, many intellectuals in the Enlightenment persisted in claiming that faith and science are at odds. One specific point of contention involving Scripture was the matter of miracles. Some advocates of science in this era denied that miracles could happen. In their view, a scientific mindset required a complete refusal to admit that God could intervene in any way that went beyond the natural workings of the world. Given that Scripture is replete with miracles and that the Catholic Church has officially recognized many miracles associated with the saints, this view is genuinely incompatible with the Catholic faith. The miracles that accompanied Jesus's ministry were important because they "attest that the Father has sent him. They invite belief in him." They "strengthen faith in the One who does his Father's works" and "bear witness that he is the Son of God" (*CCC*, 547–548). Miracles are thus one sign pointing to the truth of Jesus's teaching and therefore to the reliability of the Church that he founded.

Galileo Galilei before the Court of Inquisition.

The most famous confrontation between the Church and science in the Enlightenment was the Galileo affair. While it's true that the astronomer Galileo Galilei (d. 1642) fell under suspicion from Church officials and was disciplined by the Inquisition, it is inaccurate to view the episode as a case of "faith versus science." Galileo had many supporters among churchmen, including cardinals and popes, and he got into trouble not because he held the view that the earth revolved around the sun (the theory proposed decades earlier by Copernicus) but because he refused to admit that the view remained a questionable theory in the absence of definitive evidence. In the late twentieth century, Pope John Paul II admitted that the Church was wrong to punish Galileo for his views, but this mistake cannot fairly be construed as reflecting an overall hostility on the part of the Church toward astronomy or science in general.

The Church and the Enlightenment

Some Enlightenment ideas are entirely compatible with Catholic doctrine. The idea that the natural universe is intelligible—can be explored and understood by human intelligence—is not only consistent with Catholic doctrine

The Gregorian Calendar

The calendar that most of the world uses today, consisting of twelve months composed of twenty-eight to thirty-one days, was developed for use in the Roman Empire. Because it was made more accurate during the reign of the Roman emperor Julius Caesar (d. 44 BC), the system that prevailed across Europe for the next 1,500 years was known as the *Julian calendar.*

A major challenge of any calendar, and of the Julian calendar in particular, was to keep the solar year in line with the calendar year. The Church was keenly interested in the matter, because her principal feast of Easter was dated according to the timing of the *vernal equinox*, the spring day when the tilt of the earth results in equal hours of day and night. If the calendar did not line up well with the solar year, then Easter could end up far away from its normal date in early spring.

By the Middle Ages, it was clear that the Julian calendar year was drifting noticeably from the solar year and needed to be modified. The Council of Trent encouraged a solution to the problem, and Pope Gregory XIII (1572–1585) commissioned a task force to deal with it. Christopher Clavius, a German mathematician teaching at the Jesuit Roman College and an expert in the field of calculating dates, took the lead in correcting the old system. In addition to implementing regular corrections to the calendar by changing the system of leap years that was already in place in the Julian calendar (eliminating three leap days every four hundred years), it was also necessary to make a dramatic one-time adjustment in the calendar by subtracting ten days. The pope decreed that the change would go into effect at midnight following October 4, that is, that October 5 would become October 15 instead. Most Catholic countries, such as Spain where St. Teresa died, accepted the reform immediately. Eventually, the Gregorian calendar spread throughout the world.

but implied by it. The Church holds that religion and science, faith and reason, are complementary. God is reasonable and created a world that is "good" and ordered toward his providential plan. The created human mind, though clouded by sin, is capable of grasping the truth about God and the world. Pope Francis wrote that faith

> illumines the material world, trusts its inherent order and knows that it calls us to an ever widening path of harmony and understanding. The gaze of science thus benefits from faith: faith encourages the scientist to remain constantly open to reality in all its inexhaustible richness. Faith awakens the critical sense by preventing research from being satisfied with its own formulae and helps it to realize that nature is always greater. By stimulating wonder before the profound mystery of creation, faith broadens the horizons of reason to shed greater light on the world which discloses itself to scientific investigation. (*Lumen Fidei*, 34)

Faith assists reason in coming to the truth, but *reason also assists faith* in understanding and articulating one's beliefs. The Church insists that human beings have the rational capability of "coming to a knowledge of the existence of a personal God" (*CCC*, 35), but also that, impaired by sin and reliant on the imperfect data of our senses, we stand "in need of being enlightened by God's revelation" (*CCC*, 38) so as to come to know God more intimately and to know the truths of morality and salvation reliably.

The Catholic intellectual Blaise Pascal (d. 1662) exemplified the harmony of faith and reason. Pascal was a world-class mathematician and physicist who interacted with other French intellectuals who were skeptical about the reasonableness of Christianity. For a time, Pascal struggled to understand the role of God in the universe, but he eventually concluded that reason has limits, and that faith can assist the mind and the will in knowing and pursuing the good. In his famous *Pensées*

Philosopher Blaise Pascal once argued that the Catholic Church's claim to divine origin had to be true because the Church established herself in a hostile world and spread throughout the world despite harsh persecution.

CONSENT
OF THE
Governed

The idea that people should have a say in their own government is compatible with Catholic teaching. In the post-Reformation period, the "divine right of kings" theory emerged. It sought to justify the exercise of absolute power by kings and queens by positing that they derived their authority directly from God and therefore could not be subject to any other earthly authority. This theory was opposed by popes and major Catholic thinkers, including St. Robert Bellarmine (d. 1621), who insisted that even kings and queens are subject to the moral authority of the Church, and that, while God is the ultimate source of all power, earthly rulers derive their right to rule not directly from God but only through the consent of the governed, the people. In his *Treatise on Civil Government*, Bellarmine stated that "it depends on the consent of the people to decide whether kings, or consuls, or other magistrates are to be established in authority over them," and he therefore held that the people have the right to remove oppressive governments and establish new ones if necessary.[8]

St. Robert Bellarmine

(Thoughts), Pascal identified the twin errors of modernity and called them "two extremes." These were "to exclude reason, to admit reason only."[9]

Immanuel Kant

Other Enlightenment-era ideas were more obviously contrary to Catholic teaching. Besides Voltaire, who viewed the Church as an obstacle to human progress, there was the German philosopher Immanuel Kant (d. 1804), who sought to make reason the measuring stick for religion. For Kant, the human mind did not need to conform to what God had revealed through Jesus Christ; instead, he held that an individual could judge whether various Christian beliefs were "reasonable" or not.

The English political theorist John Locke (d. 1704) promoted the democratic principle of the "consent of the governed," but in his zeal to avoid religious strife he encouraged the complete separation of religion from political life. As one scholar put it, "Locke's philosophy of toleration was the first step toward removing religion from the public square and privatizing it."[10] In contrast, while the Church does not demand political power for itself as an institution, it insists that Gospel values must influence political life so that the state serves the common good of all people.

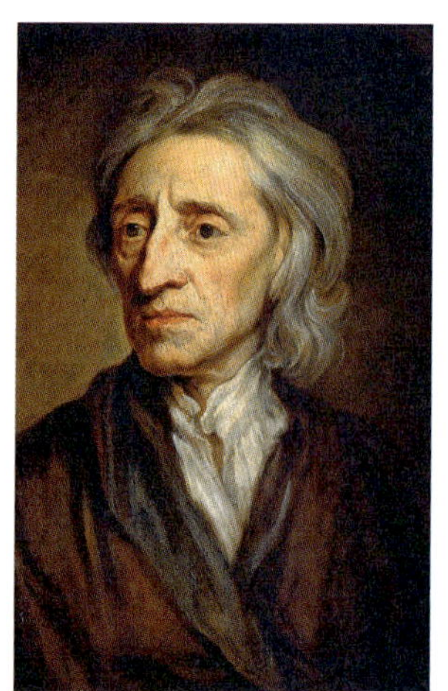
John Locke

In their participation in civic life, Catholics have a responsibility to uphold the truth concerning the nature of the human person. A common situation today, according to the Congregation for the Doctrine of the Faith, is that "citizens claim complete autonomy with regard to their moral choices, and lawmakers maintain that they are respecting this freedom of choice by enacting laws which ignore the principles of natural ethics and yield to ephemeral cultural and moral trends, as if every possible outlook on life were of equal value."[11] In contrast to this view, the Church exhorts Catholics to defend the right to life of all persons at all stages of life; the dignity of all persons irrespective of race, religion, or economic status; and the importance of marriage and family as the building blocks of society.

SECTION Assessment

Comprehension

1. What was the event that kicked off modernity or the Enlightenment?

2. What evidence did Voltaire have for his negative opinion of Christianity?

3. How did the Church's definition of progress differ from the understanding of Enlightenment thinkers?

4. Name one important contribution by a Catholic scientist during the modern period.

5. How was it that St. Teresa of Ávila died on October 4 and her funeral was held the following day on October 15?

6. Explain the Galileo affair.

7. How did John Locke distort the notion of the "consent of the governed"?

Vocabulary

8. From a Catholic perspective, identify one positive and one negative aspect of *modernity*.

Reflection

9. "Miracles do not necessarily contradict science." Explain the truth of this statement.

10. Pope John Paul II wrote that "faith and reason are like two wings on which the human spirit rises to the contemplation of truth." Explain this statement in your own words.

MARY: BEACON OF RENEWAL IN THE CHURCH

In spite of the challenges of any particular era of history, the Church is never in despair. She is always protected from any heresies, sinfulness, and contradictions the secular world throws at her. Standing willing and ready at all times to come to the Church's aid is Mary, the Mother of God and the Mother of the Church. Authentic devotion to her never distracts Christians from the saving work of Jesus. Mary is only able to be the Mother of the Church because she is filled with God's grace, which was present to her from the moment of her conception.

Catholic devotion to Mary was strong in the nineteenth century. In 1854, Pope Pius IX declared Mary's Immaculate Conception an infallible teaching of the Church (see subsection "The Magisterium: Teaching Office of the Church" in Chapter 3, Section 2). Be clear, however, that this dogma of the faith has existed for far longer than two centuries. There are many Christian beliefs that are implicit, or unstated, for a while and then become explicit—fully understood or fully articulated—over the course of time. This often happens when there is confusion or debate about some matter, so the Church examines the question more closely and then issues a decision.

Regarding the Immaculate Conception, Christians in the early centuries of the Church recognized that Mary had been granted special graces in preparation for her role as Mother of God, but the exact nature of those graces was not formally defined. By the seventh century, Christians in some places were celebrating a "feast of Mary's conception," and this local feast gradually spread through much of the Church. Theologians in the Middle Ages debated

actual sin As distinguished from Original Sin, any evil act contrary to God's law and God's will committed freely by a person. Categories of actual sin are *mortal* (deadly) sin and *venial* (lesser) sin.

whether she was preserved from Original Sin from the moment of her conception or was instead purified from Original Sin during the time of her gestation. All agreed that Mary never committed **actual sin** during her earthly life. The Magisterium did not make a clear ruling on the question until the time of Pope Pius IX. The eventual decision was supported by a miraculous occurrence around the same time.

Marian Devotions and Beliefs

Apparitions to St. Bernadette at Lourdes were just one example of a widespread revival of Marian devotion across the Catholic world in the nineteenth century.∞ Besides Lourdes, Church-approved **Marian apparitions** also occurred at Paris (Our Lady of the Miraculous Medal to St. Catherine Labouré); at La Salette and at Pontmain in France; at Knock, Ireland; at Gietrzwald, Poland;

Marian apparitions Supernatural appearances of Mary to a person or group of people on earth. There have been thousands of reported Marian apparitions over the centuries but very few Church-approved Marian apparitions. The local bishop where the alleged apparition has occurred carefully investigates an apparition based on criteria set by the Dicastery for the Doctrine of the Faith.

∞ Note

On February 11, 1858, while walking outdoors near Lourdes, France, Bernadette Soubirous heard a gust of wind and saw an apparition of a "lady dressed in white with a blue belt and yellow rose on each foot." Over the course of the next four months, the lady appeared to Bernadette eighteen times, praying the Rosary and giving her messages. When Bernadette asked the lady's name, she replied, "I am the Immaculate Conception." The dogma of the Immaculate Conception had been solemnly defined by Pope Pius IX just four years earlier. Ever since Bernadette's vision, Lourdes has become an immensely popular pilgrimage site. Thousands of visitors participate in a daily candlelight Rosary procession, and thousands of miraculous healings have been reported over the decades. In response to the cascade of reported cures, a medical bureau was established at the shrine. Managed by credentialed medical doctors, the bureau examines all cases submitted through a scientific, three-stage process, including a determination whether "there was an indisputable change from a precise medical diagnosis of a known illness to a situation of restored health." From 1862 to 2018, seventy reported healings have been officially recognized.

and at Champion, Wisconsin, to Adele Brise (see Faithful Disciple profile "Adele Brise" in this chapter).

The Assumption, *by Lu Hung Nien.*

From the earliest days of the Church, Christians have venerated Mary as the mother of Jesus. As noted in Chapter 3, the Council of Ephesus in 431 declared Mary to be the Mother of God, and a basilica in honor of Mary was erected in Ephesus around that time. Many devotions to Mary developed over the centuries, including an array of prayers and hymns. The best known is the Hail Mary prayer, whose first section derives from the Annunciation to Mary recorded in Luke 1:26–38. Related to the Immaculate Conception, the *Annunciation*, or announcement that the sinless Mary would give birth to the Savior, connects her also with the first woman, Eve, who had sinned. Mary's response to the angel's announcement that she would conceive the Son of God without the partnership of a human father was "May it be done to me according to your word" (Lk 1:38). In this way, she expressed her obedience to God's plan for the Incarnation and for human salvation.

Marian devotion is a reflection of our belief that Mary is the perfect disciple of Jesus and therefore an exemplary Christian. As such she is a model of the Church and has always played a key role in the life of the Church. As Mother of the Church, Mary is the "mother of the members of Christ" because she has "by her charity joined in bringing about the birth of believers in the Church, who are members of its head" (*CCC*, 963, quoting *Lumen Gentium*, 53). By her complete openness to the will of God, she became the conduit for the Incarnation, for God's coming into the world in human flesh. In the words of the second-century Church Father St. Irenaeus, "Being obedient she became the cause of salvation for herself and for the whole human race" (*CCC*, 494, quoting *Against Heresies*, 3, 22, 4).

Just as Mary was the vessel for Christ's coming into the world, so she was the vessel for the beginning of the Church. Mary's motherhood to all believers was confirmed by Jesus himself, when from the Cross he gave his mother to all of us through the Apostle John. "He said to his mother, 'Woman, behold, your son.' Then he said to the disciple, 'Behold, your mother'" (Jn 19:26–27). "Jesus is Mary's only son, but her spiritual motherhood extends to all men whom indeed he came to save" (*CCC*, 501).

Mary's spiritual motherhood is consistent with her *perpetual virginity*, the doctrine that Mary did not engage in sexual relations either before or after the birth of Jesus. Mary's virginity "manifests God's absolute initiative in the Incarnation. Jesus has only God as Father" (*CCC*, 503). Mary's perpetual virginity preserved her holiness. Her perpetual virginity has been a belief of the Church since the time of the Apostles. The Gospels share that the virginal conception of Jesus was the work of the Holy Spirit and a fulfillment of the Old Testament prophets: "Therefore the Lord himself will give you this sign: the virgin shall be with child and bear a son, and shall name him Immanuel" (Is 7:14, *New American Bible*). Mary's perpetual virginity teaches us several

Assumption of Mary into Heaven *painting in Maryam Kebran Church, Ethiopia.*

things about the power of God and the meaning of holiness. Here are five of them:

1. Jesus has only one Father, who is in heaven.

Jesus was never separated from his Father, even during his life on earth.

2. From his virginal conception, Jesus is filled with the Holy Spirit.

The Holy Spirit caused Mary to conceive the Second Person of the Blessed Trinity, who was thus anointed with the Holy Spirit from the beginning of his human existence. "From his fullness we have all received, grace in place of grace" (Jn 1:16) that communicates to us what we need to reach heaven.

3. The virgin birth of Jesus signifies a new birth for humanity, an offer of salvation.

This new birth takes place in the Holy Spirit through faith. In fact, this new birth is only accessible to those with faith who understand how all of the mysteries associated with the life, Death, and Resurrection of Christ are connected.

4. Mary's virginity is a sign of her faith.

Mary's virginity allows the world to witness her blessedness.

5. Mary's perpetual virginity is symbolic of the Church.

The Church "by receiving the word of God in faith becomes herself a mother" (*Lumen Gentium*, 64).

Finally, Mary's virginity is a sign of "her undivided gift of herself to God's will" (*CCC*, 506). She is totally committed to God and united to him as a bride. She is thereby a model of the Church, which is the Bride of Christ (see subsection "The Holiness of the Church" in Chapter 4, Section 2).

Mary Embodies Holiness and Shows Our Destiny

While all of us struggle to avoid sin and increase our holiness, we look to Mary as the model of holiness. She embodies holiness. Like the Holy Spirit, who was conceived as the love between the Father and the Son, Mary, too, is conceived purely and without sin, becoming the embodiment of the Holy Spirit. St. Maximilian Kolbe called Mary the "created Holy Spirit." "In the most Blessed Virgin the Church has already reached that perfection whereby she exists without spot or wrinkle. . . . [I]n her, the Church is already the 'all-holy'" (*CCC*, 829). In this way, Mary is both an example to follow and a real manifestation of the Church's holiness.

God rewarded Mary for her life of holiness with "a singular participation in her Son's Resurrection and an anticipation of the resurrection of other Christians" (*CCC*, 966), who are her children. This reward is known as the *Assumption of Mary*, which professes that Mary was taken up (assumed) body and soul into heaven at the end of her earthly life.∞ By her Assumption, Mary's body was preserved from the corruption that is common to the physical remains of human beings. As that corruption is a result of sin, it is appropriate that the all-holy, sinless Mother of God did not undergo it.

The Assumption of Mary sculpture from the Parish of Santa Maria Aranda, Spain.

∞ Note

As with the Immaculate Conception, belief in the Assumption of Mary circulated among Christians for years, dating back at least to the sixth century. In 1950, then, Pope Pius XII simply clarified and added certainty to a truth that most Christians had believed and that was implied in other teachings about Mary. The Assumption of Mary into heaven is celebrated on August 15 as a holy day of obligation.

Models of Faith

Focus Question: What are common challenges to practicing one's faith in a society hostile to religion?

Marian devotion was but one marker of renewal across the Catholic world in the nineteenth century. Nowhere was new life in the Church as obvious as in France, the site of the terrible persecutions of the revolution and the home of St. Bernadette at Lourdes.

St. John Vianney (1786–1859) was born three years before the French Revolution began. His seminary studies were disrupted when he was drafted into Napoleon's army, but he managed to avoid military service and was ordained a priest in 1815. Assigned to a parish in the small village of Ars in the French countryside, Fr. Vianney found the religious life of the people of the area to be in a deplorable state. Although the simple peasants of his parish probably weren't reading Enlightenment philosophers, the spirit of the Enlightenment—a life without God—was on display in their lives. In addition, the Catholics of Ars had gone years without any **catechetical** training. The new pastor threw himself into his work of spiritual regeneration with total dedication. He preached blunt but heartfelt homilies, urging the people to turn away from sin and back to God. As the people began to strive for holiness, he spent hours each day hearing confessions, during which he showed astounding insight into

catechetical From the Greek word *catechesis*, a term referring to instruction, usually religious instruction.

St. John Vianney

in the Modern Era

the spiritual needs of souls. He visited his parishioners in their homes and comforted the poor. He created a home for girls who needed guidance.

By his life, St. John Vianney offered a model for what a Catholic priest should be: totally dedicated to God and his people. He did not seek a life of ease, wealth, or power, but found fulfillment in doing the will of God and serving the people of the Church. Pope Pius XI canonized him in 1925 and in 1929 designated him patron saint of all parish priests.

Two years before St. John Vianney was ordained a priest, Frédéric Ozanam (1813–1853) was born to a French family in Milan, Italy. He went to college in Lyon and then in Paris, where he participated in debates with other students about the truth of the Catholic faith. At the beginning of his college studies, having encountered skeptical Enlightenment writers such as Voltaire, Ozanam was doubtful about Catholicism. But through discussions with an intellectual French priest and others, he came to embrace the faith wholeheartedly.

Frédéric Ozanam

Ozanam believed that the Gospel must not only be believed but be put into action. Troubled by the poverty of those he encountered in the streets of Paris, Ozanam resolved to put his faith into action by helping those in need. "The earth has become a chilly place," he lamented. "It is up to us Catholics to rekindle the flame of human warmth going out."[12] In 1833, he joined with a group of other students to form an organization devoted to the material and spiritual assistance of the needy. They collaborated with a religious order, the Daughters of Charity, who were already working among the destitute of Paris. The Daughters of Charity had been founded by St. Vincent de Paul (d. 1660) and St. Louise de Marillac (d. 1660), so the new organization took St. Vincent as its patron. The Society of St. Vincent de Paul spread through France and around the world. Today, its eight hundred thousand members help over thirty million people a day.

The "social Catholicism" practiced by Frédéric Ozanam could be found in Germany as well, where Bishop Wilhelm von Ketteler (d. 1877) argued that those who possessed much property were obligated to use it in a way that benefited all people. Bishop von Ketteler insisted on the centrality of charity in the Church and defended the rights of working-class people, but he rejected the path of "class conflict" and the abolition of private property that thinkers such as Karl Marx, the author of *The Communist Manifesto*, were propounding around the same time. In 1891, Pope Leo XIII drew in part on Ketteler's ideas in his encyclical *Rerum Novarum* (*Rights and Duties of Capital and Labor*), which inaugurated the Church's modern *social teaching*, her effort to address the social and economic problems of the modern world.

Bishop Wilhelm von Ketteler

In England, where Catholics had been persecuted for centuries, the Church was reborn. With the lifting of legal restrictions on Catholic activity, Catholics were once again free to worship in public. In 1850, Catholic dioceses were reestablished for the first time since the sixteenth century, and Catholic bishops returned to England. Five years earlier, St. John Henry Newman, a brilliant Anglican priest, had joined the Catholic Church. Newman's conversion was part of a broader phenomenon known as the Oxford Movement, which resulted in many Anglican conversions to Catholicism.[13] Newman's sophisticated theology, in particular his articulation of "development of doctrine," was an important contribution to the Church's engagement with modernity.

Further Study and Reflection

- Look up a local St. Vincent de Paul center. Summarize its mission or "About Us" statement.
- Read Pope John XXIII's statement on the hundredth anniversary of St. John Vianney's death, *Sacerdotii Nostri Primordia* (*On St. John Vianney*), and write down one statement you found interesting. Explain why you found it so.
- Where would it be more difficult for you to practice your faith: in a society that opposed all religion or a society that opposed only your religion? Explain.

Mary's sharing of the fruits of redemption is a foreshadowing of the reward promised to all who strive for holiness. We too will receive an incorruptible, glorified body and soul if we reach heaven.∞ What will our resurrected, glorified bodies be like? They will have the same characteristics as Christ's glorified body. We know from the Gospels that the Risen Jesus was recognizable to his disciples (see, for example, John 20:16), that he passed through locked doors (see John 20:19), and that he ate food (see John 21:12–13). We can imagine the same for ourselves. Our glorified bodies will also be incapable of suffering, sickness, and dying. They will be incorruptible and no longer bound by space and time. St. Thomas Aquinas taught that they will be impassible, subtle, agile, and filled with clarity.[14] Perhaps most exciting for us to consider now is that our resurrected bodies will be radiant and beautiful as God intended from the time he first thought of us and fashioned us. Jesus himself said, "The righteous will shine like the sun in the kingdom of their Father" (Mt 13:43).

Mary is a sign of the perfection that is to come for us in heaven: "Just as the Mother of Jesus, glorified in body and soul in heaven, is the image and beginning of the Church as it is to be perfected [in] the world to come, so too does she shine forth . . . as a sign of sure hope and solace to the people of God during its sojourn on earth" (*Lumen Gentium*, 68). In union with Mary, we, as members of her Church, are already perfect, all-holy, and present with Christ. Mary's Assumption to heaven reveals our future destiny.

SECTION Assessment

Comprehension

1. Why was it unusual for the dogma of the Immaculate Conception to be formally defined less than two centuries ago?

2. Name two things Mary's perpetual virginity teaches about the power of God.

∞ Note

We state this belief in the Nicene Creed: "I believe in . . . the resurrection of the body."

Vocabulary

3. Name two other Church-approved *Marian apparitions* in the nineteenth century besides Our Lady of Lourdes.

4. What is the difference between Original Sin and *actual sin*?

5. Why did St. John Vianney find the people of Ars lacking in *catechetical* training?

Reflection

6. Explain what hope you find for yourself in Mary's Assumption into heaven.

THE CHURCH BALANCES INDIVIDUALISM AND COMMUNION

The strong focus of the Enlightenment on individual rights led to views that opposed the Christian understanding of personhood. A radical *individualism* sees the person as the fundamental unit of society, disconnected from family, church, and community. Western culture has often celebrated this idea, as for example represented in the early-twentieth-century ideal of "rugged individualism."

The spirit of individualism reverberated from another revolution that shook the world a few years before the French Revolution. This revolution began in the towns of Lexington and Concord in the colony of Massachusetts and in its course produced a Declaration of Independence and a new nation, the United States of America. Like the French Revolution, the American Revolution sought liberty and the right of the people to have a say in their own government. The American colonists aimed to escape the rule of kings and queens and establish a representative system of government in which people would vote for their leaders.

The Church is in accord with principles that support more individual freedom, including political and economic freedom. Indeed, the Church has in recent times "rejected the totalitarian and atheistic ideologies associated . . . with 'communism' and 'socialism' because of their limits on personal freedom." However, "she has likewise refused to accept, in the practice of 'capitalism,' individualism and the absolute primacy of the law of the marketplace over human labor" (*CCC*, 2425), a partial result of the revolutions in the United States and France.

More accurately, the Catholic view of the person understands all people as inherently oriented toward *community*. As the Genesis account of creation relates, when God saw Adam by himself in the garden, he said, "It is not good for the man to be alone" (Gn 2:18). People are designed by God to be in relationship with others, to love and be loved. In our material lives, we are not utterly independent and self-reliant: we depend on others to build, make, and do all the things we are incapable of doing due to lack of time, expertise, or skill. Similarly, in our spiritual lives we rely on the encouragement, support, and example of others.

This is one reason why the Catholic Church emphasizes the necessity of communal worship. You may have heard—or used yourself—something like this as a reason to miss Sunday Mass: "I can pray alone. I might take a walk in nature where I feel God's presence." This thought is faulty. When you miss Mass, you deprive yourself of a source of grace that builds necessary communion with God and others. In particular, the Eucharist

✠ brings you to greater, more intimate union with Christ;

✠ separates you from sin (forgives **venial sin**); and

✠ builds up the Church through your relationships with others.

The *Catechism of the Catholic Church* teaches that a primary grace of participation at Mass is that "the celebration of the Eucharistic sacrifice is wholly directed toward the intimate union of the faithful with Christ through communion" (1382). While personal, private prayer is important, it cannot replace the *communal liturgy*, worship in company with others. The word *liturgy* derives from an ancient Greek term that means "work for the people." This notion of working together has sometimes been lost in the era when people's quest for individualism left them slaves to other masters, like work, money, and social standing.

The Church's call to community in the name of Jesus Christ is meant to balance the tide of individualism. As far as Sunday Mass attendance goes, the Church, the Body of Christ, is not complete when her members are missing.

---

venial sin Personal sin that weakens but does not kill a person's relationship with God. Venial sin is the failure to observe in lesser matters the obligations of moral law.

American Revolution

Unlike the French Revolution, the American Revolution never devolved into complete lawlessness and bloodletting. There were instances of violent reprisals against loyalists (American colonists who supported the king), but American cities never sank into the vicious cycle of revenge symbolized by the guillotine.

After the American Revolution, the colonies were able to come together in an orderly system of laws, which gave a large number of people substantial participation in government. There were serious imperfections in this system, such as the lack of voting rights for many citizens, including women, that would be addressed in time. Native Americans were often treated cruelly and their ancestral lands overtaken. And the revolution did not eradicate the terrible institution of slavery, which systematically denied the rights of millions of Black Americans and which would only be destroyed in the course of a devastating Civil War. Nonetheless, the result of the revolution was a fundamentally stable order based on the Constitution, with a Bill of Rights designed to protect essential human rights. This system has endured down to the present and has served as a model for systems of government in many nations across the world.

Although they were a very small percentage of the American colonists, Catholics did join in the American Revolution. Charles Carroll of Carrollton, Maryland, was the most prominent Catholic patriot. A wealthy landowner, Carroll argued publicly against the injustice of British taxation of the colonies. He participated in the Continental Congress leading up to the Declaration of Independence and was the only Catholic to sign that historic document. At the time of his death in 1832, he was the last surviving of the fifty-six signers.

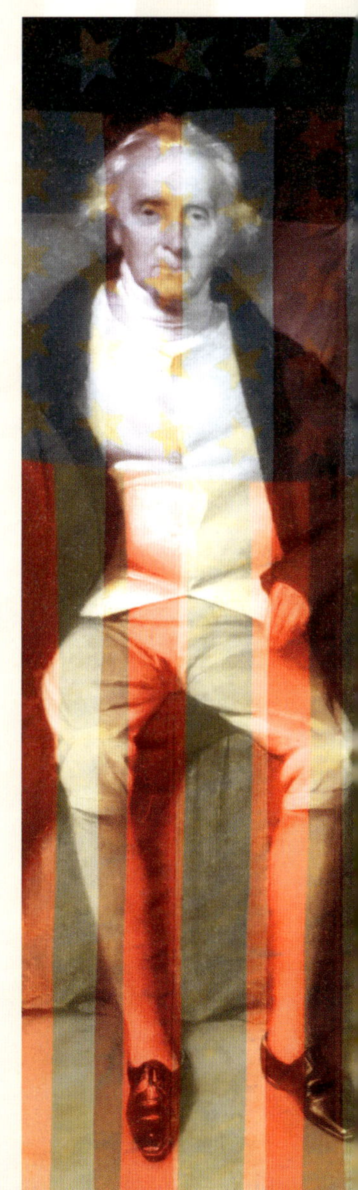

Charles Carroll was the only Catholic to sign the Declaration of Independence.

The Source and Summit of the Christian Life

The *Catechism of the Catholic Church* defines the Eucharist as "the source and summit of the Christian life" (1324, quoting *Lumen Gentium*, 11). It is the *source*, because the Eucharist makes us present at the actual events of the Last Supper leading to Jesus's saving Death on the Cross. It is the *summit* because when we participate in the Eucharist and receive the Body and Blood of Christ, we have a foretaste of eternal life in heaven. Unity with Christ is the principal fruit or positive outcome of the sacrament. The Risen Lord is truly present at Mass.

Celebration of the sacraments also brings the members of the Church into communion with one another. In fact, recall that the original meaning of the term *liturgy* is "public work" or "service done on behalf of people." The

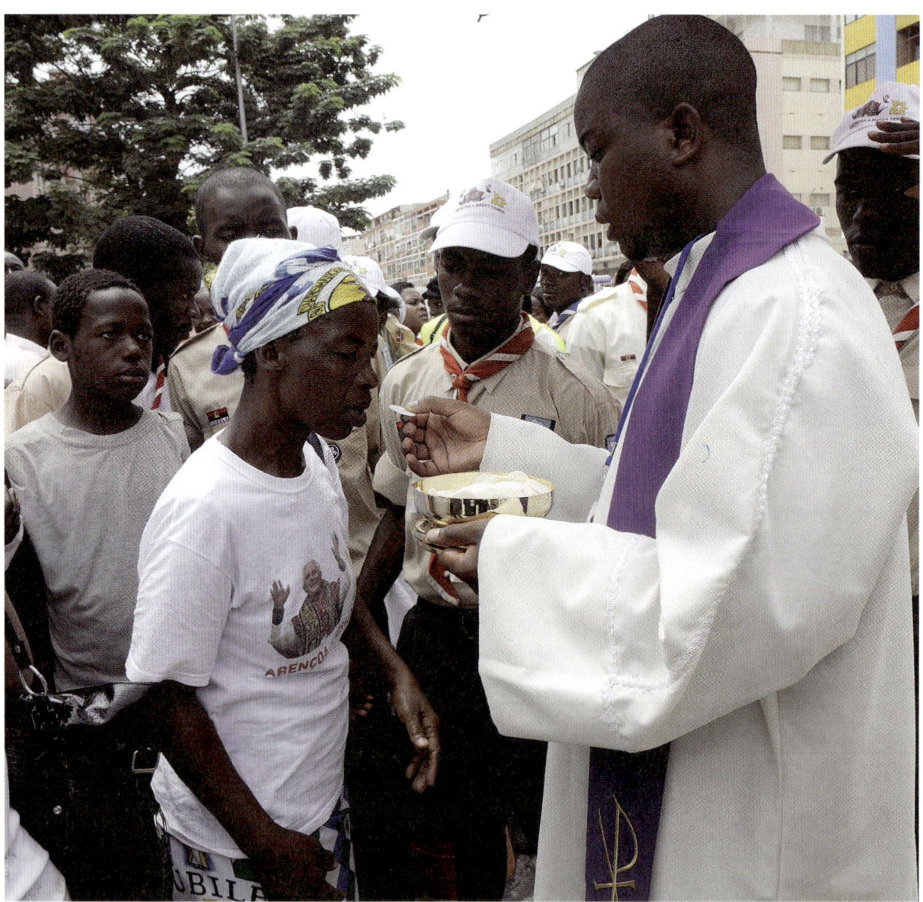

Angolans receive Communion outside Sao Paulo Church in Luanda, Angola.

Eucharistic liturgy, then, involves the participation of the Church in the "work of God." This has been true since the earliest days of the Church. According to the first-century text of the *Didache* (see Chapter 2, Section 4), the Eucharist is a meal that forms the Church into the new People of God: "Even as this broken bread was scattered over the hills, and was gathered together becoming one, so let your Church be gathered together from the ends of the earth into your Kingdom."[15]

In the early Church, no one came to the Eucharist without having resolved any disagreements that might prevent the Church from being truly united in the Lord. Jesus taught, "Therefore, if you bring your gift to the altar, and there recall that your brother has anything against you, leave your gift there at the altar, go first and be reconciled with your brother, and then come and offer your gift" (Mt 5:23–24).

There are many specific parts of the liturgy where the unity of the Church is highlighted. One of these is during the intercessions of the Eucharistic Prayer. The intercessions are prayed by the priest offering the Mass on behalf of the whole Church in heaven and on earth (the living and the dead): for the pope, bishop, and all the clergy, for Catholics in need ("the prayer of the family you have gathered here before you"), and for those who have died ("welcome into your kingdom our departed brothers and sisters, and all who have left this world in your friendship").

The Lord's Prayer also promotes unity with God. It acknowledges the identity of all people as God's adopted children and as brothers and sisters to one another: "When we pray to the Father, we are *in communion with him* and with his Son, Jesus Christ" (*CCC*, 2781).

Finally, the reception of Holy Communion is so intimate that Christ becomes part of those who receive, and they of him. This grace of the sacrament is one-of-a-kind and cannot be replicated with a prayerful walk in the park or with anything else. Jesus said: "Whoever eats my flesh and drinks my blood remains in me and I in him" (Jn 6:56). Assuming the person is properly disposed, the Church recommends that a Catholic receive Communion at every Mass. At the very least, Catholics are obliged by the Church to receive Communion once a year.

Unity with the Church of Heaven and Earth

It can be easy to forget that the Church is not made up solely of people living on earth in the present. The Church on earth is also united with pilgrims in **Purgatory** and with the saints in heaven, and it is especially in the liturgy where this union is realized. The three states of the Church have traditionally gone by these names: the Church Militant on earth, the Church Suffering in Purgatory, and the Church Triumphant in heaven. It is in the liturgy that "with combined rejoicing we celebrate together the praise of the divine majesty; then all those from every tribe and tongue and people and nation who have been redeemed by the blood of Christ and gathered together into one Church, with one song of praise[,] magnify the one and triune God" (*Lumen Gentium*, 50).

The intercession of the saints in heaven helps to strengthen the weakness of those on earth and bring everyone closer to Christ, who is the fountain of all grace. This relationship with the saints is not meant to be one-way: Those on earth should imitate the virtues of the saints. And from her earliest days, the Church has also remembered, honored, and prayed for those in Purgatory to reach heaven.

This unity among the Church of heaven, Purgatory, and earth represents our participation in the one family of God. When you love others and join as the communion of the Church of heaven, Purgatory, and earth in praising the Holy Trinity, you are faithful to your deepest vocation in the hope that you will eventually share in the richness of heaven.

SECTION Assessment

Comprehension

1. In general, how did the Enlightenment thinkers' understanding of personhood differ from the Christian understanding?

2. Name three graces of the Sacrament of the Eucharist.

Purgatory The state of purification that takes place after death for those who need to be made clean and holy before meeting the all-holy God in heaven.

3. Explain how the Eucharist is both the source and summit of the Christian life.

4. What is the minimum frequency with which a Catholic should receive Holy Communion?

Vocabulary

5. Define *venial sin.*

6. What is required of people on earth for those in *Purgatory*?

Reflection

7. Explain how important communal worship on Sunday is to you.

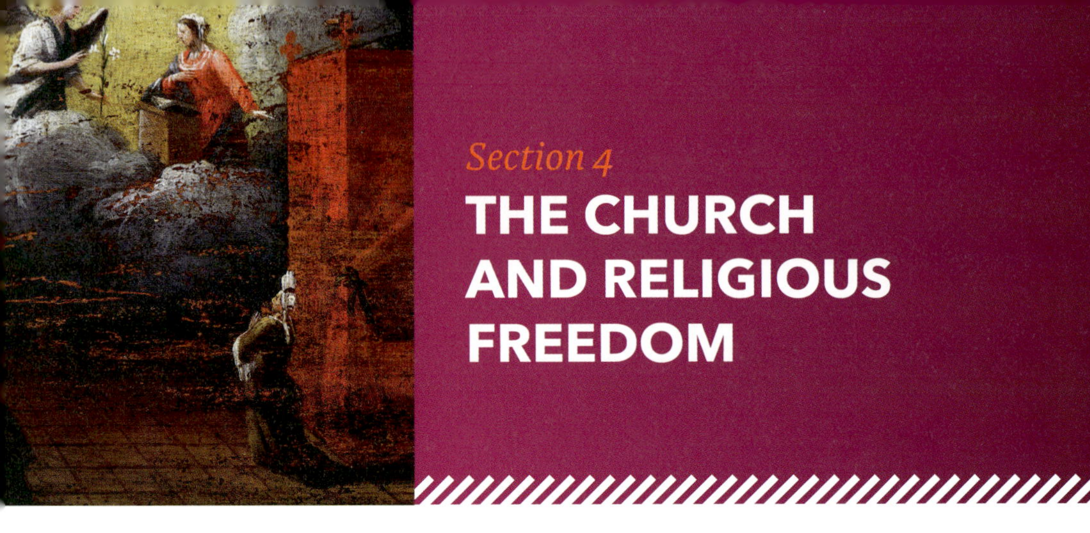

Section 4
THE CHURCH AND RELIGIOUS FREEDOM

Freedom is the power to make the choices that will enable us to fulfill our potential and become the people we are created to be. Anything that makes us less than God intended us to be is not really freedom. Pope John Paul II recognized that freedom is "an essential part of that creaturely image which is the basis of the dignity of the person. Within that freedom there is an echo of the primordial vocation whereby the Creator calls man to the true Good, and even more, through Christ's revelation, to become his friend and to share his own divine life. It is at once inalienable self-possession and openness to all that exists, in passing beyond self to knowledge and love of the other. Freedom then is rooted in the truth about man, and it is ultimately directed towards communion" (*Veritatis Splendor*, 86).

For hundreds of years, a majority of Catholics lived in predominantly Catholic nations that were ruled by Catholic monarchs and in which the Church enjoyed the support of the government. Although there was much conflict between the Church and the monarchs of Europe through the centuries, in most cases the rulers at least recognized the Church's right to exist and conduct her mission with substantial freedom. Revolutions and other upheavals caused widespread change such that by the end of the nineteenth century, most countries were secular democracies. The Church gradually adapted to this new world, reorienting her thought and structure to continue her mission in countries that were variously open, hostile, or indifferent to the Church's freedom to exist and of individual Catholics to practice their religion.

The relationship between the rise of democracy and the Catholic Church is complicated. For a time, it wasn't clear that democratic governments would uphold the rights of the Church, and the Church remained skeptical of the development. As the Enlightenment spread through Europe and its colonies, anti-Catholicism also spread. So it seemed reasonable to associate democracy—one dimension of Enlightenment thought—with another of its dimensions, hostility toward religion. This view gained traction through the Church's experience of the French Revolution, which turned violently against the Catholic faith and obstructed individual Catholics' freedom to pursue the practice of their faith. In France, for example, besides the Reign of Terror, priests were forced to become employees of the state, and the new government confiscated Church property.

The Papal States as they appeared in 1796, just before the Napoleonic War, during which they were divided up to become modern Italy.

The Church's apprehension regarding the fruits of the Enlightenment also grew through what happened to the papacy in the nineteenth century. For a thousand years, the pope had been a "king" as well, the ruler of the **Papal States** in central Italy. As democratic revolutions spread across Europe, they also came to Italy. Pope Pius IX was initially favorable to political reforms that granted more freedom to the people, but as in France, the movement in Italy radicalized and turned hostile toward the Church. Italian revolutionaries wrested the Papal States from the control of the pope and, in the process, created a new, united Italian nation. The experience made it

Papal States The territory in present-day central Italy that was overseen by the pope from the eighth century until 1870.

difficult for the popes to look on democratic governments as compatible with Catholicism.∞

At the same time, the Church appreciated the positive aspects of a democratic government. In some countries, including the United States, the rise of democracy led to *increasing* freedom for the Church. This allowed the Church to boldly proclaim and support the fundamental dignity and value of each person as made in the image of God, which is the indispensable foundation for human freedom. By the end of the nineteenth century, with the Church in the United States growing rapidly under the protection of the Constitution, Pope Leo XIII wrote that he saw in the emergence of the Church in the United States "some design of divine Providence." Referring to President George Washington and Archbishop John Carroll of Baltimore, Pope Leo XIII continued: "At the very time when the popular suffrage placed the great Washington at the helm of the Republic, the first bishop was set by apostolic authority over the American Church. The well-known friendship and familiar intercourse which subsisted between these two men seems to be an evidence that the United States ought to be conjoined in concord and amity with the Catholic Church."[16]

Pope Leo attributed the American Church's growth, in part, to the nation's favorable laws. "Thanks are due," he wrote, "to the equity of the laws

religious freedom A term that promotes human dignity and recognizes and defends the fundamental human right to be free from coercion in religious matters. The Church extends the understanding of religious freedom to indicate that all people are called in freedom to accept Jesus Christ and his Church, which has a divine mission oriented to one's salvation.

∞ Note

At the foundation of the Republic of Italy, the new government did not interfere with Church governance within the Vatican walls. However, other Church property around Rome and Italy was confiscated by the government. Pope Pius IX (1846–1878) was the last ruler of the Papal States. He and his immediate successors did not recognize the Italian king's right to rule Rome, and they remained within the Vatican compound until the dispute was resolved in 1929 with the Lateran Treaty, which established the independent state of Vatican City and reaffirmed Catholicism as the national religion of Italy.

which obtain in America and to the customs of the well-ordered Republic." The Church in the United States, he observed, was "fettered by no hostile legislation, protected against violence by the common laws and the impartiality of the tribunals," and therefore "free to live and act without hindrance." While he praised the American system's respect for the freedom of the Church, Leo invoked the older European model of cooperation between the government and the Church. The state and the Church ought not to be "dissevered and divorced," he insisted; the Church "would bring forth more abundant fruits if, in addition to liberty, she enjoyed the favor of the laws and the patronage of the public authority."

Pope Leo's letter shows that the Church was adjusting gradually to a new world characterized by **religious freedom** and democratic government, but that it still saw the ideal state as one that officially supported the activity of the Church. Determining how best to navigate this new world would continue to be a challenge for the Church into the twentieth century and beyond.

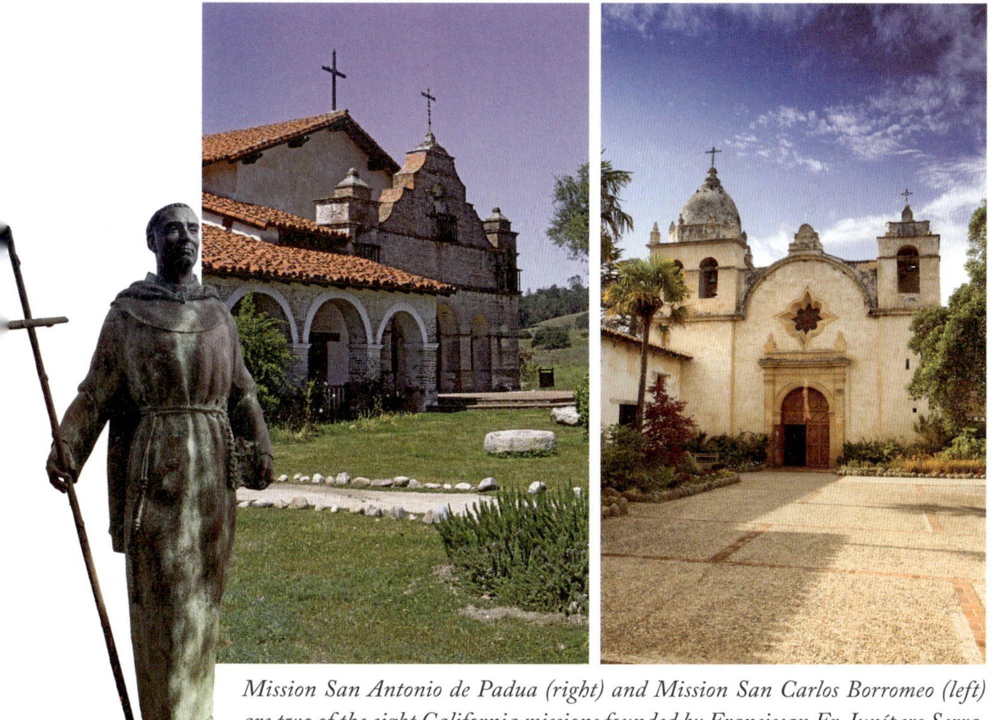

Mission San Antonio de Padua (right) and Mission San Carlos Borromeo (left) are two of the eight California missions founded by Franciscan Fr. Junípero Serra.

More Challenges in the Americas

Recall from Chapter 5 that missionary activity in the Americas occurred alongside the conquest and colonization of the New World by the Spanish, Portuguese, and French Empires. Catholic missionaries faced many challenges in passing on the faith, including some they brought on by their own actions and circumstances. For example, some missionaries took indigenous people as slaves, often treating them harshly. Also, Jesuit missionaries from France carried diseases with them that caused sickness and death to many tribes. When the native peoples connected the diseases to the presence of the missionaries, the missionaries often dismissed them as being "superstitious." Yet in spite of challenges, the Gospel message did take hold. Many people of the New World were baptized.

How did the missionaries do it? You might wonder how they were able to share the faith with people whose native languages were complicated and different from their own, with the additional challenge of using Latin, the official language of the Church, to celebrate the sacraments, including the most essential Sacrament of the Eucharist. The Jesuits had success due to their persistence in learning native languages, translating Christian materials, and immersing themselves in the native cultures. Most often the missionaries were accompanied by translators. They often began by preaching common human beliefs (e.g., that murder and stealing were morally wrong) and applying those to Christian commandments. At times they also accommodated Christian beliefs to native beliefs—for example, the indigenous concept of *Manitou* that held there was one supernatural force that pervaded the natural world. The missionaries used this as a starting point for teaching about **monotheism** and belief in the one, true God. From there, the missionaries worked on instilling, according to sixteenth-century Jesuit missionary José de Acosta,

> the most essential points of our faith, especially those which they ignore most, such as unity of one God, and that we must not worship more than one God, that Jesus Christ is God and man, and

---

monotheism From the Greek words *monos* (one) and *theos* (God), the belief in one all-powerful God. Judaism, Christianity, and Islam are the three great monotheistic religions.

Pope Francis delivered the Mass of Canonization of St. Junípero Serra at the Basilica of the National Shrine of the Immaculate Conception in Washington, DC, in 2015.

the only savior of men, that through sin man loses heaven and is damned forever, that to free oneself from sin, one has to get baptized, or to confess all sins; that God is Father, Son, and Holy Ghost, that there is another life and eternal damnation for the wicked and eternal glory for the just.[17]

Enlightenment ideas spread to these colonies as well, bringing dramatic change to the environment in which the Church operated. Around or shortly after the American Revolution, other Central and South American nations declared independence. In the early nineteenth century, Spain was expelled from Mexico with a revolution. Although most Mexicans remained Catholic and most Mexican priests were on the side of the revolutionaries, the Church as an institution was attacked as an ally of the Spanish Crown. The missions—including those in California, which was still a part of Mexico—were "secularized," meaning that they were removed from the control of the Franciscan order and assigned to diocesan priests. Practically speaking, this resulted in their neglect and eventual dissolution. A similar pattern prevailed throughout Central and South America. Independence from European empires brought political freedom and democracy to the people of these regions, and most continued to identify as Catholic, with many remaining devout in the practice of their faith. However, many Catholic institutions, at least for a time, suffered during the turmoil as anti-Catholic sentiment was allowed free rein.

Although Catholicism remained popular and influential in Latin American culture, the Church no longer had direct access to political power. In the former lands of the Spanish and Portuguese Empires, the governments, shaped by Enlightenment ideas of separation of church and state, were now wary of the Catholic Church as a political force. Many political leaders saw the Church not as a contributor to the common good but as a threat to social and economic progress. This fundamental tension between modern governments and the Church would shape the experience of the Church in the twentieth century.

The Church Perseveres in Society

In the face of government opposition and widespread apathy, the Church continues to insist on her indispensable role in society. This role is based not on the merits of the Church's members but on recognition of God's plan for the Church in the history of the world, as revealed in the life and teaching of Jesus Christ. The sanctification of the world—the building of the Kingdom of God on earth—depends on the action of the Church. "No one can bestow grace on himself; it must be given and offered. This fact presupposes ministers of grace, authorized and empowered by Christ" (*CCC*, 875).

The proclamation of the Good News of salvation is a function of the Church, and "no one can give himself the mandate and the mission to proclaim the Gospel—the one sent by the Lord does not speak and act on his own authority, but by virtue of Christ's authority" (*CCC*, 875). The good that the Church brings to the world—the very life of Christ conferred by grace—cannot be replaced by material wealth, technology, or secular humanitarianism. The Church recognizes the benefits of modernity, but modernity without the Church is hollow and aimless.

SECTION Assessment

Comprehension

1. How did the democratic governments of the eighteenth and nineteenth centuries both help and hinder the Church's freedom and individuals' freedom?

2. What was Pope Leo XIII's idea of an ideal state?

3. What was one method that the Jesuits had for sharing the Gospel with indigenous peoples of the New World?

4. Why were priests distrusted in Mexico after the Mexican Revolution?

Vocabulary

5. What happened to the *Papal States* after the Italian revolution?

6. On a scale of 1 to 10, with 10 meaning "most," rate the United States today in terms of *religious freedom*. Explain.

Reflection

7. Describe how you believe the Church and the state should function together.

8. List three ways you find the Church indispensable for society.

Section Reviews

Focus Question

What are common challenges to practicing one's faith in a society hostile to religion?
Complete one of the following:

- Briefly report on the similarities and differences between the US Bill of Rights, the English Magna Carta, and the French Declaration of the Rights of Man and of the Citizen. Then compare all three to the seven themes of Catholic social teaching (see www.usccb.org).

- Based on your study of this chapter and previous knowledge, list five positive reasons a person would want to belong to the Catholic Church. Rank the reasons from least (5) to most (1) important. Share an explanation of the reasons you ranked 1 and 5.

- Find and cite two examples of discrimination against the Catholic Church occurring today.

Introduction
Turmoil and Opportunity Coincide

Review

The political change that swept the world in the eighteenth and nineteenth centuries impacted the Church. Some viewed the Church as part of the old order and wanted her influence swept away. Yet the faith of Catholics persisted, allowing for great saints, martyrs, and missionaries to flourish in this period. The Church looked for new opportunities as democratic governments emerged.

Assignment

Research and write down a quotation from St. John Vianney, St. Bernadette Soubirous, or Blessed Frédéric Ozanam that you find inspiring. Explain why you find it so.

Section 1
Enlightenment and Revolution

Review

The Enlightenment mentality of hostility to religion, skepticism about Christian truths, and clinging to reason alone ran against God's plan for creation. The chief aim of the world is not technological, scientific, or economic progress, but rather the salvation of all people. Nevertheless, the Church does not oppose science or reason; rather she encourages the cooperation of both with faith. Many Catholics have been pioneers in the field of science.

Assignment

Research and write down one interesting fact about the lives of at least two of the Catholic scientists listed in the subsection "The Church Is a Pioneer of Science, Not an Enemy of Science" in Chapter 6, Section 1.

Section 2
Mary: Beacon of Renewal in the Church

Review

Marian devotion is based on our belief that Mary is the perfect disciple of Jesus and therefore the model of our faith. As the Mother of the Church, she is our mother because we are part of Christ's Body. Conceived immaculately, she was the vessel for bringing God's Son into the world. She is also the vessel for the beginning of the Church. She was perpetually a virgin, and God rewarded her at the end of her life by assuming her body and soul directly into heaven. Mary enables and emboldens our own holiness. There were several Marian apparitions in the nineteenth century that witnessed to her motherhood to all believers.

Assignment

Compose a short prayer or poem to Mary. Include in it a mention of her motherhood to you and the Church.

Section 3

The Church Balances Individualism and Communion

Review

The Church values and respects individuals' freedom to choose their own destiny while understanding all people as inherently oriented to community. This belief is best practiced by Catholics in the communal worship of the Sacrament of the Eucharist, which is the source and summit of our faith. Celebration of the Eucharist brings Catholics into communion with God and with others, including the Church in heaven and in Purgatory.

Assignment

Write a letter (not an email) to a relative or friend who has been away from the Church. You can tell the person that your letter is part of a school assignment if you wish. Be sure to share something about your life and the importance of your faith. Invite the person to attend Mass with you.

Section 4

The Church and Religious Freedom

Review

Freedom is an essential part of the Christian vocation. For the most part, freedom flourished under the rise of democratic governments in the nineteenth century. With the rise of democracy came more societal and religious freedom. The Church was initially skeptical of democracy because it came with attacks on the Church in places such as France and Italy. The Church's missionary efforts continued in the New World, with the Jesuits often taking the lead in the difficult task of communicating the Gospel to indigenous peoples.

Assignment

Research the Church's position on the accommodation of the faith by Jesuit missionaries to people in China.

Chapter Projects

Choose and complete at least one of the following projects to assess your understanding of the material in this chapter.

⚙ 1. Create an Our Lady of Guadalupe Notebook

Answer each of the following questions concerning Mary's apparitions to St. Juan Diego near Mexico City in 1531. Print each question and your written response on a separate lefthand page of a paper notebook. On the righthand page opposing it, draw the requested illustration.

- *Write*: Where was St. Juan Diego going when the Lady first appeared to him?
- *Draw*: Mary's appearance to Juan Diego on Tepeyac Hill.
- *Write*: Why do you think the Lady wanted Juan Diego to inform the bishop of the apparition?
- *Draw*: Juan Diego opening his tilma before the bishop and having the roses fall out.
- *Write*: Quote some of the actual words that Our Lady spoke to Juan Diego in one of her apparitions.
- *Draw*: The famous image of Our Lady of Guadalupe.
- *Write*: When was the Basilica of Our Lady of Guadalupe in Mexico City completed?
- *Draw*: The front of the basilica and its public square.

⚙ 2. Introduce Famous Catholic Missionaries to the United States

Do *one* of the following assignments.

- Write a three-page report detailing the life of one of the missionaries listed below. Include information about the missionary's early life, how the person came to America, the goal and results of the mission, how the person's life ended, and his or her legacy.

- Prepare a flash slideshow or PowerPoint presentation displaying each of the missionaries listed below in chronological or geographical sequence. Include two slides for each person. On one of the slides, include biographical information in the caption. On the other slide, include a quotation from the missionary.

Partial List of Catholic Missionaries in the United States

Juan Baptista de Segura: One of eight Jesuit missionaries killed by natives near the future site of Jamestown, Virginia, in 1571

Georgia Martyrs: Six Franciscans killed near their mission base of St. Augustine, Florida, in 1597

St. Isaac Jogues: With the other North American Martyrs, was put to death by the Iroquois in the seventeenth century

Andrew White: English Jesuit who was known as the "Apostle of Maryland"

Sébastien Râle: Jesuit missionary who ministered to the indigenous Abenaki people around Maine at the beginning of the eighteenth century

Eusebio Kino: Jesuit martyr who founded twenty-four missions in Mexico and the southwestern United States

Ferdinand Farmer: Eighteenth-century German Jesuit priest who ministered to Catholics in eastern Pennsylvania, New Jersey, and New York

Jacques Marquette: French Jesuit priest who traveled with Louis Jolliet on his exploration of the Mississippi River and founded the first European settlement in Michigan

Gabriel Richard: French priest who became a delegate to the United States House of Representatives from the Michigan Territory in the early eighteenth century

Frederic Baraga: First bishop in the Upper Peninsula in Michigan

Stephen Badin: First priest ordained in the United States; explored Kentucky and the Ohio Valley in the early nineteenth century

St. Elizabeth Ann Bayley Seton: Religious sister and first American saint; was instrumental in laying the groundwork for the Catholic school system in the United States

Demetrius Gallitzin and Peter Henry Lemke: Helped Catholics to settle in western Pennsylvania

St. Junípero Serra and Fermín de Lasuén: Spanish Franciscans who founded twenty-one missions in California

Pierre de Smet: Traveled nearly 180,000 miles in the western United States to minister to Native Americans; known as a friend of Sitting Bull

St. Katharine Drexel and Venerable Samuel Mazzuchelli: Focused on missions to Native Americans and African Americans

St. Damien of Molokai and Blessed Marianne Cope: The first missionaries in Hawaii, focusing eventually on the leper colony there

Venerable Fulton J. Sheen: Head of the Society for the Propagation of the Faith in the 1950s and 1960s who also had a nationally televised program of evangelization

⚙ *3. Design Word Puzzles Using Chapter Vocabulary Words*

Create three different word puzzles using vocabulary and other key words in and related to this chapter, for example, *Enlightenment, Galileo, monotheism, Vianney, Badin, venial, democracy, Bernadette, Marquette, Purgatory, Guadalupe, Napoleon, modernity, Voltaire, pluralism, apparition*, and many more. You may also choose terms related to topics in this chapter (e.g., monotheism versus deism). Each puzzle should include a minimum of ten words. You can repeat the same words in the different puzzles. You can choose your own type of word puzzle. Examples include word search, word ladder, anagram, crossword, brain teaser.

⚙ *4. Explain Why We Need the Church*

Christian faith cannot be separated from a relationship with the Church, because where the Church is, God is. There are many specific reasons why we need the Church. Make a chart like the one below. Read the *Catechism of the Catholic Church* paragraphs listed in the first column. In the second column, write summaries of the paragraphs (the first one is completed for you). In the third column, write your answers to each of the reflection questions.

CATECHISM PARAGRAPHS	SUMMARY	REFLECTION
CCC, 760	God wants to be present with us as members of his family. The Church was made for that purpose.	Q: What image best describes your vision of Church? Why? A:
CCC, 875		Q: Who is a Catholic who has modeled servant leadership to you? A:
CCC, 820		Q: What is something that you can personally do to repair Christian unity? A:
CCC, 1140–1141		Q: Describe a liturgy that made you feel at home in the Church. A:
CCC, 1322–1324		Q: Which name for Eucharist best describes how you feel about the sacrament? Explain. A:
CCC, 1093–1097		Q: How do you understand yourself fitting into salvation history? A:
CCC, 871–874; 876–879		Q: Imagine choosing religious life for yourself. Who would be the first person you would tell? What would you say? How would the person respond? A:

⚙ *5. Help the Missionary Childhood Association*

A motto of the Missionary Childhood Association (MCA) is "Children helping children." One of the Pontifical Mission Societies in the United States, the Missionary Childhood Association was founded by the French bishop Charles de Forbin-Janson in order to help the missionary needs he had witnessed firsthand while in the United States. He had observed on a visit to New York that "there is not yet a minor or major seminary, and this diocese is larger than all of England." A common way children of the United States support the MCA is by offering prayers and financial help after learning about the needs of the poor children of the world. You may have once contributed your gift of coins and dollars to one of the MCA boxes during Lent. Besides this help, there are other things you can do to support mission awareness and the MCA. Choose and complete one of the following options. Write a three-page report summarizing your role in the event you chose in support of the Missionary Childhood Association.

- Sponsor a living Rosary at your school where students wear shirts, hats, or bandanas representing various colors of the mysteries of the Rosary. Pray for the poor children of the world. Arrange a financial donation that can be collected and given to the MCA.

- Sponsor an "international hat parade" in which students wear hats that represent a country in the world. Parade together to other classrooms during the school day. Have each person in your group prepare a brief report on the poor in the country he or she represents. Collect donations from the students for the MCA.

- Sponsor a lunchtime or after-school walkathon in support of the missions. Arrange for businesses and individuals to support the participants with donations for laps or yards walked. Share a short presentation at the beginning of the walkathon about a famous missionary. Point out that the participants will be "walking in step with the missionaries," who have always shared the Gospel with others.

Faithful Disciple
Adele Brise

Adele Brise

December 8, 2010, the Feast of the Immaculate Conception, was a momentous day for the Church and for the United States of America. It was on that day that Bishop David Ricken of Green Bay issued a decree that authenticated the nineteenth-century apparitions of the Blessed Virgin Mary to a young woman, Adele Brise, in the farmlands near Champion, Wisconsin. A shrine built there, now known as the National Shrine of Our Lady of Champion, reminds the Church that the apparitions of Mary to Adele Brise are worthy of belief in the same way that those at Guadalupe in Mexico, Lourdes in France, and Fatima in Portugal are because of their approval by a local bishop. Mary's appearances to Adele Brise are the first Marian apparitions approved by the Church in the United States.

Adele Brise's story is a remarkable one. The oldest of four children of Belgian immigrants, she came with her family in 1855, at the age of twenty-four, to the Green Bay peninsula. Her father purchased 240 acres of land in the town of Red River for 120 dollars. Adele had intended to join a religious community when she came to America, but her first years in Wisconsin were taken up with the hard work of farming and pioneer life.

Adele's life changed in early October 1859. While she was carrying grain to a mill about four miles from her home, Mary appeared to her. A few days later, on October 9, while she was walking to Sunday Mass in Bay Settlement, about eleven miles from home, Mary appeared to her again. After

Mass, Adele told the pastor about what she had seen. He told her to ask in God's name who it was and what it desired of her. On the way home, Mary appeared a third time, and Adele asked the question the pastor had suggested. Mary responded, "I am the Queen of Heaven who prays for the conversion of sinners and I wish you to do the same. Gather the children in this wild country and teach them what they should know for salvation. Teach them their catechism, how to sign themselves with the Sign of the Cross, and how to approach the sacraments."

Adele Brise dedicated the rest of her life to doing what Mary instructed. She gathered the children near her home and taught them the faith. She also traveled to other farms, sometimes as far as fifty miles away, to do the same. She faced the challenges of the forest and weather, which were often easier to handle than the ridicule she received from those who didn't believe that Mary had really appeared to her.

Eventually, a school and chapel were built at the site of the appearances. Most of the students were orphans. Adele, who gathered a lay community known as the Sisters of Good Help around her, often went begging for what she and the school needed. When food was scarce, Adele would pray to Mary

The National Shrine of Our Lady of Champion in New Franken, Wisconsin.

for help. Inevitably someone would drop by a sack of flour or some meat to get them through the next days.

A huge forest fire known as the Peshtigo Fire threatened the area on October 8, 1871 (the same day as the Great Chicago Fire). People brought animals and their families to the grounds of the chapel. Adele carried a statue of Mary around the perimeter of the grounds. On the outer portion of the perimeter everything burned. The fire did not advance inside the five-acre section near the school and chapel. Many considered this a miracle. Every year since, pilgrims have gathered on October 8 to reenact the original procession.

Bishop Ricken began looking into Mary's appearances to Adele in 2009, and much of his investigation involved the life of Adele Brise. The bishop said this about her: "What has struck me about the story of the life of Adele Brise is her lifelong fidelity to what the Blessed Mother asked her to do with her life. She dedicated her life to prayer, especially for the conversion of sinners, and to the catechesis of children. She made great sacrifices and attracted other young women to follow her in fidelity to the Blessed Mother's call."

Comprehension

1. What is unique about the location of Mary's appearance to Adele Brise?
2. What did Mary ask of Adele?
3. Describe the miraculous event that convinced others to believe that Mary had truly appeared to Adele.

Reflection

Imagine that you are teaching younger children about what they should know for their salvation. What would you tell them?

Prayer

A morning offering is meant to be prayed first thing upon waking up. The purpose is to focus on and dedicate one's day to God. The morning offering listed below was composed by Fr. François-Xavier Gautrelet in 1844. By referring to the Sacred Heart of Jesus and the Immaculate Heart of Mary, it reflects a devotion linking the two devotions that was first formalized in the seventeenth century by St. John Eudes. Other, more recent devotions grew from this idea: in the twentieth century, St. Maximilian Kolbe described consecration to Mary as in actuality being "to Jesus through Mary."

Morning Offering

O Jesus through the Immaculate Heart of Mary,
I offer you my prayers, works, joys, and sufferings of this day,
in union with the Holy Sacrifice of the Mass throughout the world.
I offer them for all the intentions of your Sacred Heart:
the salvation of souls, the reparation for sin, the reunion of Christians;
and in particular for the intentions of the Holy Father this month.
Amen.

The Church Faces a More Hostile World

Cloud of Witnesses

Br. Mickey McGrath

Br. Mickey McGrath, a member of the Oblates of St. Francis de Sales near Philadelphia, insisted on doing things his own way and in his own time from his earliest days as a child. That spirit has carried over to his artwork, where he has dabbled in painting in a variety of techniques and styles. One of his trademarks is that he paints people who don't always look like him: a white American male who grew up in a suburban neighborhood during the early stages of the civil rights movement of the 1960s. "I never witnessed it firsthand, but I watched it on the news," he said. "Water cannons and vicious Southern policemen with snarling dogs were just as scary to me as Nazi storm troopers and SS commandants."

It was art—in the mediums of radio, film, and eventually painting—that rescued Br. McGrath from his doldrums. "I was awakened by beauty and art and all those things that unite us as a human family." During his time as an art major at Moravian College, his scope of characters and styles expanded. "In the beginning, Black, Jewish, Puerto Rican, and Asian teens were as new to me as ink, paint, charcoal, and clay." Eventually, Br. McGrath began to focus on topics associated with social justice along with multicultural issues. Many of his paintings have been used by Catholic Relief Services in various promotions and resources.

In *Cloud of Witnesses*, pictured here, Br. McGrath paints swirling Catholic disciples in bright colors. They are, clockwise starting from the top left, St. Francis de Sales, St. Thérèse of Lisieux, Servant of God Nicholas Black Elk, Venerable Augustus Tolton, Servant of God Dorothy Day, and Servant of God Thea Bowman. All of these people have connections with the Church's social teaching; after completing this painting, Br. McGrath created separate paintings focusing on each of these people individually.

Cloud of Witnesses is symbolic of Br. Mickey McGrath's own life: "As I envision the long and winding road of my adult spiritual journey, I see it lined with my favorite cloud of witnesses, a beloved communion of saints creating a litany of holy woke-ness across the ages of Church history—and I want to be in that number when they go marching in."[1]

If you would like to delve more into colorful painting and research the modern Catholic disciples in this painting, see Chapter 7 Review, Chapter Project 1.

How does the Church bring greater unity to our family, faith, and world?

Introduction

The Church Is Unchanging in a Changing World

Section 1

The Foundation of the Church's Formal Social Doctrine

Section 2

The Church Works to Increase Unity

Section 3

The Church and Totalitarianism

Section 4

The Importance of Family

THE CHURCH IS UNCHANGING IN A CHANGING WORLD

Even after Jesus ascended into heaven and even after the death of the last Apostle, the next generation of Christians understood that Christ still lives and is still present to the Church. As Christians, we await no new public revelation, but rather seek to grasp the full meaning of what the Lord has already revealed. For example, throughout the ages, the Church has recognized certain "private" revelations, such as the appearances of the Blessed Virgin Mary at Lourdes and Fatima. However, as the *Catechism* reminds us, it is not the role of these private revelations "to improve or complete Christ's definitive revelation, but to help live more fully by it in a certain period of history" (*CCC*, 67). Jesus himself is the fullness of God's revelation to humankind. As Sacred Scripture teaches, "Jesus Christ is the same yesterday, today, and forever" (Heb 13:8).

Likewise, part of the Church's own mystery is that she is also unchanging. The Body of Christ, the Church, is constant in her permanent apostolic structure established by Jesus; her permanent moral teachings, which likewise are rooted in the teachings of Jesus; and her permanent dogma, those absolute truths that were revealed by Christ and are so indispensable to the Christian faith that their essence can never be changed.

Yet the Church's understanding of God's revelation has increased throughout history. Although Jesus Christ is the absolute and complete self-communication of God to humanity, the Church's understanding of Jesus and the truth that he revealed is constantly growing and deepening. The role of the Church as the Body of Christ guided by the Holy Spirit is to continue to reveal the presence of God and to lead all people to unity with the Father, just as Jesus did. It is the task of the Church to interpret what is going on in today's world in light of the Gospel.∞

For example, in the modern period that stretched approximately from the sixteenth to the nineteenth century (see Chapter 6), the Church was forced to confront a new world, one in which a multitude of religious beliefs circulated and any religious belief at all was often challenged. While these developments did not change the essence of the Church, which is constant even as Christ himself is constant, they did induce the Church to adapt her approach to the world she lived in and ministered to. As the twentieth century opened and progressed, even more new and unforeseen historical, scientific, and cultural changes rocked society and demanded new responses from the Church.

The Church Speaks Out on Social Issues

As ideologies and political systems outside the Church's control continued to rise to power in the nineteenth century and into the twentieth century, the Church sought to remind the world that the true path to social welfare, economic fairness, and world peace is following the teachings of Christ. A systematic definition of the Church's teachings on how to apply the principles of the Gospels to changing social situations was needed. The Church's emphasis on taking care of those in need was not new; Jesus himself had commanded his followers to do so, and care for the poor, sick, and suffering had been a central concern of Christianity since the apostolic era. In the modern world, in which many people were no longer receptive to the Gospel delivered as an explicitly religious message, however, the Church's social outreach was

∞ Note

The Second Vatican Council pastoral constitution *Gaudium et Spes*, promulgated by Pope Paul VI in 1965, well understood the changing times that the world has experienced ever since. One of its opening paragraphs stated that "the Church has always had the duty of scrutinizing the signs of the times and of interpreting them in the light of the Gospel. Thus, in language intelligible to each generation, she can respond to the perennial questions which men ask about this present life and the life to come, and about the relationship of the one to the other. We must therefore recognize and understand the world in which we live, its explanations, its longings, and its often dramatic characteristics" (*GS*, 4).

increasingly important as a lived demonstration of the potential of the Gospel to bear good fruit for all people. A written body of social doctrine based in the Gospel was indeed formulated in this age, and Pope Leo XIII (see Section 1 of this chapter) was at the forefront of these efforts.

New social dimensions were also prominently on display in the Church in the United States, where the Church grew rapidly in the twentieth century in a predominantly non-Catholic environment. Maintaining intact Catholic belief while trying to thrive in a non-Catholic nation was a challenge, and the growth of the Church in the United States was not without difficulty. The necessity of interacting with Protestants and more others in the American context challenged the Church to reflect on and articulate her relationship with non-Catholic Christians and those of other faith traditions. The United States became an important venue for the practice of *ecumenism* (see subsection "Teachings and Tasks of Ecumenism" in Section 2 of this chapter) and dialogue with non-Christian religions.

The Church Remains a Pilgrim People

Confronted by a world increasingly hostile to her teachings, the Church was forcefully reminded of her true role on this earth. The image of the Church as a "pilgrim people" is rooted in the Scriptures and reinforced throughout the writings of the saints. The First Letter of Peter states: "Beloved, I urge you as aliens and sojourners to keep away from worldly desires that wage war against the soul. Maintain good conduct among the Gentiles, so that if they speak of you as evildoers, they may observe your good works and glorify God on the day of visitation" (1 Pt 2:11–12).

As pilgrims, Catholics are on a journey, on their way to a destination at which they have not yet arrived. The Church is striving toward perfection, toward deeper communion with God through Christ. At the same time, she recognizes that this perfect communion of the Church with God will never occur in this world. The Church's destination is beyond this world; she "will attain its full perfection only in the glory of heaven, when there will come the time of the restoration of all things" (*Lumen Gentium*, 48). From the perspective of the Church, this life is not all there is. While the Church seeks to proclaim the Gospel and build the kingdom, her goal is not worldly success. Rather, the Church's goal is the sanctification of her people, so that they will find salvation through Christ and thus find their way home to him in heaven.

The twentieth century underscored the Catholic Church's character as a pilgrim people. While the Church continued to spread across the world and grew to encompass a billion believers, in many places she faced hostility from governments, the societal elite, and dominant cultural and intellectual movements. Totalitarian regimes under the influence of communist and Nazi ideologies persecuted Christians who refused to cede to the state all authority over every aspect of life. In other places, false ideas about wealth, status, marriage, and family came to dominate the culture, undermining the Church's efforts to guide her people on the way of true happiness. Through everything, the Church strove to be faithful to her vocation as the Bride of Christ: to form and nurture the family of God, particularly through the **domestic church**, on her pilgrim journey toward eternal life with God.

---

domestic church A name for the Christian family. In the family, parents and children exercise their priesthood of the baptized by worshipping God, receiving the sacraments, and witnessing to Christ and the Church by living as faithful disciples.

SECTION Assessment

Comprehension

1. In what three ways is the Church unchanging?

2. Why was it necessary for the Church to focus on the social dimension of the Gospel beginning in the nineteenth century?

3. What does 1 Peter 2:11–12 teach about the Church operating as a "pilgrim people"?

Vocabulary

4. What is meant by the *domestic church*?

Reflection

5. On a scale of 1 to 10, how much effort do you put into reaching worldly goals? How much effort do you put into reaching the goal of heaven? Explain both of your ratings.

THE FOUNDATION OF THE CHURCH'S FORMAL SOCIAL DOCTRINE

Why does discussion of the Church's formal social doctrine usually begin with Pope Leo XIII in the nineteenth century, even though the Church has cared for the poor in all ages? The answer is fairly simple. Before the nineteenth century, there was little perceived need for a social doctrine that was any more explicit than that found in the Gospels. It was enough to feed the hungry, tend the sick, clothe the naked, and share what one had with the poor. However, at the dawn of the Industrial Revolution with its new structures, society began to change as the "Gospel encountered modern industrial society with its new structures for the production of consumer goods, its new concept of society, the state and authority, and its new forms of labor and ownership" (*CCC*, 2421). Pope Leo XIII and others understood that the Church had an important role to play in evaluating and shaping the new society. There was a need for a systemic teaching that would help apply the principles of the Gospel to changing social situations.

In *Rerum Novarum* (see the feature "Models of Faith in the Modern Era" in Chapter 6, Section 2) Pope Leo addressed concern about the rise of *ideologies*—systems of thought—that undermined the faith and were also harmful to the well-being of the world's people. He criticized **laissez-faire capitalism**, which held that material wealth and economic efficiency were the chief aims of society and might be pursued at the expense of the dignity of individual persons. He insisted that workers be paid a just wage and that public policy support the formation and maintenance of strong families. He likewise condemned socialism and communism, which violated the right of individuals

laissez-faire capitalism An economic theory from the eighteenth century that opposes any government intervention in the business market. *Laissez-faire* is a French term for "let it be."

to own property and neglected the importance of individual initiative in economic activity.

Despite Pope Leo's warnings, errors that emanated from the Industrial Revolution continued to spread and cause widespread suffering throughout the twentieth century.[∞] On the fortieth anniversary of *Rerum Novarum* in 1931, Pope Pius XI issued another social encyclical, *Quadragesimo Anno* (*On Reconstruction of the Social Order*). The *Great Depression*, a severe worldwide economic downturn, was then underway, and Pope Pius located the cause of financial distress in the greed of the wealthy and powerful, who had failed to practice justice and charity toward those in need. The pope described the ultimate consequences of the individualist spirit in economic life this way: "Free

competition has destroyed itself; economic dictatorship has supplanted the free market; unbridled ambition for power has likewise succeeded greed for gain; all economic life has become tragically hard, inexorable, and cruel" (*Quadragesimo Anno*, 109).

Pope John XXIII issued two social encyclicals: *Mater et Magistra* (*Mother and Teacher*) in 1961 and *Pacem in Terris* (*Peace on Earth*) in 1963. In 1963, when Pope John wrote *Pacem in Terris*, the world was recovering from two devastating world wars over the previous fifty

Free soup distributed by the Salvation Army Soup Kitchen, Gateshead, England, 1934.

∞ Note

The Industrial Revolution changed the societal roles of individuals and families. Working conditions were often inhumane. The advent of industrialization increased the production of goods but moved the workforce to crowded cities, away from small, local shops and farms. Human rights violations were rampant. Living wages were disregarded. There were few employer savings or pension programs. Most despicably, children as young as six years old were made to work long days—sometimes up to nineteen hours per day—in cramped buildings known as *sweatshops*.

years. While history had seen destructive natural disasters and plagues, World War I and World War II produced human-caused violence on an unprecedented scale, not to mention the physical damage to cities and landscapes and the spiritual damage inflicted both on people who perpetrated violence and on those who were victims of it. It is estimated that World War II caused the deaths of at least seventy million people.

Yet World War II did not bring lasting peace. In the 1960s, the world was locked in a "Cold War" between the United States and the Soviet Union. Both nations possessed large numbers of nuclear weapons, a technology whose destructive potential had been demonstrated to terrible effect when the United States dropped atomic bombs on the Japanese cities of Hiroshima and

Mother *and* Teacher

In *Mater et Magistra* (*Mother and Teacher*), Pope John XXIII wrote that the Church "was entrusted by her holy Founder the twofold task of giving life to her children and of teaching them and guiding them—both as individuals and as nations—with maternal care" (*MM*, 1). Mary is a model for and an image of the Church, in part because she is the model of motherhood, and the Church is our mother, nurturing us as we grow and mature in our faith. ("Holy Mother Church" is a phrase that used to be common among Catholics.) Even as human mothers are also teachers, instructing their children in countless ways through word and example, so the Church is both mother and teacher.

Nagasaki to end World War II. "In this age which boasts of its atomic power," Pope John wrote, "it no longer makes sense to maintain that war is a fit instrument with which to repair the violation of justice." The quest for alternatives to war, the pope continued, provided grounds for hope: "We are hopeful that, by establishing contact with one another and by a policy of negotiation, nations will come to a better recognition of the natural ties that bind them together as men. We are hopeful, too, that they will come to a fairer realization of one of the cardinal duties deriving from our common nature: namely, that love, not fear, must dominate the relationships between individuals and between nations" (*Pacem in Terris*, 127, 129).

Pope John Paul II continued to stress the themes of his predecessors, urging the world to avoid the errors of socialism and unrestrained capitalism. In 1991, he commented on the fall of communism in the Soviet Union and Eastern Europe, celebrating the new possibility of increased political and economic freedom for the people who had been oppressed by communist regimes. But those freed from totalitarianism would trade one mistaken ideology for another, he warned, if they embraced the consumerism and individualism that were rampant in noncommunist nations: "The crisis of Marxism does not rid the world of the situations of injustice and oppression which Marxism itself exploited and on which it fed," Pope John Paul II observed. Marxist communism had presented itself as one answer to the search for true freedom, but the pope reminded the world that true liberation only comes through accepting the saving message of Jesus: "To those who are searching today for a new and authentic theory and praxis of liberation the Church offers not only her social doctrine and, in general, her teaching about the human person redeemed in Christ, but also her concrete commitment and material assistance in the struggle against marginalization and suffering" (*Centesimus Annus*, 26).

Throughout the twentieth century, the Church continued her long tradition of providing care and assistance to those in need. In doing so, she reflected and pointed the way to the love of Christ. In the United States, for example, the Church built a massive system of charitable institutions consisting of thousands of hospitals, homes for the elderly, international aid organizations, soup kitchens, immigrant aid agencies, adoption agencies, and other services. While attempting to live the words of *Mater et Magistra*, the Church as *mother* fostered among her people the works of charity that showed the world this better way in practice; the Church as *teacher* tried to remind the world of the way to human flourishing.

The Church Continues to Guide God's Revelation

To understand the proper course of our personal and communal actions, the Church insists that both reason *and* revelation are essential. In a modern world where we are surrounded by innumerable opinions concerning the nature of God and morality, looking to revelation through the sure guidance of the Church is more necessary than ever. The alternative is confusion and aimlessness. Without the light of revelation, Pope John Paul II wrote in *Veritatis Splendor* (*The Splendor of Truth*), "man's capacity to know the truth is . . . darkened," and so, "giving himself over to relativism and skepticism, he goes off in search of an illusory freedom apart from the truth itself" (*VS*, 1). For example, consider how human reason alone might offer up answers to these questions:

- Does a woman's right to choose what to do with her body really trump the right of an innocent unborn human to live?

- Are the poor of another nation really our responsibility?

- Are unnatural, scientific means to conceive a child acceptable?

- Do same-sex couples have a right to marry?

Modern culture often tells us these answers are clear. But are they really? How we answer them could have a big impact on our lives. We need to get the answers right. God did not leave us on our own to search for—and perhaps never to find—the truth. The Church, the living Body of Christ, offers truly clear and objective answers.

Thus, we see the need for the Church as evangelist and teacher. For "Jesus Christ, the 'light of the nations,' shines upon the face of his Church, which he sends forth to the whole world to proclaim the Gospel to every creature (cf. Mk 16:15)." And so the Church, "attentive to the new challenges of history and to mankind's efforts to discover the meaning of life, offers to everyone the answer which comes from the truth about Jesus Christ and his Gospel" (*Veritatis Splendor*, 2).

The Church Confronts Modernism

Questions like those posed in the previous subsection seem confined to today. But the truth is that these difficult issues began to arise early in the twentieth century with the rise of *modernism*. Do not confuse modernism with modernity. Modernism of the late nineteenth and early twentieth centuries was a movement that attempted to reduce or limit what the Church could teach about advances in history, science, and biblical research. Whereas certain aspects of *modernity* are compatible with Catholicism, *modernism* is a set of ideas that cannot be reconciled with the Catholic faith.

Pope Pius X (1903–1914), Pope Leo XIII's successor, looked critically at the development of modernism. The modernism that Pope Pius attacked was

The Descent of the Modernists, *by E. J. Pace, first appearing in his book* Christian Cartoons, *published in 1922.*

in a way a continuation of the Enlightenment error concerning the nature of human reason. The pope criticized the idea that "reason is confined entirely within the field of . . . things that are perceptible to the senses" and therefore can determine nothing about God or the supernatural (*Pascendi Dominici Gregis*, 6). You may have heard statements along these lines: that science is "rational" while religion is "irrational"; or that we can know with certainty things about the natural world, but religion is just a "personal thing," a private belief based on opinions or feelings.

Pope Pius X pointed out that this way of understanding reality is the philosophical foundation for *agnosticism*, the belief that nothing can be known with certainty about God. In this view, religion is based not on reasonable apprehension of the truth about God, Jesus, and the Church, but on *sentiment*—feelings about who God is and what his plan is for our lives. This approach makes religious truth merely *subjective*, a matter for each individual to decide based on his or her own experiences and feelings. The common phrases "my truth" and "your truth" reflect this mistaken notion about reality—that two contradictory beliefs can both be true at the same time. Yet God either exists or he does not. The truth of his existence is independent of what we think about it. The task of human reason is not to create truth but to conform our beliefs to reality: to accept the things we find to be true, even if they make us uncomfortable or force us to reevaluate the way we live.

While experience and feelings are important aspects of the spiritual life, they are an uncertain guide. Yet another Pope Pius reminded the modern world of the Church's indispensable role in guiding human thought and action. Pope Pius XII (1939–1958) reaffirmed that "human reason by its own natural force and light can arrive at a true and certain knowledge of the one personal God, Who by His providence watches over and governs the world," but he also cautioned that the human intellect is hampered in its search for the truth by the effects of Original Sin. He wrote, "It is for this reason that divine revelation must be considered morally necessary so that . . . religious and moral truths . . . may be known by all men readily with a firm certainty and with freedom from all error" (*Humani Generis*, 2–3).

The Church's social teaching and her appraisal of modernism are examples of the way she constantly scrutinizes the "signs of the times," the new developments and ideas that emerge in human history, and interprets them in the light of the Gospel. It is the Church's task to distinguish what is good from what is harmful in contemporary ideas and movements. In doing so, the Church continues her mission of proclaiming salvation in Christ, preserving and handing on his teaching to every generation. The Church nurtures and instructs. She is truly both mother and teacher.

SECTION Assessment

Comprehension

1. What led to the need for the Church to record a systematic definition of her teachings on social situations in the nineteenth century?

2. What led Pope John XXIII to conclude that war is not a viable solution to conflict in the modern world?

3. Rather than a new political or economic source for liberation, what alternative did Pope John Paul II suggest?

4. Why are both reason and revelation essential to guide personal and communal actions?

5. How does modernism differ from modernity?

6. How does the Church interpret the "signs of the times"?

Vocabulary

7. Define *laissez-faire capitalism*.

Reflection

8. How do you imagine some alternatives to war as Pope John XXIII alluded to in *Pacem in Terris*?

9. What do you think it means when someone claims his or her own "personal truth"? What is the danger of this perspective?

THE CHURCH WORKS TO INCREASE UNITY

The wounds to Church unity, exacerbated in the years since the Protestant Reformation, remained present at the turn of the twentieth century. Unity, or oneness, as one of the marks of the Church, is something that should never be abandoned over an unwillingness to dialogue and heal divisions. The Church, like any family, has breaks in her unity. Today, there remain different ecclesial or church communities—for example, Baptists, Methodists, and Presbyterians—that profess belief in Jesus Christ but are not fully united with the Catholic Church. These divisions must always be addressed with prayer. Throughout the twentieth century, more and more efforts were begun on all sides to forge discussion and agreement as well.

Among the separated Protestant communities, the commitment to work toward Christian unity began in 1910 with the World Missionary Conference in Edinburgh, Scotland, where a focus was, according to news reports, "to exchange views on the ways and means of executing the Gospel to the whole creation." Pope Pius XI later spoke out against the conference. Although he acknowledged that superficially the goals and efforts of the conference were worthy, he was concerned that those in attendance would fail to understand the mystical nature of the Catholic Church as the true Church of Christ. Instead, they might name a visible Church as only "a Federation, composed of various communities of Christians, even though they adhere to different doctrines, which may even be incompatible with each other" (*Mortalium Animos*, 6).

Another reason why the Church in the United States did not participate in the World Missionary Conference may have been because Catholicism was viewed with suspicion by the country's Protestant majority. American Catholics tended to keep a low profile in the early decades of the nation's history. In the mid-nineteenth century, this began to change, as millions of

Catholic immigrants began arriving—first from Ireland and Germany, later from Poland, Italy, Canada, Mexico, and elsewhere. The Church grew rapidly in the late nineteenth and early twentieth centuries. The increased prominence of the Church, and especially the political importance of Catholic voters, provoked worry among some non-Catholic Americans that "foreign" influence, especially that of Catholics who looked to Rome for the leadership of their Church, would undermine American ideals and perhaps even destroy the country. A rash of anti-Catholic activism broke out in the 1920s, including the resurgence of the Ku Klux Klan (which in its original iteration was primarily anti-Black, anti-Jewish, and anti-Catholic) and the passage of federal laws severely restricting immigration that aimed to reduce numbers coming from Catholic countries.

By the 1920s, however, the Catholic Church in the United States was large and influential enough that it could no longer be cowed into passivity. Across the small towns of the Midwest; in major cities such as San Francisco, Boston, New York, New Orleans, St. Louis, and Cincinnati; in historic Catholic enclaves in rural Maryland, Kentucky, Pennsylvania, and Texas; and in many other places, Catholic communities were thriving. Their lives revolving around parish life, Catholics joined social organizations such as the Knights

Clerical procession during the International Eucharistic Congress at Soldier Field, Chicago, Illinois, 1926.

of Columbus and Sodalities of Our Lady, attended parish schools, and participated in novenas and other devotions. At the heart of parish life was sacramental ministry, especially Sunday Mass.

In 1926, Catholics in the United States celebrated this thriving community by hosting the twenty-eighth International Eucharistic Congress.∞ The site of the congress, Chicago, had rocketed to world-class status in the late nineteenth century as a transportation and food-processing hub. Catholic immigrants poured into the city from around the world, creating some of the world's largest parishes. Chicago was symbolic of the extraordinary growth of both the American nation and the American Catholic Church.

The idea of an International Eucharistic Congress had been born in France in 1881. Congresses were held every year or two, mostly in European cities. The 1926 event in Chicago was the first on American soil. Railroad companies made special arrangements to transport the massive number of people who would flock to the city. Delegations came from Mexico, France, Germany, Poland, and Italy. The highlights of the five-day schedule were the public Masses, usually held at the recently built Soldier Field football stadium. A children's Mass featured a choir of sixty thousand students, and six thousand nuns attended the Mass for women's day. Onlookers were amazed at the colorful processions of hundreds of priests and bishops, including Vatican dignitaries. Even Soldier Field couldn't hold the crowd for the final Mass of the Congress, which took place on the spacious grounds of Saint Mary of the Lake Seminary north of the city. Attendees (estimates for the closing Mass ranged between five hundred thousand and one million) celebrated Mass and formed a two-mile-long Eucharistic procession around the seminary campus. One of the city's newspapers called it "the most stupendous one-day pilgrimage on record in history."[2] Chicago's International Eucharistic Congress was a palpable expression in America of the strength of Catholic community and Eucharistic devotion.≈

The Eucharist is both an important source of communion, with both God and fellow believers, and a source of grace for calling all people to communion with God and one another. The Church's public witness of the Eucharist

∞ Note

In 2024, the fifty-third International Eucharistic Congress was held in Quito, the capital of Ecuador, to commemorate the 150th anniversary of the consecration of Ecuador to the Sacred Heart of Jesus.

attracted the attention of many non-Catholics and contributed to encouraging many Christians of other communities to seek out the Church on their own. One of these was a college professor named Thomas Merton, who would later convert to Catholicism and become a Cistercian monk and one of the century's greatest Catholic writers (see Faithful Disciple profile "Thomas Merton" in this chapter).

Events like the International Eucharistic Congress also helped to pave the way for the Church to participate fully in the ecumenical movement with other outreach efforts, including a continuation of the Church's social justice teaching, new focus on biblical scholarship highlighted by Pope Pius XII's encyclical *Divino Afflante Spiritu* (*Inspired by the Divine Spirit*), and a recognition of the dangers of blending missionary work with colonialism. These and other efforts were precursors to the announcement in 1959 by Pope John XXIII of the Church's twenty-first ecumenical council, the Second Vatican Council.

Teachings and Tasks of Ecumenism

Although the relationship between Protestants and Catholics in the United States has often been tense, over the course of the twentieth century those

Pope Francis leads an ecumenical prayer ahead of the opening of an Ordinary General Assembly of the Synod of Bishops.

≈ Note

In July 2024, the tenth National Eucharistic Congress, and the first in eighty-three years, took place in Indianapolis, Indiana.

relations generally improved, and Catholics and Protestants found more common ground. During the civil rights movement of the 1960s, for example, Catholic priests, sisters, and laypeople marched arm in arm with the Reverend Martin Luther King Jr. and other Protestant ministers, together inspired by a call for justice for Black Americans. Beginning in the 1970s, Protestants, Catholics, and many of other faiths cooperated in the pro-life movement, working together in the common conviction that unborn persons deserve legal protection.

A major official focus of the Second Vatican Council was forging efforts for greater Christian unity. The Council's *Unitatis Redintegratio* (*Decree on Ecumenism*), while reaffirming that the Catholic Church is entrusted with the fullness of the means of salvation, committed the Church to the ecumenical movement and affirmed the many positive qualities in other ecclesial communities. It taught that those who grow up in other ecclesial communities should not be treated as if they themselves caused the rift in Christianity. Rather, Christians in these communities cannot be accused of any sin involving the break in Christian unity "and the Catholic Church embraces . . . them . . . with respect and affection. For [those] who believe in Christ and have been truly baptized are in communion with the Catholic Church even though this communion is imperfect" (*Unitatis Redintegratio*, 3).

Unitatis Redintegratio was a landmark statement in many ways. First, the decree acknowledged that both sides shared in the blame for divisions that occurred in the Great Schism between East and West and during the Protestant Reformation. Second, the decree focused on what Catholics have in common with other Christians, for example, Scripture, celebration of at least some of the sacraments, work for justice and peace, and aspirations for holiness and discipleship in Christ. In these separated Christian communities there are many elements of sanctification and truth that indeed come from Christ. These elements are calls to Christian unity. Pope Benedict XVI mentioned this common bond among Christians in the introduction to his first encyclical, *Deus Caritas Est* (*God Is Love*): "Being Christian is not the result of an ethical choice or a lofty idea, but the encounter with an event, a person, which gives life a new horizon and a decisive direction" (*DCE*, 1). It is primarily in the Divine Person of Jesus Christ that Christians find unity.

God calls the entire Church to participate in these efforts of unity by asking all individual Catholics to examine their own consciences, as suggested both by *Unitatis Redintegratio* and later by Pope John Paul II in his encyclical *Ut Unum Sint* (*That They May Be One*), and keeping in mind the words from

Working toward Unity

Focus Question: How does the Church bring greater unity to our family, faith, and world?

Pope Francis pointed out two important anniversaries, each in 2025, relating to the ongoing quest for Christian unity. The year was both the 1,700th anniversary of the First Council of Nicaea and the 500th anniversary of the Augsburg Confession, the declaration of the basic beliefs of Lutherans. The pope noted that the "Trinitarian and Christological confession" of Nicaea is meant to unite all Christians. "For it is Christ," Pope Francis said, "whom the men and women of every time . . . are seeking, however unconsciously." The pope noted that during a time of growing divisions in Christianity, the Augsburg Confession tried unsuccessfully to preserve unity. He also reminded us that "the path to unity is important" and that "it is also good that we, God's faithful people, go on the journey together."[3]

Several times in his pontificate, most specifically in *Ut Unum Sint*, Pope John Paul II said that the work toward Christian unity involves everyone, laity and clergy alike, while acknowledging that the reconciliation of all Christians into the Catholic Church remains the work of God. The greatest ecumenical effort any of us can take on is to pray along with Christ for the Church. Pope John Paul II also named these other areas where all Christians can work toward greater unity:

You must renew and be faithful to your Christian vocation.

Your vocation, given at Baptism, is to seek out the Kingdom of God and arrange your life according to the Kingdom by following God's will.

You must live a holier life according to the Gospel.

Holiness is a perfection of love. You are called to "be perfect, just as your heavenly Father is perfect" (Mt 5:48).

You must pray with and for separated Christians.

You can pray both privately and in ecumenical prayer services for the unity of Christians. Pope John Paul II regarded this as the "soul of the whole ecumenical movement" (*Ut Unum Sint*, 21, quoting *Unitatis Redintegratio*, 8).

You must grow in knowledge of people in other ecclesial communities and their beliefs.

Without abandoning your own convictions, you must recognize Christ's presence in these communities. Pope John Paul II described this dialogue as an ecumenical "exchange of gifts" (*Ut Unum Sint*, 28, quoting *Lumen Gentium*, 13). This exchange often takes place through participation together in social and service activities.

You must form yourself in the faith.

You can do this by studying the Catholic faith so that you can comfortably share your knowledge of it with others. For example, you should understand Mary's role in your life and in the life of the Church and be able to share about it when a non-Catholic confronts you with the claim that "Catholics worship Mary." You should also pray for priests and seminarians and all who minister in the Church as they grow in their own knowledge of the faith.

You must remain informed about the latest dialogues among theologians and meetings among different churches and communities.

Follow the news of ecumenical meetings and dialogues. Read up on statements on ecumenism from recent popes and the United States Conference of Catholic Bishops.

You must work together with other Christians in efforts of service to all people, especially the poor.

Oftentimes common opportunities arise around the holidays—for example, serving Thanksgiving meals to the homeless or providing Christmas gifts to families in need.

Further Study and Reflection

- Choose two of Pope John Paul II's suggestions for participating in the Church's ecumenical efforts that you can take part in and provide examples of how you can do each.
- Summarize the Church's "Practice of Ecumenism" from paragraphs 7 to 12 of the Second Vatican Council's *Unitatis Redintegratio* (*Decree on Ecumenism*). Write one sentence to summarize each of the paragraphs.
- Choose a specific Protestant ecclesial community (see Chapter 5, Section 2). Research and report on any recent dialogue that has taken place between Catholic leaders and leaders of that community.

the First Letter of John: "If we say, 'We are without sin,' we deceive ourselves, and the truth is not in us" (1 Jn 1:8).

Since the Second Vatican Council, the Church has also engaged in formal dialogue with Lutherans, Anglicans, the Orthodox, Reformed churches, Pentecostals, Methodists, and Disciples of Christ, among others. As a result of these formal dialogues, some significant disagreements have been overcome. For example, in 1999, the Catholic Church and the Lutheran World Federation declared an agreement about the essential truths regarding the justification of human beings. Other times, the Church has simply apologized for any wrongs she has caused. Pope John Paul II did this by meeting frequently with other religious leaders and asking that they forgive the Roman Catholic Church for causing any pain in the cause of Christian unity throughout history. Likewise, Pope Francis asked for forgiveness of other Christians for wrongs committed by the Church.∞

Religious leaders from Judaism, Islam, and the Catholic Church, meet in Brussels, Belgium, to send a joint message for peace and unity.

∞ Note

In 2015, Pope Francis asked the Waldensian Church, which was founded in the twelfth century and whose members were persecuted by Catholics during the Middle Ages, for forgiveness. "On the part of the Catholic Church, I ask your forgiveness, I ask it for the non-Christian and even inhuman attitudes and behavior that we have showed you," said Pope Francis.

The Task of Interreligious Dialogue

While ecumenism begins with a common belief in Jesus Christ, Baptism, and other tenets of Christianity, *interreligious dialogue* occurs as the Church reaches out in good will toward people of non-Christian faiths. Sometimes this dialogue occurs naturally and providentially among individual members of various faiths, as was the case in a human-interest story involving a Catholic priest, Jewish rabbi, and two Protestant ministers that attracted worldwide attention in 1943 (see the feature "A Common Witness to Love" in this section). However, in the absence of such direct providential occurrences bringing different religions together, the process of formal interreligious dialogue tended to move slowly up to and through most of the twentieth century.

For Catholics, dialogue with Judaism must always take precedence. As the religion out of which Christianity emerged (see Chapter 1), Judaism holds a special place in the Church's ecumenical efforts. The Jews, said Pope John Paul II, are our "elder brothers" in the faith.[4] The Church recognizes her own historic link to Judaism and that the Jewish faith "is already a response to God's revelation in the Old Covenant" (*CCC*, 839). Despite this common heritage, from the Jewish persecution of Christians in the first century to the Christian persecution of Jews in the Middle Ages and beyond, the relationship between Judaism and Catholicism has often been troubled by misunderstanding and even violence. In recent decades, Church leaders have striven to overcome this troubled past by listening to the perspective of Jewish leaders and making efforts to adjust various Catholic practices.

For example, in 1959 Pope John XXIII deleted the adjective *perfidis* from the prayer for Jews that was part of the Good Friday liturgy. (Most Catholic liturgies were conducted in Latin at that time.) The term was interpreted by many to mean "perfidious," which is associated with "treacherous" or "deceitful." While popes had clarified that it should be taken instead as "unbelieving,"

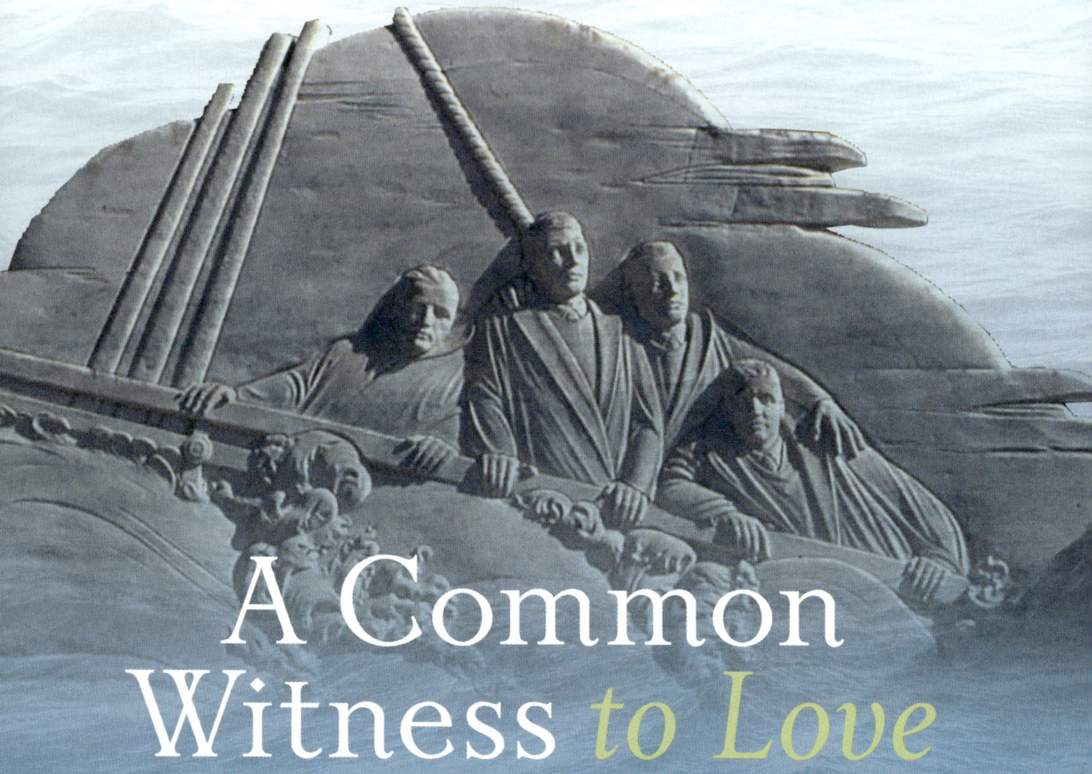

A Common Witness *to Love*

In the winter of 1943, the world was deeply embroiled in war. Nine hundred young men boarded the SS *Dorchester* in New York to be transported across the Atlantic Ocean to participate in the Allied war effort against Nazi Germany. On February 3, a German submarine torpedoed the ship and it began to sink. Panic set in aboard the transport as the soldiers stared death in the face and scrambled frantically for life jackets. There weren't enough for everyone.

Amid the confusion, four passengers remained calm, praying with and comforting the others. They were army chaplains: Methodist minister George Lansing Fox, Jewish Rabbi Alexander Goode, Dutch Reformed (Protestant) pastor Clark Poling, and Catholic priest Fr. John Washington. The four had become good friends in their brief time together preparing for chaplaincy at the Army Chaplains School at Harvard University.

When they discovered the life jacket shortage, the four men gave their vests to others. "It was the finest thing I have seen or hope to see this side of heaven," one survivor later declared. The chaplains voluntarily remained with those who were unable to get off the ship as it sank beneath the waves. Survivors reported hearing prayers rise up in different languages, including

Rabbi Alexander Goode, Fr. John Washington, Rev. Clark Poling, and Rev. George Fox

Jewish prayers in Hebrew and Catholic prayers in Latin. "I could hear men crying, pleading, praying," one survivor recalled. "I could also hear the chaplains preaching courage. Their voices were the only thing that kept me going."[5]

Another witness described the chaplains' final actions: "They quieted the panic, forced men 'frozen' on the rail toward the boats and over the side, helped men adjust life jackets and at last gave away their own. They themselves had no chance without life jackets. I swam away from the ship and turned to watch. . . . The last I saw, the chaplains were up there praying for the safety of the men. They had done everything they could. I did not see them again."[6]

The chaplains went down with the ship. Many other men perished in the frigid water. Just 230 of the 900 were rescued. Yet the example offered by the faith leaders was a bright spot in an otherwise dark tragedy. Congress awarded the four the Purple Heart and the Distinguished Service Cross, as well as a Special Medal for Heroism. Inspired by their sacrifice, the Four Chaplains Memorial Foundation was formed "to impart the principles of selfless service to humanity without regard to race, creed, ethnicity, gender, or religious beliefs."

In an address at the dedication of the Chapel of the Four Chaplains in Philadelphia, President Harry S. Truman said, "They obeyed the divine commandment that men should love one another. . . . They were not afraid of death because they knew that the word of God is stronger than death. Their belief, their faith, in His word enabled them to conquer death."[7] The four chaplains, supported by a vital faith in God, found unity amid religious difference: unity in witnessing to the reality of God's love.

that is, not accepting Christ, misunderstanding among Catholics and Jews continued. So Pope John removed the term completely; the current Good Friday prayer (in English) begins simply, "Let us pray also for the Jewish people." Catholic worship aids and preaching emphasize that the role of the Jews in the Death of Jesus, as recounted in the Gospels, is not to be interpreted as reason to blame the Jews *as a people* for Jesus's Crucifixion, nor as reason to foster bitter relations between the two faiths.

The relationship between Islam and Christianity also has a long, contentious past. History is replete with conflict between the Christian nations of Europe and the various Muslim empires of North Africa and the Middle East, most notably the Crusades during the Middle Ages and the **Reconquista of Spain** (ca. 800–1500). The rise of Muslim extremism in some places, which has resulted in violent attacks on Christians in Nigeria, Egypt, Iraq, and elsewhere, has made interreligious dialogue with Islam more challenging (recall the story of Akash Bashir from Chapter 2).

But here, too, the Church has made strides. The Church sees that Muslims "together with us . . . adore the one, merciful God, mankind's judge on the

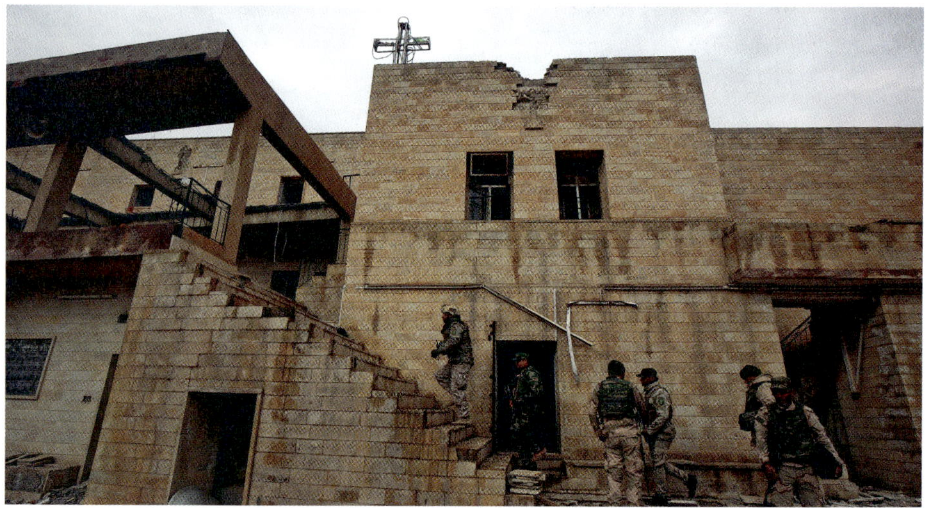

The debris of St. George's Monastery, a historical Chaldean Catholic church on the northern outskirt of Mosul, Iraq.

Reconquista of Spain A series of campaigns by Christians to recapture territory on the Iberian Peninsula between Spain and Portugal from Muslims. The reconquest of this territory took over eight centuries, from the eighth century to the fifteenth century.

last day" (*Lumen Gentium* 16, quoted in *CCC*, 841). Catholics recognize that violent extremists represent a scant minority of Muslims and have found ways to cooperate with Muslim believers of good will. In 1992, Catholic bishops in the Middle East stated, "We [Christians and Muslims] share in a unique heritage in a civilization that we have both enriched by bringing to it our own contributions. . . . The Arab Christians are an integral part of the cultural identity of Muslims, just as Muslims are an integral part of the cultural identity of Christians. . . . We are responsible for each other before God and humanity."[8]

In a message to Muslims issued at the close of the Islamic holiday of Ramadan in 2013, Pope Francis affirmed the need for mutual respect and dialogue between Christians and Muslims, noting that they can work side by side without having to discuss theological differences: "It is clear that, when we show respect for the religion of our neighbours or when we offer them our good wishes on the occasion of a religious celebration, we simply seek to share their joy, without making reference to the content of their religious convictions."[9] In a beautiful example of such cooperation, Muslims and Christians worked together in 2017 to rebuild a historic Chaldean Catholic monastery in Iraq after the building was badly damaged by the terrorist group ISIS.[10]

The Church willingly enters into dialogue with any religious group that is open to it. Other non-Christian religions are recognized by the Church for their own goodness and truth, which prepares them "for the Gospel . . . given by Him who enlightens all men so that they may finally have life" (*Lumen Gentium*, 16). The Catholic Church invites all people, including non-Christians,

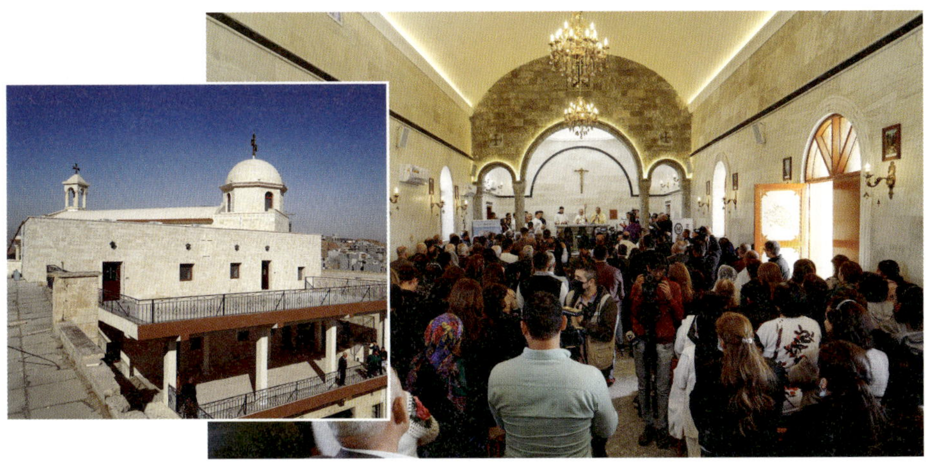

A rite held during a reopening ceremony of St. George Chaldean Monastery after it was rebuilt seven years after being destroyed by the terrorist group ISIS.

to reach out to her like a bark in the sea. The Church continues to affirm that there is no salvation outside her (see subsection "All Who Are Saved Are Connected with the Church" in Chapter 5, Section 3), meaning that everyone who is to be saved is to be saved through Christ the head of the Catholic Church, the universal sacrament of salvation.

SECTION Assessment

Comprehension

1. Why did Pope Pius XI not allow Catholics to support the findings of the World Missionary Conference?

2. Why was *Unitatis Redintegratio* a landmark statement?

3. Why should interfaith dialogue for Catholics begin with Jews?

4. Which non-Christian religions is the Church willing to dialogue with?

Vocabulary

5. How are the *Crusades* and the *Reconquista of Spain* sources of conflict between the Church and Muslims?

Reflection

6. Imagine participating in a public display of your Catholicism like the 1926 International Eucharistic Congress. Name three emotions that you might experience at such an event.

7. Tell about an interfaith social or service event that you have participated in (or would like to participate in). What was it like (or what do you think it would be like)?

8. Explain how the Church's asking for forgiveness as a first step in ecumenism is similar to your asking for forgiveness as a first step in making up with a person you have a disagreement with.

9. How do you understand the image of the Church inviting others to reach out to her "like a bark in the sea"?

THE CHURCH AND TOTALITARIANISM

The Fourth Commandment—"Honor your father and your mother"—also requires Catholics to "honor all who for our good have received authority in society from God" (*CCC*, 2234). That being said, the political authorities are required to respect the fundamental rights of the human person. One of the most fundamental rights is freedom, and in particular religious freedom. This right is based on human nature because we are made by God to freely choose to know him and to ascend to his divine truth. Political authorities are obliged to allow their citizens freedom to pursue the practice of religion.

The Church herself is not a political society, nor is she bound to any government. The primary duty of the Church is the *spiritual* needs of her people, whereas governments are responsible for managing temporal affairs. Because of the necessity of religious freedom, no government should interfere with the Church's mission. For her part, the Church respects the legitimate autonomy of the democratic order and is not entitled to express preferences for what type of government or political structure is in power, except in connection with her mission. However, while the Church does not promote a singular form of government, she is very clear that political communities that uphold democratic values—that is, ones that call for the involvement of citizens—are integral for upholding human rights and religious freedom.

These days, as with many other times in history, the Church faces several actions by political authorities that threaten religious freedom. For example, since the mid-2010s, the Church in Nicaragua has been persecuted severely. President Daniel Ortega took on the role of dictator and censored the Church, and Catholics have had most of their religious freedoms stripped away. In 2023, he sentenced Bishop Rolando Álvarez to more than twenty-six years in prison, accusing him of conspiracy against the government. Government troops had previously abducted the bishop and held him for three months. Ortega also expelled priests, nuns, seminarians, and the papal *nuncio* (representative) from the country. The persecutions occurred because the Church was the last group of Nicaraguan citizens to speak out against the brutality of the government. Ortega's dictatorship had eradicated the media, civil and nonprofit organizations, and any public spaces where free speech took place. Inside of churches, homilies were recorded by the government. The Church, as is usually her way, did not advocate for violent insurrection against the government, only an opportunity to dialogue with Ortega and his cabinet with the chance to secure justice and freedom for all citizens.

The Rise of Totalitarianism

In what seems a 180-degree reaction against democratic governments, many regimes diametrically opposed to such governments arose in several places in the twentieth century. These often extreme, **totalitarian** forms of government opposed most forms of personal and religious freedoms.

One example in the early twentieth century was in Mexico. The country's president, Plutarco Calles, fearing that the Catholic Church was trying to regain the political power she had lost since the time of Spanish colonization, began persecuting the Catholic Church. It wasn't long before devout Catholics formed an army of soldiers. One of these was José Sánchez del Río, a fourteen-year-old boy from western Mexico who was allowed to participate in the so-called **Cristeros** as a flagbearer. During a battle in 1928, José was captured by government troops. While he was in prison, José prayed devoutly and expressed his willingness to give up his life for Jesus. He was brutally tortured by the Mexican authorities, who assured him that he would be set free if he would only say, "Death to Christ the King." But José refused, shouting instead, "Viva Cristo Rey!" (Long live Christ the King!), which was the battle cry of the Cristeros. On February 10, 1928, José was executed by the Mexican government in a public park. In 2016, Pope Francis canonized José Sánchez del Río with six other saints, of whom the pope said, "They prayed mightily; they fought and they were victorious."[11]

---

totalitarian A term to describe a government with total control by an authoritarian leader or a hierarchy.

Cristeros A Spanish word for "soldier of Christ."

A woman shows a poster of St. José Sánchez del Río before a canonization mass led by Pope Francis on October 16, 2016, at St. Peter's Square.

The Mexican government in the 1920s was just one example of a number of governments that became hostile toward religion in general or Catholicism in particular. Anti-Catholic leaders embraced various ideologies, including

- liberalism in Mexico;

- fascism in Italy;

- national socialism (Nazism) in Germany; and

- communism in Russia.

In these places and others, Catholics were frequently persecuted, and the Church struggled to survive and continue her mission.

Nazism and communism are extreme forms of totalitarianism, a concept of society that sees the state as *total*, controlling every aspect of a nation's existence. Under these forms of government, religion must be either absent or utterly controlled by the state. Because the Catholic Church must remain faithful to the mission conferred by Jesus Christ, she cannot accept this view of the relationship between the Church and government. In order to shape her teachings and actions in accordance with the Gospel, the Church must be catholic (accepting of all people) and apostolic (true to the teaching of Jesus handed down by the Apostles and their successors). Because of this fundamental conflict, totalitarian rulers try to stamp out Catholicism wherever they assume power. If the Church is too large or popular to destroy immediately, the rulers try to restrict or control the Church's activities and eliminate any Church leaders who refuse to cooperate.

This is what happened, for example, in Nazi Germany in the years preceding and during World War II. Although there were Catholics in Germany, even some priests and bishops, who were sympathetic to Nazism, the relationship between Nazism and Catholicism became increasingly hostile as Nazism's anti-Christian character and horrific program of imprisoning and exterminating Jews and other so-called "inferior" people became clear. Thousands of Catholic priests and sisters were interned and murdered in Nazi death camps—including St. Maximilian Kolbe (see sub-subsection "To Die in His Place" in Chapter 1, Introduction).

St. Teresa Benedicta of the Cross was another Catholic victim of Nazi persecution, though her path to martyrdom was very different from St. Maximilian's. Edith Stein was born into a devout Jewish family in eastern Germany (present-day Poland). She was intellectually gifted and pursued the study of philosophy at German universities. By the time she went to college, she had abandoned her Jewish faith and come to doubt the existence of God.

Edith studied under prominent European philosophers and, despite facing discrimination for being a woman and a Jew, achieved distinction. Through the example of Christian friends and her reading of Christian literature—especially St. Teresa of Ávila's autobiography—she became convinced of the truth of the Catholic faith. She was baptized in 1922 and in 1933 entered the Carmelite order that had been reformed by St. Teresa of Ávila herself (see the feature "St. Teresa of Ávila" in Chapter 5, Section 3).

Also in 1933, Adolf Hitler was appointed chancellor of Germany and began enacting anti-Jewish laws. Although Edith Stein, who had taken the name Sr. Benedicta of the Cross, was now Catholic, anyone of Jewish descent was vulnerable in Nazi Germany. To protect her, the Carmelites transferred Sr. Benedicta to one of their houses in the Netherlands. She was safe there until 1940, when Germany invaded and occupied the Netherlands. In 1942, the Dutch Catholic bishops issued a public letter of protest against the Nazi persecution of Jews; in response, the Nazi commander ordered all Jewish converts to Catholicism to be rounded up and sent to death camps. Sr. Benedicta was arrested and put on a train to the infamous Auschwitz concentration camp, where she was killed in a gas chamber.

"There is a vocation to suffer with Christ and thereby to cooperate with him in his work of salvation," Sr. Benedicta had written the year before she was exiled from Germany. "When we are united with the Lord, we are members of the Mystical Body of Christ: Christ lives on in his members and continues to suffer in them. And the suffering borne in union with the Lord is his suffering, incorporated in the great work of salvation and fruitful therein."[12] For St. Teresa Benedicta of the Cross, the Church as the Mystical Body of Christ (see subsection "The Writing of St. Paul" in Chapter 2, Section 2) was not merely a novel idea; it was a lived reality that entailed suffering on behalf of others.

St. Teresa Benedicta did not deserve the suffering she experienced, but she chose to unite her pain and death with the Cross of Christ, and thereby participated with him in the work of salvation. This is what the Apostle Paul meant when he wrote, "Now I rejoice in my sufferings for your sake, and in my flesh I am filling up what is lacking in the afflictions of Christ on behalf of his body, which is the church" (Col 1:24). Christ's sacrifice—the offering of the Son of God—was enough to save the world, but he allows us the privilege of

Sculpture of Edith Stein in Cologne, Germany, depicts her as a young Jew with a Star of David, as a young scientist, and as a Catholic nun.

participating in that act of salvation by offering our own sacrifices and sufferings in union with his.∞

The Light of Faith Provides True Freedom

The lives and deaths of Sts. José, Maximilian, and Teresa Benedicta illustrate the difficulty that the Church faced in modern states that were hostile to the faith. Yet even in these awful conditions, Catholics are called to be light. Where the night of suffering is darkest, the light of faith appears brighter. Where oppression, suffering, and falsehood are most severe, the Church's ministry of compassion and truth can be most brilliant.

Freedom itself—the ability to move freely, express opinions out loud, and seek pleasure—is not the real objective of a Christian's freedom. Instead, a Christian's freedom is to discover God in all places and situations—even in the direst conditions of war or the suffering of a concentration camp. Even those facing such sufferings can achieve a sense of interior freedom while being restricted and abused with inhumane treatment. A Jewish psychiatrist, Victor Frankl, who was imprisoned at Auschwitz and later Dachau during World War II discovered that his happiness or lack thereof was not related to being deprived of freedom in prison, but that inner happiness could be achieved anywhere, and that is what brought about true freedom. In his book *Man's Search for Meaning*, published after his release from prison, he noted that those prisoners who had a rich interior and spiritual life "may have suffered much pain but the damage to their inner selves was less. They were able to retreat from their terrible surroundings to a life of inner riches and spiritual freedom." Frankl discovered that love perseveres and is the source of true freedom. "The salvation of man is through love and in love," he wrote.[13]

∞ Note

Human suffering is given new meaning because of Christ's redemptive suffering on the Cross. Wrote Pope John Paul II: "Each one is also *called to share in that suffering* through which the Redemption was accomplished. He is called to share in the suffering through which human suffering has also been redeemed. In bringing about the Redemption through suffering, Christ *has* also *raised human suffering to the level of the Redemption*. Thus each man, in his suffering, can also become a sharer in the redemptive suffering of Christ" (*Salvifici Doloris*, 19).

A statue and mural of Monsignor Hugh O'Flaherty are both located in Killarney, Ireland.

Irish-born Monsignor Hugh O'Flaherty exemplified the power of love in his actions during World War II. As a long-time resident of Rome working as a Vatican diplomat in Nazi-occupied Rome, he knew the city intimately and had many contacts there. He used these assets skillfully during the Nazi occupation, as increasing numbers of escaped Allied prisoners of war sought his assistance in evading the Germans.

Msgr. O'Flaherty established a network of hiding places and conspirators who would help transport the soldiers to safety. He perfected the art of disguise, sneaking around Rome in various costumes. O'Flaherty's work became even more dangerous when the Nazis decided to round up Rome's Jews for deportation to—and likely death in—German concentration camps. O'Flaherty then used his network to hide and transport Jews, often to Catholic churches and convents for hiding. Thanks to the efforts of this Irish priest and many others, some 80 percent of Rome's Jews survived the war—a far higher rate than elsewhere in Nazi-occupied Europe.

O'Flaherty's charity extended even to the foes who had hunted and attempted to kill him. After the war, the Nazi commander of Rome, Herbert Kappler, was imprisoned for war crimes. Over many years in prison, Kappler had few visitors, but one of them was Msgr. Hugh O'Flaherty. When Kappler decided to become Catholic, he was received into the faith by Msgr. O'Flaherty.∞

∞ Note

Msgr. O'Flaherty's story has been dramatized as a television miniseries: *The Scarlet and the Black* (CBS, 1983). See also J. P. Gallagher, *The Scarlet Pimpernel of the Vatican* (London: Souvenir, 1967), and Brian Fleming, *The Vatican Pimpernel: The Wartime Exploits of Monsignor Hugh O'Flaherty* (Cork, Ireland: Collins, 2008).

By persevering in her purpose—to proclaim the Good News of salvation—even in the face of persecution and suffering, the Church reminds all people of their eternal destiny. The Church also reminds us that suffering, injustice, and death will come to an end. Through the Church we are able to perceive this truth and find the strength to endure our pilgrimage on earth as we make our way toward heaven.

SECTION Assessment

Comprehension

1. What is a democratic value that is essential to religious freedom?

2. What are two extreme forms of totalitarianism?

3. What did the Mexican authorities ask of José Sánchez del Río in order for his life to be spared?

4. How did St. Teresa Benedicta of the Cross live the reality of the Mystical Body of Christ?

5. What did Msgr. Hugh O'Flaherty accomplish in Rome during World War II?

Vocabulary

6. Explain the root word of *totalitarian* and how it relates to governments of that name.

7. What is the English translation of *Cristeros*?

Reflection

8. Name a contemporary issue in your country where the Catholic Church has recently been threatened by the government. Do you feel called to speak out in protest over this issue? Why or why not?

9. Explain the meaning of this saying: "I sought happiness in freedom only to find freedom in happiness."

THE IMPORTANCE OF FAMILY

The Church asks that any government refrain from interfering in the lives of individuals and families as much as possible. The term **subsidiarity** is related to the state's or the government's role in our personal lives. The principle teaches that justice and human welfare are best achieved at the most immediate level. Individuals, families, and local communities should be given the freedom and resources to address the challenges they face. Larger social or political structures, such as the state or local government, should only intervene when individuals, families, or local communities are unable to help themselves. For example, in the United States, the standards and operations of public schools are typically left to the local communities. However, if the school system is not serving its citizens (e.g., dropout rates are high, students are not prepared for college), the state government may intervene. Or subsidiarity may encourage a more refined solution, with families taking on added influence over their child's education in a private, charter, or homeschool arrangement.

The family itself is a concrete example of the Church. The Church is present in family life. This has been true since the beginning of creation when man and woman came together as one. This was also true in the early years of the Church when the Eucharist was celebrated in family homes (see Chapter 2). Also, the vocations of those who become priests and members of the consecrated life have always been nurtured and developed through family life. The family is the first place for education in prayer and the practice of prayer. The family is the domestic church and the "original cell of social life" (*CCC*, 2207), and it must always be protected, including against cultural threats that may be supported by governments.

---

subsidiarity A social principle that stipulates that social matters should be taken care of at the lowest, most local level of authority, if possible.

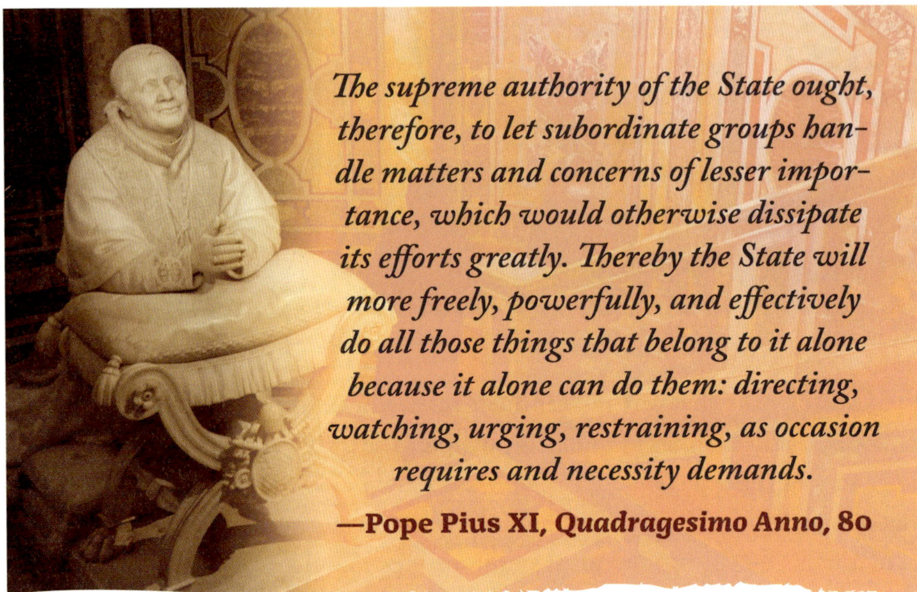

Married Life Is the Foundation of Family Life

The union of a man and a woman in the Sacrament of Matrimony constitutes the beginning of what the Second Vatican Council called "an intimate partnership of married life and love" and, hence, family life (*Gaudium et Spes*, 48). Marriage is also the root of the domestic church, the "church of the home," which ordinarily bears the fruit of the couple's love in the children they will welcome and raise, but even couples who are unable to have children form a family and must see that their love is put to the service of others.

Along with Holy Orders, Matrimony is one of the **Sacraments at the Service of Communion**. In marriage, the husband and wife focus on each other. It is this self-giving love that brings them their holiness and salvation. Through their service to each other and through their intimate union, a husband and wife "experience the meaning of their oneness and attain to it with growing perfection day by day" (*Gaudium et Spes*, 48).

The effects of the Sacrament of Matrimony are an encounter with God's grace. This is not something that happens only on the wedding day. In fact, it

---

Sacraments of Service Sacraments whose primary purpose is to create, build, and maintain the Church community. The Sacrament of Holy Orders and the Sacrament of Matrimony are the two Sacraments of Service.

is the very ordinariness of married life that witnesses to the graced character of a sacramental marriage. Daily activities like preparing dinner, shopping for groceries, folding laundry, picking up the children at school, and listening to a spouse share the events of his or her day can be moments of grace that lead to the perfection of holiness. These activities can also be done by single people, but they take on a different meaning when engaged in by a married couple. These simple actions become expressions of the meaning of the sacrament because they are lifelong and unconditional. They become symbolic actions that say, in effect, "In this simple act of care, I want you to know that I am now and will always be concerned about your needs."[14]

The sexual relationship of a husband and wife is the more profound example of the sacramental reality of marriage. When a husband and wife make love, they consummate or seal their sacramental commitment. The love and union between the two of them, expressed in their sexual sharing, is also intended to be fruitful—that is, open to children.

Catholic married couples are called not only to ensure the other's happiness but to ensure the other's *holiness* as well. This takes place through sharing the kind of love that is concerned with the care and well-being of another. A Greek word used in the New Testament for this kind of love is *agape*. This kind of love goes beyond romantic desires and fantasies, offering ways to celebrate an ever-deepening intimacy. It leads the spouses to grow in holiness and work toward salvation in partnership with one another. Thus, in marriage the husband and wife are truly holy companions.

Modern Threats to Family Life

Given the centrality of the Christian family to the life of the Church, the Church has an interest in maintaining a vibrant family culture. In the twentieth century, the Church confronted a series of crises in family life. Society is currently dealing with the consequences of these crises, and restoring strong families remains one of the most important tasks of the contemporary Church. In the late twentieth century, Pope John Paul II wrote:

> At a moment of history in which the family is the object of numerous forces that seek to destroy it or in some way to deform it, and aware that the well-being of society and her own good are intimately tied to the good of the family, the Church perceives in a

more urgent and compelling way her mission of proclaiming to all people the plan of God for marriage and the family, ensuring their full vitality and human and Christian development, and thus contributing to the renewal of society and of the People of God. (*Familiaris Consortio*, 3)

The union of husband and wife is meant to reflect the union of Christ and his Church. St. Paul wrote: "Husbands, love your wives, even as Christ loved the church" (Eph 5:25). Note that God's love came first and the love between spouses images it. Through their agreement in the covenant of marriage, the two spouses "are no longer two, but one flesh" (Mt 19:6), and they "render mutual help and service to each other through an intimate union of their persons and of their actions. . . . As a mutual gift of two persons, this intimate union and the good of the children impose total fidelity on the spouses and argue for an unbreakable oneness between them" (*Gaudium et Spes*, 48). The Church thus holds that the bond of marriage is "unbreakable." This belief was widespread in the Christian nations of Europe and the Americas until the twentieth century. Its legacy is still reflected in the common wedding

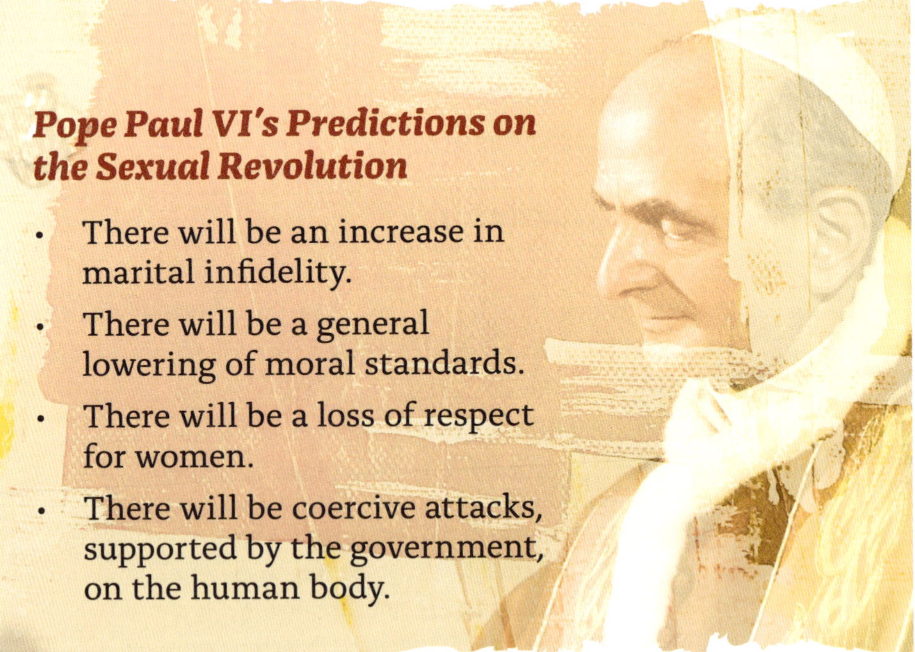

Pope Paul VI's Predictions on the Sexual Revolution

- There will be an increase in marital infidelity.
- There will be a general lowering of moral standards.
- There will be a loss of respect for women.
- There will be coercive attacks, supported by the government, on the human body.

vows pledging to remain faithful "for better or for worse, for richer, for poorer, in sickness and in health . . . until death do us part." In the past century, however, divorce has become increasingly common, and the Catholic understanding of marriage has weakened. Many couples get married without a serious commitment to preserving their relationship in the face of difficulties.

For a true marriage, spouses entering into the marriage must do so with full understanding and full freedom of consent. In light of this, the Church recognizes that sometimes marriages that appeared to be valid are not in fact true marriages because of some deficiency in the consent given by one or both of the spouses. In such cases, the Church can grant a **declaration of nullity**, or an annulment. The Church also recognizes the necessity of separation when one of the spouses is abusive. Yet the principle remains that marriages freely entered into are by their nature permanent and indissoluble.

When God's design for marriage is flouted, family life suffers. Divorce is emotionally and financially draining on spouses and their

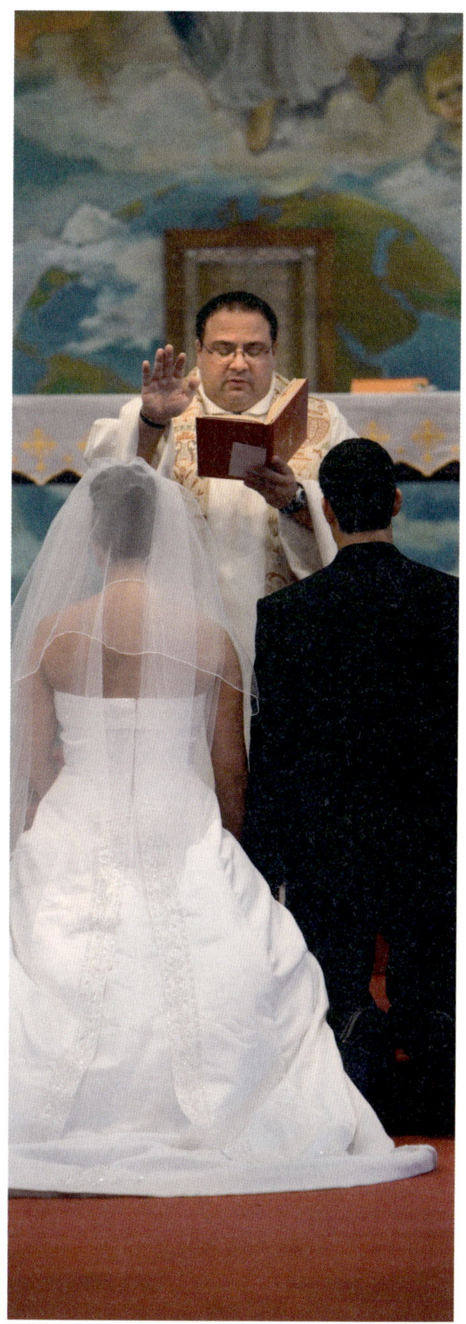

---

declaration of nullity The Church's declaration that a particular marriage, whether presumed to be a sacramental body or simply a natural body, was never valid.

families. Children experience feelings of rejection and betrayal when their parents separate. Churches, schools, and communities are weakened when families dissolve.

One important dimension of the unity of husband and wife is conjugal, or sexual, union. Because sex is such a powerful means of union and because it is designed by God as the means for bringing new life into the world, the Church has always held that only spouses committed to marriage are to partake of the gift of conjugal union. Although Catholics and others have always fallen short of this ideal, this too was the dominant view throughout the Christian world until the twentieth century.

The "sexual revolution" of the 1960s in large part destroyed this common understanding of the connection between sex and marriage. For many, sex became a recreational activity for consenting adults, with increasingly few limits placed on it. Sins against the Sixth Commandment—"You shall not commit adultery"∞—not only became increasingly common but were also defended as harmless or even beneficial. In the face of opposition from the dominant culture, the Church continues to insist on God's design for sex and marriage. The truth of the Church's teaching has been borne out in the negative psychological, medical, and spiritual fallout from widespread extramarital sexual relationships.

The popularization of artificial forms of contraception, especially the birth-control pill, empowered the cultural changes of the sexual revolution. As the connection between sex and marriage was weakened, the connection between sex and babies was broken. Proponents of contraception promised that it would ensure a better family environment for children and lower rates of abortion, because couples would get pregnant only when they wanted to. Both claims proved to be false. Instead, the predictions of Pope Paul VI in his 1968 encyclical *Humanae Vitae* (*On the Regulation of Birth*) proved true. He wrote that the easy availability of contraceptives would "open wide the way for marital infidelity and a general lowering of moral standards"; men would "forget the reverence due to a woman, and, disregarding her physical and emotional equilibrium, reduce her to being a mere instrument for the satisfaction of his own desires, no longer considering her as his partner whom he should surround with care and affection" (*HV*, 17).≈

The permissiveness of the sexual revolution, to which the acceptance of contraception contributed, led to a massive increase in nonmarital pregnancies, which in turn led to an increase in abortion. The rise in abortion rates was abetted by abortion's legalization in many places, including the United

∞ Note

Note that offenses against the Sixth Commandment include all offenses against chastity, including lust, masturbation, fornication (sex between an unmarried man and unmarried woman), pornography, prostitution, and rape. All people—single and married—are called to keep the Sixth Commandment through the practice of the virtue of chastity.

≈ Note

Pope Paul VI made several other accurate warnings of what would occur as result of the widespread acceptance of contraception. He warned of "the danger of this power passing into the hands of those public authorities who care little for the precepts of the moral law" (*HV*, 17). Abortions, sterilizations, and a general antichild mentality have been present since. Pope Paul's final warning was that contraception would lead man to think that he had unlimited dominion over his own body (see *Humanae Vitae*, 2). Besides sterilization and euthanasia, note the movement of the medical field to promote body-altering surgeries to deal with gender dysphoria.

States, where the Supreme Court decisions *Roe v. Wade* and *Doe v. Bolton* (1973) overturned all state-level abortion restrictions and made abortion legal throughout pregnancy in all fifty states. (The Court's 2022 *Dobbs v. Jackson Women's Health Organization* decision reversed *Roe v. Wade* and largely returned control of abortion laws to the states.)

Another potent deterrent to Christian family life that gained strength in the twentieth century was *materialism*, a focus on wealth and material goods as the path to happiness. The sexual revolution and materialism reinforced each other. The care of children requires the outlay of financial resources and other forms of parental sacrifice. Spouses could use contraception to avoid having children and to enable them to focus on careers and material gain. Recourse to abortion could help parents avoid the inconvenience of caring for a child and continue to pursue education or careers without interruption.

In contrast to the sexual revolution, the Church continues to propose what many now view as a radical understanding and practice of sex, marriage, and family. Faithful to God's intention for creation and upholding the love, fidelity, generosity, and fruitfulness exemplified by the union of Christ and his Church, Catholic teaching exhorts us to a vision of marriage as the union of one man and one woman, sharing in an unbreakable covenant of love, giving totally of themselves to each other and open to the creation of new life in cooperation with God's plan. To be sure, God's plan for marriage requires discipline and sacrifice, but as exemplified in the dramatic witness of many saints and other disciples, it is through sacrifice that we find joy; through giving that we receive; through dying that we gain eternal life.

Seen this way, the Church's vision of family life is not oppressive or limiting but empowering and inspiring. "The joy of love experienced by families is also the joy of the Church," wrote Pope Francis. Therefore, the Church's teaching on the family is "good news indeed" (*Amoris Laetitia*, 1). The Church also recognizes that "no family drops down from heaven perfectly formed" and that we must not "judge harshly those who live in situations of frailty" (*AL*, 325). The Gospel of the family is not a stick to beat someone with in condemnation but an offering of God's mercy and an invitation to a better and more joyful way. Finally, family life itself, even when it is harmonious and supportive, is not the end goal.

Hope in the Christian Family

The role of the family as a building block of the Church is so vital because the Church herself is a family, the "family of God." When St. Paul wrote to those who had become Christian in the city of Ephesus, he assured them that "you are no longer strangers and sojourners, but you are fellow citizens with the holy ones and members of the household of God" (Eph 2:19). The Apostle John exulted in the privilege accorded to those who follow Jesus and connected that privilege with family life: "See what love the Father has bestowed on us that we may be called the children of God. . . . Beloved, we are God's children now" (1 Jn 3:1–2).

By learning to be members of their human family, Catholics learn to be members of a divine family. "The Christian family is a communion of persons, a sign and image of the communion of the Father and the Son in the Holy Spirit" (*CCC*, 2205). In the family,

- we learn the meaning of love;

- we learn to want the good of another;

- we learn how to place ourselves at the service of others and thereby find meaning in our own lives; and

- we learn how to put God at the center of our existence.

For those who are isolated or without a loving human family, the Church extends an invitation to join in a community of unconditional love. "No one is without a family in this world: the Church is a home and family for everyone, especially those who 'labor and are heavy laden'" (*Familiaris Consortio*, 85). All of us are called to keep striving toward something greater than ourselves and our families, and every family must feel this constant impulse.

SECTION Assessment

Comprehension

1. Name one way that the Church is present in family life.

2. What are two requirements of a true marriage?

3. Name one way that the Church advocates for a radical understanding of the practice of sex, marriage, and family life.

Vocabulary

4. According to the principle of *subsidiarity*, which level of government should sponsor a public library?

5. What are the two *Sacraments of Service*?

Reflection

6. Give an example of the graces of married life you have witnessed in the relationship of a married couple you know.

7. What is your reaction to Pope Paul VI's predictions about the sexual revolution?

8. Choose one of the four things listed above that we learn by being part of a family and explain how you have found it to be mostly true.

Section Reviews

Focus Question

How does the Church bring greater unity to our family, faith, and world?
Complete one of the following:

- Develop a short oral presentation with at least four slides of images and quotations from an actor, politician, business leader, or other well-known person who was raised Catholic. Search for quotations where the person credits their Catholic upbringing for developing their values and character and furthering their later success in forging a career. Add a closing slide with your own quotation and image that tell what you believe to be the value of being raised a Catholic (or of receiving a Catholic education).

- Comment in writing on the following issue faced in several Catholic churches. Then ask a parish priest his opinion and record his responses as well. *There is no standard pattern of sitting, standing, and kneeling for worship. It has become the practice for people to do whatever they want and are most comfortable with. Some people are complaining that the lack of unity distracts them from worship.*

- Research and report on the Cursillo Movement. *Cursillo* is a Spanish word for "workshop" or "course." The Cursillo Movement offers short courses on Christianity. Answer this question as part of your report: How does the Cursillo Movement further the ecumenical and interreligious efforts of the Church?

Introduction

The Church Is Unchanging in a Changing World

Review

The twentieth century brought unprecedented social, economic, scientific, and several other kinds of change. The Church remained constant in the preaching of the Gospel of Christ and in extending her boundaries to add new members on her mission as a "pilgrim people." This era featured the formal writing of the Church's social doctrine, which was intended to set parameters so that the world's underserved would be treated fairly. The Church also continued to speak of the importance of the family, the domestic church.

Assignment

What are the bonds of unity of the pilgrim Church? Summarize paragraph 815 of the *Catechism of the Catholic Church*.

Section 1
The Foundation of the Church's Formal Social Doctrine

Review

Abuses and greed that accompanied the beginning of the Industrial Revolution and two world wars challenged the Church in the late nineteenth and twentieth centuries. She remained steadfast as she consistently endeavored to share the Gospel while continuing to foster a spirit of hope and act as both mother and teacher. This period was known for the foundation of the Church's formal doctrine, beginning with the encyclical *Rerum Novarum* of Pope Leo XIII and continuing with encyclicals by succeeding popes.

Assignment

What do the following people have to do with the advancement of workers' rights around the time of the Industrial Revolution? Look up and write one sentence for each Catholic clergyman that tells his role: Bishop Wilhelm Emmanuel von Ketteler, Cardinal Henry Edward Manning, Cardinal James Gibbons, and Fr. Joseph Cardijn.

Section 2
The Church Works to Increase Unity

Review

Modern times have witnessed some healing to the wounds to Christian unity that began in earnest at the time of the Protestant Reformation. Ecumenical efforts of both Protestants and Catholics have yielded some success. Also, unity around the Eucharist, including at International Eucharistic

Congresses, has provided a visible witness to Christ's active presence in the world. It is the task of all Catholics to strive to improve unity with other Christians. Interreligious dialogue also increased in the twentieth century, beginning with the Jews, who are our ancestors of faith. The work of ecumenism and interreligious dialogue has sometimes begun with making and accepting apologies.

Assignment

List the themes or focuses of the most recent International Eucharistic Congress and the most recent National Eucharistic Congress.

Section 3
The Church and Totalitarianism

Review

The Church does not promote one government over the other, but she asks that the state respect the human rights and religious freedom of all. Over the years, the Church has clashed several times with governments that attempt to restrict these rights and freedoms. In the twentieth century, a number of totalitarian regimes impacted the Church, including Nazi and communist governments. Many brave Catholics stepped up in these countries to support the Church and victims of the regimes. True freedom is the result of an inner happiness that can be achieved anywhere, even in the darkest conditions of imprisonment.

Assignment

Print Jesus's prayer for unity from John 17:20–21 on art paper in stylish printing. Decorate the borders around the prayer. Keep the copy of the prayer and pray it after you receive it back from your teacher.

Section 4

The Importance of Family

Review

The role of the family is accented by the principle of subsidiarity, which stipulates that decisions for individuals and families should be made at the most local level possible. Marriage is the foundation of family life, and the Church teaches its indissolubility. Married couples are in service of each other and of each other's holiness. They are also to be open to having children. There are currently growing threats to family life, many relating to the sexual revolution that arose around the time of the increase in artificial birth control. In family life, we learn many skills, most especially the meaning of love and how to love. By learning to be members of their human family, Catholics learn to be members of a divine family.

Assignment

Write your answer to the following question: Based on the principle of subsidiarity, why is the family essential?

Chapter Projects

Choose and complete at least one of the following projects to assess your understanding of the material in this chapter.

⚙ 1. Depict and Describe Saints Devoted to Catholic Social Teaching

Catholic social teaching is a name for the body of Church doctrine, beginning with Pope Leo XIII's 1891 encyclical *Rerum Novarum* (*The Condition of Labor*), that applies Jesus's Gospel to society, including its institutions and political structures. Other than St. Francis de Sales, who died in 1622, the other people featured in the painting *Cloud of Witnesses* by Br. Mickey McGrath all lived in either the nineteenth or the twentieth century. Complete the following assignment for each of these modern Catholics: St. Thérèse of Lisieux, Servant of God Nicholas Black Elk, Venerable Augustus Tolton, Servant of God Dorothy Day, and Servant of God Thea Bowman.

- Write a two-paragraph biography.
- Include a quotation on social justice from the person.
- Use colored pencils to draw the person either in the style of Br. McGrath or in your own style.

⚙ 2. Report on the Importance of Christian Names

Choosing Christian names is a practice that dates back in popular practice to the fourth century and perhaps earlier, when records show girls named for the Blessed Mother and boys named for the Apostles. According to Pope Benedict XVI, a Christian name signifies that in Baptism "every baptized person" has acquired a new character and an "unmistakable sign that the Holy Spirit gives birth anew." Complete all of the following:

- Research a list of the most popular names of boys and girls for concurrent decades over at least the past fifty years. Develop a chart or graph that compares and contrasts the choice of Christian names (e.g., saints, Christian feasts, etc.) with non-Christian names.
- Detail some information about your own name. What does your name mean? How was your name chosen?

- If you were named for a saint (first name or middle name), write a short profile of the saint. Tell about some qualities of the saint that you admire and how the saint is a model for your life. If you were not named for a saint, choose a favorite saint to write about.

⚙ *3. Write "Pray-Reflect-Act" Scripts for Religious Freedom Issues*

In recent years, the United States Conference of Catholic Bishops (USCCB) has supported religious freedom by marking a week devoted to the issue, typically beginning on June 22, the Feasts of St. Thomas More and St. John Fisher, two English Catholics who gave their lives for this cause. Read several ways that the USCCB encourages Catholics to pray, reflect, and act on various issues around religious freedom, such as religious freedom at work, in other nations, at school, and in healthcare. Examine the format for "Pray-Reflect-Act" scripts at www.usccb.org under religious liberty. Write three of your own scripts for the issues suggested or those of your own choice.

⚙ *4. Answer Questions about Challenges Faced by the Church Today*

Presented here are ten challenges faced by the Church today. Read through the list. Then choose five of the challenges. Write a detailed answer to the question associated with each challenge you choose. Each of your answers should include at least one citation to and reference for an outside source that helped you to formulate your answer.

1. *Ecumenism and interreligious dialogue.* How can Catholics reach out to other Christians and to members of other religions, including Islam?
2. *Gospel witness.* How can Catholics remain true to the vision of Jesus in a pluralistic and increasingly secular society that accepts behaviors and lifestyles contrary to the Gospel as "normal"?
3. *Immigrants.* How can the Church help immigrants, especially the fast-growing number of Latinos, adjust to American society and give them important roles in the Church herself?
4. *Leadership.* How can the bishops most effectively share the best of America's societal and cultural values with the universal Church?

5. *Parish life.* How can the Church reanimate people in the pews through a better appreciation of the Eucharist?

6. *Religious education.* How can the Church reach out to Catholics of all ages, especially to disaffected Catholics who have dropped out of the Church?

7. *Schools.* What is the future of Catholic schools on all levels: elementary, secondary, and collegiate? What is their specific Catholic identity and mission?

8. *Vocations.* How can the Church call and train priests to provide vision for the laity, who will assume even greater roles of leadership? How can the Church mobilize the laity to support those in religious life?

9. *Women.* What role should women have in the Church?

10. *Self-identity.* How can Catholicism in America remain faithful to the Roman Catholic Church as she continues her life and witness in the pluralistic American culture?

⚙ *5. Write a Position Paper on the Subject of Marriage*

A position paper is a type of writing that supports the author's position or presupposition on a certain topic through the presentation of statistics, facts, and other pieces of well-researched and current evidence. The objective of a position paper is to clearly and concisely explain why you believe what you do about a topic. Choose one of the following positions, and research relevant information to support it:

- Married couples who follow the teachings of the encyclical *Humanae Vitae* have happier and more satisfying marriages.

- There are several examples of married saints who are worth emulating.

- Because of Christ and the founding of the Church, women were given more esteem and value in married life than ever before.

- Divorced Catholics have served the Church well in ministry.

Write a five-hundred-word position paper supporting one of these positions. Cite specific evidence to support your claims.

Faithful Disciple
Thomas Merton

Thomas Merton

Thomas Merton had a cosmopolitan upbringing as the son of artists from New Zealand and the United States. Born in 1915, he lived and went to school in France, England, and the United States, training to be a writer. Through his adolescence he had little exposure to religion and considered himself agnostic, not caring much about whether God existed or not. He immersed himself in a life of pleasure: parties, alcohol, and women.

Even though he pursued it relentlessly, Thomas did not find happiness. He had "walked out into the world that I thought I was going to ransack and rob of all its pleasures and satisfactions," Merton wrote later. "I had done what I intended, and now I found that it was I who was emptied and robbed and gutted. . . . In filling myself, I had emptied myself. In grasping things, I had lost everything. In devouring pleasures and joys, I had found distress and anguish and fear."[15] Disappointed by what the world had offered, Thomas began exploring religion.

Eventually, he found himself in a Catholic church in New York City. He was struck by the piety of the congregation. A pretty teenager caught his eye. "I was very much impressed to see that someone who was young and beautiful could with such simplicity make prayer the real and serious and principal reason for going to church. She was clearly kneeling that way because she meant it, not in order to show off." He was also impressed by the priest's homily, a clear and forceful presentation of the doctrine of Jesus Christ as truly God and truly man, and of the need for grace to come to belief in him. When the time came for the consecration, Merton sensed the power and mystery of the Eucharist and fled the church. As he walked down Broadway, "my eyes looked about me at a new world. I could not understand what it was that had happened to make me so happy, why I was so much at peace, so content with life."[16]

Even though he didn't yet understand the working of grace, Thomas had felt its effect. Over the next few months, he read more about Catholicism and began to change his behavior. In November of 1938, as he was nearing completion of his master's degree at Columbia University, Thomas became Catholic. But his journey was not over. He would hear another call.

Merton thought God was calling him to the priesthood, but at first he couldn't find his way. He considered the Jesuits. He tried the Franciscans. Finally, he decided to make a retreat at a Trappist monastery. As Thomas prepared for his retreat, he perused an encyclopedia article about monks such as the Trappists. "What I saw on those pages," he recounted, "pierced me to the heart like a knife." He was struck by their lives of work and prayer, of poverty and simplicity and love of God. "The thought of those monasteries, those remote choirs, those cells, those hermitages, those cloisters, those men in their cowls, the poor monks, the men who had become nothing, shattered my heart. In an instant the desire of those solitudes was wide open within me like a wound."[17]

Resigning himself to God's will, Thomas Merton entered the Abbey of Gethsemani near Bardstown, Kentucky. "The monastery is a school," he wrote, "a school in which we learn from God how to be happy." Merton had spent much of his life running toward what he thought would bring happiness but didn't. When he stopped chasing pleasure, he opened his heart to hearing God's call. When he answered that call, he found the satisfaction for which he had been searching. "Our happiness consists in sharing the happiness of God, the perfection of his unlimited freedom, the perfection of his love."[18]

While in the monastery, Merton began to keep a journal. At first, he felt guilty about writing and thought it detracted from his life as a monk. But his superiors encouraged him, and he began to write biographies of saints and to translate texts for his community. In two-hour intervals between prayer, Merton also wrote his autobiography, which was published as a popular text in 1948 and titled *The Seven Storey Mountain*. It became a bestseller. Merton wrote spiritual works the rest of his life.

Thomas Merton was killed while on retreat in Bangladesh in 1968. He was electrocuted while taking a bath when a fan fell in the tub. His writings have lived on, including many works that were found unpublished after he died.

Comprehension

1.   What led Thomas Merton to begin exploring religion?
2.   How did Merton discover the Trappist monks?
3.   How did Merton define happiness?
4.   Why was Merton initially hesitant to continue writing as a monk?

Reflection

Thomas Merton was attracted to the authenticity of the prayerful demeanor of a young woman in church. Who is a person you know who is authentic in his or her faith? Tell about the person's faith life and why you find it authentic.

Prayer

The United States Conference of Catholic Bishops produced this prayer for unity inspired by the reflections of Pope Benedict XVI in paragraph 89 of *Sacramentum Caritatis* (*The Sacrament of Charity*). The main subject of Pope Benedict's apostolic exhortation is the Eucharist and the various ways it brings about unity.

Prayer for Unity, to Overcome Division

Christ Jesus,
who gave yourself for the good of all,
we come before you
as brothers and sisters
but we are divided
and at times, even hostile—
tearing one another down.
We approach the altar unworthily
and ask for your forgiveness.
Move us, instead, towards
Encounter
listening
dialogue
reconciliation, and
a commitment to build your kingdom
for the good of all.
Heal us, restore us,
unite your divided family, Lord.
Through the power of the Eucharist, overcome our divisions.
Give us sincere hearts that
make us open, not closed,
and willing to encounter,
ready to listen.
In your broken body, given for all, may we find unity
and peace in you.
Amen.

The Church Continues Her Mission

▶ *Twelfth-century fresco, unknown artist*

Christ Pantokrator is an image in iconography that depicts the Almighty, or all-powerful, ruling Lord. The Greek word *Pantokrator* literally translates to "ruler of all."

The *Apse of Sant Climent de Taüll* is a Romanesque fresco of the Pantokrator which was painted in the early twelfth century in a church by the same name in a village in the Catalan Pyrenees in what is now northeastern Spain by anonymous artists known collectively as the Master of Taüll. The mural of this fresco covered the entire **apse** surrounding the church altar. To preserve the mural as much as possible, it was transferred in the early 1920s to the National Art Museum of Catalonia. A replica of the mural remains in the church, as well as some of the original decorations that can still be seen in some places on the walls.

In the *Apse of Sant Climent de Taüll*, Christ sits on a band of gold. A white halo surrounds his head. The book he holds in his left hand reveals the words "I am the light of the world" in Latin. The first and last letters of the Greek alphabet, alpha and omega, are painted above his shoulders, signifying that he is the first and the last, the beginning and the end. Christ is surrounded by the four evangelists, Matthew, Mark, Luke, and John, along with their symbols. Below the image of Christ are other saints and Mary, the Mother of God. Mary holds a bowl with red rays emanating from it, symbolizing the Blood of her Son.

Appearing as it does today on a reproduction of the curved church apse, the painting show's Christ's body as proportional; if it were on a flat surface, his lower body would seem much smaller than his upper body.

The image, in various forms, of Christ Pantokrator has come to represent Christ as the stern but fair judge who will review our life at the time of our **particular judgment** to determine our worthiness for heaven.

If you would like to learn more about what the Church teaches about our particular judgment, see Chapter 8 Review, Chapter Project 1.

apse A semicircular or polygonal termination to the choir or nave of a church, in which the altar is placed. It is the place where the clergy are typically seated at Mass.

particular judgment The individual's judgment right after death, when Christ will rule on one's eternal destiny to be spent in heaven (after purification in Purgatory, if needed) or in hell.

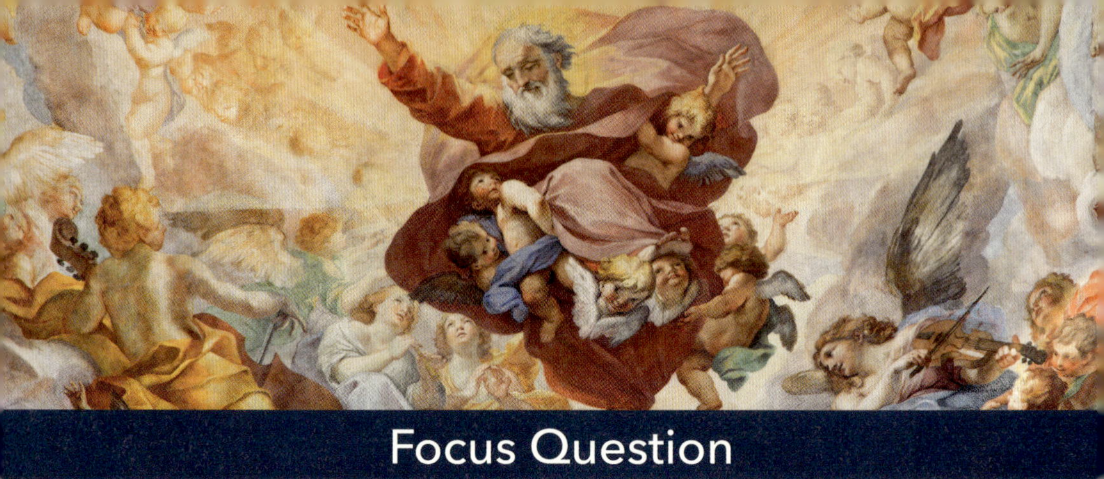

How is the Church renewed and reformed in modern times?

Introduction
The Uninterrupted Voice of the Church

Section 1
The Power of the Sacred Liturgy

Section 2
God's People Live Their Vocations

Section 3
Ways to Read, Study, and Pray with Scripture

Section 4
Joy and Hope for the Future

THE UNINTERRUPTED VOICE OF THE CHURCH

When in January of 1959, only three months after his election, Pope John XXIII announced his plan to call an ecumenical council, many bishops were unsupportive. Some felt that councils should only be called to deal with pressing questions or particularly dangerous heresies; others believed that since papal infallibility (see subsection "The Magisterium: Teaching Office of the Church" in Chapter 3, Section 2) had been declared in the nineteenth century, councils had become a thing of the past and the pope could rule the Church alone.

Nonetheless, Pope John XXIII called the Second Vatican Council, expressing his view that the Church needed to be "updated" so that it could respond more effectively to the world of the twentieth century. When the Council opened on October 11, 1962, in St. Peter's Basilica, Pope John was there to give the opening address. Although a main intention was to present the Gospel in new ways to people living in a time of momentous and sweeping changes, the pope began by paying homage to the Church's history:

> The voice of the past is both spirited and heartening. We remember with joy those early popes and their more recent successors to whom we owe so much. Their hallowed, momentous words come down to us through the councils held in both the East and the West, from the fourth century to the Middle Ages, and right down to modern times. Their uninterrupted witness, so zealously given, proclaims the triumph of Christ's Church, that divine and human society which derives from its divine Redeemer its title, its gifts of grace, its whole dynamic force.

At the same time, the pope called for a renewal of enthusiasm for embracing and sharing the faith in new ways to reach the contemporary world more effectively:

Four Constitutions of the Second Vatican Council

Historically, documents of ecumenical councils, including constitutions, would include both positive expressions of Church teaching and canons condemning false propositions. The constitutions and other documents of the Second Vatican Council are unique in that they contain only positive doctrine and no canons. To be made official, a constitution must be formally approved by the pope. The four constitutions of the Second Vatican Council were approved by Pope Paul VI, as Pope John XXIII died before the Council ended. They are named and described as follows:

Sacrosanctum Concilium

(*Constitution on the Sacred Liturgy*; December of 1963) underlines the importance of the full participation of both the clergy and the laity in the liturgy. This constitution emphasizes that the liturgy is the pinnacle of the Church's activity, stresses the vital importance of the Eucharist, and introduces permission to use vernacular languages in the liturgy, instead of only Latin, although Latin remains the official language of the Church.

Lumen Gentium

(*Dogmatic Constitution on the Church*; November of 1964) speaks of the Church as mystery. This constitution gives special attention to the image of the Church as the People of God: lay, consecrated religious, and ordained. It teaches that all members of the Church have a responsibility for carrying out the Church's mission.

Dei Verbum

(*Dogmatic Constitution on Divine Revelation*; November of 1965) encourages all Catholics, especially the laity, to read, study, and pray with the Bible. It also reinforces the close relationship between Sacred Scripture and Sacred Tradition. This constitution emphasizes revelation as God's disclosure of himself.

Gaudium et Spes

(*Pastoral Constitution on the Church in the Modern World*; December of 1965) stresses that although the Church's mission is ultimately directed to eternal life in heaven, her earthly members are present in this world and are called to shape it in light of the Gospel. In the words of the document, the Church "serves as a leaven and as a kind of soul for human society" (*GS*, 40). Every member of the Church is called to bear witness to Christ and to help in his or her own way to bring about the transformation of the world.

The Second Vatican Council also produced three declarations and nine decrees. One of the decrees, *Unitatis Redintegratio* (*Decree on Ecumenism*), while reaffirming that the Catholic Church is entrusted with the fullness of the means of salvation, committed the Church to the ecumenical movement. One of the declarations, *Nostra Aetate* (*Declaration on the Relation of the Church to Non-Christian Religions*), affirmed many positive qualities of other religions. The Church understands that every person in the world is in some way connected to the Body of Christ because all people are called to salvation.

There are choices families and individuals make on where to spend their Sundays.

> What is needed, and what everyone imbued with a truly Christian,
> Catholic and apostolic spirit craves today, is that this doctrine shall
> be more widely known, more deeply understood, and more pene-
> trating in its effects on men's moral lives. What is needed is that
> this certain and immutable doctrine, to which the faithful owe obe-
> dience, be studied afresh and reformulated in contemporary terms.[1]

Over the course of four years, the Council Fathers would debate how to implement Pope John's mandate. They would formulate and approve sixteen documents, including four constitutions, the most theologically important of the documents. The remaining sections of this chapter explain more about the central themes of these constitutions.

The Second Vatican Council was by far the largest ecumenical council ever, attended by more than 2,600 bishops, of which 42 percent were from Latin America, Asia, and Africa.[2] This large attendance of non-European bishops at an ecumenical council for the first time brought concerns for the poor and the oppressed to the forefront. The Second Vatican Council offered the most wide-sweeping changes to the Church since the sixteenth century's Council of Trent—changes that continue to be discerned and implemented today.

The Second Vatican Council Shapes the Church Today

The teachings of the Second Vatican Council set the tone for the recent history of the Church. In the constitutions on the liturgy, the Church, Divine Revelation, and the Church in the modern world, the Council reiterated venerable Catholic teachings while emphasizing certain aspects of the Church's message that the bishops deemed especially relevant to our times.

In the years since the Council, the Church's engagement of the world has had a diverse array of effects, good and bad. The liturgy has become more accessible through the use of local languages and congregational singing, but many Catholics do not attend Mass regularly, and in many areas there is a shortage of priests. The empowerment of the laity is everywhere on display, as the nonordained have taken on leadership roles in the Church, advanced in society through education and economic progress, and created important apostolates to assist both Catholics and non-Catholics in various ways. At the same time, in some places, many Catholics have not learned the Church's teaching well and neglect Catholic moral principles. Many Catholics have gained an appreciation for the Bible, and cooperation with non-Catholics has increased, but large numbers of Catholics have left the Catholic Church in favor of other Christian denominations or abandoned altogether the practice of religious faith. Positively, the fruits of the Second Vatican Council have continued to remind Catholics and all people to look at the world with joy.

At this moment in the twenty-first century, the challenge of the missionary mandate of the Gospel remains. Even though the world that Peter and the Apostles encountered at the birth of the Church on Pentecost two thousand years ago seems in many ways so different from ours, the fundamental task of the Church is the same. Even in regions where Christianity has a long history and most people have heard of Christ, the urgency of the Great Commission—"Go, . . . make disciples of all nations"—persists. The peoples of the world—Christian, Jewish, Muslim, Hindu, atheist—still need to hear the message of the Gospel, and Catholics themselves need to become better disciples through the continual process of repentance and reform.

SECTION Assessment

Comprehension

1. Why was the Second Vatican Council convened? How did this reason differ from why other ecumenical councils were convened?

2. What makes the constitutions of the Second Vatican Council unique compared to those of previous councils?

3. In one or two words, summarize the subjects of each of the four Second Vatican Council constitutions.

Reflection

4. What did *Gaudium et Spes* teach about the role of the Church in the modern world?

5. Which challenge resulting from the Second Vatican Council discussed in this section most resonates with you? Explain.

THE POWER OF THE SACRED LITURGY

Recall the story of the conversion of spiritual writer and Trappist monk Thomas Merton. In the 1930s, he was awed by the mystery of the Eucharist after wandering into a church where Mass was taking place, spurring his deeper research into and eventual conversion to Catholicism. About sixty years later, around the turn of the century, the Eucharist was instrumental in another, even greater (in number of people) conversion. Nearly the entire congregation of Detroit's Maranatha Church along with their fiery Pentecostal pastor, Alex Jones, began their entrance into the Catholic Church.

Pastor Jones led the movement. In 1998, he began reading about the early Church Fathers in order to establish a worship service at his church that closely resembled that of those earliest Christians. He soon discovered that what he was trying to recreate was nearly exactly what he knew of the Catholic Mass. Jones asked his congregation if they would like to accompany him with his studies and on his journey of discovery. One of the things that they did was attend an Easter Vigil Mass at a local Catholic Church. Many were moved by the experience, while others were uncomfortable and left Jones's congregation. The ones who stayed joined with Jones to begin the initiation process at St. Suzanne's Catholic Church in September of 2001. Alex Jones was ordained a permanent deacon in the Catholic Church in 2005.

The change was monumental and one that Jones wrote about in his autobiography *No Price Too High*. "All of what I had before may have seemed perfect," he said, "but it was not complete." Gloria Yarber, one of those whom Jones persuaded to make the move to the Catholic Church, explained why she did: "The love of the presence of Christ in the Eucharist, the sacraments and the Church. That's why we came into the Catholic Church: the traditions."[3]

The Masses that Thomas Merton and Alex Jones attended were quite different in some ways because the Catholic Mass in most places changed noticeably between the 1930s and the 1990s as a result of reforms called for by the Second Vatican Council. Even so, as the experiences of Merton and Jones indicate, the essential character of the Mass endures. The Mass is an act of communal worship whereby we hear the Word of God, renew the sacrifice of Jesus on Calvary, and seek communion with the triune God.

A Call for Active Participation

Before the Second Vatican Council, the Mass was normally said in Latin. The altar servers, not the congregation, responded to the priest's invocations. Most Masses (i.e., **low Mass**) did not have music. The typical **high Mass** did have music, but most or all of the singing was done by choirs and ministers, not the congregation. *Sacrosanctum Concilium* recommended that more of the Mass be presented in the *vernacular* language (the language spoken by the people in a region, such as English in most of the United States). It also called for "dialogue" Masses, where the people would join the servers in giving the responses.∞ And it encouraged more congregational singing. The goal of all these reforms was "that all the faithful should be led to that fully conscious, and active participation in liturgical celebrations which is demanded by the very nature of the liturgy" (*SC*, 14).

> **∞ Note**
>
> Think about how most parts of the Mass are a dialogue between the priest and the congregation. Even the longer Eucharistic Prayer, which seems to be a monologue given by the priest, is actually a dialogue. The congregation responds with its agreement to what the priest has prayed in the Eucharistic Prayer with the "Great Amen."

low Mass A Mass that is entirely read or spoken by the celebrant. No parts of the Mass are chanted or sung. Sometimes soft music may be played during certain aspects of a low Mass, and hymns may be sung by the congregation and choir.

high Mass A Mass that has some parts chanted or sung by the celebrant, including some parts that are sung in response by the congregation. A high Mass is more prominent than other Masses celebrated on the same day, and more people are expected to attend it.

Parishioners accompanied by their pets attend Mass on St. Francis of Assisi Day in São Paulo, Brazil.

In the years following the Council, *Sacrosanctum Concilium* was applied in different ways in various places. The changes described above were implemented virtually everywhere, but other practices that had not been prescribed by the Council also became common—for example, receiving Communion in the hand and the priest facing the people (*versus populum*, "toward the people") rather than facing the altar with the people (often called *ad orientam*, "to the east"; or *ad Deum*, "toward God").∞ In some places, the changes gave Catholics a sense that "experimentation" was now permitted in the liturgy, and a variety of unapproved practices appeared. At the same time, some Catholics resisted the changes entirely, insisting that the "old Mass" was fine as it was.

∞ Note

Ad orientam orientation is sometimes viewed as the priest "having his back to the people." However, more concretely, the priest and people are united as one, according to Pope Benedict XVI (writing before he became pope), "in a common act of trinitarian worship. . . . Where priest and people together face the same way, what we have is a cosmic orientation and also an interpretation of the Eucharist in terms of resurrection and trinitarian theology. Hence it is also an interpretation in terms of parousia [end of the world], a theology of hope, in which every Mass is an approach to the return of Christ" (Joseph Ratzinger, *The Feast of Faith* [San Francisco: Ignatius Press, 1986], 140–141).

The debates and differences over the liturgical reform emerging out of the Second Vatican Council explain why, still today, people may experience very different kinds of Masses depending on which Catholic church they attend. In some churches, parts of the Mass may be said in Latin, while in others everything is in English (or Spanish or another modern language). In some, an organ may accompany ancient hymns, while in others guitars accompany contemporary worship songs. The priest may face the altar with his back toward the people, or he may face the congregation. Communicants might receive the Body of Christ on their tongues, possibly while kneeling, or they may receive in their hands while standing.

The Source and Summit

Despite any outward differences in how the Mass is celebrated, the Eucharist is, according to *Lumen Gentium*, the "source and summit of the Christian life" (*CCC*, 1324, quoting *LG*, 11). All of the liturgy, and especially the Eucharist, is the heart of Catholic prayer life and the primary means by which we are united to each other and to Christ. Whether it is in Latin, English, Spanish, or Chinese, the Mass is a reenactment of the Passion of Jesus. Whether we stand or kneel to receive the host, it is the Real Presence, the Body and Blood of Christ. Whether the songs we sing are a thousand years old or were composed in the twenty-first century, the purpose of our singing is to worship God. In a global Church that encompasses people of all races, languages, and cultures, the "common celebration of divine worship" is one of the "visible bonds of communion" (*CCC*, 815) that assure the unity of the Church—one of her four essential marks. Christians in the first century celebrated the Mass, and fellow Catholics across the world today celebrate the Mass; it is the link that connects the People of God across time and space.

Considering the importance of the Mass as a means of union with God and each other, it is imperative that Catholics attend Mass regularly. Yet statistics show that the number of Catholics who go to church on Sunday has been declining in recent decades. Around 55 percent of Catholics attended Mass weekly in 1970, but just over 23 percent did in 2015. (Numbers were even lower in 2020–2021, but those figures are skewed by the coronavirus pandemic.)[4] With so many Catholics rarely or never availing themselves of the graces available in the sacraments, the vitality of their spiritual lives, and therefore the life the Church, cannot reach its full potential.

Catholic pilgrims participating in the Hat Mass where a priest blesses their hats after the closure of All Souls' Day celebrations in Juazeiro do Norte, Brazil.

However, many Catholics do draw spiritual sustenance from the Mass, and they attest to the power of the Eucharist. Fr. Mike Schmitz, the personality behind *The Bible in a Year* podcast, was not always enthusiastic about the faith. "I was raised Catholic, but I didn't really care about the Catholic Church," he recalls. "Had to go to Mass every Sunday . . . hated going to Mass every Sunday. Went to Mass at Catholic elementary school . . . hated going to Mass at Catholic elementary school." But when he was fifteen, "everything changed for me." The experiences that ignited his faith revolved around Confession and the Eucharist. He remembers picking up a book that was lying around his house and reading a chapter on the Eucharist. "My mind was blown. This is real. What we've been doing at Mass. When the priest says this is my Body, this is my Blood, that bread becomes the Body of Christ. The wine becomes the Blood of Christ. That changed everything." As a teenager, Fr. Mike gained a deep faith in the presence of Jesus in the Church. He realized, "The Eucharist we've had in every Catholic church for the last two thousand years is really Jesus."

Fr. Mike now sees the liturgy as the center of the Christian life. "This teaching is worth living for; this teaching is worth dying for," he says. "This teaching is worth giving up hockey tournaments to make sure you get to Mass every single Sunday!" He sees the Eucharist as "the heart of Christianity," reflecting the message of John 3:16: "God so loved the world that he gave his only Son." The Son, Fr. Mike continues, "so loved the world that he gave his very self as food." Jesus's generosity has a very practical effect in our spiritual lives. "He gives his very self so you're never alone, so you never walk through this world in isolation. Every step you take is *Immanuel*, God with us—with Jesus, the bread of life, with a God who gave everything to be close to you." Fr. Mike believes that the Eucharist can have the same impact on others that it had on him: "This teaching has the ability to change your life."[5]

SECTION Assessment

Comprehension

1. What led Alex Jones and his congregation to attend a Catholic Mass?

2. How were the Masses that Thomas Merton and Alex Jones attended both different and the same?

3. Name an example of a practice not explicitly prescribed by the Second Vatican Council that has become part of the Mass in some places.

4. Explain the difference between Masses celebrated *versus populum* and *ad orientam*.

Vocabulary

5. Differentiate between *low Mass* and *high Mass*.

Reflection

6. Compare and contrast how the Mass is celebrated in two different parishes in your area.

7. What does the Mass mean to you?

GOD'S PEOPLE LIVE THEIR VOCATIONS

Chapter 2 of *Lumen Gentium* (*Dogmatic Constitution on the Church*) is devoted to the description of the Church as the "People of God." The constitution traces the formation of the Church as the People of God from the beginning of **salvation history**. The People of God includes those of every role in the Church: popes, bishops, priests, deacons, religious men and women, and the laity. A person is initiated into the People of God—the Church—through Baptism. *Lumen Gentium* states: "The baptized, by regeneration and the anointing of the Holy Spirit, are consecrated as a spiritual house and a holy priesthood, in order that through all those works which are those of the Christian man they may offer spiritual sacrifices and proclaim the power of Him who has called them out of darkness and into His marvelous light" (10).

The vocation given to Catholics in Baptism is part of the **common priesthood of the faithful**. Living this gift is "exercised by the unfolding of the baptismal grace—a life of faith, hope, and charity, a life according to the Spirit" (*CCC*, 1547). The Sacrament of Baptism calls all Catholics to live holy lives and, further, to consider how the vocations of the ordained ministry, consecrated life, marriage (see subsection "Married Life Is the Foundation of Family Life" in Chapter 7, Section 4), or a single life dedicated to a life of chastity and service to others are connected with holiness and their individual purpose in the Church.

In fact, Chapter 5 of *Lumen Gentium* emphasizes that holiness is universal and not limited to any one state of life. Before the Second Vatican Council,

salvation history The account of God's saving activity and intervention on behalf of humanity.

common priesthood of the faithful The priesthood of the baptized. Christ has made the Church a "kingdom of priests" who share in his priesthood through the Sacraments of Baptism and Confirmation.

consecrated religious (sisters and brothers) and ordained men (priests) were sometimes viewed as the only ones called to and capable of living a holy life. According to *Lumen Gentium*, "Everyone whether belonging to the hierarchy, or being cared for by it, is called to holiness, according to the saying of the Apostle: 'For this is the will of God, your sanctification'" (*LG*, 39 quoting 1 Thes 4:3). To this day, holiness is lived out by Catholics through vocations that have been present in the Church from her earliest days, albeit with different emphases. Two vocations, the ordained ministry and consecrated life, are presented in the following sections.

Holiness of the Ordained Ministry

For men called to the ministerial priesthood, the vocation offers several graces, both for personally living a holy life and for helping others to a life of holiness as well. Realize that the ministerial priesthood is different from the common priesthood. The ministerial priesthood is directed toward serving the common priesthood by "unfolding . . . the baptismal grace of all Christians" (*CCC*, 1547). Through the life of the Catholic priest, Christ builds up and leads the Church. For that reason, the ministerial priesthood has its own sacrament, the Sacrament of Holy Orders.

Men who are ordained to the priesthood in the Sacrament of Holy Orders are consecrated to serve the Church in three basic ways:

I   preaching the Gospel;

II   celebrating divine worship; and

III   providing pastoral governance, typically as the pastor of a parish.

In fulfilling these roles in the Spirit of Christ, priests grow in their own holiness and build up the laity so they can live lives of faith, hope, and love, and reach for perfection.

In receiving the fullness of the Sacrament of Holy Orders, bishops share in a similar role of consecrated service to the Church. Priests function in their ministry only because of their relationship to their local bishop. Each may administer the sacraments, although only a bishop can administer the

The Church Responds to a Modern Crisis

Focus Question: How is the Church renewed and re-formed in modern times?

Time and again throughout history, the Church has found herself in need of renewal and reform, and individual members of the Church are always in need of conversion and repentance. *Lumen Gentium* speaks of the simultaneous presence of holiness and sinfulness in the Church: "While Christ, holy, innocent and undefiled, knew nothing of sin, but came to expiate only the sins of the people, the Church, embracing in its bosom sinners, at the same time holy and always in need of being purified, always follows the way of penance and renewal" (*LG*, 8).

Christ did not leave his Church without the means for dealing with sin. The purpose of the Sacrament of Penance and Reconciliation is to provide a way to recognize our sin, turn away from it, and make our way back toward God. *Lumen Gentium* states, "Those who approach the sacrament of Penance obtain pardon from the mercy of God for the offence committed against Him and are at the same time reconciled with the Church, which they have wounded by their sins, and which by charity, example, and prayer seeks their conversion" (*LG*, 11). Through our sins, we offend God, harm ourselves, and damage our relationships with others, including the community of the Church. The Sacrament of Penance and Reconciliation assists us in healing all those wounds.

In recent times, the reality of the Church's weakness and the pressing need for healing have been manifested in the clergy sexual abuse crisis. Beginning in the early 2000s, it gradually came to light that hundreds of Catholic priests over the course of decades (the worst period was the 1970s and 1980s) had acted unchastely, betrayed the trust of parishioners, and violated the dignity of their victims by engaging in sexual acts, often with children or teenagers of both sexes, but mostly with boys.

On top of the original sinful actions, bishops and other priests in positions of authority too often neglected the immoral and criminal acts. Sometimes they refused to believe accusers. Sometimes, even when they knew the accusations to be true, they simply reassigned abusive priests to other parishes and schools. Too often they trusted advisors and counselors who assured them that

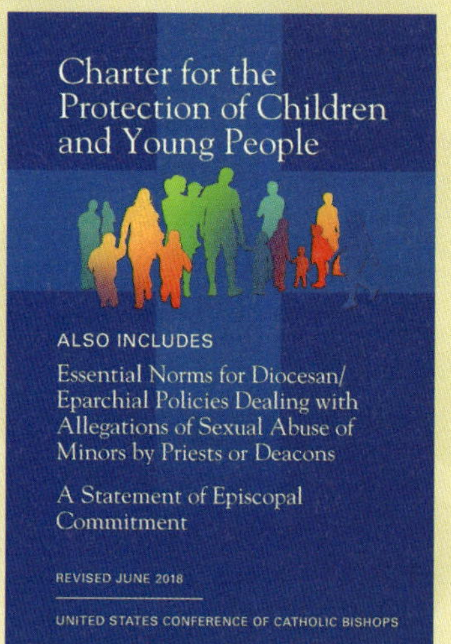

the troubled priests had reformed and could return to active ministry. When legal action was taken by victims against the Church, leaders sometimes treated the victims, who were often faithful Catholics, as opponents to be attacked. Bishops focused on hiring public relations and legal firms rather than on repenting, asking forgiveness, and seeking the healing of the victims.

In time, however, the Church did come to grips with the scale and severity of the crisis in her midst. In 2002, the US bishops instituted the Charter for the Protection of Children and Young People, also known as the "Dallas charter," which aimed to coordinate efforts to minimize the possibility of abuse in Church institutions or by Church personnel. The charter has been updated several times since it was first released. The Church also established a National Review Board of independent experts who would oversee the Church's programs in this area and offer criticism and recommendations for improvement. Many Catholics continue to debate whether enough has been done to rectify past mistakes and how to best prevent future abuse, but it is widely agreed that the Catholic Church has been more transparent and proactive in confronting this problem than had been the case in the past.

Sexual abuse is a scourge across many institutions—public education, government, business, non-Catholic religious bodies—and American society has yet to address the matter adequately. Catholic dioceses in the United States have implemented programs to train all adults who interact with children, teaching them to recognize signs of abuse and report suspected abuse to authorities. These efforts led the author of a 2012 article on the crisis to conclude, "Whatever its past record, the Catholic Church in the US has made unparalleled strides in educating their flock about child sexual abuse and ensuring that children are safe in Catholic environments."[6]

In 2019, Pope Francis issued a *motu proprio*, a document affecting Church law, which revised and tightened the Church's procedures for handling sex-abuse cases. "The crimes of sexual abuse offend Our Lord, cause physical, psychological and spiritual damage to the victims and harm the community of the faithful," the pope wrote. To prevent future abuse, he went on, "a continuous and profound conversion of hearts is needed, attested by concrete and effective actions that involve everyone in the Church, so that personal sanctity and moral commitment can contribute to promoting the full credibility of the Gospel message and the effectiveness of the Church's mission."[7]

Sexual abuse, like all kinds of sin, will never disappear completely, and much

Protesters hold a cross with names of accused priests as they stand outside the Cathedral of the Holy Cross in Boston.

---

motu proprio Latin for "of his own accord," a papal document promulgated on the pope's own initiative.

Protesters hold quilts bearing portraits of young children outside the Cathedral of Our Lady of the Angels in Los Angeles, California, one day after the release of personnel files of priests accused of sexual misconduct.

work remains for Church leaders to demonstrate amendment and rebuild trust, but declining rates of abuse within the Church in recent years seem to indicate that progress is being made. The Church on earth suffers because of all the sinfulness and failings of her members. This is why the People of God collectively must continue to repent and to strive toward sanctification. The Church herself, thanks to the goodness of God, possesses the resources to aid us in this quest, especially through the Sacrament of Penance and Reconciliation, which restores our connection to God; and the Sacrament of the Eucharist, which draws us closer to him and gives us the grace to resist temptation and to relate to others in genuine love.

Further Study and Reflection

- Investigate the "Protection of Children and Young People" portion of the USCCB website (www.usccb.org). Report on at least five ways the Church is committed to protecting people from sexual abuse.
- Share an important lesson about protection from and accountability for sexual abuse from your own parish or diocesan website.

Sacrament of Holy Orders, and he is also the ordinary minister of the Sacrament of Confirmation. Whereas the priest is responsible for sharing in the governance of a parish, the bishop is the ordinary pastor of his diocese and therefore has responsibility for all of the ministries in the diocese that are oriented toward building up the Church in holiness.

Deacons, too, receive the Sacrament of Holy Orders, but unlike the bishop and priest, deacons are ordained not for priesthood but for service. In the Rite of Ordination, the deacon promises obedience to the bishop. He serves at liturgy and is also in service to the needs of the entire Church and world. While until recently the diaconate was almost exclusively a transition to priestly ordination, many deacons today remain in the diaconate permanently. They may be mature single or married men. A single man ordained to the permanent diaconate may not marry. A married man ordained to the permanent diaconate may not remarry if his wife should die. Pope John Paul II praised the ministry of the deacon, saying that "such a ministry, whether in the form of the simplest acts of charity or the most heroic witness to the radical demands of the Gospel," is much needed in today's world.[8]

All Catholics are called to live the **evangelical counsels**. For consecrated religious, this takes the form of a vow. Some, but not all, members of the *clergy* (bishops, priests, and deacons) are consecrated religious. Each of the counsels stands in opposition to a temptation that can draw a person away from God. A commitment to *poverty* frees one from the temptation to sin for the sake of material wealth. A commitment to *chastity* frees one from the temptation to sin for the sake of physical pleasure. In the Latin Church, *celibacy*, the state of being unmarried for the sake of the Kingdom of God, is required for bishops and priests. A commitment to *obedience* frees one from the temptation to sin for the sake of power. These evangelical counsels also make up the heart of consecrated, or religious, life, described in the following subsection.

Holiness of Consecrated Life

There have always been Christians who have renounced worldly goals and pleasures for the sake of God's Kingdom. Some of them have made vows or

---

evangelical counsels When related to vows taken by a religious, promises of personal poverty, chastity (understood as a lifelong celibacy), and obedience to a bishop or superior of a religious community.

promises committing themselves to the evangelical counsels. Today, there are still both men and women who live a life consecrated to God, typically in religious communities. You may consider this an extreme way to live a life of holiness. In many ways it truly is. This radical form of discipleship has roots in the words of Jesus, who, in explaining the lifetime commitment of marriage, said, "Some are incapable of marriage because they were born so; some, because they were made so by others; some, because they renounced marriage for the sake of the kingdom of heaven. Whoever can accept this ought to accept it" (Mt 19:12).

Lumen Gentium addresses the reformation of religious life around the universal call to holiness given at Baptism. More specifically, the constitution recognizes several distinctive dimensions of religious life, including the following:

- ***Religious life is devoted to the welfare of the Church through the practice of the evangelical counsels.*** The practice of these counsels through various ministries performed by religious always leads to charity, which inspires others to seek out Christ and the Church. Likewise, religious life, *Lumen Gentium* teaches, is "not an intermediate state between the clerical and lay states. But, rather, the faithful of Christ are called by God from both these states of life so that they might enjoy this particular gift in the life of the Church and thus each in one's own way, may be of some advantage to the salvific mission of the Church" (*LG*, 43).

- ***Religious life is a sign of the bridge between heaven and earth.*** In a secular world in which the minds of many are primarily on the cares of this time and space, religious sisters, brothers, and priests[9] are asked to keep in mind "the fact that the Church presents Christ to believers and non-believers alike in a striking manner daily through them" (*LG*, 46).

As the Council concluded, many religious communities took the opportunity to reflect on these dimensions and renew their communities in different ways. Many communities looked back into their histories to recover their original charisms and learn more about their founders. In the process, religious life changed. Some communities adapted religious habits, and many expanded their ministries. Before the Second Vatican Council, a majority of sisters and many brothers were teachers in Catholic schools. After the Council, the expansion of new ministries often centered on other ways to directly serve the poor and those in most need.

In an address to religious in 2017, Pope Francis spoke of a vision of religious life in which religious sisters, brothers, and communities become an "eloquent and joyful" witness that attracts people to God. He also addressed the declining numbers of those who seek out this vocation today, offering this advice:

If consecrated life is to maintain its prophetic mission and its appeal, continuing to be a school of faithfulness for *those near and far* (cf. Eph 2:17), it must maintain its freshness and the novelty of Jesus' centrality, the appeal of spirituality and the strength of mission, show the beauty of following Christ, and radiate hope and joy. Hope and joy. This shows us how a community is doing, what is inside.∞

There are other forms of consecrated life that have thrived since the Second Vatican Council as a part of Church life that are ways to holiness. Members of *secular institutes* are men or women who consecrate themselves to God through the profession of vows, particularly to celibacy, but generally do not live in community. Rather, they dedicate themselves to evangelization and promoting the

∞ Note

Pope Francis, Address to the Participants in the Plenary Assembly of the Congregation for Institutes of Consecrated Life and Societies of Apostolic Life, Clementine Hall, January 28, 2017.

Gospel through secular careers. Members of *apostolic societies* are faithful Catholics who pledge to live the evangelical counsels but do not take formal vows. *Consecrated virgins* are women who dedicate themselves to virginity or perpetual chastity. Members of *third orders* are laypeople who live according to the rules of a religious order but don't necessarily live in community. Living lives of prayer, penance, and apostolic service, they are consecrated by the bishop as an image of the heavenly bride and of the Kingdom of God that is to come.

The Church Is One People of God

"God created the world for the sake of communion with his divine life, a communion brought about by . . . the Church" (*CCC*, 760). As the People of God, the Church is a chosen race, a kingdom of priests, a nation of prophets, and a royal people. The individual personalities within the People of God have not been given to us as a means of separating us, but rather as a means of uniting us more completely. All people are called to be members of the People of God; none are to be excluded. Our differences in personality and vocation are complementary. We are all meant to work together to build the Kingdom of God.

In Baptism, you receive God's grace. The priestly work for you to do is to live in Christ. The New Testament Letter to the Hebrews describes Jesus as "high priest forever according to the order of Melchizedek" (Heb 6:20). By his sacrifice on the Cross, a single offering, Jesus merited all the grace for the salvation of humankind. He established a new understanding for priestly living which all who are baptized in his name are to participate in.

When Christ took on the role of the High Priest who offers not another victim but himself as the one sacrifice, he ended the need for human beings ever to offer sacrifice to God again (see Hebrews 9:11–14).∞ Christ was not offered as a victim by another person in order to appease God; Jesus freely offered himself as both priest and victim. His offering, together with his Resurrection, demonstrated that his self-giving love triumphs over sin and death.

∞ Note

In the Old Testament, priestly living had different connotations than it does for Catholics today. Jewish priests performed a number of roles, but over time their primary ministry was restricted to the Temple, where they offered animal sacrifices on behalf of all of God's People.

When you are baptized, you take on an actual share in the Paschal Mystery and membership in the common priesthood of the faithful. How are you to live out the common priesthood of the faithful? Put simply, you are to participate in the one sacrifice of Christ, whether in the ordained priesthood if you are a man, consecrated or religious life, marriage, or the dedicated single life.

SECTION Assessment

Comprehension

1. What are four ways that Catholics can live out their vocation to holiness?

2. Name three ways that priests serve the Church.

3. Who can administer the Sacrament of Holy Orders?

4. What are two tasks of deacons?

5. Can a priest also be a religious? Explain.

6. Differentiate between apostolic societies and third orders.

7. What is one difference between the animal sacrifices offered by Old Testament priests and the sacrifice offered by Jesus on the Cross?

Vocabulary

8. What is meant by *salvation history*?

9. Who belongs to the *common priesthood of the faithful*?

10. Name the *evangelical counsels*.

Reflection

11. Explain how you envision the Church as the People of God.

12. Is the description of religious life as "radical" apt? Explain why or why not.

WAYS TO READ, STUDY, AND PRAY WITH SCRIPTURE

Many people, Catholics and non-Catholics alike, are surprised when they realize how deeply rooted in the Bible Catholic doctrines and practice are. Some converts to Catholicism from Protestant traditions cite the testimony of Scripture as one of the factors that led them to see the fullness of the faith in the Catholic Church. John Bergsma, a professor of theology with special expertise in Scripture, is one: he titled his account of discovering the link between the Church and the Bible *Stunned by Scripture*.

Bergsma was raised in the Christian Reformed tradition, a variety of Calvinist Protestantism. He believed that "the Catholic Church was largely a false church that ignored—and was ignorant of—Scripture." A devout young man, he discerned a call to the ministry, was ordained as a Reformed pastor, and went to work in a small inner-city church. His seminary studies had given him knowledge of Greek, the original language of most of the New Testament, and later he went to the University of Notre Dame to obtain a doctorate in Old Testament studies. At Notre Dame he met a fellow doctoral student who "was highly intelligent, filled with the Holy Spirit, and Catholic." As Bergsma got to know his new friend, he began raising his objections to Catholic theology. "To my surprise," Bergsma recalled, his friend "responded to my apologetic attacks on the Catholic Church by citing Scripture." On several points of doctrinal disagreement,

John Bergsma

Bergsma explained, his friend "could show that the plain sense of Scripture better supported Catholicism!"

One of the key questions Bergsma had about Catholicism was the Real Presence of Jesus under the appearances of bread and wine in the Eucharist. When Bergsma looked at the writings of early Christians such as the Church Fathers, he found strong support, *based on Scripture*, for the doctrine of the Real Presence of Jesus. Another difficult issue for him was the pope. "After all," Bergsma wrote, "if there is one thing Protestants don't like about the Catholic Church, it is the papacy." But here, too, Bergsma found that the testimony of Scripture favored the Catholic view. His analysis of the original language used in important Gospel passages (for example, Matthew 16:18, when Jesus calls Peter the rock on which he will build his Church) led him to accept the position that Christ had intended Peter to be the head of the Church.

Bergsma would have more work to do, trying to understand the scriptural basis for ideas such as the Catholic view of Mary, but he gradually came to see that Scripture supported rather than undermined Catholic theology. He and his family became Catholic, and Bergsma today writes and speaks on many aspects of the relationship between the Bible and Catholicism.[10]

John Bergsma's experience points to the fact that Sacred Scripture stands at the heart of the Church, and that Catholics have a duty to explore its texts in order to understand their faith more fully. Beyond its doctrinal importance, however, the Bible is a rich source of spiritual sustenance, a means of praying and of meditating on the goodness of God. In fact, *Dei Verbum* (*Word of God*), the Second Vatican Council's Dogmatic Constitution on Sacred Scripture, says that Sacred Scripture should be venerated by the Church

> just as she venerates the body of the Lord, since, especially in the sacred liturgy, she unceasingly receives and offers to the faithful the bread of life from the table both of God's word and of Christ's body. . . . For in the sacred books, the Father who is in heaven meets His children with great love and speaks with them; and the force and power in the word of God is so great that it stands as the support and energy of the Church, the strength of faith for her sons, the food of the soul, the pure and everlasting source of spiritual life. Consequently these words are perfectly applicable to Sacred Scripture: "For the word of God is living and active" (Heb 4:12) and "it

> has power to build you up and give you your heritage among all those who are sanctified" (Acts 20:32). (*Dei Verbum*, 21)

This passage's quotation from the Letter to the Hebrews points out that Sacred Scripture is different from any other text because it is "living and active." The Second Vatican Council urged all Catholics to "remember that prayer should accompany the reading of Sacred Scripture, so that God and man may talk together" (*Dei Verbum*, 25). This was something new for many Catholics in the 1960s, when the Council was taking place. Many Catholics did not even own a Bible at the time, and the only time they heard anything from the Bible in their own language was when small snippets of Scripture would be read to them at Mass.

Inspired by the Spirit and Interpreted by the Church

Recall from Chapter 3 how Sacred Scripture emerged from the Church herself, how the Church set its canon, and how the teaching of the Church is a sure guide to the interpretation of God's Word. The Second Vatican Council affirmed these tenets in *Dei Verbum*, the Council's longest constitution.[∞]

In fact, all of Sacred Scripture is inspired by the Holy Spirit and is free of error. This means that Scripture contains the truth God intends to be shared and that "everything asserted by the inspired authors or sacred writers must be held to be asserted by the Holy Spirit" (*Dei Verbum*, 11). The Old Testament is the inspired written testimony of the people of Israel. The New Testament preserves the memory of the Apostles and those close to them. This memory includes what Christ revealed to them about God and his plan for salvation.

The Catholic Church teaches that Sacred Scripture must always be interpreted. Scripture is inerrant because it is the Word of God, but it is the Word of God expressed in human words and written by human authors. Like all human words and human beings themselves, it is shaped by human circumstances and limitations. Scripture is valid for all times and all generations, but

∞ Note

Dei Verbum has a preface and six chapters: I. Revelation Itself; II. Handing on Divine Revelation; III. Sacred Scripture, Its Divine Inspiration and Interpretation; IV. The Old Testament; V. The New Testament; VI. Sacred Scripture in the Life of the Church.

it was written in a particular time and for a particular group of people. In order to understand Scripture, the Church considers how Scripture was intended for its original audience.

To do this, the Church values the contributions of modern Scripture scholarship. Biblical scholars examine the context and audience of a particular writing. They also study literary forms (e.g., poetry, genealogies, parables, etc.) to understand the meanings of a passage. However, since Sacred Scripture is inspired, the Church teaches that it "must be read and interpreted in light of the same Spirit by whom it was written" (*CCC*, 111, quoting *Dei Verbum*, 11). Examining Scripture in these three ways requires the following:

1. Paying attention to the Bible as a whole, not just individual passages or even books.

The entirety of Scripture is a unity of God's plan, and Christ is at the center of it.

2. Reading the Bible in light of the Sacred Tradition of the Church.

The Holy Spirit inspired the authors of Scripture. Scripture remains alive because it is interpreted by the Holy Spirit through the Church. It must be read from the perspective of the Church rather than individualistically, that is, you must consider what the Church says about its meaning.

3. Being attentive to the analogy of faith.

The hierarchy of truths of faith, of which the Scriptures are a part, must be placed in the context of the whole of God's revelation. The Scriptures must be understood within the whole plan of God's revelation.

Another point to remember is that there are two main ways of looking at and interpreting Scripture. These are the two main senses of Scripture: the literal and the spiritual (see subsection "How the Church Understands Sacred Scripture" in Chapter 3, Section 4).

---

analogy of faith The doctrine that all individual statements (e.g., Scripture passages) must be understood in light of the Church's entire objective body of faith.

As the guardians and conveyors of the truth given them by Christ, the Apostles were also the preservers of unity in the early Church, the authorities to whom the followers of Christ looked for authentic teaching. In the same way, the Apostles' successors—the bishops, with Peter's successor, the pope, at their head—sustain the unity of the Church today. The bishops continue to take up the role of shepherds of the flock, leaders who care for and protect the members of the Church. The vast and diverse People of God find unity by together holding fast to the doctrines taught by the successors of the Apostles. The truths of Christ thus come to us through the teaching of the bishops as well as through the biblical text—through both Sacred Tradition and Sacred Scripture.

The third chapter of *Dei Verbum* clearly explains the role of the Church in being the final judge of the authentic interpretation of Sacred Scripture. This too has often been a roadblock for Protestant Christians, who prefer to be able to personally interpret the Bible. Another Catholic convert from Protestantism, theologian and apologist Scott Hahn, admits that non-Catholics and some dissenting Catholics have disagreed with having to submit to the Magisterium for interpretation of Scripture, thinking of it as a "demotion." Hahn disagrees: "It's actually a promotion. Who, after all, is more powerful, the mayor of the village or the vice-president of a nation? We are actually more powerful when we place ourselves in the service of a greater power." He explains that since we can rely on the Magisterium, we can go deeper in our Bible study. "Since we're able to avoid certain errors, we can explore the Bible with greater freedom, power, and assurance."[11]

Returning to the Scriptures

Although the Bible has always been central to Catholic prayer and liturgy,[∞] individual Catholics have not always cultivated knowledge of Scripture and

---

∞ Note

Many common Catholic prayers are based on Scripture, for example, the Hail Mary (Luke 1:26–28; 39–45) and the Our Father (Matthew 6:9–13 and Luke 11:1–4). Similarly, the prayers and invocations in liturgy are mostly derived from Scripture. Also, Felix Just, SJ, reports that 13.5 percent of the Old Testament (not counting the Psalms), 54.9 percent of the non-Gospel New Testament, 89.8 percent of the Gospels, and 71.5 percent of the entire New Testament are read in the three-year cycle of Sunday Mass and the two-year cycle of daily Mass readings.

LECTIO DIVINA

Lectio divina means "divine reading" in Latin. You can also think of it as "prayerful reading." St. Benedict of Nursia left instructions in his sixth-century *Rule of St. Benedict* for doing divine reading. They can be divided into three steps:

I. The first step, *lectio* (reading),

involves selecting a spiritual reading, in this case Scripture. Once you select a passage, read the passage until a verse or phrase strikes you. At this point, stop and begin your meditation.

II. The second step, *meditatio* (meditation),

asks you to pause and to let the meaning sink into your mind and heart. Mentally repeat the words over and over. Let them become part of you. Appreciate what they are saying. After spending some time pondering the meaning of the words, turn to prayer.

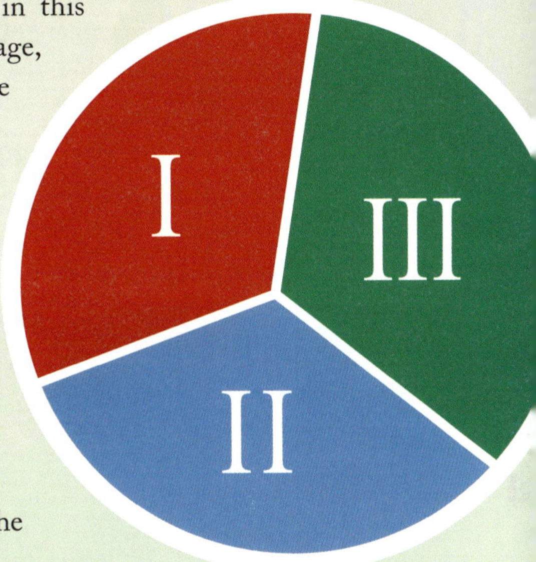

III. The third step, *oratio* (prayer),

has you speak to God about the phrase, or simply sit in God's presence and let him speak to you. When you find that you have exhausted your prayer, or when you become distracted, return to the passage again, and begin to read until you come to another phrase that seems to be speaking directly to you. Then continue the process as before.

Prayer is the key ingredient to growing in friendship with Jesus. The Bible is the source for prayer. Studying Scripture is an exercise in knowing God, and adding prayer is helpful for meeting Jesus and knowing him intimately.

devotion to reading it. The Council encouraged all Catholics, laity and religious alike, to renew their study of and appreciation for the Word of God contained in the Bible. According to *Dei Verbum*, "Easy access to Sacred Scripture should be provided for all the Christian faithful. . . . The bride of the incarnate Word, the Church taught by the Holy Spirit, is concerned to move ahead toward a deeper understanding of the Sacred Scriptures so that she may increasingly feed her sons with the divine words" (*DV*, 22–23).

To this end, the Council encouraged not only personal reading of Scripture but also its formal study by seminarians and scholars: "This should be so done that as many ministers of the divine word as possible will be able to effectively provide the nourishment of the Scriptures for the people of God, to enlighten their minds, strengthen their wills, and set men's hearts on fire with the love of God" (*DV*, 23).

In recent decades, there are signs that Catholics have in fact gained a renewed appreciation for the Bible, and the Bible has often been an instrument of unity. A recent "State of the Bible Survey" by the American Bible Society found that 77 percent of Catholics want to read the Bible more, an

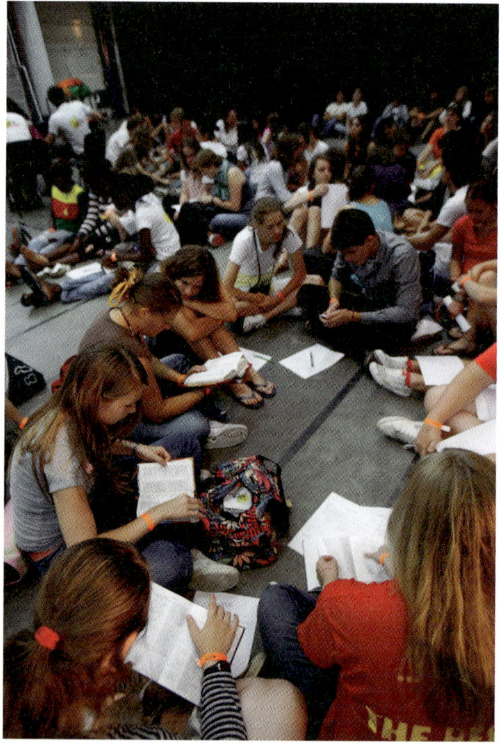

increase of 8 percentage points since the time immediately before Pope Francis's election in 2013. Many Catholics have joined in-person or online Bible studies, including greater participation in the ancient practice of *lectio divina*.[12] On teachings such as Mary, the papacy, and the Eucharist, Catholics have rediscovered the extensive biblical material relating to these themes, as well as the writings of the Church Fathers and other important figures in the Church's past. Sacred Scripture and Sacred Tradition under the one Deposit of Faith (see subsection "Sacred Scripture Is

Only Part of the Deposit of Faith" in Chapter 3, Section 4) are ancient sources of revelation, but their unending depths provide riches to be discovered and rediscovered in every age. A key in reading the Bible is not to go it alone. It is important to consult trusted biblical scholars and theologians to help you understand key passages and the Magisterium to keep you from making any serious errors.

SECTION Assessment

Comprehension

1. What surprised John Bergsma about how his new friend defended Catholicism?

2. Explain the process of Scripture scholarship used by the Church.

3. Why is Scripture study essential for both seminarians and scholars?

Vocabulary

4. What does it mean to be attentive to the *analogy of faith* when studying Scripture?

Reflection

5. What is an example of a Catholic prayer based on Scripture? Cite its Gospel reference.

6. How do you understand the Bible to be a book that is "living and active"?

7. Explain one benefit of relying on the Magisterium to interpret Sacred Scripture.

JOY AND HOPE FOR THE FUTURE

Interestingly, the Second Vatican Council took a different tack in addressing the problems around modernism than Pope Pius X had done in outright condemning it several decades earlier (see subsection "The Church Confronts Modernism" in Chapter 7, Section 1). The Council's final constitution, *Gaudium et Spes* (*Joy and Hope*), was the only pastoral constitution of the Council, meaning that it was intended for all people, not only Catholics. As with the other constitutions, the title of *Gaudium et Spes* comes from its opening words in Latin. The first sentence in English reads: "The joys and hopes, the griefs and anxieties of the men of this age, especially those who are poor or in any way afflicted, these are the joys and hopes, the griefs and anxieties of the followers of Christ."

Remember that the Church herself had participated in an era of two world wars, the rise of communism, and fast-moving technological advances. *Gaudium et Spes*, and really the entire Second Vatican Council, was the Church's effort to face modernism head on and to address the many new problems associated with it. *Gaudium et Spes*'s message of joy and hope to the world centers around finding consolation in Jesus Christ and a home in the People of God.

Many people still need to hear the teachings that can change their lives. In his opening address to the Second Vatican Council, Pope John XXIII said that it is "an overwhelming source of grief to us to know that, although Christ's blood has redeemed every man that is born into this world, there is still a great part of the human race that does not share in those sources of supernatural grace, which exist in the Catholic Church." Pope John reaffirmed that the life and love of Christ are intended for everyone: "The Church sheds her light everywhere."[13]

People today, like people in all times, seek to understand in the depths of their souls that they are made for higher things. Speaking on October 11,

2022, the sixtieth anniversary of the opening of the Second Vatican Council and on the feast day of Pope St. John XXIII, Pope Francis said that the purpose of Vatican II was to "rekindle [the Church's] love for the Lord," calling us to be a Church "madly in love with its Lord and with all the men and women whom he loves" and "*in the midst* of the people, not *above* the people."[14] *Gaudium et Spes* reaffirms that the Church's missionary mandate has not expired. The world's need to hear and witness the message of the Gospel is as imperative today as it was in the first century. The Catholic Church must always be a missionary church.

The Church Is Always Missionary

The Great Commission Christ gave to the Apostles to make disciples of all nations applies to every member of the Church in every era. We have seen how well-known missionaries such as St. Paul and St. Francis Xavier have responded to this command. But it is in fact the duty of all Catholics to evangelize others; it is part of our baptismal call to be "prophets."[15] This duty is rooted in the nature of our faith, which holds that God's invitation to salvation extends to all people. The purpose of evangelization is to bring others to

Catholic priest and missionary Jose Antonio Benitez (left) poses with a migrant at Las Rehoyas parish in Las Palmas de Gran Canaria. Benitez left a lifetime in education to throw himself full-time into helping migrants.

"share in the communion between the Father and the Son in their Spirit of love" (*CCC*, 850).

The way Catholics take on the task of evangelization will differ according to our particular calling and state of life. Some will be called to be missionaries in the mode of Francis Xavier, going to the far corners of the world and sharing the Good News through preaching or service to those in need. Others will be called to dedicate themselves in their local communities to apostolates such as education, assistance to the poor or disabled, or support for pregnant mothers or those addicted to harmful substances. Many will be called to be missionaries in their own families: as parents training their children in the teaching of the Church and promoting the faith among their friends and relatives.

Even in historically Christian nations such as the United States, there is ample opportunity for evangelization. The fastest-growing "religious group" in the country is "nones," people who identify as agnostic, atheist, or "nothing in particular" when asked about their religious identity. In 2007, 78 percent of Americans identified as "Christian" while 16 percent were "nones." By 2021, the same categories were 63 percent and 29 percent, respectively.[16] Many of the nones who abandon traditional organized religion continue to seek answers to the deepest questions of life, which leads them to movements that are non-Christian or that embrace a distorted view of Christianity. Some **New Age** techniques, for example, resemble Catholic practices like meditative prayer but do not have as their aim the Christian goal of union with God through Christ. Charismatic religious leaders of many varieties attract followings but do so outside the structure of the Church. They lack the guarantee of truth provided by the Holy Spirit through the guidance of Sacred Scripture and Sacred Tradition.

In fact, the United States and other modern nations have entered into an era that can be called **post-Christian**. Even among those who do identify

---

New Age A broad movement characterized by alternative approaches to culture and religious practice, with focus on spirituality and mysticism; typically does not include worship of or belief in God.

post-Christian A term often applied to Western cultures and nations that were historically Christian but now reject the authority of the Church in particular, and Christianity in general. The language and cultural references to Christianity that were once part of the society are less present and often only superficial.

as Christian and Catholic, there are many who do not pray or attend church regularly, do not accept the teachings of the Church, or do not try to live according to Gospel morality. There is plenty of missionary work available for a person willing to be countercultural, for the more post-Christian our era becomes, the more countercultural being a Christian, and especially a Catholic, will be.

A New Evangelization

Recall from Chapter 5 that the task of "re-Christianizing" regions and cultures that were historically Christian is different from preaching the Gospel to people who have never heard it. In a 1990 encyclical, Pope John Paul II spoke of "the *new evangelization* of those peoples who have already heard Christ proclaimed" (*Redemptoris Missio*, 30). The United States Conference of Catholic Bishops explains that "the new evangelization is focused on 're-proposing' the Gospel to those who have experienced a crisis of faith" due to secularization. The Church's effort to re-evangelize those who have rejected or drifted from the Gospel of Jesus does not require travel to distant lands, adapting to different cultures, or speaking new languages. However, just like the "old

Young Catholics gather for Pope Francis's final Mass of World Youth Day 2023 at Tagus Park in Lisbon, Portugal.

J. R. R. TOLKIEN

J. R. R. Tolkien, a devout Catholic, evangelized in his personal life. His friendship and discussions with another well-known author, C. S. Lewis, the author of *The Chronicles of Narnia*, were important factors in the formerly agnostic Lewis's becoming a believing Christian, but Tolkien also evangelized through his vocation of writing. While he did not write explicitly about Jesus, morality, or the Church in his tales about hobbits and elves, his stories nonetheless reflect the truths of the Gospel.

For example, Tolkien's virtuous king, Aragorn, displays the qualities of Christian kingship, including mercy and serving others rather than lust for power. Another hero, the wizard Gandalf, is a model of sacrifice, willing to lay down his life for his friends. The preeminent hero, the hobbit Frodo Baggins, exhibits courage, humility, and perseverance, virtues that are central to the Christian life. Tolkien's books exalt honesty and integrity and condemn deception and corruption. Jay Richards, a philosopher who teaches at the Catholic University of America, credits Tolkien's works in part for his own conversion to Catholicism. He asserts that Tolkien's fictional writing has "evangelistic significance" and that it "tended and nurtured my moral and aesthetic intuitions" by portraying a "sacramental understanding of reality."[17] Tolkien and many other Christian figures in the last century have demonstrated the potential for evangelization through the arts and literature.

evangelization" of St. Paul and St. Francis Xavier, it does require hard work and creativity, and all Catholics are responsible for the effort. J. R. R. Tolkien, the famous fantasy author who wrote *The Hobbit* and *The Lord of the Rings*, is one modern Catholic who practiced "creative evangelization," not only in his personal life, but in his writing.

As the Church and the world move deeper into the third millennium, evangelization remains a vital task for young people to take up. Pope John Paul II, recognizing the testimony of the past, noted that "in the Church's history, missionary drive has always been a sign of vitality, just as its lessening is a sign of a crisis of faith" (*Redemptoris Missio*, 2). The Church will be more perfectly what she is intended to be—the presence of Christ on earth—when she once again becomes a missionary Church.

Our Final Destination

In Chapter 1, we met Takashi Nagai, a Japanese physician who converted to Catholicism through the example of his wife, Midori. In the years that followed, Takashi and Midori had two children and enjoyed a happy family life. Takashi became a pioneer in the medical study of radiation. He used X-rays extensively to diagnose the ailments of other patients, but in the early days of this technology when its effects were not well understood, he did not take adequate measures to protect himself from the radiation emitted during these tests. Takashi found that cancer had developed in his own body. He knew that he did not have long to live, and that a painful death awaited him. It was June of 1945.[18]

For the previous three years, as the Japanese military had fought the American military across the waters and islands of the Pacific Ocean, a secret research program was underway in the New Mexico desert and other American sites. The Manhattan Project brought together top scientists to develop the military capabilities of atomic energy. By mid-1945, the United States had successfully produced an atomic bomb. The war in Europe came to an end with Germany's surrender in May, but the conflict with Japan dragged on through the summer. Fearing a terrible battle for the Japanese mainland, American leaders decided to use their new weapon on Japanese cities, hoping to convince the empire's leaders that the cost of continuing to fight against atomic power would be too high.

The remains of the Catholic cathedral that was destroyed after an atomic bomb was dropped in Nagasaki, Japan, on August 8, 1945.

On August 6, 1945, the first atomic bomb was dropped over the city of Hiroshima. The world had never seen manmade devastation on this scale. The extent of the Hiroshima catastrophe was not reported in the Japanese media, but Takashi and Midori sent their two children out of the city to a relative's house, in case their hometown might be next. Three days later, the second bomb was detonated on Nagasaki, the heart of Catholic Japan and the home of Takashi and Midori Nagai.

Takashi was at work at the hospital when it happened. Protected by the heavy walls, he survived the blast, though he was seriously injured when he was thrown across the room and blanketed in shattered glass. Thousands of Nagasaki residents were incinerated instantly. Midori, at home awaiting her husband's return, was among them. Takashi found her charred remains later. Her rosary beads, melted by the explosion, were in her hands. She had been in the kitchen, working and praying. Three months later, in November of 1945, on behalf of the laity, Takashi addressed Catholics at an open-air Mass at the ruins of Nagasaki's Catholic cathedral. He told them that Nagasaki was "the chosen victim, the lamb without blemish, slain as a whole burnt offering on an altar of sacrifice for the sins of all the nations during World War II."

In the six years of life remaining to him, Takashi spread the Good News of Jesus Christ and the Church far and wide. He wrote many books and gave many speeches promoting peace and forgiveness between nations and among all people. Takashi's faith gave him an eternal perspective, a deep-seated hope that he sought to pass on to his children as he prepared for his own death. "My death will leave you orphans," he wrote to them, "vulnerable and alone in the world." He continued in his writing:

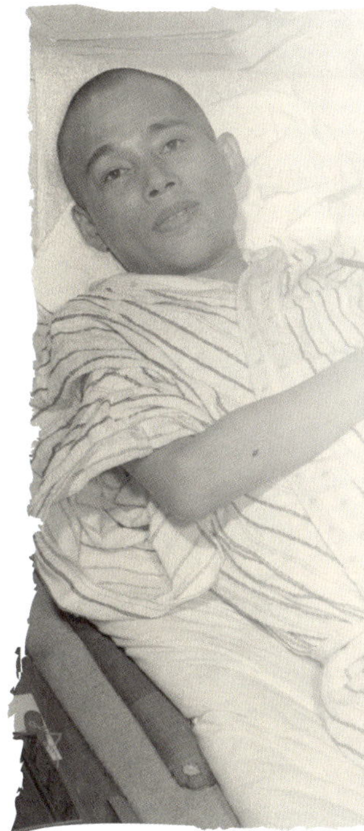

You will weep. Yes, you might even weep your hearts out, and that is good—provided you weep before your Father in heaven. We have it on the authority of his Son, and I have experienced the truth of it personally: "Happy are those who weep, for they shall be comforted." . . . I must be honest with you, children. You will drink a bitter chalice as orphans. . . . He has asked the three of us to accept a bitter drink. This is our "way" to peace and participation in his great plan, the one Jesus saw when he spoke of the lilies of the field and of the sparrows that are precious in the eyes of the Father. . . . But persevere! He is fitting us for eternal companionship with him and our loved ones in heaven.

The *Salve Regina* (see subsection "Prayer" in the Chapter 8 Review), a venerable Catholic prayer to Mary, speaks of this world as a "valley of tears." Takashi Nagai lived in the conviction that this valley of tears, the suffering of this life, is preparation for another world, where God "will wipe every tear from [our] eyes, and there shall be no more death or mourning, wailing or pain" (Rv 21:4). The purpose of the Church is to call all people together to follow Christ into this paradise. The heavenly Kingdom of God is the final destination of the Church.

SECTION Assessment

Comprehension

1. Why is *Gaudium et Spes* called a "pastoral" constitution?

2. What issue did *Gaudium et Spes* and the entire Second Vatican Council seek to address?

3. Who is the primary audience for the Church's new evangelization?

Vocabulary

4. What is meant by a *post-Christian* society?

Reflection

5. Why do you think there are so many "nones" among your peers?

6. J. R. R. Tolkien evangelized through his writings. How can you use one of your own talents for evangelization?

7. Imagine the Church in heaven that Takashi Nagai entered. What does it look like to you?

Section Reviews

Focus Question

How is the Church renewed and reformed in modern times?
Complete one of the following:

- Look up and write down the definition of the term *moral relativism*. Name some ways that you witness this ethic in the world today. Tell how it connects with aspects of a post-Christian society.

- List five reasons, based on your study in this course, why it is important to belong to the Catholic Church. Rank the reasons from most important (1) to least important (5). Write an explanation of your 1 and 5 rankings.

- Think of some family members, friends, and peers who are in need of the Church's efforts at the new evangelization. Name some effective strategies for reaching these groups with the truth of the Gospel.

Introduction
The Uninterrupted Voice of the Church

Review

Pope John XXIII convened the Second Vatican Council to look for new ways to present the Gospel to the modern world. The Council was attended by bishops from previously underrepresented areas and produced four central constitutions around the liturgy, the Church, Divine Revelation, and the Church in the modern world. The Council reemphasized the Church as missionary and called on all Catholics—clergy, religious, and laity—to go out and make disciples of the world.

Assignment

Review a recent day and list all the ways you brought the Gospel in your words and actions.

Section 1

The Power of the Sacred Liturgy

Review

Originating with the Second Vatican Council constitution *Sacrosanctum Concilium*, several changes in the liturgy have taken place, including the use of the vernacular to complement or replace Latin for prayers and the addition of songs. The Eucharist remains the "source and summit of the Christian life." The Mass and the presence of Christ in the liturgy are constant aspects of the Church from the first century through today. Numbers of Catholics participating in the Mass are down from earlier generations; without their participation the Body of Christ is incomplete.

Assignment

Read paragraphs 52–58 of *Sacrosanctum Concilium*, on "The Most Sacred Mystery of the Eucharist." Write five takeaways about the Mass you learned from this reading. What did you find most surprising? Why?

Section 2

God's People Live Their Vocations

Review

Catholics live out their personal vocations that emanate from Baptism in the ordained ministry, consecrated life, married life, and committed single life. All of these particular vocations are ordered toward growing in holiness personally, as well as sharing holiness with others in the world. The Second Vatican Council constitution *Lumen Gentium* describes the formation of the Church as the People of God and outlines the hierarchy and common mission of these vocations.

Assignment

Explain which particular vocations (bishop, priest, deacon, consecrated religious, married person, single person) are most connected to the following tasks. Connect one task with each vocation: *evangelical counsels, dedicated career focus, governance, service, preaching,* and *domestic church.*

Section 3

Ways to Read, Study, and Pray with Scripture

Review

Sacred Scripture is one part, along with Sacred Tradition, of the Church's Deposit of Faith. The Second Vatican Council encouraged all Catholics to prayerfully read Scripture while also recognizing the Magisterium's authoritative role in interpreting Scripture. The Church teaches that Scripture "must be read and interpreted in light of the same Spirit by whom it was written."

Assignment

Define *analogy of faith* in your own words. Describe how you would explain this term to a peer who has never heard it before.

Section 4

Joy and Hope for the Future

Review

The purpose of the Church is to call all people home to heaven. The Second Vatican Council document *Gaudium et Spes* was the only pastoral constitution of the four constitutions, meaning it was addressed to the entire world. It encourages all people to seek joy and hope even amid the ever-changing culture that is growing more hostile to religion, Christianity, and Catholicism. In the midst of that reality, Catholics are called to the new evangelization, to reshare the Gospel with those who have previously heard it but have drifted away from the Church. There are plenty of opportunities to live new forms of radical Catholicism and to call all people to Jesus Christ and his Church.

Assignment

Think of some family members, friends, and peers who are in need of the Church's efforts at the new evangelization. Name some effective strategies for reaching these groups with the Gospel of Jesus Christ.

CHAPTER 8 REVIEW

Chapter Projects

Choose and complete at least one of the following projects to assess your understanding of the material in this chapter.

✿ 1. *Read and Write about the Particular Judgment*

An immediate judgment after death is based on Divine Revelation. This particular judgment is right after death, when Christ will determine whether we go to heaven immediately, need purification in Purgatory, or must suffer eternal damnation and punishments in hell. Complete each of the following assignments to learn more about the meaning of the particular judgment:

- Read and write a one-sentence summary of 2 Corinthians 5:10.

- Read the parables of the rich man and Lazarus (Lk 16:19–31) and the judgment of the nations (Mt 25:31–46). Write three to four paragraphs comparing and contrasting these parables and explaining what they teach about the particular judgment.

- Read paragraphs 1021–1022 of the *Catechism of the Catholic Church* and write a one-paragraph summary of this teaching on the particular judgment.

- Reflect on your own life, and write your responses to these three questions once posed by St. Ignatius of Loyola: (1) What have you done for Christ? (2) What are you doing for Christ? and (3) What will you do for Christ?

✿ 2. *Survey the Religious Beliefs of Your Peers*

Research current information on religious beliefs and practices among your peers. Focus your research on the following: (1) the religious affiliation of those surveyed and (2) their level of religious participation. Use information gleaned from the Pew Forum on Religion and Public Life and the Center for Applied Research on the Apostolate. Focus your research further by naming a question for which you would like data. For example, "How often do you pray?" "Who can be saved?" "What is your attitude about faith?" Supplement these official findings with two other data elements: (1) an anecdotal story told by one of your peers related to the main topic of your survey and (2) a sample survey using the same focus questions, but this time with data that you personally collect from the target age group. Display all results in an appropriate format. Write a summary of your study.

⚙ *3. Develop a Promotion for Vocations*

Prepare a project to support the Catholic vocations of the ordained ministry, consecrated life, and marriage. Choose one of the following:

- Compile a resource notebook with positive news articles about priests or religious that share the joy and scope of their vocation. The articles might refer to their ministry, their hobbies, their call, or even their obituary. Just make sure the articles provide an interesting and inspiring view of the vocation.

- Gather personal correspondence from priests, religious, and married couples that speaks of some aspect of their vocation. Begin by sending a handwritten letter to people in these vocations that explains this assignment and asks them to share some aspects of their life, both the rewards and the challenges.

- Interview priests, religious, and married couples, and video record the interviews. Edit and plan for a showing.

- Arrange for a "vocations panel." Invite people representing each vocation to address classmates at your school or parish around the topics already mentioned.

⚙ *4. Make a Chart with Counterpoints against the Post-Christian Culture*

The post-Christian culture is upon us. It is a culture in which Christianity and the Church have been marginalized and ridiculed. Taking a stand against the post-Christian culture will take courage and creativity. Make a chart with at least fifteen examples of evidence of a post-Christian culture present today. In the second column, enter suggestions for combatting each example. Two examples are given below.

POST-CHRISTIAN CULTURE ADVOCATES . . .	CHRISTIANS RESPOND . . .
putting off having children or not having children at all.	as a married couple, by practicing Natural Family Planning and welcoming children into the family as a blessing.
producing and supporting entertainment that degrades the human body via sexuality and violence.	by choosing entertainment that builds up and does not tear down either men or women, like participating in sports, taking hikes, reading classic books.

⚙ 5. Share an Oral Presentation on the New Evangelization

All Catholics share in the Church's apostolic mission. It is the task of all Catholics to share the Good News of Jesus Christ to the ends of the earth. Outline a plan for participating in the new evangelization by doing the following:

- Read St. John Paul II's apostolic letter *Novo Millennio Ineunte* at the Vatican website.

- Create a reading model to outline one of the pastoral priorities named in Chapter 3, "Starting Afresh in Christ." Begin by selecting one of the pastoral priorities.

- Set up an organizer like the one below that (1) lists the priority you have chosen, (2) summarizes the pope's teaching on the priority, (3) shares how the priority is being enacted in your local parish or community today, and (4) tells how you can personally enact the priority in your life. The organizer should look like this:

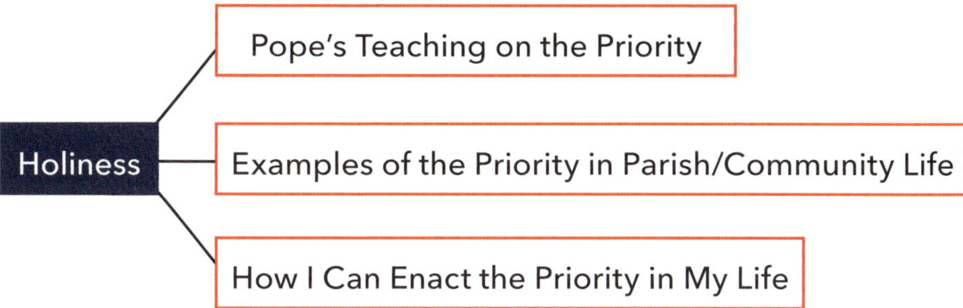

Finally, combine all of these elements into a five- to seven-minute oral presentation. Include at least four accompanying slides, one of which depicts your organizer. Video record your oral presentation in a format approved by your teacher for sharing.

CHAPTER 8 REVIEW

Faithful Disciple
Blessed Karl von Habsburg

Blessed Karl von Habsburg

Blessed Karl von Habsburg was the last emperor of Austria and the last apostolic king of Hungary. He died in 1922. He was born into the ancient Habsburg family, a dynasty that had ruled as Holy Roman emperors and kings of Austria and Hungary for seven hundred years. The assassination of his uncle, Archduke Franz Ferdinand, is often seen as the spark that ignited World War I. With his uncle's death, Karl was next in line to the throne of the Austro-Hungarian Empire. In 1916, he ascended to that office in the midst of the horrendous bloodshed of World War I.

Before and during the war, Pope Benedict XV was the world's foremost advocate for peace. His proposals for peace were ignored by the leaders of most nations, but not by Karl of Austria. Karl "saw his office as a commission from God" and "as a holy service to his people." During the war, he established an extensive network of social programs to care for those in need. Karl, who had fought in the army before succeeding to the throne, understood how devastating war was, and he agreed with the pope that the best way to serve the good of the people of Europe was to bring about a swift end to the conflict.

The French novelist Anatole France, whose beliefs and style of living were very different from Karl's, nonetheless praised him as "the only decent man to have come out of the war." The Austrian emperor "sincerely wanted peace, and therefore was despised by the whole world." According to Cardinal Christoph Schönborn of Vienna, Karl's "modesty, kindness and spirit of

Blessed Karl von Habsburg, also known as Charles I of Austria, with his wife Zita and their children in exile in Switzerland.

reconciliation have been held against him—particularly by cynics in power—as weakness, even stupidity."

In the aftermath of the war, democracy was extended to several European nations, including Austria, and Karl was removed from power. He and his family went into exile and ended up on the Portuguese island of Madeira. There, Karl, who had been a wealthy and powerful man, lived in poor conditions, neglected and forgotten by most of the world. Yet he continued to work for God's kingdom within the domestic church of his own family. On the day after he married his wife, the Empress Zita, he had said to her, "Now we must help each other get to heaven." They had eight children, and Karl "strove personally to ensure that his children received religious education, and he guided them in the truths of the faith and taught them their prayers." His behavior as a husband was "completely upright and faultless."[19]

Karl von Habsburg died of pneumonia at the age of thirty-four in 1922. His granddaughter, Princess Maria-Anna Galitzine, spoke of the devotion that has developed around him: "When they see a picture of Blessed Karl, they see a young man. . . . They see a family man. A man with tremendous

CHAPTER 8 REVIEW

responsibility on his shoulders. Yet, he was devout. He always took time for prayer. In fact, his wife, Servant of God Empress Zita, described him as being 'in another place' when he was at prayer."[20]

Pope John Paul II elevated Karl to the title of "Blessed" in 2004.[∞] The pope recognized him as both a man of peace and a husband whose life testified to being a husband and a father. In both areas, "his chief concern was to follow the Christian vocation to holiness." Blessed Karl von Habsburg's feast day is October 21, his and Empress Zita's wedding anniversary.

Comprehension

1. Why is it appropriate to call Karl von Habsburg "the only decent man to have come out of the war"?
2. Name two significant facts about Karl von Habsburg's becoming emperor of the Austro-Hungarian Empire.
3. What caused Karl to lose his position as emperor?
4. What happened to him after he was no longer emperor?

Reflection

Karl von Habsburg said upon marrying Empress Zita: "Now we must help each other get to heaven." Name three ways that husbands and wives today can do what he suggested.

∞ Note

Empress Zita of Bourbon-Parma (1892–1989) was elevated to Servant of God when her cause for canonization was opened in 2010.

Prayer

The *Salve Regina* (Hail, Holy Queen) is a Marian antiphon typically sung at the close of Compline, the final office of the Liturgy of the Hours (Divine Office). It was composed sometime during the Middle Ages, and its author is unknown. The current form of the *Salve Regina* is from the twelfth century at the Benedictine Abbey at Cluny, where it was sung as part of processions on Marian feast days.

Salve Regina

Hail, Holy Queen, Mother of Mercy,
our life, our sweetness and our hope.
To thee do we cry, poor banished children of Eve.
To thee do we send up our sighs,
mourning and weeping in this valley of tears.
Turn then, most gracious advocate,
thine eyes of mercy toward us,
and after this our exile,
Show unto us the blessed fruit of thy womb, Jesus.
O clement, O loving,
O sweet Virgin Mary.
V. Pray for us, O holy Mother of God.

R. That we may be made worthy of the promises of Christ.

Appendix

THE NICENE CREED

I believe in one God,
the Father almighty,
maker of heaven and earth,
of all things visible and invisible.

I believe in one Lord Jesus Christ,
the Only Begotten Son of God,
born of the Father before all ages.
God from God, Light from Light,
true God from true God,
begotten, not made, consubstantial
    with the Father;
through him all things were made.
For us men and for our salvation
he came down from heaven,
and by the Holy Spirit was incar-
    nate of the Virgin Mary,
and became man.

For our sake he was crucified under
    Pontius Pilate,
he suffered death and was buried,
and rose again on the third day
in accordance with the Scriptures.
He ascended into heaven
and is seated at the right hand of
    the Father.
He will come again in glory
to judge the living and the dead
and his kingdom will have no end.

I believe in the Holy Spirit,
the Lord, the giver of life,
who proceeds from the Father and
    the Son,

who with the Father and the Son is
    adored and glorified,
who has spoken through the
    prophets.

I believe in one, holy, catholic, and
    apostolic Church.
I confess one baptism for the for-
    giveness of sins
and I look forward to the resurrec-
    tion of the dead
and the life of the world to come.

Amen.

A TIMELINE OF CHURCH HISTORY

"The world was created for the sake of the Church."
—attributed to Christians of the first century

The Early Church (AD 33–early fourth century)

Following the events of the Paschal Mystery—the suffering, Death, Resurrection, and Ascension of Christ—the Apostles awaited the fulfillment of Christ's promise to send them an Advocate. That promise was fulfilled on Pentecost. From that day forward, the Apostles took up Jesus's command to "go, . . . make disciples of all nations" (Mt 28:19). Thus began the development and growth of the young Church in the Roman Empire.

Pentecost, 33

During the Feast of Weeks, the Apostles and Mary were gathered in a small upper room of a house in Jerusalem. The Holy Spirit came down upon them, giving the Apostles the grace to begin their preaching ministry.

Martyrdom of Stephen, 34

Stephen, a deacon, was stoned to death by an angry mob that included Saul, later to become St. Paul.

Conversion of St. Paul, 35

Paul, previously known as Saul, was a persecutor of Christians. After his conversion following an encounter with Christ, he became one of the early Church's greatest missionaries, traveling throughout the Roman Empire to establish and provide support to church communities.

Council of Jerusalem, 49

At this meeting, the leaders of the Church decreed that Gentiles can be baptized into the Church and are not subject to Jewish regulations regarding circumcision and diet. This decision contributed to the rapid growth of Christianity throughout the Roman Empire.

St. Peter emerges as the bishop of Rome, ca. 55

Because the Church in Rome had primacy among the other centers of Christianity, St. Peter had primacy over the other bishops. Rome became the see (from the Latin word *sedes*, or "seat") of Peter, and therefore the seat of the Church.

Persecution of Christians begins under Emperor Nero, 64

When a fire destroyed most of Rome, Nero, who is believed to have set the fire himself, blamed Christians, inciting mass persecutions. Both Sts. Peter and Paul were martyred during this time (Peter in 64 and Paul in 67).

Gospels are written, 65–100

Mark's Gospel is believed to have been the first written, between 65 and 70. John's is believed to have been the last written, around 90–100. A number of Paul's letters are believed to have been written before the Gospels, around 50–60.

Destruction of the Temple in Jerusalem, 70

The Roman army conquered Jerusalem and destroyed the Jewish Temple.

Didache is written, ca. 100

Written anonymously, the *Didache* is a pastoral manual of teachings and practices. Lost in the early centuries of the Church, this document was rediscovered in 1873.

Canon of the New Testament is established, early second century to fourth century

Under the guidance of the Holy Spirit, the leaders of the early Church discerned the official canon of the New Testament, recognizing that the authors of the sacred books were inspired by the Holy Spirit and that the writings were apostolic, that is, based on the teaching of the Apostles or their closest disciples. The Councils of Hippo (393) and Carthage (397) were instrumental in forming the canon of Sacred Scripture for both the Old and New Testaments.

Gnostic heresy emerges, early second century

Gnostics denied the goodness of the created world and claimed that only a select few can have the knowledge needed for salvation. St. Irenaeus (ca. 130–ca. 200), bishop of Lyon, responded with his *Against Heresies*, a treatise comprising five books.

Tertullian and other apologists explain the faith, second century–early third century

The early apologists were writers who defended and explained Christianity to nonbelievers. Tertullian (ca. 160–ca. 220) was the first of the apologists to write in Latin. He defended Christianity against charges of immorality and subversion. St. Justin Martyr (ca. 100–ca. 165) also made a great contribution. His writings include his *First Apology* and *Second Apology*. He also wrote extensively about the Eucharist.

Waves of persecution of Christians continue in the empire, through the third century

Persecutions were carried out under various emperors, including Domitian (81–96), Hadrian (117–138), and Marcus Aurelius (161–180). Christianity was often punishable by death. Perhaps the most severe persecutions took place under the emperor Diocletian (284–305), whose aim was to uproot Christianity from the empire.

Monastic movement is established, third century

The founding of Christian monasticism is traditionally attributed to St. Anthony of Egypt (251–356). Around age twenty, Anthony withdrew from society and went to live as a hermit in the desert. His way of life attracted many followers. Around 320, Pachomius, one of Anthony's contemporaries, organized the first monastery.

Edict of Milan establishes toleration for Christianity, 313

In 312, Constantine became Roman emperor following a victory in battle that also led to his eventual conversion. In 313, shortly after assuming power, Constantine and his Eastern counterpart, Licinius, issued the *Edict of Milan*, a decree that proclaimed religious toleration in the empire and legalized Christianity. As a result, Christian worship became public, and Christian missionaries could preach the faith without fear of retribution.

Arian controversy begins, 315

Arianism, a teaching promoted by the presbyter Arius of Alexandria (ca. 250–336), denied Christ's divine nature and therefore his power to redeem us. This heresy posed one of the first major threats to the Church's doctrine.

Emperor Constantine commissions the construction of the Basilica of St. Peter in Rome, ca. 318

Pope Sylvester I consecrated the basilica in 326.

Emperor Constantine defeats Emperor Licinius and becomes the sole Roman emperor, 324

Constantine moved the seat of government from Rome to Byzantium (today's Istanbul, Turkey), renaming it Constantinople. The empire now had two centers of power, Rome and Constantinople. Different styles of celebrating the sacraments and the liturgy, as well as different styles of church architecture, emerged in each.

Age of the Fathers (early fourth century–fifth century)

After the Edict of Milan, *Christianity could be practiced and witnessed to publicly. As the Church continued to thrive and grow in this new environment, it also faced new threats from within: heresies promulgated by bishops and other leaders. Church Fathers, such as St. Jerome and St. Augustine, and ecumenical councils played an essential role in defending the Church's doctrine.*

Constantine convenes the First Council of Nicaea, 325

To respond to the teachings of Arius, Constantine convened the Church's first ecumenical council in Nicaea. The bishops developed the Nicene Creed (see the Appendix) in response to the Arian heresy.

First Council of Constantinople, 381

Because the First Council of Nicaea had not clarified the nature of the Holy Spirit, this became a new source of division within the Church. This council firmly affirmed the divinity of the Holy Spirit.

Conversion of St. Augustine, 387

Before his conversion, Augustine lived a life of dissipation. Following his conversion, he became one of the most important Church Fathers. He was the bishop of Hippo, in present-day Algeria. His writings, which include *The City of God* and his *Confessions*, continue to influence Christian thought.

Publication of St. Jerome's Latin translation of the Bible, ca. 400

In 382, Pope Damasus I commissioned St. Jerome to begin a Latin translation of Scripture from its original Hebrew and Greek. His translation became known as the Vulgate, the Church's official version of the Scriptures.

Council of Ephesus, 431

This third ecumenical council was convened by the emperor Theodosius II. The council reaffirmed that Jesus is both God and man and that Mary is *Theotokos*, that is, "God-bearer," or the Mother of God.

Council of Chalcedon, 451

In response to the heresy of Monophysitism, which said that Jesus's human nature was lost in his divine nature, this council declared Christ's two natures as undivided, unchangeable, and inseparable.

Pope St. Leo the Great halts the attack of Attila the Hun, 452

Pope Leo took the title *Pontifex Maximus*, meaning "supreme pontiff." In 452, at the request of the Roman emperor, Pope Leo intervened to make peace with Attila the Hun, who was threatening to invade Rome.

Fall of the Roman Empire in the West, 476

After decades of continuing invasions and decline, the Western Roman Empire collapsed in 476, when the emperor was deposed by a barbarian chieftain.

Early Middle Ages (Dark Ages) (476–1000)

With the fall of the Roman Empire in the West, Europe faced an authority vacuum, weakened civil rulers, and an absence of services to meet the needs of citizens. The Church stepped in to fill the void and frequently brought order to the chaos.

St. Benedict of Nursia establishes a monastery at Monte Cassino, 528

Benedict (480–550), who has come to be known as the Father of Western Monasticism, established a monastery at Monte Cassino and developed a rule of life for monasticism that emphasized prayer and work (*ora et labora*). Eventually a group of women, led by Benedict's twin sister, St. Scholastica, formed a monastic community not far from Monte Cassino.

Pope St. Gregory the Great introduces key reforms and sponsors missions to Great Britain, 590–604

Pope Gregory, a Doctor of the Church, developed a system for providing charitable aid to the poor, oversaw the development of seminaries, and introduced liturgical reforms that still influence the Church's liturgical celebrations. He is also remembered for sponsoring missions to Great Britain, as well as for the development of an unaccompanied style of liturgical singing known as Gregorian chant.

St. Augustine of Canterbury evangelizes Great Britain, 596–604

Sent by Pope Gregory the Great to evangelize the Angles and Saxons native to the region, this Benedictine monk is credited with the Christianization of England. His missionary work resulted in the baptism of thousands. He became the first archbishop of Canterbury.

Development of Islam and Islamic conquests of Christian lands, seventh century

Islam was founded by Muhammad early in the seventh century and then quickly established as the religion of the Arabian Peninsula. A Muslim army marched eastward and westward, conquering many previously Christian areas. The first major cities to fall were Damascus and Antioch (636 and 637) in Syria, followed by Jerusalem (638) and Alexandria (642). In 711, Muslim armies invaded the Iberian Peninsula.

St. Boniface evangelizes the Germans, 716–718

Known as the "Apostle to the Germans," St. Boniface is credited with bringing Christianity to the Frankish Empire, in what is Germany today.

Iconoclast Controversy begins, 730

When Byzantine Emperor Leo III gave orders to remove an image of Christ from the Great Palace of Constantinople, the removal of all holy images from Eastern Churches ensued. The conflict between those who venerated holy images, or *icons*, and those who opposed them was resolved by the Second Council of Nicaea in 787.

Venerable Bede writes *Ecclesiastical History of the English People, ca. 731*

In this famous work, the English monk known as the Venerable Bede demonstrated the growth and history of the Catholic Church in Great Britain.

Battle of Tours, 732

In this key battle, Charles Martel, a prince of the Franks, defeated Muslim invaders, halting their expansion in Europe. Although most of the Iberian Peninsula was by then under Muslim control, the Christian identity of lands north of the Pyrenees Mountains was preserved.

Founding of the Papal States, 756

In 751, Pepin the Short, son of Charles Martel, became king of the Franks, beginning the Carolingian Dynasty. In 756, in the Donation of Pepin, he gave Pope Stephen II control over the middle regions of Italy, establishing the Papal States, which existed until 1870.

Charlemagne is crowned Holy Roman emperor, 800

Charlemagne, Pepin's son, became king of the Franks in 768. He engaged in military campaigns throughout Europe and created a vast empire. On Christmas Day in 800, Pope Leo III crowned him Holy Roman emperor, cementing the alliance between the crown and the Church. Charlemagne believed he ruled by divine right and actively involved himself in Church affairs. His crowning as Holy Roman emperor increased tensions between East and West.

Sts. Cyril and Methodius begin evangelizing the Slavic peoples, 862

The missionary brothers Cyril and Methodius developed the Glagolitic alphabet, a predecessor of the Cyrillic alphabet still used today, and translated the Bible into Slavonic. Known as the "Apostles to the Slavs," they successfully evangelized the Slavic people.

Abbey at Cluny is founded, 910

This monastery in Cluny, France, became a fountainhead for monastic and eventually Church reform. It was free of the corrupt control of lords and bishops. It had free elections of abbots and was answerable only to the pope. The Cluniac reform spread throughout France, Italy, Spain, and England.

High Middle Ages (1000–1300)

The period beginning around 1000 was one of intense activity in European society and the Church. Key developments for the Church include the founding of the university system, the development of Gothic architecture, and the birth of new religious orders.

Muslims destroy the Church of the Holy Sepulchre in Jerusalem, 1009

The church was extensively damaged, and the fourth-century shrine long believed to have been built over Jesus's burial place was destroyed. This act of desecration fueled the call for a crusade to retake the Holy Land.

Great Schism, 1054

Following centuries of growing differences and tensions over doctrine, liturgical practices, and politics, the Churches of the East and the West issued a mutual excommunication. In 1965, Pope Paul VI and Patriarch Athenagoras I lifted the excommunications. Ecumenical efforts continue, in the hope that one day the two Churches will be united.

University of Bologna is founded, 1088

This founding of the first university in Europe was followed by the founding of the University of Paris (1150) and the University of Oxford (1167). By the start of the fourteenth century, more than eighty universities had been established in Europe.

First Crusade, 1096–1099

In 1070, Seljuk Turks had conquered Palestine and begun a campaign of persecution of Christian pilgrims to the Holy Land. In 1095, Pope Urban II called for a crusade to reclaim the Holy Land from Muslims. A series of major and minor crusades followed. Militarily, the Crusades were of limited success. Jerusalem and Asia Minor ultimately remained under Muslim control. A positive consequence of the Crusades was the exchange of ideas, scholarship, and scientific advances between East and West.

Concordat of Worms, 1122

Especially beginning in the eleventh century, some bishops had become subservient to secular leaders, leading to the practice of lay investiture, in which secular leaders appointed bishops throughout their domains. The Concordat of Worms established the pope's authority to appoint bishops and abbots and invest them with spiritual authority. The emperor, in turn, was responsible for temporal rule.

Murder of St. Thomas Becket, 1170

For refusing to cooperate with the attempts of England's King Henry II to gain control of the Church courts, St. Thomas was murdered in Canterbury Cathedral.

Development of Gothic architecture, beginning in twelfth century

Magnificent cathedrals and abbey churches built between 1100 and 1400 symbolize the spirit and grandeur of the medieval Church. Each cathedral contained the bishop's *cathedra* (chair), symbolizing his teaching authority and

power. The Cathedral of Notre Dame in Paris, constructed in the Gothic style, was built over two centuries, from 1163 to 1345.

Fourth Lateran Council, 1215

Among other decrees, this ecumenical council defined transubstantiation, the transformation of the bread and wine into the Body and Blood of Christ during the consecration at Mass.

Founding of mendicant orders, early thirteen century

With the decline of feudalism, mendicant, or "begging," orders emerged to serve the Church by witnessing to simple Gospel values. The Carmelites and Augustinians began at this time as well, but the two most important new orders were the Dominicans, founded by St. Dominic (1170–1221), and the Franciscans, founded by St. Francis of Assisi (1181–1226). St. Clare of Assisi (1194–1253), a friend of St. Francis, left her rich family to found an order of religious women known as the Poor Clares.

Medieval Inquisition begins, 1231

In response to the development of several heretical groups, Pope Gregory IX established this inquisition, also known as the Papal Inquisition. Inquisitors served as investigators and judges. Some found guilty of heresy were condemned to death. Most sentences were "canonical" penances, such as fasting and making pilgrimages.

St. Thomas Aquinas writes the *Summa Theologiae*, 1265–1274

In this treatise, St. Thomas Aquinas makes an argument for the existence of God and clarifies how we can know God through human reason. The unfinished *Summa*, a twenty-one-volume work, remains one of the greatest works of theology and philosophy.

Late Middle Ages (1300–1450)

Although this was a period of continued growth and development, it was also marked by strife and suffering, most notably resulting from the Black Death.

Avignon papacy, 1309–1377

In 1309, Pope Clement moved the Church's headquarters from Rome to Avignon, France, where it remained for nearly seventy years. Seven popes lived there, until Pope Gregory XI returned to Rome.

Black Death strikes Europe, 1347

This epidemic of bubonic plague is estimated to have killed more than a third of Europe's population. The plague permeated the medieval mindset. Because of the constant presence of death, the Sacrament of Penance and Reconciliation came to dominate the Catholic experience.

Western Schism, 1378–1418

When Pope Gregory XI died in 1378, French cardinals deposed the newly elected pope, Urban VI. They elected a new pope, known as an antipope, to replace him. Named Clement VII, the antipope reestablished the papal court at Avignon. The conflict continued for nearly forty years, with three rival claimants to the papacy at times. The conflict was resolved at the Council of Constance (1414–1418).

St. Joan of Arc is burned at the stake, 1431

A peasant girl from northeastern France, Joan had visions of God telling her to lead her nation to reclaim their land in a victory over England. She led her troops to a number of victories, but at the age of nineteen she was captured by the English and burned at the stake as a heretic. Twenty-five years later, the charges against Joan were nullified by the Church.

Invention of the printing press, 1440

Johannes Gutenberg's invention of a printing press that used moveable type revolutionized the way information was disseminated, and its availability to the masses. The earliest major mass-produced book printed in Europe was the Bible.

Renaissance and Reformation (1450–1650)

During the Middle Ages, society was ordered around religion and the Church. In the fifteenth century, focus began to turn to human achievement, often expressed through art.

Spanish Inquisition is established, 1478

Queen Isabella and King Ferdinand of Spain established an inquisition to ensure conformity to Catholicism. In 1492, the monarchs issued a decree requiring all Jews and Muslims to convert or leave Spain.

Construction begins on a new St. Peter's Basilica, 1506

Begun under the direction of Pope Julius II, St. Peter's was built over the next century. In 1508, Michelangelo started painting the ceiling of the Sistine Chapel in the Apostolic Palace, the pope's official residence.

Spanish colonizers arrive in South America and Mexico, early fifteenth century

As Spanish explorers arrived in the New World, they set out to conquer the natives: Aztecs and Maya in Mexico and Incas in South America. The explorers often brought Catholic missionaries with them. Along with working to convert and baptize the native peoples, the missionaries often also became their advocates and defenders. In the Americas, Bishop Bartolomé de las Casas (1484–1566), a Dominican friar, worked for the rights of native people of the West Indies and other conquered territories. St. Peter Claver

(1581–1654), a Jesuit priest, ministered to the slaves in Colombia. St. Martin de Porres (1579–1639), a Dominican lay brother, did the same in Peru.

Martin Luther posts his *Ninety-Five Theses* on a church door in Wittenberg, Germany, 1517

Although Luther (1483–1546) had not intended to start a movement, the posting of the *Ninety-Five Theses* became the spark that ignited the Protestant Reformation. One of Luther's chief complaints was against the practice of selling indulgences. Initially, he intended to engage Church leaders in examining the issues. When the Church was slow to respond, Luther broke with the Church. Luther advocated Scripture over Tradition, the priesthood of the laity, and the doctrine of justification by faith alone. He criticized the papacy and taught that there were only two valid Sacraments: Baptism and Eucharist. Luther was excommunicated.

Christianity in Europe further splits into different branches, sixteenth century

After the formal establishment of Lutheranism (1530), other protestors followed. Ulrich Zwingli (1484–1531) established Protestantism in Switzerland, where he encouraged a church with democratic rule. John Calvin (1509–1564), known for the doctrine of *double predestination*,∞ developed his own version of Protestantism, known as Calvinism. John Knox (ca. 1514–1572) brought Presbyterianism, a brand of Calvinism, to Scotland.

Our Lady of Guadalupe appears to Juan Diego, 1531

The Blessed Mother appeared to an Aztec peasant in Mexico. As a miraculous sign, Mary's image was imprinted on his cloak. A church was

∞ Note

Double predestination is the idea that not only does God predetermine some people who will be saved, but he also predetermines some who will be damned.

built in her honor. As word of the apparitions and miracle spread, millions of Mexicans were baptized.

King Henry VIII breaks with the Church, 1534

The Protestant Reformation came to England not over a doctrinal dispute but because the pope would not allow King Henry VIII to divorce his wife, Catherine of Aragon. In response, Henry declared himself head of the Church in England through Parliament's Act of Supremacy. He dissolved all monasteries in England and seized all Church property. He also required an oath of allegiance to himself. A few Catholics refused this oath, most notably Cardinal John Fisher and St. Thomas More, both of whom were beheaded for the offense in 1535.

Society of Jesus (the Jesuits) is founded, 1534

St. Ignatius of Loyola (1491–1556) founded the Society of Jesus. Along with the traditional religious vows of poverty, chastity, and obedience, the Jesuits took a fourth vow: obedience to the pope.

Council of Trent, 1545–1563

This council was the Church's response to the Protestant reformers. The council reaffirmed Church teaching on papal supremacy, the doctrine of transubstantiation, the sacrifice of the Mass, the Sacrament of Penance and Reconciliation as the normal means of forgiveness for sin committed after Baptism, the number of sacraments, and the necessity of both faith and good works for salvation.

Missionaries arrive in the Far East, sixteenth century

The greatest missionary to the Far East was Jesuit St. Francis Xavier (1506–1552), who brought Christianity to India and Japan. Another Jesuit, Matteo Ricci (1552–1610), helped the Gospel take root in China.

St. Teresa of Ávila writes her spiritual masterpiece, *The Interior Castle*, 1577

Teresa of Ávila also undertook important reforms of her religious order, the Carmelites.

St. Isaac Jogues and his companions are martyred, 1646

Eight Jesuit missionaries to the native populations of North America were killed by Mohawk Indians in what is now upstate New York.

The Age of Reason (seventeenth and eighteenth centuries)

Also known as the Enlightenment, this period saw the rise of philosophers and scholars who denounced religion and the Church, and encouraged the view that only human reason, separated from religious beliefs, can provide the truth.

Rise of rationalism and empiricism, eighteenth century

Rationalist and empiricist philosophers posited that all knowledge could come from science and human experience, and rejected beliefs based on faith.

St. Junípero Serra establishes the first California missions, 1769

Franciscan missionary Serra (1713–1784) established the first nine of California's thirty-one missions.

French Revolution, 1789

In addition to abolishing the monarchy, revolutionary leaders called for sweeping changes to the Church in France. Church property was nationalized, religious men and women were forced out of their convents, and laws were passed that prohibited the taking of religious vows. Nearly forty thousand priests were forced into exile, and many were killed.

John Carroll becomes America's first bishop, 1790

Among Carroll's achievements were the establishment of the first seminary in America and the founding of Georgetown University.

The Modern Era (nineteenth century through the present)

This period is marked by dramatic social and economic changes, as well as two world wars. These events resulted in changes in the way that the Church interacts with the world.

The Church in America grows through immigration (nineteenth and twentieth centuries)

The first wave of Irish immigrants to the United States arrived between 1830 and 1860, increasing the Catholic population in America by 800 percent. The Irish wave was followed by an influx of German Catholics (1860–1890), and Italians and Eastern Europeans (1890–1920). Over two million Catholics immigrated to the United States in the first decade of the twentieth century. In the nineteenth century, Catholic immigrants in America faced prejudice. The Know Nothing nativist political movement of the 1850s questioned the patriotism of Catholics. The Ku Klux Klan, a nativist group, targeted African Americans as well as Catholics during periods of the nineteenth and twentieth centuries.

Dogma of the Immaculate Conception, 1854

Pope Pius IX declared dogmatically that Mary was preserved from Original Sin from the moment of her conception.

Lourdes apparitions, 1858

The Blessed Mother appeared to St. Bernadette Soubirous (1844–1879) in Lourdes, France, under her title of the Immaculate Conception.

First Vatican Council, 1869–1870

Pope Pius IX convened the Church's twentieth ecumenical council to affirm papal authority in spiritual matters. The council defined the doctrine of papal infallibility, which says that the pope is preserved from error when teaching *ex cathedra* on matters of faith and morals.

Loss of the Papal States, 1870

When Italy was unified in 1861, most of the Papal States were seized from the Church. The last Church territory was claimed by Italy in 1870.

Pope Leo XIII releases *Rerum Novarum* (*On the Condition of Workers*), 1891

In response to the labor conditions and economic inequality caused by the Industrial Revolution, Pope Leo XIII issued the first modern social encyclical. *Rerum Novarum* formed the early framework of Catholic social teaching.

Pope Pius X permits First Communion at the age of reason rather than at twelve, 1910

Pope Pius also encouraged frequent reception of Holy Communion.

Our Lady of Fatima apparitions, 1917

From May to October, Our Lady appeared to three peasant children in Fatima, Portugal.

Codification of canon law, 1917

Pope Pius X commissioned the revision and codification of *canon law*, or Church law. The work was completed under his successor, Pope Benedict XV. For the first time, Church law was gathered in a single volume.

Lateran Treaty establishes Vatican City, 1929

A treaty signed by Benito Mussolini and Cardinal Pietro Gasparri established the independent state of Vatican City. Vatican City is the smallest sovereign state in the world.

The Church responds to World War II (1939–1945)

In response to the suffering, death, and mass atrocities carried out by the Nazi regime during World War II, Pope Pius XII (1939–1958) worked, often behind the scenes, to save the lives of thousands of Jews. The Vatican also used diplomacy to encourage an end to the global conflict.

Second Vatican Council, 1962–1965

Pope John XXIII (1958–1963) convened the Church's twenty-first ecumenical council. The Council enacted many changes, including the change of the celebration of the liturgy from Latin to the *vernacular*, or the local language. The Council issued sixteen documents, mainly concerning the Church, her inner workings, and her relationship to the world. Pope John XXIII died before the end of the Council, which was closed by Pope Paul VI (1963–1978).

Pope John Paul II elected, 1978

Karol Jozef Wojtyla became the first Polish pope and the first non-Italian pope in 450 years. Not long after his election, he was the victim of an assassination attempt. He played an important part in the fall of communism in Eastern Europe, especially in his native Poland, where he encouraged workers to stand up for their rights and supported a workers' movement known as Solidarity. On his death on April 2, 2005, millions of pilgrims traveled to Rome to pray and pay their respects. He was declared a saint by Pope Francis in April of 2014.

First World Youth Day is held, 1986

Since Pope John Paul II instituted World Youth Day in 1986, it has been held every two to three years in countries around the world, with attendance in the millions.

Publication of the *Catechism of the Catholic Church*, 1992

Commissioned by Pope John Paul II, the *Catechism* became the official catechism of the universal Church.

St. Teresa of Calcutta dies, 1997

Mother Teresa served the poor and dying in the streets of Calcutta, India, founding the Missionaries of Charity in 1950. The religious order now numbers in the thousands and serves in all parts of the world. Mother Teresa was declared Blessed by Pope John Paul II in 2003 and canonized by Pope Francis in 2016.

US bishops issue the Charter for the Protection of Children and Young People, 2002

After years of investigation, the full body of Catholic bishops of the United States approved the charter as a response to numerous cases of sexual abuse against minors committed by members of Church leadership.

Luminous Mysteries added to the Rosary, 2002

Pope John Paul II added the Luminous Mysteries, or the Mysteries of Light, to the Rosary, bringing the total to twenty.

Kateri Tekakwitha canonized, 2012

St. Kateri (1656–1680), known as the "Lily of the Mohawks," became the first Native American saint.

Pope Francis elected, 2013

Cardinal Jorge Mario Bergoglio of Buenos Aires, Argentina, became the first pope from the Americas. He was also the first Jesuit pope.

Synod on Synodality, 2021–2024

Initiated by Pope Francis, this multiyear, worldwide synod opened to all Catholics the opportunity to submit feedback to their local dioceses about questions and issues facing the Church. To conclude the synod, the pope invited many Church representatives to Rome to dialogue on topics and comments from the survey.

GLOSSARY

abbot The title given to the leader of a community of twelve or more monks. *Abbot* derives from *Abba*, the Hebrew word meaning "Father." The equivalent for female leaders is *abbess*.

actual sin As distinguished from Original Sin, any evil act contrary to God's law and God's will committed freely by a person. Categories of actual sin are *mortal* (deadly) sin and *venial* (lesser) sin.

analogy of faith The doctrine that all individual statements (e.g., Scripture passages) must be understood in light of the Church's entire objective body of faith.

Anglican The name for the Church of England established by King Henry VIII. Although their clergy and liturgical practices appear similar to those of Catholics in many respects, Anglicans do not validly celebrate the Sacrament of the Eucharist or Holy Orders.

apologetics The defense and explanation of the teachings, beliefs, and practices of the Catholic faith. Its purpose is to remove objections to the faith, explain different principles, and win people over to Christ and the Church.

apostates Baptized Christians who deny Christ and repudiate the Christian faith.

apostolic tradition Another name for Sacred Tradition; refers to Church teachings that have been passed down by the popes and bishops, the successors of the Apostles.

apse A semicircular or polygonal termination to the choir or nave of a church, in which the altar is placed. It is the place where the clergy are typically seated at Mass.

asceticism Strict self-denial as a means of spiritual discipline. Christian ascetics imitate Christ's life of self-sacrifice in order to live the Gospel more faithfully.

Book of Kells An illuminated manuscript of the four Gospels that was produced by the monks of St. Columba in Iona, Scotland, before being brought to Kells, Ireland, in about 795 to keep it safe from Viking marauders. It is believed that the priests who read from the Book of Kells had the passages memorized and would hold the images facing the congregation so that they could learn from the beauty of the work.

Calvinist Follower of John Calvin, who denied the Catholic understanding of the sacraments and condemned the papacy, monasticism, and clerical celibacy. Calvinists believe in double predestination, which falsely teaches that God wills that some people go to hell in advance of any wrongdoing on their part.

canon A name for those books of the Bible that have been accepted as normative for the faith.

canon law The official body of rules (canons) that provide good order in the Catholic Church. It was the first modern Western legal system. Canon law has been revised several times, most recently in the Latin Church in 1983 and in the Eastern Church in 1991.

catechetical From the Greek word *catechesis*, a term referring to instruction, usually religious instruction.

catechumens People who are undergoing a period of study and spiritual preparation before receiving the Sacrament of Baptism.

college of bishops Also known as the Ordo (Order) of Bishops; a term to denote the bishops who are in communion with the pope. Just as the Apostles with St. Peter made up one apostolic college, so do the bishops and the pope.

common priesthood of the faithful The priesthood of the baptized. Christ has made the Church a "kingdom of priests" who share in his priesthood through the Sacraments of Baptism and Confirmation.

communion of saints The unity of all people who have been redeemed by Christ, both the living and the dead.

covenant A binding and solemn agreement between humans or between God and people, holding each to a particular course of action.

Cristeros A Spanish word for "soldier of Christ."

Crusades A series of military expeditions in the eleventh, twelfth, and thirteenth centuries made according to a solemn vow by Christians to return the possession of the Holy Land from the Muslims to the Church.

declaration of nullity The Church's declaration that a particular marriage, whether presumed to be a sacramental body or simply a natural body, was never valid.

disciples From the Latin for "learners," those who learn from and follow Jesus Christ and who accept a share of his ministry in the world.

dogma The name for truths that the Church teaches that have been specifically revealed by God. Acceptance of dogma is essential for complete faith and the deepest possible relationship with God. Denial of dogma is heresy.

domestic church A name for the Christian family. In the family, parents and children exercise their priesthood of the baptized by worshipping God, receiving the sacraments, and witnessing to Christ and the Church by living as faithful disciples.

ecumenical councils Gatherings of all Catholic bishops of the world under the authority of the pope to discuss and make decisions about teachings and practices that apply to all local churches (dioceses).

ecumenism The movement, inspired and led by the Holy Spirit, that seeks the full and visible unity of all Christians.

Enlightenment Name for a period in Europe that began in the late seventeenth century that was also known as the *Age of Reason*. The term *Enlightenment* implies that religious people of the Middle Ages were in the dark and that only human reason separated from religious beliefs could bring them into the light.

epistles From the Greek word for "letters," books in the New Testament in the form of letters. Some of the epistles attributed to St. Paul and others are known as catholic, or universal, epistles.

evangelical counsels When related to vows taken by a religious, promises of personal poverty, chastity (understood as a lifelong celibacy), and obedience to a bishop or superior of a religious community.

evangelization The bringing of the Good News of Jesus Christ to others through words and actions.

four marks of the Church The attributes (also called notes) of the Church mentioned in the Nicene Creed: "We believe in one, holy, catholic, and apostolic Church."

grace A free and unearned favor from God, infused into our souls at Baptism, that adopts us into God's family and helps us to live as his children.

Gregorian chant A monophonic, sacred form of song sung in Latin that arose in the ninth and tenth centuries and was named for St. Gregory the Great.

hagiography A Greek term for the biography of a saint; *hagio* comes from a term that means "holy" or "saintly," and *graphy* means "to write."

high Mass A Mass that has some parts chanted or sung by the celebrant, including some parts that are sung in response by the congregation. A high Mass is more prominent than other Masses celebrated on the same day, and more people are expected to attend it.

holy days of obligation The days in the Church Year when all Catholics are obliged to participate in Mass. In the United States, the holy days of obligation are January 1, the

Solemnity of Mary, the Holy Mother of God; Thursday of the Sixth Week of Easter, the Solemnity of the Ascension of the Lord; August 15, the Solemnity of the Assumption of the Blessed Virgin Mary; November 1, the Solemnity of All Saints; December 8, the Solemnity of the Immaculate Conception of the Blessed Virgin Mary; and December 25, the Solemnity of the Nativity of the Lord.

indefectibility Regarding Church teaching and the Church herself, a term meaning that the Church and her teachings are incapable of failure and decay to the end of time.

Inquisition A Church tribunal established in the early thirteenth century that was intended to curb heretical teachings and beliefs. In collaboration with secular authorities, papal representatives employed the Inquisition to judge the guilt of suspected heretics with the aim of getting them to repent. Unfortunately, many abuses crept into the process.

justification Describes the state of cleansing from sin through faith in Jesus Christ and Baptism and by the grace of the Holy Spirit and being made right with God. Justification not only frees us from sin but sanctifies us in the depth of our being.

laissez-faire capitalism An economic theory from the eighteenth century that opposes any government intervention in the business market. *Laissez-faire* is a French term for "let it be."

liturgy The public worship of the Church, which includes the celebration of the Eucharist and the other sacraments, as well as the Liturgy of the Hours, or Divine Office, the official prayer of the Church. The word *liturgy* literally means "public work." In Catholic tradition, *liturgy* means the participation of the People of God in the work of God.

low Mass A Mass that is entirely read or spoken by the celebrant. No parts of the Mass are chanted or sung. Sometimes soft music may be played during certain aspects of a low Mass, and hymns may be sung by the congregation and choir.

Magisterium The living, teaching office of the Church whose task it is to interpret the Word of God; the bishops in communion with the successor of Peter, the bishop of Rome (the pope). Jesus bestowed the right and power to teach in his name on Peter and the Apostles and their successors.

Marian apparitions Supernatural appearances of Mary to a person or group of people on earth. There have been thousands of reported Marian apparitions over the centuries but very few Church-approved Marian apparitions. The local bishop where the alleged apparition has occurred carefully investigates an apparition based on criteria set by the Dicastery for the Doctrine of the Faith.

modernity A movement of the late modern period that began in the late eighteenth century and lasted through the twentieth century that attempted to reduce or limit Church teaching to modern advances in history, science, and biblical research.

monotheism From the Greek words *monos* (one) and *theos* (God), the belief in one all-powerful God. Judaism, Christianity, and Islam are the three great monotheistic religions.

mortal sin A serious violation of God's law of love that results in the loss of God's life (sanctifying grace) in the soul of the sinner. For a sin to be mortal, it must concern grave matter, there must be full knowledge of the evil done, and there must be full consent of the will.

motu proprio Latin for "of his own accord," a papal document promulgated on the pope's own initiative.

New Age A broad movement characterized by alternative approaches to culture and religious practice, with focus on spirituality and mysticism; typically does not include worship of or belief in God.

New Covenant The climax of salvation history; the coming of Jesus Christ, who is the fullness of God's revelation.

novena A set form of prayers for nine consecutive days in preparation for a feast and in petition of a favor from God.

orans A Latin word meaning "praying or pleading"; commonly refers to the posture of prayer with one's hands extended. Traditionally, this is a posture reserved for the priest at Mass.

Order of Christian Initiation of Adults (OCIA) The process through which non-Catholic adults learn about and join in full communion with the Catholic Church by receiving the sacraments of Baptism (if they have not already received Christian Baptism), Confirmation, and Eucharist.

papacy The supreme rule and ministry of the pope as the shepherd of the whole Church. The pope is the successor of St. Peter, the bishop of Rome, and the Vicar of Christ.

papal nuncio A formal representative of the pope who has both political and ecclesial power. He is an ambassador to local governments and reports on the conditions of the Church in the nation where he has been assigned by the pope.

Papal States The territory in present-day central Italy that was overseen by the pope from the eighth century until 1870.

papists A name, sometimes used in a derogatory way, for Catholics that express their loyalty to the pope.

particular judgment The individual's judgment right after death, when Christ will rule on one's eternal destiny to be spent in heaven (after purification in Purgatory, if needed) or in hell.

patriarch The name for bishops of one of five *episcopal sees*, the name for the places of residence of bishops: the Eastern patriarchates of Jerusalem, Antioch, Constantinople, and Alexandria, and the Latin patriarchate of Rome. From the time of St. Peter, the bishop of Rome (the pope) was acknowledged as the principal patriarch.

Paschal Mystery Christ's work of redemption, accomplished principally by his Passion, Death, Resurrection, and glorious Ascension. The mystery is commemorated and made present through the sacraments, especially the Eucharist.

Peace of Augsburg A treaty between the Catholic Holy Roman emperor and an alliance of Lutheran princes that the leader (whether a prince or a king) of each region of Germany could choose either the Catholic faith or the Lutheran faith as the one official religion for his area of political control. A Catholic bishop who converted to Lutheranism had to give up his property. Those who did not want to participate in the religion of the region were expected to migrate to an area where their religion was practiced.

Peace of Westphalia A series of treaties that ended the Thirty Years' War between Catholics and Protestants in Germany, legalized Calvinism in Germany, and gave Protestantism equal status with Catholicism.

Pentateuch Meaning "five books" in Greek, the first five books of the Old Testament: Genesis, Exodus, Leviticus, Numbers, and Deuteronomy.

post-Christian A term often applied to Western cultures and nations that were historically Christian but now reject the authority of the Church in particular, and Christianity in general. The language and cultural references to Christianity that were once part of the society are less present and often only superficial.

precepts of the Church Five key Church laws that Catholics are required to keep: (1) you shall attend Mass on Sundays and on holy days of obligation and rest from servile labor, (2) you shall confess your sins at least once a year, (3) you shall receive the Sacrament of the Eucharist at least during the Easter season, (4) you shall observe the days of fasting and abstinence established by the Church, and (5) you shall help to provide for the needs of the Church.

presbyters The Greek name (meaning "elders") for priests, that is, members of the order of priesthood. Presbyters, or priests, are coworkers with their bishops and assist them in priestly service to the Church.

presbytery The part of the cathedral with raised steps that is reserved for the clergy during the celebration of Mass. Today, especially in Catholic churches, the presbytery is known as the *sanctuary*.

Purgatory The state of purification that takes place after death for those who need to be made clean and holy before meeting the all-holy God in heaven.

Real Presence "The unique, true presence of Christ in the Eucharist under the species or appearances of bread and wine" (*CCC*, Glossary).

Reconquista of Spain A series of campaigns by Christians to recapture territory on the Iberian Peninsula between Spain and Portugal from Muslims. The reconquest of this territory took over eight centuries, from the eighth century to the fifteenth century.

Reign of Terror A horrific time of persecutions in France that began in September of 1793. Before it ended in July 1794, the king and queen had been beheaded, and thousands of nobles, priests, nuns, and brothers had been executed. Other clergy had to sign a pledge of allegiance to the radical government. Also, the government attempted to set up a state religion, the Christian calendar was replaced by a secular calendar, and Catholic churches were seized and converted into "Temples of Reason" with religious statues replaced with statues of revolutionary philosophers.

relativism A belief that knowledge, truth, and morality exist only in relation to culture, society, or individuals and are not objective or absolute.

religious freedom A term that promotes human dignity and recognizes and defends the fundamental human right to be free from coercion in religious matters. The Church extends the understanding of religious freedom to indicate that all people are called in freedom to accept Jesus Christ and his Church, which has a divine mission oriented to one's salvation.

Roman Canon The name for Eucharistic Prayer I in the Mass of Paul VI, which came into existence after the Second Vatican Council. The Roman Canon, or Canon, has its origins in the sixth century during the pontificate of St. Gregory the Great.

Sacraments of Service Sacraments whose primary purpose is to create, build, and maintain the Church community. The Sacrament of Holy Orders and the Sacrament of Matrimony are the two Sacraments of Service.

Sacred Tradition The living transmission of the Church's Gospel message found in the Church's teaching, life, and worship. It is faithfully preserved, handed on, and interpreted by the Church's Magisterium.

salvation history The account of God's saving activity and intervention on behalf of humanity.

sanctification Means "being made holy." The first sanctification of a person takes place at Baptism. The second sanctification takes place from how the person lives his or her life in growing in the likeness of God. The third sanctification takes place when the person enters heaven and is fully united with God for all eternity.

Seven Sacraments "Efficacious [effective] sign[s] of grace instituted by Christ and entrusted to the Church, by which divine life is dispensed to us through the work of the Holy Spirit" (*CCC*, Glossary). The Seven Sacraments are Baptism, Confirmation, Eucharist, Penance or Reconciliation, the Anointing of the Sick, Holy Orders, and Matrimony.

subsidiarity A social principle that stipulates that social matters should be taken care of at the lowest, most local level of authority, if possible.

totalitarian A term to describe a government with total control by an authoritarian leader or a hierarchy.

transubstantiation Church teaching that holds that the substance of the bread and wine is changed into the substance of the Body and Blood of Christ at the consecration at Mass.

venial sin Personal sin that weakens but does not kill a person's relationship with God. Venial sin is the failure to observe in lesser matters the obligations of moral law.

Vulgate The name for St. Jerome's fifth-century AD translation of the Bible into Latin, the common language of the people of his day.

NOTES

1. The Church Gives Life

1. John Paul II, Letter to Families, *Gratissimam Sane*, February 2, 1994, https://www.vatican.va/content/john-paul-ii/en/letters/1994/documents/hf_jp-ii_let_02021994_families.html, 19.

2. Patricia Treece, *A Man for Others: Maximilian Kolbe, Saint of Auschwitz* (Libertyville, IL: Marytown Press, 1999).

3. Pietro Molla, *Saint Gianna Molla: Wife, Mother, Doctor* (San Francisco: Ignatius Press, 2004).

4. Augustine, *The Confessions*, trans. J. G. Pilkington, in *Nicene and Post-Nicene Fathers*, First Series, vol. 1, ed. Philip Schaff (Buffalo, NY: Christian Literature Publishing Co., 1887), rev. and ed. for New Advent by Kevin Knight, http://www.newadvent.org/fathers/1101.htm. Quotes: "I searched about . . . ," bk. 3; "All the darkness . . . ," bk. 8; "Our hearts . . . ," bk. 1.

5. *Letters of St. Cyprian*, 75:2.

6. Andrew Greeley, "Catholicism: Here Comes Everyone," *Baltimore Sun*, August 24, 1993.

7. There are several other descriptions of the Kingdom of God in the Gospels; for example, Matthew 13:31–32; Matthew 13:33; Matthew 18:1–5; Matthew 18:23–25; Mark 4:26–29; and Luke 7:18–23.

8. Ignatius of Antioch, *To the Smyrnaeans*, 8:2.

9. *Shepherd of Hermas* 2.4.1.

10. Pope Francis, General Audience, September 18, 2019, https://www.vatican.va/content/francesco/en/audiences/2019/documents/papa-francesco_20190918_udienza-generale.html.

2. The Church Sets Her Foundation

1. Walter J. Ciszek, SJ, with Daniel L. Flaherty, SJ, *He Leadeth Me: An Extraordinary Testament of Faith* (New York: Image, 1975; repr. San Francisco: Ignatius Press, 1995), 26, 28, 31.

2. John Evangelist Walsh, *The Bones of St. Peter: The First Full Account of the Search for the Apostle's Body* (Garden City, NY: Doubleday, 1982; repr. Manchester, NH: Sophia Institute Press, 2011).

3. US Census Bureau, "Historical Estimates of World Population," last updated December 5, 2022, https://www.census.gov/data/tables/time-series/demo/international-programs/historical-est-worldpop.html.

4. St. James the Greater was the first Apostle to be martyred. His martyrdom is recorded in Acts 12:2.

5. Richard Dawkins, *The God Delusion* (Boston: Houghton Mifflin, 2006), esp. chap. 8. For a reasoned response to Dawkins, see Alister E. McGrath, *Dawkins' God: From* The Selfish Gene *to* The God Delusion (Chichester, UK: Wiley, 2015).

6. Abigail Rine Favale, *Into the Deep: An Unlikely Catholic Conversion* (Eugene, OR: Cascade, 2018), 41.

7. Tim Drake, "Hard to Believe but Yes, There Are More Martyrs Today Than in 1st Centuries," *Aleteia*, March 5, 2019.

8. As quoted in Edwin M. Yamauchi, "On the Road with Paul," *Christian History*, no. 47 (1995), https://christianhistoryinstitute.org/magazine/article/on-the-road-with-paul.

9. Katie Yoder, "Akash Bashir, Who Died Protecting Catholic Worshippers in Pakistan, Named a Servant of God," Catholic News Agency, February 1, 2022, https://www.catholicnewsagency.com/news/250275/akash-bashir-who-died-protecting-catholic-worshippers-in-pakistan-named-a-servant-of-god; Kamran Chaudry, "Pakistan's Servant of God Inspires Catholics to Confront Terror," Union of Catholic Asian News, February 22, 2022, https://www.ucanews.com/news/pakistans-servant-of-god-inspires-catholics-to-confront-terror/96198#.

10. *The Passion of the Holy Martyrs Perpetua and Felicity*, chap. 6, trans. R. E. Wallis, in *Ante-Nicene Fathers*, vol. 3, ed. Alexander Roberts, James Donaldson, and A. Cleveland Coxe (Buffalo, NY: Christian Literature Publishing Co., 1885), rev. and ed. for New Advent by Kevin Knight, http://www.newadvent.org/fathers/0324.htm.

11. "To the Emperor Trajan," no. 97 in *The Letters of Pliny*, trans. William Melmoth, rev. by F. C. T. Bosanquet, Project Gutenberg (2001, updated 2016), https://gutenberg.org/files/2811/2811-h/2811-h.htm.

12. *The Martyrdom of Polycarp*, chap. 9, trans. Alexander Roberts and James Donaldson, in *Ante-Nicene Fathers*, vol. 1, ed. Alexander Roberts, James Donaldson, and A. Cleveland Coxe (Buffalo, NY: Christian Literature Publishing Co., 1885), rev. and ed. for New Advent by Kevin Knight, http://www.newadvent.org/fathers/0102.htm.

13. *Martyrdom of Polycarp*, chap. 11.

14. Gregory A. Smith, "About Three-in-Ten U.S. Adults Are Now Religiously Unaffiliated," Pew Research Center, December 14, 2021, https://www.pewforum.org/2021/12/14/about-three-in-ten-u-s-adults-are-now-religiously-unaffiliated/; David Masci and Gregory A. Smith, "7 Facts about American Catholics," Pew Research Center, October 10, 2018, https://www.pewresearch.org/fact-tank/2018/10/10/7-facts-about-american-catholics/.

15. "Frequently Requested Church Statistics" ("Adult Converts to Catholicism," 2020), Center for Applied Research in the Apostolate (CARA), https://cara.georgetown.edu/frequently-requested-church-statistics/; Mark M. Gray, "The Reverts:

Catholics Who Left and Came Back," *Nineteen Sixty-four* (CARA Research blog), June 19, 2012, republished at Catholic Education Resource Center, https://www.catholiceducation.org/en/controversy/common-misconceptions/the-reverts-catholics-who-left-and-came-back.html.

16. Aaron Milavec, *The Didache: Faith, Hope, and Life of the Earliest Christian Communities, 50–70 C.E.* (New York: Newman, 2003).

17. *The Didache, The Lord's Teaching through the Twelve Apostles to the Nations*, trans. Roberts and Donaldson, Early Christian Writings, http://www.earlychristianwritings.com/text/didache-roberts.html.

18. *The Apology of Aristides*, trans. D. M. Kay, in *Ante-Nicene Fathers*, vol. 9, ed. Allan Menzies (Buffalo, NY: Christian Literature Publishing Co., 1896), rev. and ed. for New Advent by Kevin Knight, http://www.newadvent.org/fathers/1012.htm.

19. Mike Aquilina, *The Mass of the Early Christians*, 2nd ed. (Huntington, IN: Our Sunday Visitor, 2007), 18.

20. Rodney Stark, *The Rise of Christianity: How the Obscure, Marginal Jesus Movement Became the Dominant Religious Force in the Western World in a Few Centuries* (Princeton, NJ: Princeton University Press, 1996; repr. San Francisco: HarperCollins, 1997), chap. 1.

3. The Church Grows and Defines Herself

1. Eusebius, *Life of Constantine*, bk. 1, chap. 41. This early Church historian provides the fullest contemporary account of Constantine's vision and its effects. In *Nicene and Post-Nicene Fathers*, second series, vol. 1, trans. Ernest Cushing Richardson, ed. Philip Schaff and Henry Wace (Buffalo, NY: Christian Literature Publishing Co., 1890), rev. and ed. for New Advent by Kevin Knight, https://www.newadvent.org/fathers/25021.htm.

2. See, for example, Timothy D. Barnes, *Constantine: Dynasty, Religion and Power in the Late Roman Empire* (Malden, MA: Wiley-Blackwell, 2011). Although he notes errors and embellishments in the classic accounts of Constantine by the early Christian writers Lactantius and Eusebius, Barnes affirms the authenticity and general reliability of these authors.

3. Mark Kurlansky, *Salt: A World History* (New York: Walker, 2002), chap. 22 et passim.

4. Ivor J. Davidson, *The Birth of the Church: From Jesus to Constantine, AD 30–312*, The Baker History of the Church, vol. 1 (Grand Rapids, MI: Baker, 2004), chap. 9, 321.

5. Tertullian, *Apology*, 39.

6. See the extensive discussion of these matters in Davidson, *Birth of the Church*, chap. 4.

7. Congregation for the Doctrine of the Faith, *Notification on the Works of Jon Sobrino, SJ*, November 26, 2006, https://www.vatican.va/roman_curia/congregations/cfaith/documents/rc_con_cfaith_doc_20061126_notification-sobrino_en.html, no. 4.

8. Pope Pius IX, Apostolic Constitution on the Immaculate Conception *Ineffabilis Deus* (December 8, 1854), https://www.newadvent.org/library/docs_pi09id.htm. A description of the ceremony, written by Irish bishop John Mac Hale, can be found in *The Bull "Ineffabilis" in Four Languages*, trans. and ed. Rev. Ulick J. Bourke (Dublin: John Mullany, 1868), 85–93.

9. Mike Aquilina, *The Fathers of the Church: An Introduction to the First Christian Teachers*, exp. ed. (Huntington, IN: Our Sunday Visitor, 2006), 15.

10. John Chrysostom, "Homily 7 on Colossians," trans. John A. Broadus, in *Nicene and Post-Nicene Fathers*, first series, vol. 13, ed. Philip Schaff (Buffalo, NY: Christian Literature Publishing Co., 1889), rev. and ed. for New Advent by Kevin Knight, http://www.newadvent.org/fathers/230307.htm.

11. Hans von Campenhausen, *The Fathers of the Church* (originally published as two volumes in German, 1955, 1960; trans. 1959, 1960; repr. Peabody, MA: Hendrickson, 1998), 89–90.

12. Ambrose, Letter 51, in *Letters of St. Ambrose*, trans. H. De Romestin, Library of Nicene and Post Nicene Fathers, 2nd series, vol. 10 (New York: 1896), 450–453, online at Medieval Sourcebook, Fordham University, https://sourcebooks.fordham.edu/source/ambrose-let51.asp.

13. Augustine, *The City of God*, vol. 1, trans. Rev. Marcus Dods (Edinburgh: T&T Clark, 1871), bk. 11, chap. 1 (p. 437); bk. 2, chap. 3 (p. 51), online at Project Gutenberg, https://www.gutenberg.org/files/45304/45304-h/45304-h.htm.

14. Augustine, *The City of God*, vol. 2, bk. 22, chap. 1 (p. 473), https://www.gutenberg.org/files/45305/45305-h/45305-h.htm.

15. Marcellino D'Ambrosio, *When the Church Was Young: Voices of the Early Fathers* (Cincinnati: Servant Books, 2014), 2.

16. Henry G. Graham, *Where We Got the Bible: Our Debt to the Catholic Church; Together with His Conversion Story: From the Kirk to the Catholic Church* (B. Herder, 1911; repr. San Diego: Catholic Answers, 1997).

17. Bernard of Clairvaux, *Sermons on the Song of Songs*, in *Selected Works*, trans. G. R. Evans (New York: Paulist, 1987), Sermon 1, no. 8 (p. 213).

18. John Cassian, *Conferences*, as quoted in Pauline A. Viviano, "The Senses of Scripture," United States Conference of Catholic Bishops website, 2008, https://www.usccb.org/bible/national-bible-week/upload/viviano-senses-scripture.pdf, 3.

19. Augustine, *The Literal Meaning of Genesis*, as quoted in Viviano, "Senses of Scripture," 3.

4. The Church Rises to Prominence

1. G. K. Chesterton, "The True Middle Ages," *Illustrated London News*, July 14, 1906.

2. Steve Weidenkopf, *The Church and the Middle Ages (1000–1378): Cathedrals, Crusades, and the Papacy in Exile* (Notre Dame, IN: Ave Maria Press, 2020), xxii.

3. John Wortley, *An Introduction to the Desert Fathers* (Cambridge: Cambridge University Press, 2019), 3.

4. Mother Dolores Hart, OSB, with Richard DeNeut, *The Ear of the Heart: An Actress' Journey from Hollywood to Holy Vows* (San Francisco: Ignatius, 2013).

5. The entire Rule in English translation (London: SPCK, 1931) can be found at https://www.solesmes.com/sites/default/files/upload/pdf/rule_of_st_benedict.pdf.

6. Henry G. Graham, *Where We Got the Bible: Our Debt to the Catholic Church; Together with His Conversion Story: From the Kirk to the Catholic Church* (B. Herder, 1911; repr. San Diego: Catholic Answers, 1997), 50.

7. Greg Peters, *The Monkhood of All Believers: The Monastic Foundation of Christian Spirituality* (Grand Rapids, MI: Baker Academic, 2018), 154, 145.

8. Leah Libresco, *Arriving at Amen: Seven Catholic Prayers That Even I Can Offer* (Notre Dame, IN: Ave Maria Press, 2015), 13.

9. Thomas Dubay, SM, *Saints: A Closer Look* (Cincinnati: Servant Books, 2007), 9.

10. Mother Teresa, *Come Be My Light: The Revealing Private Writings of the "Saint of Calcutta,"* ed. Brian Kolodiejchuk (New York: Doubleday, 2007), 192–3.

11. Quoted in Malcolm Cardinal Ranjith, "Addressing Objections to Adoration," in *From Eucharistic Adoration to Evangelization*, ed. Alcuin Reid (London: Burnes & Oates, 2012), 165.

12. Mother Teresa, Acceptance Speech, Nobel Prize, https://www.nobelprize.org/prizes/peace/1979/teresa/acceptance-speech/.

13. See Ephesians 4:12. The NABRE reads "holy ones," but many other translations use "saints."

14. Thomas Dubay, SM, *Saints: A Closer Look* (Cincinnati: Servant Books, 2007), 36.

15. Simon Yarrow, *The Saints: A Short History* (Oxford: Oxford University Press, 2016), 150.

16. See Peter King, *Western Monasticism: A History of the Monastic Movement in the Latin Church* (Kalamazoo, MI: Cistercian Publications, 1999), chap. 4.

17. Irenaeus, *Against Heresies*, trans. Alexander Roberts and William Rambaut, in *Ante-Nicene Fathers*, vol. 1, ed. Alexander Roberts, James Donaldson, and A. Cleveland Coxe (Buffalo, NY: Christian Literature Publishing Co., 1885), bk. 3, chap. 3,

no. 3. Rev. and ed. for New Advent by Kevin Knight, http://www.newadvent.org/fathers/0103303.htm.

18. The Latin meaning of the word *pastor* is literally "shepherd."

19. Catherine of Siena, Letter 74, To Pope Gregory XI in Avignon (1376), https://web.mit.edu/aorlando/www/SaintJohnCHI/Church%20History%20Readings/Catherine%20of%20Siena%20Letter%2074.pdf.

20. Eamon Duffy, *Saints and Sinners: A History of the Popes* (New Haven, CT: Yale University Press, 2006), 194.

21. Paul Johnson, *Art: A New History* (New York: HarperCollins, 2003), 153.

22. Barbara Tuchman, *A Distant Mirror: The Calamitous 14th Century* (New York: Ballantine, 1978), 528.

23. Graham, *Where We Got the Bible*, 161–2.

24. Graham, *Where We Got the Bible*, 127.

5. The Church Readdresses Her Unity

1. Julie Swenson, "This I Seek: To Dwell in the House of the Lord," in *Surprised by Truth: Eleven Converts Give the Biblical and Historical Reasons for Becoming Catholic*, ed. Patrick Madrid (San Diego: Basilica, 1994), 135–160.

2. Quoted in Charles Butler, *The Lives of Don Armand-Jean le Bouthillièr de Rancé . . . and of Thomas à Kempis* (London: Luke Hansard and Sons, 1814), 76.

3. Dr. Keith Mathison, "The Five Solas," Reformation Bible College blog, October 20, 2021, https://reformationbiblecollege.org/blog/the-five-solas.

4. Cf. *Westminster Larger Catechism*, Q. 70.

5. Information in this feature is taken from Brandon Vogt, *What to Say and How to Say It, Volume 3: Even More Ways to Discuss Your Faith with Clarity and Confidence* (Notre Dame, IN: Ave Maria Press 2022).

6. *Butler's Lives of the Saints*, concise edition, revised and updated, ed. Michael Walsh (San Francisco: HarperCollins, 1991), 336.

7. Teresa of Ávila, *The Interior Castle*, trans. Kieran Kavanaugh, OCD, and Otilio Rodriguez, OCD (New York: Paulist, 1979), 194.

8. "Doctrine Touching the Sacrament of Matrimony," 24th Session, November 11, 1563, in *The Canons and Decrees of the Council of Trent*, trans. Theodore Alois Buckley (London: George Routledge, 1853), online at Capdox (Capuchin Franciscan Friars Australia), https://www.capdox.capuchin.org.au/reform-resources-16th-century/sources/the-canons-and-decrees-of-the-council-of-trent/#post-2439-_Toc529040242.

9. Various accounts of the Skull of Wardley Hall differ in some details. See, for example, David W. Atherton and Michael P. Peyton, "Saint Ambrose Barlow: His Life, Times, and Relics," unpublished paper at Academia.edu, https://www.academia.edu/40099004/Saint_Ambrose_Barlow_His_life_times_and_relics; "The Skull of

Wardley Hall," British Histories blog, February 26, 2022, https://britishhistories.com/f/11-the-skull-of-wardley-hall; and Michala Hulme, "The Screaming Skull of Wardley Hall," in *Bloody British History: Manchester* (History Press, 2016).

10. Quoted in Antonio Spadaro, "A Big Heart Open to God: An Interview with Pope Francis," *America*, September 30, 2013.

11. Jens Manuel Krogstad, Joshua Alvarado, and Besheer Mohamed, "Among U.S. Latinos, Catholicism Continues to Decline but Is Still the Largest Faith," Pew Research Center Report, April 13, 2023.

6. The Church Enters the Modern World

1. Alejandra Molina, "Chronicling Los Angeles' Iconic Virgin of Guadalupe Street Art," Religion News Service, February 10, 2023. https://religionnews.com/2023/02/10/theyre-not-religious-but-they-chronicle-los-angeles-iconic-street-art-of-the-virgin-of-guadalupe/.

2. Story from Block Club Chicago, July 30, 2018. https://blockclubchicago.org/2018/07/30/pilsen-mural-of-virgen-de-guadalupe-vandalized-its-really-disrespectful/. https://blockclubchicago.org/2018/07/31/pilsen-artist-and-a-stranger-restore-graffitied-virgen-de-guadalupe-mural/.

3. "The Blessed Martyrs of Compiègne," Carmel of the Annunciation website, https://www.thicketpriorycarmel.org/blessed-martyrs-of-compiegne. The story of the Compiègne Martyrs is told in the form of a novel in Gertrud von Le Fort, *The Song at the Scaffold*, trans. Olga Marx (Sheed and Ward, 1933; San Francisco: Ignatius Press, 2011).

4. Voltaire, Letter 156, To Frederick the Great, January 5, 1767, as quoted in Clara A. B. Joseph, *Christianity in India: The Anti-Colonial Turn* (London: Routledge, 2019).

5. Quoted in Dominic Aquila, *The Church and the Age of Enlightenment: Faith, Science, and the Challenge of Secularization* (Notre Dame, IN: Ave Maria Press, 2022).

6. Quoted in "Alessandro Volta," Society of Catholic Scientists, https://catholic-scientists.org/scientists-of-the-past/alessandro-volta-2/.

7. There is debate about who obtained the first computer science doctorate; see Ralph L. London, "Who Earned the First Computer Science Ph.D.?" Communications of the ACM, January 15, 2013, https://cacm.acm.org/blogs/blog-cacm/159591-who-earned-first-computer-science-phd/fulltext.

8. Robert Bellarmine, *De Laicis* (Treatise on Civil Government), chap. 6; full text at Sensus Fidelium, https://sensusfidelium.com/apologetics/de-laicis-the-treatise-on-civil-government-by-st-robert-bellarmine/de-laicis-chapter-vi-the-same-inference-is-drawn-from-the-efficent-cause-st-robert-bellarmine/.

9. *Pascal's Pensées* (New York: E. P. Dutton, 1953), no. 253; online at Project Gutenberg, https://www.gutenberg.org/files/18269/18269-h/18269-h.htm#SECTION_II.

10. Aquila, *Church and Enlightenment.*

11. Congregation for the Doctrine of the Faith, "Doctrinal Note on Some Questions Regarding the Participation of Catholics in Political Life," November 24, 2002, https://www.vatican.va/roman_curia/congregations/cfaith/documents/rc_con_cfaith_doc_20021124_politica_en.html, 2.

12. "Blessed Frederic Ozanam Biography (III)," Vincentian Formation Network, November 13, 2013, http://vincentians.com/en/blessed-frederic-ozanam-biography-iii/.

13. The Oxford Movement was also the forerunner of Anglo-Catholicism, a "High Church" movement within the Church of England that incorporated many Roman Catholic practices.

14. *Summa Theologiae*, Supplement, 82–85.

15. *Didache*, 9.4.

16. Pope Leo XIII, Encyclical Letter on Catholicism in the United States *Longinqua*, January 6, 1895, https://www.vatican.va/content/leo-xiii/en/encyclicals/documents/hf_l-xiii_enc_06011895_longinqua.html, 4; subsequent quotes from 6.

17. *Terceo catechismo*, 3–4.

7. The Church Faces a More Hostile World

1. Quotations taken from Mickey McGrath, "Is There Such a Thing as 'Woke' Saints?" *National Catholic Reporter*, June 7, 2023.

2. Quote is from the front page of *Chicago Daily News*, June 24, 1926, https://encyclopedia.chicagohistory.org/pages/11319.html. Stephanie Shreffler, "Eucharistic Congress 1926: A Watershed Moment for Chicago, Catholicism," Marian Library, University of Dayton, September 20, 2021, https://udayton.edu/blogs/marianlibrary/2021-09-20-eucharistic-congress-1926.php; "1926 Eucharistic Congress Brings 'Sense of Wonder,'" Chicago Catholic, September 6, 2017, https://www.chicagocatholic.com/chicagoland/-/article/2017/09/06/1926-eucharistic-congress-brings-sense-of-wonder-.

3. Christopher Wells, "Pope: Search for Christian Unity Must Be a Journey Together," *Vatican News*, January 17, 2022, https://www.vaticannews.va/en/pope/news/2022-01/search-for-christian-unity-must-be-a-journey-together-says-pope.html.

4. Greetings by His Holiness Pope John Paul II, Visit to Israel, March 23, 2000, Jewish Virtual Library, https://www.jewishvirtuallibrary.org/pope-john-paul-ii-s-visit-to-israel-texts-of-speeches-and-statements.

5. Four Chaplains Memorial Foundation, http://fourchaplains.org/four-chaplains/.

6. Quoted in Daniel A. Poling, "A Protestant's Faith," *Life*, November 7, 1949, 114–116.

7. Harry S. Truman, "Address in Philadelphia at the Dedication of the Chapel of the Four Chaplains," February 3, 1951, Teaching American History, https://teachingamericanhistory.org/document/address-in-philadelphia-at-the-dedication-of-the-chapel-of-the-four-chaplains/.

8. Pastoral Letter of the Catholic Patriarchs of the Orient, "Christian Presence in the Orient: Witness and Mission," Easter 1992, n. 48; as quoted in Archbishop Paul Nabil Sayah, "Christian-Muslim Relations in the Middle East," Address at Special Assembly of Asian Bishops, Rome, May 8, 1998, accessed online at CatholicCulture.org, https://www.catholicculture.org/culture/library/view.cfm?id=503.

9. Francis, Message of Pope Francis to Muslims throughout the World for the End of Ramadan ('Id al-Fitr), June 10, 2013, https://www.vatican.va/content/francesco/en/messages/pont-messages/2013/documents/papa-francesco_20130710_musulmani-ramadan.html.

10. "Muslims and Christians Unite to Rebuild Mosul Monastery," Catholic News Agency, June 5, 2017, https://www.catholicnewsagency.com/news/36160/muslims-and-christians-unite-to-rebuild-mosul-monastery.

11. Homily of Pope Francis at the Holy Mass and Canonization of the Blesseds: Salomon Leclerq, José Sánchez del Río, et al., St. Peter's Square, October 16, 2016, https://www.vatican.va/content/francesco/en/homilies/2016/documents/papa-francesco_20161016_omelia-canonizzazione.html.

12. Edith Stein, Letter 129, December 26, 1932, in *Self Portrait in Letters, 1916–1942*, The Collected Works of Edith Stein, vol. 5, trans. Josephine Koeppel (Washington, DC: ICS Publications, 1993), 128.

13. *Man's Search for Meaning* (page 36) by Victor Frankl, quoted in "Don't Make Freedom a False God" by Kenneth Howell, Catholic Answers, August 30, 2022.

14. Some of this material on marriage is taken from Richard R. Gaillardetz, "The Sacrament of Marriage: Three Dimensions of a Daring Vocation," *Liguorian* 92 (May–June, 2004): 10–15.

15. Thomas Merton, *The Seven Storey Mountain* (New York: Harcourt, Brace, 1958), 163–164.

16. Merton, 209–211.

17. Merton, 317–18.

18. Merton, 372.

8. The Church Continues Her Mission

1. Pope John XXIII, "Opening Address to the Council," in *The Encyclicals and Other Messages of John XXIII* (TPS Press, 1964), 423–435; online at CatholicCulture.org, https://www.catholicculture.org/culture/library/view.cfm?recnum=3233.

2. Cited in *The Story of Christianity*, by Justo L. Gonzalez (HarperCollins, 1984).

3. Brian O'Neill, "On Fire for the Catholic Church: Remembering Alex Jones," *National Catholic Register*, February 13, 2017.

4. "Catholics Who Attend Mass Every Week" data row in "US Data Over Time" graph, "Frequently Requested Church Statistics" page, Center for Applied Research in the Apostolate, Georgetown University, https://cara.georgetown.edu/frequently-requested-church-statistics/.

5. Fr. Mike Schmitz, "How the Eucharist Changed My Life," Ascension Presents (video), June 15, 2022, https://www.youtube.com/watch?v=_yKi2OJ7oqE.

6. David Gibson, "10 Years after Catholic Sex Abuse Reforms, What's Changed?" Religion News Service, June 6, 2012, https://religionnews.com/2012/06/06/10-years-after-catholic-sex-abuse-reforms-whats-changed/.

7. Pope Francis, Apostolic Letter Issued Motu Proprio *Vos Estis Lux Mundi* (May 7, 2019).

8. John Paul II, Address at Meeting with the Men Ordained to the Permanent Diaconate, Detroit, September 19, 1987, https://www.vatican.va/content/john-paul-ii/en/speeches/1987/september/documents/hf_jp-ii_spe_19870919_diaconi-perma-nenti-detroit.html.

9. Ordained men (priests) living in an order or community (e.g., Jesuits, Franciscans, Dominicans) are also religious.

10. John Bergsma, *Stunned by Scripture: How the Bible Made Me Catholic* (Huntington, IN: Our Sunday Visitor, 2018).

11. Quoted in "Vatican II 40 Years Later: *Dei Verbum*," *Zenit Daily Dispatch*, May 27, 2003.

12. Colleen Dulle, "Survey Finds Growing Interest among U.S. Catholics in Reading Bible," *Catholic Weekly*, June 8, 2016.

13. Pope John XXIII, "Opening Address to the Council."

14. Quoted in Meghan J. Clark, "'Gaudium et Spes' Offers Wisdom for a Divided Church," *U.S. Catholic*, January 16, 2023.

15. Baptism confers on us the offices of priest, prophet, and king. The task of the prophetic office is to proclaim the Word of God and witness to the faith. All Catholics are called "to teach in order to lead others to faith" (*CCC*, 904, quoting St. Thomas Aquinas).

16. Gregory A. Smith, "About Three-in-Ten U.S. Adults Are Now Religiously Unaffiliated," Pew Research Center, December 14, 2021, https://www.pewresearch.org/religion/2021/12/14/about-three-in-ten-u-s-adults-are-now-religiously-unaffiliated/.

17. Jay Richards, "Tolkien and the Catholic Imagination," video clip, Coming Home Network, February 15, 2019, https://chnetwork.org/insights/tolkien-and-the-catholic-imagination-jay-richards/. Much has been written concerning the Catholic or more generally Christian character of Tolkien's work—for example,

Bradley J. Birzer, *J. R. R. Tolkien's Sanctifying Myth: Understanding Middle-earth* (Wilmington, DE: ISI Books, 2002).

18. This and the following paragraphs rely on Paul Glynn, SM, *A Song for Nagasaki: The Story of Takashi Nagai* (San Francisco: Ignatius, 2009 [1988]), chapters 18–30.

19. Quotations and details of Karl's life are taken from: John Paul II, Homily at Beatification of Five Servants of God (October 3, 2004), https://www.vatican.va/content/john-paul-ii/en/homilies/2004/documents/hf_jp-ii_hom_20041003_beatifications.html; Christoph Cardinal Schönborn, OP, "Emperor and King Karl of the House of Austria: A Saint for Our Day," *L'Osservatore Romano*, October 3, 2004, trans. Nathan Cochran, OSB, https://www.emperorcharles.org/biography; Fr. George W. Rutler, "Blessed Karl von Habsburg," Catholic Education Resource Center, November 3, 2013, https://www.catholiceducation.org/en/culture/catholic-contributions/blessed-karl-von-habsburg.html; and Neil Hollander, *Elusive Dove: The Search for Peace During World War I* (Jefferson, NC: McFarland, 2013), 169.

20. Quoted in Robert Klesko, "Blessed Karl of Austria Continues to Inspire Young Catholics," *National Catholic Register*, October 21, 1922.

PRIMARY SOURCE INDEX

SCRIPTURE INDEX

CATECHISM OF THE CATHOLIC CHURCH (CCC) INDEX

PHOTO CREDITS

AlbionAndalus/Etsy page 406

Art Resource page 247

Associated Press pages 24, 52

Bridgeman Images pages 56, 136, 268

Clarke University Archives photo of Sister Mary Kenneth Keller page 303

Getty pages 4, 5, 7, 9, 11, 14, 15, 17, 21, 23, 26, 29, 31, 32, 34, 48, 49, 50, 51, 52, 55, 60, 63, 64, 66, 69, 70, 74, 75, 77, 81, 82, 85, 88, 89, 92, 93, 95, 105, 110, 112, 113, 115, 116, 118, 121, 123, 127, 128, 131, 135, 138, 139, 141, 144, 149, 158, 162, 164, 165, 166, 167, 168, 170, 171, 174, 175, 177, 178, 179, 181, 184, 189, 193, 194, 198, 199, 201, 202, 203, 204, 207, 209, 212, 213, 214, 215, 217, 218, 230, 233, 234, 235, 236, 238, 241, 244, 246, 249, 251, 253, 256, 257, 259, 260, 266, 270, 271, 272, 275, 283, 290, 291, 294, 295, 296, 299, 300, 303, 304, 305, 306, 308, 310, 313, 321, 323, 324, 328, 331, 333, 352, 353, 355, 358, 359, 366, 367, 369, 371, 372, 373, 374, 375, 377, 378, 379, 381, 383, 389, 390, 392, 394, 396, 412, 414, 415, 418, 419, 421, 423, 425, 427, 429, 431, 432, 434, 435, 438, 444, 446, 447, 449, 450, 453, 462, 463, 469, 470, 472, 473, 474, 476, 478, 479, 480, 481, 482, 483, 485, 486, 487, 488

Granger page 147

Michael O'Neill McGrath, OSFS / www.bromickeymcgrath.com page 350

National Council of the United States, Society of St. Vincent de Paul image of Frédéric Ozanam page 317

National Shrine of Our Lady of Champion page 344, 345

PortraitsofSaints/Etsy page 307

SanctifiedSouls/Etsy pages 8, 80, 226

Topfoto page 58